JEWISH PEOPLE, YIDDISH NATION
Noah Prylucki and the Folkists in Poland

Noah Prylucki (1882–1941), a leading Jewish cultural and political figure in pre-Holocaust Eastern Europe, was a proponent of Yiddishism, a movement that promoted secular Yiddish culture as the basis for Jewish collective identity in the twentieth century. Prylucki's dramatic path – from russified Zionist raised in a Ukrainian shtetl, to Diaspora nationalist parliamentarian in metropolitan Warsaw, to professor of Yiddish in Soviet Lithuania – uniquely reflects the dilemmas and competing options facing the Jews of this era as life in Eastern Europe underwent radical transformation.

Using hitherto unexplored archival sources, memoirs, interviews, and materials from the vibrant interwar Jewish and Polish presses, Kalman Weiser investigates the rise and fall of Yiddishism and of Prylucki's political party, the Folkists, in the post–First World War era. *Jewish People, Yiddish Nation* reveals the life of a remarkable individual and the fortunes of a major cultural movement that has long been obscured.

KALMAN (KEITH) WEISER is the Silber Family Professor of Modern Jewish Studies in the Centre for Jewish Studies at York University.

Jewish People, Yiddish Nation

Noah Prylucki and the Folkists in Poland

Kalman (Keith) Weiser

UNIVERSITY OF TORONTO PRESS
Toronto Buffalo London

Toronto Buffalo London
utorontopress.com

ISBN 978-0-8020-9990-7 (cloth)
ISBN 978-0-8020-9716-3 (paper)

Library and Archives Canada Cataloguing in Publication

Weiser, Keith Ian, 1973–
Jewish people, Yiddish nation : Noah Prylucki and the Folkists in Poland / Kalman (Keith) Weiser.

Includes bibliographical references and index.
ISBN 978-0-8020-9990-7 (bound) ISBN 978-0-8020-9716-3 (pbk.)

1. Priluts kki, Noah. 2. Yiddish language – Poland – History – 20th century. 3. Yiddish language – Political aspects – Poland. 4. Yiddish language – Social aspects – Poland. 5. Jews – Poland – Politics and government – 20th century. 6. Jews – Poland – Civilization – 20th century. 7. Jews – Poland – Intellectual life – 20th century. 8. Yiddishists – Poland – Biography. 9. Jews – Poland – Biography. 10. Politicians – Poland – Biography. I. Title.

PJ5111.5P76W44 2011 439'.10943809041 C2011-901391-6

University of Toronto Press acknowledges the financial assistance to its publishing program of the Canada Council for the Arts and the Ontario Arts Council.

University of Toronto Press acknowledges the financial support of the Government of Canada through the Canada Book Fund for its publishing activities.

Contents

Acknowledgments

The completion of this book, which began as my doctoral dissertation at Columbia University in New York City, would not have been possible without the support, advice, and encouragement of a number of institutions and individuals. I would first of all like to thank my professors at Columbia University and the Hebrew University in Jerusalem. I was initially encouraged to write on this subject by Rakhmiel Peltz, now of Drexel University, who guided me through the Yiddish Studies program in my early years at Columbia and instilled in me an appreciation for Yiddish culture in all of its breadth and depth. His *mentshlekhkeyt* and his unflagging enthusiasm for my academic endeavours have meant much to me since I first began my doctoral studies. My sincere thanks also go to Michael Stanislawski, who oversaw all stages of my doctoral dissertation and taught me to strive for a dispassionate and critical eye in the study of history. Professor Stanislawski's good-natured humour, his pragmatism, and his ability to arrive quickly at the crux of complex and often convoluted matters were a tremendous aid in finishing a dissertation in a timely fashion.

I thank Professors Ezra Mendelsohn (Hebrew University), David Fishman (Jewish Theological Seminary), Bradley Abrams (Columbia), and Jeremy Dauber (Columbia) for participating in my dissertation committee and for contributing discerning comments and suggestions during the defence. Professor Shaul Shtampfer (Hebrew University) also provided important guidance for reworking the dissertation into a book.

During the writing of this book I benefited from the counsel and suggestions of several teachers and colleagues. I availed myself countless times of the invaluable aid of Dr Mordkhe Schaechter, z'l, of Columbia and the League for Yiddish. His peerless knowledge of the Yiddish language and eagerness to share it with students remains a constant source of inspiration to me even after his death. I also extend my sincere thanks to Ezra Mendelsohn, whose expertise and interest in all aspects of Eastern European Jewish culture motivated me to deepen my studies of Polish Jewry during my tenure as a Lady Davis Fellow at the Hebrew University. His colleague at the Hebrew University Professor Avrom Nowersztern likewise never failed to astonish me with his encyclopedic mastery of sources and his readiness to be of assistance to students. Both scholars have made me feel most welcome whenever a guest in the Israeli academic community.

I wish also to express my sincere gratitude to the Jerusalem staff responsible for the computerized Index to the Yiddish Press, without which this research project would not have been possible: Vera Solomon, Michael Dunayevski, Noga Rubin, and, above all, Vicky Shifris. They provided me with constant intellectual stimulation and expertise in the fields of Yiddish literature and the press, as well as with genuine friendship and collegiality while conducting my research in Israel. Chaya Meller, also of Israel, was kind enough to share with me her Bar Ilan University doctoral dissertation about the Folksparty.

I would similarly like to single out colleagues whose suggestions, insights, and criticisms unquestionably enhanced the quality of this work at various stages of its conception and execution: Edward Portnoy, Phillip Hollander, Rebecca Stanton, and Scott Ury. Each helped by not only elucidating difficult matters in his or her respective areas of expertise and suggesting directions for further research but also by recommending and procuring sources for me. I also owe immeasurable gratitude to Sol Goldberg and to Scott Ury for patiently reading drafts and offering suggestions.

Friends and loved ones both inside and outside of academia provided a stimulating and supportive environment in which to conduct my work. In particular I am grateful to Marc Miller, Rebecca Margolis, Naomi Kadar, z"l, Beatrice Lang Caplan, Marc Caplan, Annie Polland, and Dror Abend for their constant encouragement and interest in my work. Mark Clamen, Sol Goldberg, and, above all, Sharon Levinas have helped to make me feel at home in Toronto and have always been available for thought-provoking discussion and intellectual exploration. I similarly thank my colleagues and students at York University for providing such a congenial academic home and for supporting my endeavours. More than once, my student Jordana de Bloeme has brought to my attention pertinent sources or details that I would have otherwise overlooked.

In New York City, the staffs of Butler Library of Columbia, the Jewish Theological Seminary, the Jewish Division of the New York Public Library, and the Joint Distribution Committee all aided me. My special thanks go the academic staff and archivists of YIVO, who have always been generous with their time and expertise. In Israel, I benefited from the assistance of the staffs of the National Library, the Central Zionist Archives, and the Central Archives of the Jewish People, all in Jerusalem, as well as the Arkhion ha-avoda in Tel-Aviv. Messieurs Eliyahu Prylucki, z"l, Mordkhe Tsanin, z"l, and Shloyme Schweitzer, z"l, permitted me to interview them, and Arkady Zeltser procured materials for me from the Yad Vashem Archives. My research in Warsaw would not have been possible without the assistance of Karen Auerbach, Joshua Zimmerman, and the staffs of the Sejm Library and Archives (especially Adam Rutkowski), the Jewish Historical Institute (ŻIH), the National Library, the Archiwum Akt Nowych, and the Municipal Archives. Materials from the Archives of the University of Vilnius were kindly obtained for me by Marcos Silber of the University of Haifa and Julija Sukys of Montreal, who was also kind enough to translate materials for me from Lithuanian.

Several institutions contributed substantial financial support without which this project would never have come to fruition. I would therefore like to thank the National Foundation for Jewish Culture, the Memorial Foundation for Jewish Culture, the Lady Davis Fellowship, and the Atran and Littauer Foundations, as well as the Center for Israel and Jewish Studies at Columbia University and YIVO for their generosity. Generous funding was also provided by the Centre for Jewish Studies at York University, the Faculty of Arts at York University, and the Social Sciences and Humanities Research Council of Canada (SHHRC).

Finally, I would like to thank my editors at University of Toronto Press and the external reviewers, whose critique significantly improved this work.

Introduction

'Noyekh Prilutski'

Fun Smotshe, Stavke, Gizke, Shliske
un fun di shtetlekh – nont un vayt –
es tsit zikh folk tsu Shvyentekzshiske,
skeynem, vayber, yungelayt.

mit peklekh un mit hoyle poles
kumt s'folk tsu noyekhn tsu geyn;

prilutskis hoyz iz ful mit goles,
mit krekhts un folkslid un geveyn.

men nemt fun yidn tsu parnose,
'oy, ratevet, her advokat';
nor do hot noyekh a bakoshe,
'zogt iber s'vertl akurat'...

prilutski shraybt, farshraybt papirn:
mishpotem – lider – rednsart;
zayn feder aylt – nisht tsu farlirn
a yidish vertl, klug un tsart.

er hert un forsht a yede mine
un zapt zikh on mit yedns tsar;
un teyl mol iz a lid, a tkhine
zayn eyntsiker un hekhster skhar

A. Almi, 'Noyekh prilutski.'[1]

Although few today recall Noah Prylucki (1882–1941), his was virtually a household name among Jews in Warsaw in the early years of Polish independence. Prylucki's career of intensive cultural and political activism spanned more than three decades in the late tsarist empire and the Second Polish Republic that emerged from it. During this time he distinguished himself with important, indeed often pioneering, contributions in the fields of Yiddish philology, folklore and folk music, and theatre criticism. News of his bold and controversial speeches defending the Yiddish language and demanding Jewish civil and national rights in the Warsaw City Council and the Polish parliament appeared regularly in the pages of the Jewish press between 1916 and 1926, the years when his Folksparty was most active.

As was common among his generation of Eastern European leaders, Prylucki's academic, political, and cultural pursuits were inextricably connected. He endeavoured to employ Yiddish culture in service of the national aspirations of the Jews in Eastern Europe and simultaneously saw the attainment of national, civil, and cultural rights for the Jews in pre–Second World War Poland as the best guarantor of the continued development and expansion of this culture. By studying the Yiddish language and its culture both synchronically and diachronically, he sought to demonstrate the existence of a Jewish nation spread across a vast terrain but united by a common tongue. Moreover, his research aimed to provide legitimization for the existence of a modern, secular Yiddish culture – relatively young and opposed by various forces internal and external to Jewish society – by locating its foundations in traditional Jewish society. Together with his colleagues in the Folksparty, a band of distinguished Yiddish writers and intellectuals responsible for the popular Warsaw Yiddish daily *Der moment* (Moment), he invested his boundless energies in the creation of the very culture that he championed in the political arena. In his final years, on the eve of the Holocaust, he saw a lifetime dream fulfilled by presiding over some of the most significant institutions of Yiddish culture and scholarship.

Given the importance of Noah Prylucki's contributions to Yiddish culture and Jewish politics, a comprehensive treatment of his life and thought is long overdue.[2] His dramatic life and riveting career as a political and cultural leader committed to Yiddish is therefore the subject of this book. It follows his path – from russified Zionist raised in a Ukrainian *shtetl* through Yiddish cultural activist and Polish parliamentarian in metropolitan Warsaw to professor of Yiddish in Soviet-occupied Vilnius during the Second World War – to illuminate the events and ideologies that radically transformed Eastern European Jewish society beginning in the late nineteenth century. Above all, it examines his contributions to the campaign for Jewish national rights in the Diaspora and to the Yiddishist movement. Its strivings and successes, disappointments and failures, and, ultimately, destruction in Europe are inextricably entwined with his own.

The Echoes of Yiddish

Once the mother tongue of the vast majority of Jews, Yiddish has left a deep and lasting impression on North American popular culture. For many, mention of Yiddish conjures images of a traditional world infused with spirituality and folk wisdom that defencelessly fell victim to the Holocaust. For others, it recalls a brief history of political radicalism and secular humanism. And, for others, poverty, ugliness, religious fanaticism, and social exclusion are the dominant impressions. For nearly all, however, it evokes a good-humoured joke. In short, the image of Yiddish is emblematic of the Eastern European Jew himself, a figure alternately celebrated and reviled but seldom taken seriously for the relevance of his complex, dynamic experience to the contemporary world.

In recent decades scholars, musicians, and artists have begun to rediscover the rich intellectual and cultural legacy of Yiddish, contributing to a flurry of Yiddish-themed festivals, books, and conferences across the world.[3] Still, many such events and publications rely on nostalgia, romanticism, and stereotypes for their appeal, divorcing Yiddish from its broader historical and cultural context. The trajectory of Yiddish, the vernacular of Ashkenazic (historically, Central and Eastern European) Jewry – a polyglot, stateless minority par excellence – and the contours of its culture remain barely traced. Among the diverse voices composing European Jewish society, Yiddishism, the movement to transform Yiddish from a folk language and culture into the focal point of a modern Jewish identity and European *Kultur* in the twentieth century, deserves special attention. Its successes in the realms of art, education, and politics, accomplished in a remarkably short span of time, remain little known today.

Questions of language and identity remain as divisive in the contemporary 'global village' as they did a century ago, and despite predictions, nationalism has failed to disappear as a major factor in world politics since the Second World War. Yiddishism represents a fascinating example of language-based nationalism in the early twentieth century, because of the uncommon linguistic situation of the territorially dispersed Jews in Eastern Europe. Once a leading current in Jewish life, it has been eclipsed in both historiography and popular consciousness by the creation of a primarily Hebrew-speaking Jewish society in Israel, on the one hand, and by the social and political integration of Jews elsewhere, on the other.

Language and Nationalism in Eastern European Jewish Society

Ashkenazic Jews traditionally formed an internally bilingual (Hebrew-Yiddish) minority that balanced expectations of messianic restoration to their ancient homeland in Palestine with a sense of rootedness in their contemporary homelands. Prior to the Second World War, they were frequently perceived (and not merely by antisemites) as a distinct, non-European racial group dwelling on the margins of non-Jewish life. Their modernization and path towards emancipation and integration into the dominant society evoked crises surrounding loss of identity and cultural integrity for both Jews and non-Jews. The rival ideologies of Hebraism and Yiddishism emerged as part of a complex of political and cultural responses to the decline of religion-centred identity and the challenge of Jewish integration in Eastern Europe. Both sought to achieve a monolingual revolution in Jewish society, mimicking patterns in general European society but in a specifically Jewish key. They faced vehement opposition from both outside and inside Jewish society, most importantly from anti-nationalist Orthodox leaders and from champions of the Jews' assimilation into non-Jewish society.

While prominent students of nationalism such as Ernest Gellner frequently devote attention to the remarkable revival of Hebrew as a spoken language in what is now the state of Israel by the Zionist movement,[4] they inexplicably ignore the parallel movement on behalf of Yiddish and on behalf of national recognition in the Jewish Diaspora. In support of his well-grounded claim that matters of status, politics, and ideology, and not of communication or even culture, lie at the heart of the nationalism of language, Eric Hobsbawm errs in arguing:

> If communication or culture had been the crucial issue, the Jewish nationalist (Zionist) movement would not have opted for a modern Hebrew which nobody as yet spoke, and in a pronunciation unlike that used in European synagogues. It rejected Yiddish, spoken by 95% of the Ashkenazic Jews from the European East and their emigrants in the west – i.e. by a substantial

> majority of the all the world's Jews. By 1935, it has been said, given the large, varied and distinguished literature developed for its ten million speakers, Yiddish was 'one of the leading "literate" languages of the time.'
>
> Conversely, as the example of Yiddish shows, and that golden age of dialect literature, the nineteenth century, confirms, the existence of a widely spoken or even written idiom did not necessarily generate language-based nationalism. Such languages or literature could see themselves and be seen quite consciously as supplementing rather than competing with some hegemonic language of general culture and communication.[5]

To the contrary, it was precisely the goal of Prylucki and his colleagues in the Yiddishist movement to induce the whole of Jewish society, including its acculturating commercial and intellectual elites, to embrace its maligned mother tongue for all social functions associated with modern living. Jews of all social classes were asked to choose the vernacular Yiddish, which was commonly denigrated as a mongrel jargon, over the scholarly and liturgical Hebrew, which had not been spoken for 2000 years, or some regional hegemonic language, namely, Russian, Polish, or German. In lieu of an ethnic homeland in Europe, language was to become the primary vehicle for the expression of a Jewish national identity and the medium for mass politics, media, education, and so on. For some, Yiddish was even to replace religious observance or ethnic descent as the measure by which to determine group membership and to mark the boundaries of an ideal cultural space. The Jewish people in Eastern Europe was to become a Yiddish nation.

In a period that romantically celebrated language as the manifestation of a people's collective genius, Yiddishists struggled to gain recognition for Yiddish as a full-fledged language in order to demonstrate to Jews and non-Jews alike that the Jews constituted a national and not merely a religious or racial community. At the same time, the Yiddishist movement maintained that, because Jews were no longer confined to their own society and were increasingly subject to non-Jewish influences, Yiddish language and culture could not be sustained without obtaining official guarantees of cultural autonomy. A number of Jewish political parties therefore strove to win recognition from governments for Yiddish as the Jews' national language and to obtain corollary rights, such as state-supported schools and courts functioning in the language, to preserve their collective identity.

Basing its platform on the ideas of the seminal Eastern European Jewish historian Simon Dubnow, Noah Prylucki's Folksparty fused Yiddishism with the political ideology known as autonomism or Diaspora Nationalism because it called for national cultural autonomy for Jews and others in multiethnic states. Unlike Zionism, which sought to remove Jews from their 'temporary' dwelling places and transfer them to a sovereign state, autonomism saw Jews as autochthonous inhabitants of Europe who were destined to remain there. It aimed to make them loyal and productive citizens of their respective states while also enabling them to preserve their cultural distinctiveness as a people transcending political boundaries. Folkism would thus effectively shift the concept of diasporic centre for Jews from the land of Israel to Eastern Europe.

Significant communities of Yiddish-speakers were to be found on virtually every continent by the early twentieth century, making Yiddish a truly global culture. Recent studies such as Tony Michael's *A Fire in the Hearts: Yiddish Socialists in New York* (2005) and David Shneer's *Yiddish and the Creation of Soviet Jewish Culture, 1918–1930* (2004) help flesh out the picture in America and the Soviet Union but few studies address Yiddishism in its heartland, pre–Second World War Poland. Moreover, scholarship tends to focus on the association of Yiddish with either the radical left or the traditionalist right, ignoring that Yiddishist ideology also found expression among middle-class moderates such as supporters of the Folksparty.

Folkist ideology found expression in a number of lands in the former tsarist and Habsburg empires but knew its greatest development in a Poland whose population comprised more than one-third non-ethnic Poles and guaranteed them national rights by international treaty. With over three million Jews making up roughly 10 per cent of its population, interwar Poland was home to the largest Jewish community in Europe and the central arena for Jewish democratic politics and cultural activity.

Despite early popularity, the Folkists, fin-de-siècle cosmopolitan intellectuals, showed only modest success in accomplishing their Yiddishist agenda. They struggled in a political and social climate increasingly hostile to both Jews and Yiddish as well as against an accelerated pace of linguistic and cultural change among Jews here and elsewhere. The result was a profound crisis of purpose among Yiddish intellectuals and despair not only over the future of Yiddish in the United States, Poland, and the Soviet Union, but over the very survival of Eastern European Jewry as war approached. This study therefore takes up the party's failure to sustain a large following for its postulates in consideration of its political, economic, and, above all, cultural activity – the true raison d'être of the Folksparty.

Indeed, among those who recall him, Prylucki is best remembered today not for his intense engagement in the tumultuous political sphere but for decades of cultural activity. In the mildly derisive description of a contemporary, he was consumed with recondite philological research requiring the 'patience of an ant that does not see around himself.'[6] In his mid-twenties, he gathered folklore and literary circles around himself in Warsaw, thereby encouraging both modern literary production and the 'salvaging' of elements of traditional Jewish life that were rapidly disappearing with the advance of industrialization and secular, cosmopolitan culture among the Jews. The emergence of modern Yiddish cultural institutions, most notably secular schools, in Eastern Europe and the establishment of Yiddish as a field of independent academic inquiry (and not merely a subset of German language and literary studies) are in no small way the fruit of his labours. Despite extensive criticism of his idiosyncratic and, it was often argued, deficient scholarly methodology, he was recognized in his own lifetime for an unsurpassed knowledge of Yiddish dialectology. In the wake of the Holocaust, the largely unanalysed data that he collected and published are an invaluable resource to linguists seeking to reconstruct features of Polish and Ukrainian Yiddish.[7]

Together with his father, Tsevi, Prylucki was also a pioneer in the creation of the Yiddish daily press, the most significant instrument for the diffusion of Jewish mass culture and politics in Poland. As feature writers and contributors to a number of Yiddish publications, he and his Folkist colleagues – most notably, the journalist and fiction writer H.D. Nomberg, the Polish and Yiddish essayist and belletrist Samuel Hirschhorn, the popular religious philosopher Hillel Zeitlin, the editor Lazar Kahan – simultaneously shaped and were shaped by the modern Yiddish culture and literary language they strove to create and popularize among everyday Jews. Accordingly, attention is devoted in this study to language planning – work to codify Yiddish as a standardized, 'national' language and enhance its prestige among both Jews and non-Jews – and the creation of mass cultural institutions by Prylucki and other Yiddishists as part of the mechanism of 'nation-building.'[8]

By chronicling Prylucki's Yiddishist career, *Jewish People, Yiddish Nation* deepens our general understanding of linguistic and cultural revival movements and offers insights into how language, economics, and religion interact in the shaping of collective and individual identities. Moreover, it sheds light on the circumstances in which linguistic minorities are able to maintain themselves in the face of pressures towards and away from assimilation in multiethnic, multicultural polities or even nation states. Finally, by contrasting the fate of Yiddish with that of Hebrew, it also helps illuminate the success of the Hebrew revival movement.

The research presented here is based on memoirs, interviews with Eastern European Jews and Yiddish scholars, and archival materials from New York, Warsaw, Vilnius, Jerusalem, and Tel Aviv. It also draws on the growing body of literature about interwar Polish politics and culture. The Folksparty left no political heirs to record its history, its archives have been destroyed by war, and none of its leaders survived the Holocaust to commemorate it. Prylucki's personal archives have also been lost, although a small portion of his materials belonging to other collections has been recovered.[9] His aristocratic aloofness, personal frictions with colleagues, and his controversial role as the head of YIVO (the Yiddish Scientific Institute) and holder of the Chair of Yiddish at the University of Vilnius at the end of his life are also likely to blame for making him a 'pariah' in the camp of Yiddish scholars who survived the Holocaust and commemorated this lost world.[10]

The most important source for this study is the vast collection of the interwar Jewish (Yiddish, Hebrew, Russian, Polish, and German) press. The Yiddish press was by far the most important vehicle for the dissemination of news, culture, commerce, and politics directed at a mass Jewish audience. It interpreted a growing world to its urbanizing readers, helped to shape new forms of community, and canvassed their support in parliamentary, municipal, and local elections. Quite naturally, as Yiddishist intellectuals, Prylucki and other Folkists regularly expressed their views through this medium more than any other. Of lesser importance to this study is the non-Jewish Polish language press. Generally antagonistic to manifestations of Jewish national 'separatism' as undermining the welfare of the Polish state and people, it devoted little attention specifically to Prylucki and his small party, whose relevance to parliamentary politics was quickly exhausted. As one might expect, while it frequently expressed dogged opposition to Yiddishist ideals and the expanded use of Yiddish in the public sphere, it had usually little to say about the inner dimensions of Yiddish culture which Yiddishists so hotly debated.

Outline of the Book

Over the course of centuries a distinct Yiddish-speaking society and culture developed among Jews in the Polish-Lithuanian Commonwealth. The first chapter, 'Jewish Life, Language, and Politics in Poland,' is meant as an optional chapter intended for the non-specialist reader to help him or her to become oriented in themes and concepts that will be explored in subsequent chapters. It examines the development of Yiddish from a sociological standpoint and positions it within a general framework of language use in pre-modern Jewish societies. It continues by surveying the evolution of Polish-Jewish relations in the modern era to comprehend how the nineteenth-century movement for the peaceful integration of Jews into the Polish nation yielded, by the twentieth century, heightened intercommunal tensions and the birth of nationalist and socialist movements increasingly organized along ethno-linguistic lines.

Chapter 2, 'The Making of a Jewish Nationalist: Noah Prylucki and the Warsaw Yiddish Press,' focuses on Noah Prylucki's early ideational development as a political activist and journalist prior to his explicit embrace of Yiddishism. Despite being the dominant tongue among Jews, Yiddish was not the obvious choice for a Jewish daily press aimed at a mass readership in Poland and the Pale of Settlement. As a result of both internal objections in Jewish society and tsarist restrictions, it appeared relatively late in comparison with a daily press in other European vernaculars. Moreover, many of its pioneers in the largest cities in Poland, including Noah Prylucki and his father, were not natives of Poland but migrants from elsewhere in the Russian Empire. Once it had emerged, however, the Yiddish press revolutionized Jewish society and drastically affected Polish-Jewish relations. This chapter follows closely the Pryluckis' travails in creating a press as a reflection of changing attitudes towards language in Jewish society as well as political and social conditions in the Russian Empire during its declining years.

Chapter 3, 'Creating Modern Yiddish Culture,' analyses the unfolding of Noah Prylucki's Yiddishist ideology and its implementation in the years between 1908 and 1914. As part of the Jewish national renaissance seeking to transform traditional Jewish life into a secularized cosmopolitan culture, Prylucki passionately engaged in a number of nation-building activities common to European nationalists of his time but still unfamiliar to Jews. Possessing a sense of his own importance, he played host to literary and folklore circles in his home and penned literary, theatre, and art criticism for the Yiddish press in addition to contributing spirited defences of Yiddish and directing its standardization. During this period, he sparred regularly in publications with friends and foes alike as he drifted from his prior commitments to Hebraism and Zionism to articulate his conviction that Yiddish represented the irreplaceable core of Jewish identity.

At the centre of the book are two chapters dealing explicitly with the Folksparty. Chapter 4, 'Cultural Politics in Action: The Birth of Folkism,' treats the creation and activity of the Folksparty by Yiddish writers and pedagogues grouped around *Der moment* who were dissatisfied with Zionism and Polish political movements during the First World War. It closely examines Folkists' activity on behalf of Yiddish culture, especially the Yiddish secular school, the cornerstone of the party's ideology. Debates such as those surrounding the basis of Jewish identity and language standardization (such as spelling, vocabulary, and pronunciation) helped to distinguish the Folkists' conception of Yiddishism from that of other currents championing Yiddish. Some of the questions which the chapter addresses, such as how to (re)define secular Jewish culture and how to define membership in the Jewish people, remain just as relevant today, particularly in the state of Israel.

Chapter 5, 'From Avant- to Arrière-garde: The Folksparty in Interwar Poland,' focuses on Prylucki's parliamentary and extra-parliamentary activity at the height of its activity, the years 1918 to 1926. During this period, Prylucki was virtually synonymous with the party and its rise and fall in the public eye were very much linked to his career as a public figure. The chapter asks why Folkism did not succeed, and what we can learn from this about the nature of interwar Polish Jewry, particularly with regard to its relationship to language. It surveys the party's history and seeks to account for its failure to draw a mass audience and its relatively rapid decline after an auspicious beginning as a reflection of the political and cultural dynamics of the time, internal disagreements, and Prylucki's own personality.

Finally, Chapter 6, 'Compromises? The Chair of Yiddish at the University of Vilnius,' seeks to explain the larger issues behind his decision to take refuge in independent Lithuania at the outbreak of the Second World War and to remain there under Soviet occupation rather than flee to safety in the West. Prylucki and his remaining colleagues at YIVO, representatives of various Yiddishist orientations, desperately debated the survival not only of Yiddish culture but also of the Jewish people itself in Eastern Europe. The concrete issue of a proposed Chair of Yiddish at the University of Vilnius provides a window into their perspectives. Their debates, amply coloured by bitter grudges and personal rivalries, reveal conflicting understandings of the dangers posed by Nazism, Communism, and capitalism for Yiddish and Jewish collective existence.

The conclusion reconsiders the achievements and failures of Folkism and evaluates Prylucki's important social role qua linguist and ideologist among Jewish nationalists. In doing so, it attempts to understand why so little attention has been devoted to Prylucki even among Yiddish scholars who survived the Holocaust and what role his personality played in the failure of his political and cultural ambitions. More broadly, the conclusion summarizes the factors which permitted Yiddish culture to exist and flourish as well as decline and disappear in order to draw conclusions about the environments in which minority languages and cultures remain viable. By examining issues of language planning, it also considers the tension between populism and elitism inherent in any nationalist movement whose leadership, in seeking to subvert regnant social and economic hierarchies in the name of the masses, paradoxically creates new elites of its own. Finally, it explains why Hebraism, in contrast with Yiddishism, succeeded and comments on the return of Yiddish to its pre-modern position in a post-Holocaust world.

A Note on the Spelling of Names

The spelling of personal and place names in Roman letters generally follows the conventions of contemporary scholarly literature. *The YIVO Enyclopedia of Jews in Eastern Europe* has served as my guide in most cases. Prylucki himself used multiple spellings and variants of his names in Roman letters (e.g., Noë, Noah, and Nojach; Prilucki, Prilutzky, Prelutzky, and Prylucki), but I have opted for Noah Prylucki. When no convention exists, an attempt has been made to render the names of primarily Yiddish-speaking individuals according to the transliteration guidelines set forth by YIVO.[11] Endnote citations, however, typically follow the language of publication. Thus, for example, Samuel Hirschhorn appears in the body of text, but Shmuel Hirshhorn appears in endnotes in Yiddish citations and Samuel Hirszhorn in Polish ones.

JEWISH PEOPLE, YIDDISH NATION
Noah Prylucki and the Folkists in Poland

chapter one

Jewish Life, Language, and Politics in Poland

Jewish Settlement in the Polish-Lithuanian Commonwealth

Beginning in the medieval period, Jews migrated from 'Ashkenaz,' as they called the German lands, to the vast Polish-Lithuanian Commonwealth (figure 1.1) and laid the foundations for what was to become the world's largest Jewish community prior to its destruction in the Holocaust.[1] They were drawn over the course of centuries by comparatively favourable circumstances and flight from persecution and discriminatory legislation. They brought with them their unique cultural identity and a way of life that distinguished them from other Jewish communities around the world. Over time these newer communities became culturally, intellectually, and materially self-sufficient, overshadowing their ancestral communities. The western Ashkenazic communities, dwarfed in size and exceeded in degree of security, now looked eastward for guidance. By virtue of their numbers and the dominance of their culture, the Ashkenazim of Poland-Lithuania presumably assimilated those non-Ashkenazic, primarily Slavic-speaking Jews whose settlement predates their arrival in Eastern Europe. The same may be assumed of later arriving Sephardic Jews, a small number of whom came following their expulsion from the Iberian Peninsula at the end of the fifteenth century and following subsequent migrations.

Jews dwelled in the highly decentralized Polish-Lithuanian Commonwealth effectively, if not in legal theory, as an ethno-religious corporation in economic symbiosis with the estates in the feudal order. Like other corporations such as the nobility and burghers, they were governed by distinct sets of privileges, laws, and responsibilities. In return for the collective payment of taxes and the performance of vital economic

1.1 The Polish-Lithuanian Commonwealth and the Partition of Poland, ca. 1795. The vast territory of the Polish-Lithuanian Commonwealth (encompassing roughly modern Poland, Lithuania, Ukraine, and Belarus) was partitioned by its neighbours – Prussia, Austria, and Russia – in the late eighteenth century. The partitions, which were completed in 1795, brought the world's largest population of Jews under the rule of three empires and contributed to Eastern European Jewry's cultural and political differentiation over time. (*Source: The YIVO Encyclopedia of Jews in Eastern Europe*)

functions, they were permitted to maintain their own traditions and institutions under the supervision of rabbinical and wealthy lay authorities.

They commonly inhabited the small towns (*shtetlekh*) that served as the commercial and administrative centres of affluent magnates' estates, especially in the eastern borderlands (*kresy*) corresponding roughly to contemporary Ukraine and Belarus. They were often excluded from residence in royal cities, where burghers – typically also 'foreigners,' mainly Germans and Armenians, although they often became polonized over the course of generations – and less affluent aristocrats objected to their economic competition and lobbied for the right not to admit Jews (*de non tolerandis judaeis*). Despite their formal exclusion and the frequent opposition of the Roman Catholic Church, some Jews lived within city limits in the private enclaves (*jurydiki*) of individual noblemen and clergymen. In an overwhelmingly rural and agricultural society, they occupied the niche of a commercial and merchant class. Their pursuits were hardly limited to trade, however, as they performed a variety of functions in the service of the kings and gentry: they served as artisans and innkeepers; worked as estate managers, lessees of estate monopolies (e.g., the production and sale of alcohol), and tax farmers; engaged in the transport and long distance trade of a number of basic commodities and luxury goods; and functioned in a variety of other ways as intermediaries linking rural, overwhelmingly agrarian, and urban economies.[2] As their welfare was of direct concern to their employers, they enjoyed for the most part peace, prosperity, and protection despite sporadic eruptions of violence, most notably devastating massacres in the times of the infamous Chmielnicki (1648–49) and Haidemak (eighteenth century) uprisings when Cossacks and peasants in Ukraine rebelled against their masters, the Polish gentry, along with the Catholic clergy and Jews who were closely associated with them.

Despite their cultural distinctiveness, the Ashkenazic Jews conformed in most ways to a general model of pre-Emancipation Jewish life as a minority in Christian and Moslem lands. Thus, like other pre-modern Jewish communities, they understood themselves to be a fragment of the people Israel, a people exiled from its ancient homeland in Palestine to the four corners of the earth. They lived by God's law as expounded by rabbis in anticipation of imminent messianic restoration in *Eretz yisrael*, the Land of Israel. The practice of Judaism informed virtually all aspects of their daily lives and distinguished them from their non-Jewish neighbours, whose religion was similarly all pervasive. Moreover, they cherished a centuries-old heritage of extraterritorial autonomy, regulating their own affairs in accordance with Jewish law and an accumulated body of tradition. In conformity with this model, they also employed within their communities a language derived from contact with non-Jews as their vernacular alongside Hebrew and Aramaic.

Language Use in Eastern European Jewish Society

Long before Jewish settlement in Europe, Hebrew had ceased to be their spoken language. By the second century CE, if not centuries earlier, it had been supplanted in Palestine itself as well as Babylonia by Jewish variants of Aramaic, the lingua franca of the ancient Near East. In the same period, Greek was spoken by much of the Jewish Diaspora in the Hellenized world and by more educated and urban sections of the Palestinian Jewish population. Later migrations of both Jews and Gentiles brought Jews into contact with additional languages, yielding a general pattern of Jews speaking as their mother tongue a 'Jewish' variant of a non-Jewish language – one recognizably related to the language of non-Jews but not necessarily mutually intelligible with it. Despite language shift, however, Jews held on to Hebrew and Aramaic as their sacred, scholarly, and scribal languages since it is in these languages that their most significant texts, the Hebrew Bible and the Talmud, as well as their liturgy were recorded. Moreover, they continued to employ Jewish script (itself an adaptation of the Aramaic alphabet) for their writing, thereby reinforcing their linguistic distinctiveness in general and adding to the distance between the norms of their vernacular literature and those of a related non-Jewish language.[3]

A relationship of complementary functionality ('diglossia') between the vernacular and the sacred tongues was the norm in pre-modern Jewish communities. Hebrew and Aramaic served higher prestige functions, such as prayer, religious study, and serious composition (Hebrew for Bible commentaries, Aramaic for Talmudic and kabbalistic writings). To be more precise, the Ashkenazim, like other Jews, did not always make a clear distinction between the two languages. Their use of the term 'language of sanctity' (*lashon kodesh* in Hebrew or *loshn-koydesh* in Yiddish) referred to an amalgam of biblical and post-biblical Hebrew and Aramaic elements. A literary rather than spoken language – it was no one's literal mother tongue – *loshn-koydesh* served as the language for communication between Jewish communities around the globe, as well as the scribal language of rabbis, communal functionaries, chroniclers, and, frequently, businessmen. It was even spoken, albeit seldom, when

Jews with no common spoken language encountered each other. In comparison with pre-modern Catholic society (in which Latin was imparted as part of a classical education to a relatively small privileged class), basic literacy in the 'high' language, that is, an acquaintance with the alphabet and the ability to decode familiar texts (although not necessarily the ability to write or to read freely), was relatively widespread.[4] It was cultivated as an integral part of a system of (ideally) universal male primary schooling, since the study of religious texts was deemed the foundation of religious piety and a religious injunction in itself.

Rote learning of the Hebrew Bible and the rudiments of Talmud in the *kheyder*, the Jewish primary school, imparted a large degree of respect and familiarity with, if not actual comprehension or fluency in, Hebrew and Aramaic among males. Regular daily encounter with liturgy and sacred texts reinforced this connection. True mastery of these languages, including the ability to compose freely, was only attained, however, by smaller circles of yeshiva graduates, and only the most erudite Jewish scholars were capable of composition in Aramaic. Since females were not religiously obliged to engage in thrice daily prayer and sacred study, their knowledge of *loshn-koydesh* was typically far more limited, although they too came in regular contact with it and respected this linguistic hierarchy.[5]

The spoken language of Ashkenazic Jews was Yiddish, an idiom that has its origins in the Middle High German dialects they learned from non-Jews in the medieval period. Quite naturally, Jews adapted these dialects over time to meet their unique religious and cultural needs, ultimately fashioning a supra-regional dialect (or dialects) of their own.[6] This Jewish vernacular based on varieties of German (itself centuries away from standardization) was greatly influenced – lexically, syntactically, and otherwise – by Jews' regular use of Hebrew and Aramaic (many forms were transmitted via pre-Yiddish Jewish languages or through textual study and prayer) as well as by the vestiges of languages Jews spoke prior to shaping this new vernacular (such as Jewish variants of Old French and Old Italian). Because of the regular interaction between languages, Yiddish also exercised an influence on the phonetics of *loshn-koydesh*, its vocabulary, and its syntax.

Internal multilingualism within Jewish society was complemented by whatever degree of competence in 'non-Jewish' languages, for example, Ukrainian and Polish, was needed by the individual Jew to communicate with Gentiles, for example, for purposes of commerce and interactions with officials. Regular contact over generations with co-territorial languages, especially Slavic languages in Eastern Europe, also left its mark on the sounds, vocabulary, syntax, and idioms of Yiddish. Multilingualism was thus the norm in Jewish society, each language serving its distinct function but also influencing others. By the late eighteenth century, Yiddish, the lingua franca of the Ashkenazic world, existed in a number of more or less mutually intelligible dialects in Eastern and Central Europe and beyond. It was known among Jews by a variety of names (e.g., *lashon ashkenaz* 'the language of Ashkenaz') before the centuries-old name 'Yiddish' (meaning 'Jewish') gained widespread acceptance in the nineteenth and early twentieth centuries.[7]

The Disappearance of the Polish-Lithuanian Commonwealth

Weakened by a century of foreign invasion and political intrigue that exploited its internal weaknesses, the Polish-Lithuania Commonwealth disappeared from the political map in the last quarter of the eighteenth century. At one time the largest state in Europe and home to a myriad of ethnic and religious communities, including Jews, it was partitioned between its politically ascendant neighbours, the Russian, Prussian, and Austrian empires, in three successive bouts of territorial plunder (1772, 1793, and 1795). While change was largely imperceptible in their daily life for decades following the partitions of Poland, the Jews of the defunct Commonwealth would be transformed over the course of the next century into the subjects of these three absolutist regimes, thus rupturing their long-standing political and cultural unity.

The largest number of those Jews affected by the partitions of Poland found themselves subjects of the Romanov dynasty. They retained a tremendous degree of linguistic, occupational, and cultural distinctiveness under Russian rule into the twentieth century. It is with cultural and political developments among them in particular that this book is concerned. The second-largest part fell under the (by the mid-nineteenth century) comparatively benign rule of the Habsburg Empire, which emancipated its Jews in 1867. Residing in the desperately poor, primarily rural Austrian province of Galicia, they continued to share much culturally, although naturally less so politically, with their brethren in neighbouring Russian Poland. The smallest part of the Commonwealth's Jews, those dwelling in its westernmost parts, underwent the most thoroughgoing transformation of identity and the greatest dissociation from the Polish-Lithuanian cultural legacy. Following the western model of emancipation and embourgeoisement, the Jews of Poznań (Posen in German) integrated into Prussian society. They often migrated to Berlin and other large cities, becoming typically staunch German burghers and fervent patriots while maintaining a religious and communal identity as Jews.

Jews in the Russian Empire, the 'Western Provinces,' and 'Congress Poland'

Historically, by the fifteenth century tsarist Russia had excluded (with few exceptions) 'the enemies of Christ' from within its boundaries for fear of their nefarious religious influence and because of the economic competition they constituted for the native merchant class.[8] Now, instead of the Jews coming to Russia, Russia had come to the Jews – along with the other inhabitants of the former Commonwealth. The territories that fell to the tsarist regime in the partitions were divided into two distinct regions. The so-called Western Provinces, corresponding to the multiethnic eastern borderlands (*kresy*) of Poland-Lithuania, were considered an integral and historic part of Russia, since Kievan Rus was held to be the cradle of Russian culture.[9] In contrast, the Kingdom of Poland (otherwise known as Congress Poland because it was established by the post-Napoleonic Congress of Vienna in 1815), was characterized by markedly less ethnic and linguistic diversity (figure 1.2). The bulk of the population, encompassing all classes of society, was ethnically and linguistically Polish and religiously Roman Catholic. The primary exceptions were the Jews and smaller numbers of Germans, who were mainly concentrated in urban areas, most prominently in Łódź. Although the Russian tsar was the ex officio King of Poland, the kingdom possessed a constitution, as well as its own currency, army, and legislature. This autonomy was considerably circumscribed, however, after the suppression of an insurrection aiming to restore Polish independence in 1830–31.[10]

Russia found itself sovereign, in the territory of the former Polish-Lithuanian Commonwealth, over millions of linguistically and religiously diverse subjects. If we permit ourselves to anachronistically assign national identities for the sake of simplicity, there were Poles, Jews, Ukrainians, Byelorussians, and Lithuanians, as well as smaller numbers of other groups. Out of respect for their social class and historical legacy (and likely to avoid revolt), the traditional Polish elites were permitted to maintain their positions of authority, their language, and their culture in the annexed territories as long as they accepted tsarist rule. They continued to exert influence, especially as landowners and members of the local intelligentsia, in the northwestern part of the Western Provinces

1.2 Congress Poland (*Source: The YIVO Encyclopedia of Jews in Eastern Europe*)

in addition to Congress Poland. Moreover, much of the Catholic clergy in the newly annexed territories was Polish or polonized. In contrast to the respect accorded to Polish, the languages and cultures of Ukrainian- and Belorussian-speaking peasants were, from the perspective of Russian authorities, not worthy of independent status but local, folkloric manifestations of one Great Russian culture and people.[11]

While the Poles, with their history of independence and demonstrated hostility to subordination, were suspect as politically unreliable to the Russian Empire, Jews were deemed a problem sui generis. In many ways, tsarist policy aimed to replicate the policies of neighbouring absolutist states, especially Austria, to intervene in communal life and acculturate and integrate the Jews. However, the unique conditions of the Russian Empire, including the resiliency of traditional Judeophobia and resistance to liberalizing reforms that threatened autocracy, were obstacles to the emancipation of the tsar's subjects. Tsarist policy towards the Jews is best characterized as ambivalent, alternating between, on the one hand, measures to break down the feudal legacy of corporate status and integrate them into pre-existing social structures (*soslovie*); and, on the other hand, measures to preserve Jewish segregation and exclude them from general society.[12]

In order to placate groups fearful of Jewish influence, the tsarist regime declared that without special permission Jews were not permitted to sojourn or reside within the Russian interior. By 1835 the boundaries of the Pale of Settlement, the region of legal residence for Jews in the Russian Empire, were defined to contain the nine western provinces of the Russian Empire corresponding to the *kresy* (see figure 1.3). Desiring to populate newly acquired territory with its subjects and mindful of the Jews' economic usefulness, the Russian regime included so-called New Russia, the southern territories Russia had gained at the expense of the Ottoman Empire, within the Pale too. Congress Poland (which comprised ten provinces), as well as the Baltic provinces of Kurland and Livland (part of today's Latvia) on the Baltic Sea – regions where Jews lived prior to the partitions – lay outside the Pale and possessed a separate status within the tsarist empire. Conditions for the population, including its Jews, differed here from elsewhere in the Empire.

Haskalah

By the late eighteenth century, small numbers of 'progressive' or 'enlightened' Jews (*maskilim*) familiar with social and political trends in

1.3 The Pale of Settlement, ca. 1855. The term refers to the territories in the Russian Empire in which Jews were legally permitted to reside. The boundaries of the Pale were delineated over the course of decades. They included within

German states and other Western lands undergoing modernization began to promote the cause of Jewish emancipation and social and cultural integration throughout Europe. They urged both external state interference and internal reform in Jewish life to bring an end to what they deemed a morally deforming and intellectually enfeebling legacy of Jewish separatism, cultural isolation, and overly narrow economic behaviour. The *Haskalah*, the Jewish analogue of the European Enlightenment, set forth an agenda emphasizing unswerving loyalty to and admiration for the emperor (replacing pragmatic alliances with local aristocrats in the decentralized Commonwealth) and promoted secular education and occupational diversification as the path to cultural and political – although not ethnic or religious – fusion with the Gentile middle and upper classes in civil society. The *Haskalah* desired a revival of aspects of human knowledge and endeavour, such as the natural sciences and humanistic studies, which it saw as not foreign to the Jewish tradition but woefully neglected, if not outright dismissed as subversive, by Ashkenazic Jewry in recent centuries.

Language, in both its communicative and symbolic dimensions, occupied a position of tremendous importance in the *Haskalah* enterprise to 'regenerate' the Jews into productive citizens and loyal brethren to their countrymen. Taking their cue from the Jewish philosopher Moses Mendelssohn and his circles in Berlin, most *maskilim* denounced Yiddish as a mongrel hodgepodge of corrupted German, Hebrew, and Slavonic elements that served to isolate the Jews and impair their thoughts. Influenced by the eighteenth-century dichotomy between 'pure' and 'impure' languages, *maskilim* disdained Yiddish for its ugly hybridity and alleged 'fall' from German. Having in large degree internalized Gentile

---

them territory annexed from the Polish-Lithuania Commonwealth plus some additional regions, such as Bessarabia. Jews considered to be economically productive or fulfilling the agenda of Jewish acculturation into Russian society were eventually permitted by tsarist authorities to reside outside the Pale or in previously restricted cities within it, such as Kiev. The Pale did not include the Russian-controlled Kingdom of Poland, where different regulations governed Jews, but Jews were permitted free movement between the two regions. Nor did the Pale include established Jewish communities in Courland province and in the cities of Riga and Shlok in Lifland province. Its provisions also did not affect long-established communities of non-Ashkenazic Jews in Central Asia and the Caucasus. (*Source: The YIVO Encyclopedia of Jews in Eastern Europe*)

perceptions of Jewish perversity and inferiority, the *Haskalah* saw in Yiddish an emblem of the physical, moral, and intellectual defects of Ashkenazic Jewry. It was to be replaced as soon as possible with a language of pan-European culture or the language of the state. In its earliest phases, German was the preferred language of the *Haskalah,* because it was in territories where German was the language of state, such as Prussia and Galicia, that the movement first took root. Moreover, the close relationship between Yiddish and German facilitated this transition.[13]

At the same time that the *Haskalah* discredited Yiddish and preached its displacement as the Jews' vernacular, it lauded biblical Hebrew as 'the daughter of Heaven' and launched a program for its cultivation in modern, secular literary genres such as poetry, journalism, and historiography for internal Jewish consumption. This adoration of biblical Hebrew, a language respected by Jew and Gentile alike, contrasted with distaste for Rabbinic Hebrew, an 'impure' language mixing various layers of post-biblical Hebrew and Aramaic. Moreover, *maskilim* frequently advocated the adoption of the Sephardic pronunciation of Hebrew, which was also used by Christian Hebraists, to replace the pronunciation tradition peculiar to Ashkenazic Jewry; they judged it more 'correct,' in part because it did not share the contemptible sound patterns of Yiddish. The early *Haskalah* thus aimed to reconfigure language relations in Jewish society: the language of the upper classes (whom Jews sought to emulate) would not only replace Yiddish as the Jews' spoken language; it would also serve as the language of elevated cultural exchange with their non-Jewish countrymen and fellow Europeans. Biblical Hebrew, whose usage hearkened back to what was imagined as pristine, pre-exilic Israelite life, would replace Rabbinic Hebrew to serve as the universal internal language of Jewish written communication. It would thus continue to unite the Jews as a transnational people despite integration into the dominant society.

Reluctantly, at least initially, the *Haskalah* also made use of Yiddish to spread its message, justifying its use with the need to reach the masses in the only tongue they knew well precisely to alert them to their current debasement and provide them with rudimentary intellectual tools to escape it. Through the use of Yiddish, particularly in satire, the ugliness and inadequacies of the language and the traditional way of life were to be exposed in order that Jewish society could be reformed. Not all literary activity in Yiddish, however, was hostile to it, even if its use was typically justified on utilitarian grounds. In the *Haskalah* lie by mid-century the origins of Yiddish and Hebrew in Eastern Europe as modern literary and journalistic language. The enterprising *maskil* Alexander

Zederbaum founded the Russian Empire's first Hebrew newspaper, *Hamelits* (The Intercessor), in Odessa 1860 with the goal of mediating between the government and Jewish society and between various sectors of the Jewish population. He introduced in 1862 a more popular Yiddish-language supplement, *Kol Mevaser* (The Heralding Voice), which dealt with social issues and pioneered the publication in instalments of modern Yiddish literature.[14]

In Western Europe the *Haskalah* agenda coincided with the shaping of nation states which out of necessity and liberal ideology emancipated and integrated their Jews. In radical republican France these ideals were pursued to their fullest, leading to the emancipation of its Jewish populations by 1791 as part of the sweeping changes that sought to create a united, culturally homogeneous and linguistically uniform citizenry under the banner of secular French universalism. The price of becoming Frenchmen was the relinquishing of judicial autonomy and acculturation in all ways, including linguistically, other than what was deemed the strictly religious sphere, that is, the confessionalization of Judaism, its reduction from an all-encompassing way of life to a religious category (parallel to forms of Christianity) subordinate to the authority of the state. Elsewhere, such as Germany (which was not united as a single state until 1871), the emancipation of the Jews entailed a longer, more drawn-out process whereby acculturation to non-Jewish norms often outpaced the removal of legal impediments and granting of political rights. In all cases, integration into the nation state required the disappearance of Yiddish and the suppression of any transnational loyalties other than, at least in theory, purely religious ones. Over the span of a few generations, Yiddish was thus supplanted throughout Central and Western Europe by the language of the state and any historical ties to the language were emphatically denied (if not simply forgotten). Yiddish, depicted as a shameful badge of medieval barbarism, was associated by Jews with Eastern Europe, a region imagined by Germans of all faiths as politically despotic, economically and culturally primitive, as well as desperately poor. The self-conscious dissociation from Yiddish and its radical, emotionally tinged rejection facilitated the construction of a specifically Western European Jewish identity distinct from the assumedly backward, religiously (or politically) fanatical *Ostjuden* (Eastern Jews) with whom the *Westjuden* (Western Jews) claimed to share merely an ancestral faith. This dissociation was especially important when large numbers of impoverished, culturally distinct, Yiddish-speaking immigrants settled in European capitals in the latter part of the nineteenth century for native

Jews feared that their distasteful foreignness jeopardized their own hard-won (and precarious) social acceptance and political gains.[15]

The *Haskalah*'s transformative vision for the Jews was hampered in nineteenth-century Russia by a state slow to modernize and lacking a well-developed native middle class and intelligentsia able and willing to absorb the Jews. It was also combated tenaciously by an ultra-conservative rabbinic leadership and compact Jewish masses reluctant to change. Arising in the eighteenth century at roughly the same time as the westernizing *Haskalah*, the mysticism-based Hasidic movement simultaneously challenged the authority of the established Jewish religious elite and shielded Jewish society from the destabilizing effects of an increasingly encroaching state and modernization in Eastern Europe. It triumphed over the attempts of its opponents (*mitnagdim*), who were focused around the personality of the charismatic scholar Elijah Gaon of Vilna, to root it out as a form of heresy and became the dominant form of Jewish religiosity in much of Poland-Lithuania and beyond by the mid-nineteenth century. In the latter half of the nineteenth century, the religious leadership of Eastern European Jewry, whether Hasidic or *mitnagdic*, was steadfast in its opposition to secularization, acculturation, and social integration as subversive of the Jews' unique vocation as upholders of the divine covenant.

Russification

In contrast with Western and Central Europe, where one language typically dominated in the state, acculturating Jews of the Romanov regime were faced with a multiplicity of choices in choosing a cultural and political orientation. Beginning in Byelorussia after the first partition of the Poland-Lithuanian Commonwealth in the late eighteenth century, the *Haskalah* among Jews in the Western Provinces of the Russian Empire preached identification with the imperial regime and Russification. There were petitions for official involvement in this endeavour, advocating military service, bans on traditional Jewish dress, and state support for Russian-language schools for Jewish children, with the expectation that these measures would culminate in a cultural rapprochement between Jews and the general, that is, Russian, population and the eventual granting of citizenship to them. This program fell on largely deaf, if not hostile ears because such measures were typically viewed with suspicion, if not as outright heresy, by Jews. Service in the Russian military, which relied on its Jewish agents (*khapers*) to draft children in the Western

Provinces as young as twelve (and even younger unofficially) for onerous terms of twenty-five years (and, in effect, more for those drafted as minors) during the reign of Tsar Nicholas I (1825–55), was not only brutal but understood as designed to undermine children's attachment to their native religion and culture. State-sponsored schools for Jewish children, which employed *maskilim* as faculty, were similarly feared as institutes for heresy and conversion.[16]

Nonetheless, by the 1840s the foundation for the emergence of a Jewish intelligentsia whose members chiefly spoke Russian and were consumers of Russian culture had been laid. State schools for Jewish children were opened in which the Jewish religion was taught in Russian in addition to general subjects. In Vilna and Zhitomir rabbinical seminaries were organized to train modern Russian-speaking rabbis who were employees of the state and would help to remake Russian Jewry in the model of their Western European co-religionists.

Official measures to encourage the acquisition of Russian language and culture were received far more favourably during the comparatively liberal reign of Nicholas' successor Alexander II (1855–81). Known as the 'tsar liberator' for emancipating the serfs in 1862, he implemented Westernizing reforms in order to attempt to bridge the gap between Russia and the West and offered a number of incentives to promote secular education and professional diversification among Jews. He also ended the notorious recruitment of Jewish minors and reduced the term of military service for Jews to the same length of time as that of other groups.

Beginning in the 1860s and 1870s, increasing numbers of Jews began to pursue occupational and residential opportunities (such as the right to domicile outside the Pale of Settlement, granted to Jews with a higher education in 1861) made available to them via Russian-language schooling. Exemptions from conscription for those knowing Russian extremely well (1874) served as further impetus for masses of middle-class Jewish children and youth to study in Russian-language schools. So great was the allure of Russian state schools that social and government circles already sought to curb the growth of the Jewish intelligentsia by the 1880s, and a *numerus clausus* was introduced in schools in 1887. Historian Yehuda Slutsky observes, 'If the masses of Jews in the 40's of the nineteenth century cried "shkoles nie zhelayem" ("we don't want schools"), their children a generation later did their utmost to enter their children in the schools that were closed to them. A sort of psychosis to study the Russian language was created on the Jewish street in all directions.'[17]

Consequently, Russian began vying with Yiddish as the language of everyday Jewish life in the Pale of Settlement and, to a much lesser extent, in Congress Poland. This was especially true of secularized Jewish intellectuals, who were almost as a rule ashamed of Yiddish as an obstacle to integration and symbol of Jewish poverty and backwardness. Having eagerly mastered the Russian language and absorbed elements of its culture, they formed a non-traditional elite clustered in St Petersburg, Odessa, and Kiev.[18] A Russian-language Jewish press espousing the cause of the *Haskalah* appeared beginning in the 1860s. But this language shift was not restricted to these small circles: with the increasing urbanization of Jews in the latter half of the nineteenth century, not only a command of spoken Russian, but Russian literacy, too, became widespread among white- and blue-collar labourers dwelling in the Russian-language environments of larger cities and on the peripheries of major industrial and commercial centres.[19]

The adoption of Russian, however, did not imply ethnic or national affiliation. From the perspective of the *Haskalah*, the acquisition of a 'European' language was consistent with its goals to integrate Jews into European culture without surrendering their unique collective identity. Moreover, despite official recognition as a religious community, Jews were effectively treated as a distinct ethnic or national group by tsarist officials. Indeed, the Russian language distinguishes between *russkii*, referring to ethnic Russians, and *rossiiskii*, a designation for those belonging to the Russian cultural and political sphere. Thus, a Jew, in the eyes of most, could no more be a Russian than a Pole or Armenian could be, regardless of his cultural orientation.[20]

Polonization

Despite the advances made by Russian in Congress Poland, Polish continued to be identified here too as the language of high culture and Europeanization by the small number of modernizing Jews. For the first generation of Polish *maskilim*, polonization meant support for state authorities and access to European culture. Alternately, many of this generation continued to use German, a respected European language, to promote their goals and express their loyalties to the emperor, seeing in this no contradiction. They clustered in Warsaw around the so-called German synagogue (established in 1802), which introduced moderate reforms into synagogue practice, including the use of German as the language of address and sermons. They also encouraged the opening in 1826 of a state rabbinical seminary, which aimed to produce a class of

Polish-speaking enlightened rabbis and supported the establishment of a second progressive synagogue whose character was more Polish than the first (which by the 1850s replaced German with Polish too). For the second generation of Polish *maskilim*, use of Polish reflected a much more personal bond. Many spoke Polish as their mother tongue and identified profoundly with Polish culture and the Polish national cause. As early as 1815, a group of self-proclaimed Jewish Poles (*Żydzi-Polacy*; the Polish places equal weight on the two components of this identity) petitioned authorities for treatment distinguishing them from the Yiddish-speaking Jewish masses in recognition of their 'superior' cultural level.[21] In contrast with the Western Provinces, Congress Poland possessed essentially a mono-ethnic national culture. In the absence of an actual Polish state to which one could give his allegiance, modernization in Congress Poland meant increasingly not simply cultural and political identification with the dominant power but identification with the nascent Polish nation itself.[22] Such associations became all the more intense as increasing tsarist oppression in response to insurrections increased the romantic appeal of the Polish language, Polish culture, and the Polish national cause. While a distinct minority of the overall Jewish population of Congress Poland, thousands of Jews sympathized enough with this cause and believed its victory would be beneficial to Jews to participate in the unsuccessful Polish rebellion against Russian rule in 1830–31.

By the 1860s, a small number of Jewish 'Progressives' or 'Assimilationists' (as they were popularly known by both their supporters and their ideological opponents) stepped forward onto the political scene as Polish patriots and enthusiastic champions of the integration of Jews into Polish society.[23] Unlike earlier *maskilim*, their devotion to Polish culture was rooted in personal identification more than in utilitarian sympathies. While professing respect for Judaism and traditional Hebrew literature, often they were little interested in Hebrew culture and did not deem the language an autonomous value. They advocated the use of Polish as a literary language among Jews because Hebrew was understood well by few Jews and its use impeded participation in a common realm of public discourse by maintaining a linguistic barrier between Jews and Gentiles. Most concentrated in Warsaw, the Assimilationists were generally intellectuals or members of the Jewish high bourgeoisie – financial, commercial, and industrial – a group composing no more than 5 to 6 per cent of the total Jewish population.[24] They considered themselves Jews by descent or religion (hence the terms 'Poles of Mosaic Confession' or 'Poles of Mosaic Descent' by which they frequently referred to themselves) but Poles by virtue of culture and nationality (even if some spoke Polish with a pronounced Yiddish accent). Their Polish-language organ, *Izraelita* (1866–1913), championed the liberal values of Polish positivism and called for the religious reform (but not conversion) of the Jews and their gradual adoption of the Polish language and culture as steps towards full integration into Polish society. More aptly described as integrationists, Assimilationists desired to follow the Western European model of recasting Judaism in mostly religious (rather than national or ethnic) terms and did not seek, contrary to the accusations of their late-nineteenth and twentieth century Jewish detractors, the complete disappearance of Jewish identity and of the Jews as a collective.[25]

Polish-Jewish relations reached their apogee in the years 1861–63, when Jews and Poles were united in a brief but memorable 'spirit of brotherhood' to wrest Poland from the hands of the tsars.[26] The Romantic attempt to restore Polish sovereignty through armed uprising was met with bloody suppression and the vindictive eradication of not only what remained of Polish autonomy but of almost all pretences to the historical legacy of an independent cultural and political tradition. No longer would Polish culture be respected as long as Poles remained politically subordinate to the tsar. Tsarist Russia resorted to severe measures to check Polish nationalist aspirations, imposing an almost entirely Russian system of education, administration, and justice upon the ten Polish provinces known as the 'Kingdom of Poland.' The pretence of the Kingdom's autonomous status within the Russian Empire, guaranteed at the Congress of Vienna in 1815 but never fully instituted, was now cast aside. The purely geographical designation 'the Vistula country' was adopted in bureaucratic parlance (although the old name continued to be used, as well, in official documents) to emphasize the territories' integration into Russia and the futility of aspirations for Polish independence. Poles were excluded from nearly all government employ in the Polish provinces (and in the nine 'Western Provinces' immediately to their east) and benefited from none of the organs of limited self-government, such as town governments and *zemstva* (elected rural organs of self-government), which reforms brought to the central Russian provinces.

Russification efforts took aim, in particular, at educational institutions. Russian was introduced as the language of secular instruction in all schools, both public and private, and in teachers' seminaries for all courses save religion and Polish grammar (as religious schools, the Jewish *kheyder* was exempt and permitted to teach in Yiddish). Students were subject to punishment for speaking Polish on school premises, and schools could be closed for what was deemed excessive Polish content in their curriculum or requesting that students speak Polish. No Polish university was permitted to function and the Polish language, now reduced to an elective 'foreign language' in certain gymnasia, found a public forum in but a few state-owned theatres. The Warsaw rabbinical seminary, a bastion of pro-Polish sympathies, was similarly closed. The names of several towns were russified and even Polish street and building signs were replaced with Russian ones as part of this effort to reinforce Russian control and forestall the recurrence of a nationalist rebellion. The Catholic Church, by the nineteenth century intimately linked in popular consciousness with Polish nationhood, was regarded by Russian authorities as an instigator of the uprising and was terrorized into submission: hundreds of priests were kidnapped and imprisoned in the depths of Russia or otherwise removed from office and often forced into emigration.[27]

For all its draconian pervasiveness, however, the russification of Congress Poland was neither well coordinated nor executed in a wholly consistent manner by tsarist officials. For most Jews, it changed life little, as they continued to speak Yiddish and send their children to religious schools. Coercive linguistic policy did result in lower levels of Polish literacy and made Polish less useful for purposes of socioeconomic mobility. Still, society in Warsaw, the symbolic capital of partitioned Poland, remained broadly Polish-speaking and a high, as well as, low culture continued to function in that language. Rather than obliterate ethnic consciousness, the tsarist program aimed primarily at neutralizing rebellious elements and promoting the institutional integration of the region into the Empire. While the tsarist regime certainly desired for all its subjects to be Russian-speaking and Orthodox, the complete assimilation of minorities was never considered necessary nor contemplated. It was, however, considered expedient to hinder the polonization of other groups, such as Jews (who were, like the Poles, considered an unreliable element) and Ukrainians. Moreover, the regime aimed to sow dissension between the peasantry, which was deemed apolitical or loyal to the tsar, and the dominant classes in Polish society, the clergy and the nobility, who were held chiefly responsible for the 1863 insurrection.[28]

Urbanization, Socioeconomic Rivalries, and Ethnic Tensions

Congress Poland underwent rapid urbanization and industrialization in the second half of the nineteenth century. Punished for their leading role in the insurrection with measures conceived to deprive them of their feudal economic base, former landowning elites of noble background often found their lot no better than that of landless peasants and migrated to the cities and towns in search of jobs. Beginning in the 1870s, they were joined by the recently emancipated serfs of the Western Provinces who, unable to survive as independent or tenant farmers, were also hungry for work.[29] Even more dramatically than their neighbours, Jews also underwent rapid urbanization in the latter half of the nineteenth century as their role in the feudal economy declined and impoverishment was exacerbated by large family size, geographical confinement, and bitter economic competition due to a lack of occupational diversification and opportunities. With the lifting of residence and employment restrictions as part of the 1862 Wielopolski Reforms granting quasi-equality to Jews with the non-Jewish population in Congress Poland, Jewish proletariats developed in cities like Łódź and Warsaw. While throughout the nineteenth century, only 15 per cent of the Christian population of Congress Poland lived in cities, by 1827 already 80 per cent of the Jewish population was urban and by 1865 this figure had reached 91.5 per cent. By 1900, both Warsaw and Łódź – dubbed the 'Manchester' of Poland for its industrial boom in the latter half of the nineteenth century – had populations that were more than 30 per cent Jewish.[30]

Despite tsarist oppression, Congress Poland became the most economically advanced region of the Russian Empire even if it remained predominantly rural and agricultural, woefully backwards in comparison with the industrial and financial powers of Western Europe. Benefiting from high protective tariffs and the Empire's large Asian market, it came to produce 25 per cent of the Empire's industrial output in the second half of the nineteenth century while only possessing 10 per cent of its population. A young urban proletariat began to emerge in addition to the historically small Polish petite bourgeoisie and an inchoate intelligentsia. Comprising practitioners of the free professions (e.g., writers, journalists, doctors, lawyers, engineers, teachers, and scholars), the intelligentsia in Poland, as elsewhere in Russia and Eastern Europe, developed as a self-conscious social class beginning in the late nineteenth century. In Poland it viewed itself as the political elite of the Polish nation and inheritors of the patriotic leadership of the *szlachta*, the nobility of the Commonwealth.

The integration of Jews into Polish society and the financial and cultural contributions of Assimilations were welcomed by the Polish Positivist movement, which rejected Polish romanticism's exaltation of armed revolt in the disastrous wake of the 1863 insurrection. As exemplified by the *Prawda* editor Aleksander Świętochowski, Positivism instead embraced 'organic work,' the pacific development of the Polish economy and culture within each of the partitioned territories of the former Commonwealth. The Positivists welcomed all who contributed to the expansion of Polish-owned industry and trade as an integral part of the nation regardless of religion. By legitimizing economic activity as a form of patriotism, Positivism broadened the definition of the Polish political nation to include the polonized, secularized Jewish intelligentsia and high bourgeoisie in a time of external, denationalizing pressures.[31] Jews contributed greatly to the development of industry, especially textiles, sugar, and tobacco. Jewish bankers, along with Jewish converts to Christianity, also supplied a substantial part of the capital for the Kingdom's expansion through their own investments and by creating a ramified network of banking and credit facilities available to other entrepreneurs.[32]

Nonetheless, despite its condemnation of antisemitism and discrimination of the Jews as irrational and harmful to Polish society, anti-clerical Positivism was not tolerant of the vast majority of Polish Jews *as they were.* Jews were expected to abandon their presumably inferior culture and adopt the patterns of the superior secularized Christian-Polish culture as a natural by-product of their eventual emancipation.[33] The Positivist vision of Jewish integration often included conversion to Christianity or, at the least, a reform of Judaism to render it more 'rational.'[34] Still, most of Polish society was not so accepting, continuing to view Assimilationists, including those who had undergone baptism, as a separate group. At the same time, converts often maintained strong social and business ties to their former co-religionists. In an age of increasing religious indifference, other Jews commonly continued to see them as 'their own' and took pride in the economic success of members of their ethnic community even if baptism was traditionally regarded as a form of betrayal of God and the Jewish people.[35]

The expanded Polish urban classes found themselves engaged in mounting economic competition with Jews and Germans, the two groups historically dominant as merchants, traders, bankers, and artisans in Poland. To its alarm, the déclassé *szlachta* found itself being eclipsed in social and political influence by a new capitalist plutocratic class in whose ranks Jews were prominent.[36] While most industry in Poland was developed by French and Germans, the presence of Jews and 'Poles of Jewish descent' in this new class was painfully felt. The alleged Jewish 'stranglehold' on commerce and industry was also a sore point for Polish nationalists, one that was exacerbated by the prominence of non-ethnic Polish and foreign elements in the rising class of bankers, large-scale merchants, and industrialists. It was frequently overlooked that members of such 'dynasties' as the families Kronenberg, Epstein, Natanson, and Wawelberg formed but a tiny elite of highly polonized Jews who acted as generous patrons and contributors to the Polish arts and sciences in the absence of culture-promoting state institutions. They were also leaders of clandestine or unofficial programs to promote education in Polish and strove to spread the Polish language (and secular learning) within the Jewish community.[37]

New rivalries emerging from the collapse of long-standing social and economic niches inflamed the traditional, clerical variety of anti-Jewish sentiment. Indeed, by the 1880s, the perceived likelihood of a Polish-Jewish rapprochement, as preached by the Positivists and Assimilationists, and of the Jews' shedding their cultural particularities had already begun to retreat. This animus manifested itself in three days of anti-Jewish pogroms, promptly denounced by Poles of all stripes, in Warsaw on Christmas Day, 1881. This followed a wave of pogroms that erupted earlier that year in Ukraine sparked by the assassination of the tsar by revolutionaries, one of whom was a rather assimilated Jew.[38]

Tensions were further exacerbated by the diffusion of more ethnically exclusive varieties of nationalism, a part of the nationalist 'awakening' occurring throughout Central and Eastern Europe in the closing decades of the nineteenth century. Of greatest concern to many Polish nationalists was the progress of the Jews and the Ukrainians, the two largest non-Polish groups within their midst. In contrast with the traditional concept of the Polish 'political nation,' which was rather open with respect to ethnic origin but included only members of the Polish and polonized (Christian) gentry, the new nationalist movement understood the nation to include ethnic Poles of all classes and aimed to draw the peasantry and growing urban proletariat under its banner.[39] Jews' disproportionately urban presence allegedly impeded the emergence of a native Polish middle class, a class which was historically lacking and which Polish nationalists claimed was necessary to be a 'complete' nation. The overwhelmingly rural Ukrainians, on the other hand, were concentrated outside Congress Poland, in the Western Provinces and, outside the Russian Empire, in Habsburg Galicia.

Some, like Polish liberal and socialist parties, desired the disintegration of a specific Jewish identity and the complete integration of the Jews into Polish civil society. They identified Jewish forms of nationalism (or 'separatism' as it was labelled by its detractors) and socialism, movements propagated by secularized Jews by the 1890s, as forces undermining this ideal. They were a factor not only depriving the Polish national cause of potential support, but one also presenting a serious obstacle to it. Others, most infamously the notoriously antisemitic middle-class party National Democracy (Narodowa Demokracja or Endecja, the popular name formed from its initials N.D.), cast doubt upon the possibility and even desirability of the Jews' complete assimilation. Led by Roman Dmowski, it emerged as the dominant Polish party by the end of 1905.[40]

Jewish Nationalism and Socialism

Following the devastating pogroms of the early 1880s, many 'progressive' Jews found their faith profoundly shaken in the possibility of cultural and social rapprochement between Jews and non-Jews and the inevitability of emancipation in the Russian Empire. The notorious May Laws instituted in the Pale by the regime blamed the mayhem on the Jews' ruthless exploitation of the unwitting peasantry, effectively punishing the victims. Their sphere of residence and means to earn a living were further constricted (even if many Jews found ways to evade its harshest strictures) by permitting no new settlement outside towns and hamlets, cancelling deeds of leasing and sale on rural real estate, and forbidding trading on Sundays and Christian holidays. In Congress Poland, the implementation of the May Laws was narrowly averted through the intervention of Assimilationist financiers.[41] Nonetheless, among Jews in both Poland and the Western Provinces, feelings of frustration, disillusionment, and a very real sense of endangerment at the hands of a hostile non-Jewish majority and regime deepened. These culminated in a number of responses to address Jewish misery and insecurity.

By the mid-1880s Jewish youth increasingly looked to nationalism and socialism as solutions to both Jewish and general problems in the Empire. Jewish nationalism began to coalesce as a coherent ideological movement at this time in the form of *Hibat-Tsion* (Love of Zion). It loosely united organizations urging Jewish colonization in Ottoman Palestine, economic productivization and occupational diversification, and forms of cultural revival centred around the Hebrew language. Radicalized Jewish youth, especially those with secular educations and competent in Russian or Polish, also joined left-wing organizations and many embraced the cause to put an end to tsarist autocracy. While only a minority of Jews, on the whole traditionally religious and opposed to socialist doctrine, took up revolutionary activity, nearly 30 per cent of political arrestees in the Russian Empire were Jews by 1900.[42] Common responses to worsening conditions also included emigration to the United State and elsewhere.

The year 1897 is particularly noteworthy as a milestone in Jewish political organization. It saw the birth in Vilna in the northeastern Pale of the 'General Jewish Workers' Alliance of Lithuania, Poland, and Russia' (the Bund), a socialist party formed by russified Jewish intellectuals that demanded the exclusive right to agitate among the Jewish masses and eventually employed Yiddish as its chief medium to propagandize among them. By 1905, it championed Yiddish as the national language of the Jews and the cause of national cultural autonomy for the Jews and other groups within the framework of the Russian Empire. The first Zionist Congress, organized by the Viennese journalist Theodor Herzl (1860–1904), was held in Basel, Switzerland, that same year. The Zionist movement, which absorbed *Hibat-Tsion*, was chiefly divided around the turn of the century between proponents of political and cultural nationalism. Herzl's plan to secure an internationally recognized charter for the creation of a Jewish state in Palestine competed with the essayist Ahad Ha'am's ('One of the People,' Hebrew pen name of Asher Ginzberg, 1856–1927) emphasis on national rejuvenation via a modernized Hebrew culture. Meanwhile, other nationalist theoreticians, most notably the historian Simon Dubnow (1860–1941), championed the cause of national cultural autonomy (often referred to as the doctrine of autonomism or Diaspora nationalism) for Jews as citizens in the lands of their contemporary residence.

Jewish parties also arose that attempted to resolve the apparent contradiction between the ideal of international class struggle and integral nationalism. The fundamental issue dividing groupings fusing socialism with Jewish nationalism was that of geography: Where should the Jewish nation dwell? In its historic homeland in *Eretz-yisrael* in agreement with Zionist thought, in any territory where it could enjoy sovereignty as proposed by territorialists, or as one of many nationalities with rights to administer its cultural and political life in the greater context of the multiethnic states of Eastern Europe as championed by autonomists? Scattered Labour Zionist groups in the Russian Empire coalesced between 1901 and 1904 into distinct territorialist, Palestine-centric, and autonomist currents and, eventually, parties. These parties also increasingly took positions regarding what would serve as the language of the Jewish future – a revived Hebrew language or a cultivated Yiddish. Many socialist Jews joined, of course, parties that were not specifically Jewish, such as the Russian Social Democratic Party (RSDP) or the Polish Socialist Party (PPS), which agitated in Yiddish as well as Polish but encouraged the assimilation of Jews into Polish society. Some Jews, partial to neither Jewish nationalism nor socialism, identified with liberal Russian and Polish parties, such as the Cadets, that favoured civil (although not national) rights for all regardless of origin.[43]

At the same time that political activity increased among Jews, however, the pace of acculturation in both its Polish and Russian forms continued undiminished into the twentieth century. Moreover, not all lost faith in the inevitability of greater tolerance and social progress and the diminution of religious and ethnic prejudices with the spread of secular education. Many russified Jews, for example, continued to believe in the possibility of liberal reform to redress discrimination and Jewish rightlessness, often seeking to use their training in faculties of law to promote this goal.[44] Most Jews, it must be stressed, however, remained traditionally religious and Yiddish-speaking. They stood aside at this time from active political involvement, which was illegal.

Modern Yiddish and Hebrew Culture

Alongside the inroads of polonization and russification into Jewish life, a modern culture finding its expression in Jewish languages also began to develop in cities such as Warsaw, Odessa, and St Petersburg by the late nineteenth century. A centre of Hebrew printing and publishing in Poland since the nineteenth century, Warsaw hosted the influential *maskilic*, later Zionist, periodical *Ha-tsefira* (The Dawn) edited by Nahum Sokolow (also briefly editer of *Izraelita*), and was home to such Hebrew luminaries as Ben-Avigdor (Avraham Leib Shalkovich) and David Frishman. With the arrival of the multilingual writer Y.L. Peretz, the city also became home to a vibrant Yiddish literary circle that coalesced around him in the years 1880–1915.

Steeped in Jewish tradition in his youth, Peretz (1852–1915) jettisoned his religious belief under the influence of Polish Positivism (he actually began his writing in 1875 with poetry in Polish and spoke with his son in this language),[45] and Russian nihilism as a young man during the 1870s. The rising tide of political oppression and antisemitism in Russia, of which the pogroms of the 1880s were the most brutal expression, shook his faith a second time. He abandoned as futile the *maskilic* ideology of cultural rapprochement as a means to achieve social and political equality for the Jews. In time he came to regard the shedding of the Jews' cultural specificity as a disgraceful endeavour and made the crusade against 'assimilation' one of the primary themes of his writing from the 1890s on. Despite having flirted with socialism and expressed a degree of enthusiasm for Jewish settlement in Palestine, he endorsed neither the Bund nor the Zionist movement, both of which he criticized freely.[46]

Like a number of other Jewish writers, Peretz was drawn to metropolitan Warsaw from his native town (Zamość) in no small measure by the possibilities it offered for a writer to earn a living thanks to its growing Jewish population in the late nineteenth century and its many Hebrew publishers and book stores.[47] Peretz came, however, to prefer Yiddish over Hebrew for the articulation of a modern, secularized Jewish culture, and eventually embraced the ideology that came to be known as Yiddishism. During this time, Peretz, the most prominent cultural personality in Yiddish-speaking Warsaw, was employed as a bureaucrat in the local *kehila* (official Jewish community), a sinecure which left him ample time to pursue his literary interests. Urging hopeful arrivals from the provinces to write in Yiddish rather than Hebrew, he served as an inspiration and mentor to successive generations of young men who had left behind traditionally religious homes to create a modernistic Jewish literature.[48]

The Press, Politics, and the 1905 Revolution

A tremendous upward surge in political activity and related violence transfigured Congress Poland during the years 1904–7 as part of the general revolutionary wave then engulfing the vast Russian Empire. Confined previously to covert existence by the Russian bureaucratic-police system, slowly incubating conspiratorial cells emerged at this time from hiding and developed into open and well-organized political factions, some of which did not eschew violence and expropriation from private businesses to achieve their aims. Until the Reaction restored civil order and crushed opposition, widespread strikes and demonstrations were the order of the day, particularly in Warsaw and Łódź. Bloody street battles in 1905 pitted rival political factions against each other in near civil war and against the soldiers of the tsarist regime.[49] The tsar's October Manifesto, which held the promise of a constitutional monarchy with guarantees for civil rights, was only temporarily implemented. Still, the creation in 1906 of the Empire's first popularly elected parliament, the Duma, provided the opportunity for political parties to compete openly to influence state policy. In an atmosphere of extreme turmoil but relaxed censorship, a burgeoning press, both Jewish and Polish, played an invaluable role in mobilizing mass readerships to previously unknown levels of political consciousness and engagement.

The more open journalistic atmosphere post-1905, as Theodore Weeks points out, permitted both Polish and Jewish newspapers to engage in polemics with each other and exchange hostile barbs. These mutual barrages helped to strengthen both national consciousness and mutual suspicion, if not outright hostility, between Jews and Poles.[50] Polish liberalism wavered by 1905 in its faith in the inevitability of assimilation – the abandonment by the Jews of their 'separatist' cultural particularities in exchange for Polish language and customs, traditions, and patriotism. Indeed, the Polish Positivist movement, which had in the aftermath of 1863 attempted to expand the concept of nation to include secular, polonized Jews and supported Jewish legal equality, began to transform by 1909 into 'progressive anti-Semitism' (antysemityzm postępowy), the antisemitism of the moderate left. As antisemitism grew more strident and gained supporters across the political spectrum (with the exception of the far left and, perhaps, ironically, the far right), Jewish voters were only more inclined to vote for Jewish candidates.[51]

Conclusion

The modernization of European society and the decline of ancient régimes had a disintegrative effect on the fabric of traditional Jewish society among the Jews of the former Polish-Lithuanian Commonwealth. The ascendancy of new modes of social, economic, and political organization – processes that had begun prior to the partitions with the rise of absolutist regimes in neighbouring states and the diffusion of Enlightenment ideals – engendered the beginnings of a profound reconfiguration of Jewish-Gentile relations throughout Europe and new perspectives among Jews regarding their own society and culture. European Jews began to integrate into an emerging civil society (especially in those places where they achieved partial or full emancipation), abandoning and adapting prior modes of behaviour and identification. They also entered into increasing economic and political competition with non-Jews as their long-standing judicial autonomy, increasingly dismantled by the centralizing state, and traditional economic niches and legal restrictions began to decline, if not disappear.

By the late nineteenth century, Jews found themselves increasingly divided into often mutually hostile camps along linguistic, religious, and political lines. At the same time, relations between Jews and Poles worsened with the intensification of economic and political competition and the spread of ethnically exclusive forms of nationalism among both groups. While Hebrew-Yiddish diglossia and religiosity, whether in its Hasidic or *mitnagdic* forms, remained the dominant patterns of life among an increasingly urbanizing Jewish population, a secularizing Jewish culture was also emerging. It found expression through a modern Jewish press in multiple languages: Polish and Russian, as well as Hebrew and Yiddish.

Even before the lifting of restrictions following the 1905 Russian Revolution, which made a legal press and theatre in Yiddish legal, Warsaw exerted an almost magnetic attraction on aspiring young talents from the Polish provinces and Pale of Settlement. In the years immediately prior to the First World War, the city was inundated with publishers, journalists, and actors eager to partake in the construction of a modern Jewish culture directed at a mass audience. By 1910, it had become the cultural capital of the Yiddish world: in addition to a wide selection of press, theatre, concerts, and popular lectures available daily, three or more theatre companies could be seen performing before large, demonstrative audiences even during the Jewish Sabbath on Friday nights and Saturdays.[52]

Of the Jewish press in all languages – Russian, Polish, Hebrew, and Yiddish – the Yiddish press, in particular, was an irritant to Polish nationalists: it stood as a blatant symbol of growing Jewish national consciousness and cultural self-assertion. Especially galling was what appeared to be the increasingly aggressive use of Yiddish in the public sphere. Even for those more favourably inclined towards Jews, the Jewish jargon, like all forms of medieval Jewish separatism and segregation, was destined to disappear into oblivion with the Jews' embrace of progressive European culture. Perhaps worst of all, the Mecca of this emerging Jewish vernacular culture was none other than Warsaw, the unofficial Polish capital. The birth of the Jewish national press in Yiddish is inextricably entwined with the careers of two russified Jewish migrants to that city, Noah Prylucki and his father Tsevi.

chapter two

The Making of a Jewish Nationalist: Noah Prylucki and the Warsaw Yiddish Press

As may be expected of a man so often in the public eye, Noah Prylucki was no stranger to controversy, and opinions of him varied dramatically. His many admirers lauded him as an exceptionally industrious, if unsystematic, autodidact, a prolific journalist, and a pioneer in the scholarly research and cultivation of diverse fields of Yiddish culture. His equally abundant detractors assailed him as an irascible dilettante who founded and commanded a political party to satisfy his own ego. A 'Jewish aristocrat' known for his distinguished appearance[1] and a fiery temperament expressed in near constant polemics and a nervous twitch,[2] he left few, if any, intimates and observers indifferent. Surrounding only one aspect of his multifaceted personality did there exist universal accord: his boundless love and devotion to the Yiddish language, which he romantically conceived of as the expression of the soul of the Jewish people and in whose dialectal diversity he located the underlying national unity of Eastern European Jewry.[3]

Nonetheless, like many other Jewish intellectuals born in late nineteenth-century Eastern Europe, in his youth Noah Prylucki shared the condescension towards, if not distaste for, Yiddish common to *maskilim* (proponents of the Jewish Enlightenment). The everyday language of the Jewish masses, it was the lowly 'handmaiden' of 'lady' Hebrew, a hallowed language that had not been spoken as anyone's mother tongue in roughly two thousand years. He turned to it after initial literary and political activity in other, more prestigious languages. Although as an adult he was celebrated as a riveting orator famous for the 'folksy' quality of his Yiddish speech, Prylucki did not consider himself a native speaker of what he later proclaimed *the* national language of the Jewish people in Eastern Europe.[4] 'My true mother tongue,' he recalled in a biographical sketch, 'was Russian, the second, Hebrew, in which I tried for years to feel at home. My Yiddish, on the other hand, was poor and raw.'[5]

At first blush, this self-appraisal sounds unusual, if not implausible at a time before Jews were commonly native speakers of Russian and the revival of Hebrew as a spoken language was at best in its infancy. How are we to make sense of it, especially when considering the career of a man so devoted to Yiddish? Beginning with a sketch of his childhood and early adulthood, this chapter traces Noah Prylucki's path to Yiddish as a reflection of changing attitudes towards language in Jewish society and of his unfolding political ideology and professional career. It focuses on his early journalistic engagement under the tutelage of his father, the trilingual newspaperman Tsevi Prylucki, and the revolutionary role of the press in 'teaching' Jews to read as a means to shape them politically and culturally.

Mother Tongue

Looking back through the adult eyes of an accomplished Yiddish journalist and philologist, Prylucki deemed the Yiddish of his youth inelegant and deficient. This comment should be regarded not as testimony to his unfamiliarity with the vernacular of Eastern European Jewry; rather, if not an instance of false modesty, it is a reflection of a lack of conscious cultivation of the language in his youth in comparison with a thorough grounding in the Russian and Hebrew literary languages. Indeed, Prylucki's initially condescending attitudes towards Yiddish were typical of a generation of middle-class Jewish youth educated in Russian-language schools at the turn of the century.

It is instructive on this point to compare Prylucki's reminiscences with those of a contemporary who was also raised in a middle-class home permeated with the spirit of the *Haskalah* in Volhyn (Ukraine). Reflecting upon his youth, Nokhem Shtif (1879–1933), who similarly went on to become a prominent Yiddish linguist and Diaspora nationalist, recalls:

> I came to literature rather late and to Yiddish literature even later. Yiddish literature was then something alien to me. In my circles in those years, the idea of Yiddish literature did not even exist. I first heard about Yiddish in a serious vein when Sholem Aleichem read his stories at Zionist gatherings in Kiev 1900–2. Though brought up in a Jewish home where Yiddish was always spoken, where I lived until I was nineteen, I believed, like all of my friends, that I did not know Yiddish, and even more certainly that I could

> not write it – so much so that when I had to write two pamphlets about the attempt on Krushevan's life, I wrote in Russian and asked someone to translate into Yiddish.[6]

Acutely sensitive to language, Prylucki reports having borne from earliest youth an abiding interest in the colourful language and rich treasury of folklore possessed by uneducated Jews in his immediate surroundings. While it is unclear what language dominated in the home of Prylucki's grandfather, where he spent his childhood, it is not to be excluded that the boy typically spoke Russian with his father (and perhaps also with his grandfather), as was commonplace then among the secularly educated Jewish bourgeoisie in the Western Provinces of the Russian Empire. It is certain, however, that the boy possessed at least a passive command of Yiddish, the language most widely spoken among Kremenets Jews, and almost certainly an active command of the language. Not only Noah and his father, but his siblings too demonstrated literary abilities in Yiddish as adults. Quite likely Yiddish was the language in which his parents communicated and in which his mother spoke to him even if he responded in Russian.[7] Most probably, Prylucki was accustomed until adolescence to hearing, speaking, and perhaps even reading Yiddish in informal settings but did not consider using it for 'higher' functions. The use of Yiddish, which was then scarcely being cultivated as a modern literary language, was virtually unthinkable in intellectual circles, even among those intellectuals who used it in their public addresses to the 'masses.' Indeed, speaking Russian (or Polish in Russian-controlled Congress Poland) was a marker of membership in educated society.[8]

It is characteristic of a generation of politically active middle-class Jews that Noah Prylucki's initial use of Yiddish in the public sphere stemmed more from practical than ideological reasons: he sought to communicate his Jewish nationalist message to the Jewish masses that knew no other language as well, and he was happy to turn a profit in doing so.[9] Over time he came romantically to conceive of Yiddish as the *mame-loshn*, the mother tongue of Eastern European Jewry, and to champion the cause of Yiddishism, the movement to make the Yiddish language the primary, if not exclusive, vehicle for the articulation of a modern, secularized Jewish identity. Throughout his life, Prylucki would frequently draw upon the wealth of Yiddish idioms and proverbs absorbed during his Volhyn childhood for use in both his philological studies and his journalistic work.[10] Critics even mocked him for what they judged an excessive love for 'folksy' turns of phrase – likely as much overcompensation by a self-proclaimed democrat and champion of the Yiddish-speaking masses for his elite origins (and hence his 'inauthenticity') as an expression of the sheer delight that he took in the language.

While a gradual but marked change in attitudes towards Yiddish is similarly observable in the biographies of many Jewish political and cultural leaders belonging to his generation, Prylucki's path towards Jewish nationalism and political engagement is less typical. Many of his peers in the forefront of Jewish politics rejected, or at the very least neglected, the ways of their fathers – whether by abandoning the strictures of Orthodoxy or by turning their backs on programs of social and cultural integration that accompanied *embourgeoisement* – when embarking upon the road that would ultimately lead them to a secular conception of Jewish nationhood. Notably absent from Prylucki's biography, however, is a tale a profound (and often painful) disillusionment or of 'conversion' from one ideology or way of life to another following a sobering encounter with antisemitism or a loss of religious faith. Among the principle founders of the Folksparty (the popular religious philosopher Hillel Zeitlin, the political philosopher Saul Stupnicki, the fiction writer Hersh-Dovid Nomberg, the Yiddish and Polish essayist and bellelettrist Samuel Hirschhorn – all writers for *Der moment*) in the summer of 1916, he alone was not a graduate of a *kheyder*, the traditional religious school for young boys which Folkists hailed as the precursor of the national elementary school. Nor was he raised on the periphery of Jewish society in an atmosphere foreign to traditional culture. From earliest childhood, rather, he was shaped by the secularized, Jewish nationalist circles of his father Tsevi and like-minded intellectuals.

Noah Prylucki was groomed by his father from adolescence for a role in the Jewish nationalist movement. His course of intellectual development as a nationalist and language ideologist entailed some meandering but few radical turns. Although in his mature years he dismissed his father Tsevi's goal of mass Jewish colonization in Palestine and the revernacularization of Hebrew as utopian dreams, he never publicly departed from a secular understanding of the Jews as a nation nor ceased to militate on behalf of their civil and national rights. At the same time, he remained a fin-de-siècle liberal and cosmopolitan, a champion of democratic values and admirer of European, especially Russian, culture.[11]

In the absence of archival materials and with limited access to sources to corroborate details, the researcher is necessarily overly reliant upon Prylucki's own memories to construct his biography, especially about his childhood and adolescence. Fortunately, these recollections, scattered across hundreds of articles and interviews over a span of more than three decades, are generous in details. He was moved to write frequently about his life on the pages of the Yiddish daily press by the practical need to fill a regular newspaper column as well as by a self-aggrandizing but not fundamentally mistaken conviction that his experiences and achievements were of lasting political, cultural, and historical import. Unlike his more reticent father, he publicly reflected upon his personal past and described in great (and sometimes suspicious) detail events that had occurred even years prior. An exercise in self-fashioning like any autobiography, his writings depict him as a precocious and talented child already imbued with enthusiasm for the Jewish nationalist cause and Eastern European Jewish folk culture long before such sentiments were in vogue.[12] With the exception of his father, mention of friends or family life beyond incidental references are few and far between. It is unclear to what to attribute this notable absence of intimate relations: a desire to protect the privacy of others, familial estrangement, lack of perceived relevance to readers or, quite simply, narcissism. It is also not unusual for Prylucki to laud his own childhood feats and to downplay or ignore the contributions of others to the early Jewish nationalist movement. This is especially true of latter-day political opponents and rivals with whom he was once active in revolutionary student circles. Among his contemporaries in the Jewish nationalist movement, however, he is hardly uniquely guilty of such 'sins' of omission: the memoirs of Zionist leaders Yitshak Grünbaum and Apolinary Hartglas, for example, similarly make little mention of Prylucki – even when they were clearly present at the same event.[13] These caveats aside, a picture of Noah Prylucki's childhood and early adulthood emerges.

Noah Prylucki's Earliest Years

The eldest of five children, Noah Prylucki was born into an affluent merchant family in the predominately Jewish city of Berdichev in Kiev province (Ukraine) on 1 October 1882. He spent his childhood, however, in Kremenets, where the famous *maskil* Isaac Baer Levinsohn, the 'Russian Mendelssohn,' was long active. Located in Volhyn province and not far from the Galician *Haskalah* centre of Brody, Kremenets was host to an intellectual Jewish milieu that had a profound impact on Prylucki's later career as both a politician and a linguist.

His father Tsevi (Hirsh-Sholem) Prylucki (1862–1942) was educated in Kremenets in the spirit of the *Haskalah* by his own father Nakhmen, a personal friend and pupil of Levinsohn. Details concerning Tsevi's early life and career are scarce. He became acquainted with both the modern press and Russian officialdom – two formative influences in shaping his future career – through the activities of his father. Nakhmen Prylucki subscribed to the Russian press as well as to the Jewish newspapers available in Hebrew, Polish, and Russian in the latter half of the nineteenth century.[14] He also maintained cordial relations with local tsarist officials, most notably military officers who enjoyed discussing politics and current events in his store.[15]

Raised in a home that valued both Jewish and general education, Tsevi Prylucki studied both traditional Jewish subjects and European languages (Russian, German, and French) in his native town prior to auditing courses in 1880 at the universities of Kiev and Berlin. In 1880, a year before the eruption of pogroms in southern Russia in 1881 that catalyzed the movement for Jewish settlement in Palestine, he contributed to the Hebrew journal *Ha-boker or* (The Morning Light) an article inspired by Byron's 'Hebrew Melodies' entitled 'Shivat-tsion' (Return of Zion).

The leading spirit of the local branch of the organization *Hibat-tsion* (Love of Zion), Tsevi Prylucki travelled throughout Volhyn in the 1880s and 1890s to preach in the exhortative style of a traditional preacher the then unconventional message of Jewish colonization in Palestine and the cultivation of Hebrew not only as a modern literary language but also a spoken idiom. In his home he regularly played host on Saturdays in the early 1890s to meetings of the society *Safa brura* (Clear Language).[16] Its members strove to converse in flowery Hebrew over a glass of tea about quotidian affairs or to read a Hebrew book or newspaper.[17] Given Tsevi Prylucki's commitment to the revival of Hebrew – members of the Kremenets chapter of *Safa brura* vowed to speak Hebrew among themselves and with their children[18] – it is not to be ruled out that he conversed with his son, at least for a time, in Hebrew despite the difficulty of such an endeavour. Indeed, by attempting to make Hebrew a language of daily exchange in Eastern Europe, Tsevi Prylucki was seen as a zealot even by his Zionist colleagues, most of whom spoke Russian at home and believed the revival of Hebrew as a vernacular to be a possibility only in Palestine.[19]

He also agitated on behalf of the *Hibat-tsion* movement, in general, and its doctrine of Jewish productivization through physical labour, in particular, on the pages of the St Petersburg Hebrew daily *Ha-melits* (The Advocate). To this end, he laboured to organize modernized *khadorim* and *talmud toyres*, Jewish community-supported schools for indigent boys in which practical subjects and trades were taught in addition to traditional religious subjects. In recognition of his endeavours, he was inducted into *Bnei Moshe* (Sons of Moses), the elite Zionist coterie founded by Ahad Ha-am.[20]

Not surprisingly, Tsevi Prylucki took great pains to inculcate in his first-born son his own passion for Jewish history and Hebrew. In addition to attending the local government school (1891–94), where he excelled in Russian language and literature, Noah received regular instruction in Hebrew and Judaica (Bible, Jewish history, the *maskil* Ze'ev Jawitz' Hebrew tales for children) from his father and other tutors.[21] Profoundly influenced by this proto-nationalist milieu, Noah Prylucki, according to his own recollection, composed at age ten his first publicistic article, a piece about Jewish colonization in Argentina written in Hebrew.[22]

After finishing his studies in the Kremenets elementary school, Prylucki remained at home for a year, reading widely in Russian and Hebrew and devoting himself to the study of Talmud, Torah, and Hebrew grammar under the tutelage of a respected local scholar. In 1896, he registered in the progymnasium (a school which prepared students for admission to secondary school, or gymnasium) in Sandomierz (Kielce province). This was his first extended stay in Congress Poland and the beginning of a long-time intimacy with Polish Jewry and Polish society. During his two years of study there, Prylucki, according to his recollection, became more closely acquainted with the 'folksmasn' (the popular Yiddish term for the broad Jewish population, especially those segments without a higher level of secular or religious education) and their manner of speaking and unique jokes. He also viewed for the first time a *purim-shpil* (a genre of plays performed as part of the celebration of the holiday of Purim), a subject which he later revisited as a scholar,[23] and transcribed the play in a notebook. After graduating with distinction from the progymnasium, Prylucki began the fifth class in Warsaw's Third Gymnasium.[24] That year, 1898, represents a turning point in the lives of both father and son, marking the beginning of four decades of journalistic collaboration. During this epoch, the infant Yiddish press developed and expanded into a powerful instrument of mass culture and politics in Poland, with no small thanks to the two of them.

Journalistic Debut

Following some bad business dealings which impaired his financial well-being, Tsevi Prylucki abandoned his dry goods store and the pursuit of itinerant Zionist activism in the provinces to relocate to the Russian imperial capital. In St Petersburg he devoted himself full-time to the Jewish nationalist and Hebraist causes as a regular staff member of the Hebrew daily *Ha-melits*, to which he contributed articles mainly about *Eretz-yisrael* and for which he eventually became editor for political affairs and author of a regular column titled *Pinkas katan* (Small Ledger). He also began to write and edit for the Russian-Jewish journal *Budushchnost'* (The Future) as well to contribute sporadically to the Hebrew publications *Ha-zeman* (Time) and *Ha-tsefira* (The Dawn).[25]

Once ensconced in the small Jewish journalistic and intellectual milieu of St Petersburg, Tsevi suggested to his eighteen-year-old son that he contribute to a new Yiddish publication, *Bleter fun a togbukh* (Pages of a Diary), to which he had himself contributed. No Yiddish newspapers could be legally printed in the Russian Empire at this time but journals managed to appear irregularly since they were considered books and therefore not subject to the same ban. Impressed by the financial success in Russia of *Der yud* (The Jew), Leon (Leib) Rabinovich, the editor of *Ha-melits*, began to publish *Bleter fun a togbukh* as a supplement to *He-melits* in June 1900 under the pseudonym Ish yehudi (Jewish man). Featuring popular scientific articles, a genre then very much in vogue among Jewish youth seeking knowledge of the natural and non-Jewish worlds, the pioneering journal avoided politics and news items in order to pass more easily the tsarist censor.[26]

In need of money for his upkeep, the adolescent Noah Prylucki was able to supplement the modest income he earned from tutoring with honoraria received for articles about the planet Mars, the importance of forests and nature, and other topics in the natural sciences. The short-lived journal marked his professional debut as a journalist in Yiddish. The following year he began to publish articles and feuilletons in *Ha-melits* on literary and Jewish topics, including a piece about the instruction of Jewish history in state middle schools for Russian Jews and the beginnings of a larger work about Spanish literature. He also reports contributing a discussion of the phenomenon of Jewish 'assimilation' in Warsaw, a subject that remained his bête-noire in the years to come.[27]

An avid reader of Russian and European literature, Noah Prylucki also took special interest in the literature that had begun to emerge in the closing decades of the nineteenth century as part of the 'Jewish national renaissance.' The movement called for the 'awakening' of the Jewish masses to self-awareness of their condition as a modern nation (and not merely as an ethno-religious group) and the cultivation of secular cultural forms common to European nationalist movements. It devoted its energies to the shaping of new Jewish culture, either in Hebrew or Yiddish or both, that would encompass science, literature, theatre, and the arts, and would rival the finest in the cultures of all other European peoples. For the benefit of russophone readers unfamiliar with the emerging body of modern Jewish belle lettres, he translated from Hebrew Peretz Smolenskin's *Nekam brit* (Avenger of the Covenant) and Y.L. Peretz's Yiddish works *Sholem bayis* (Domestic Peace) and *Der toyt fun a klezmer* (The Death of a Musician) for the St Petersburg anthology *Evreiskii ezhegodnik* (Jewish Annual) in 1902. His father contributed reports on the Zionist movement to the journal as well as articles about the poet and *maskil* Yehuda Leib Gordon and the early advocate of a Jewish national homeland Leo Pinsker.[28]

Simultaneously, Noah Prylucki tried his hand at fiction in Russian, the language whose literature he knew best and in which he had distinguished himself in the eyes of teachers and school officials through his writing talents. In contrast with his Yiddish feuilletons, which were generally well received, he considered his attempts at belle-lettres in Russian a failure and, according to his reminiscences, often burned chapters he had written only the night before. He abandoned aspirations for an artistic career despite an abiding love for Russian literature and theatre without ever seeing his fiction published in a Russian literary journal.[29]

Following a near fatal bout with scarlet fever and diphtheria in his last year of gymnasium, Prylucki graduated with a prestigious gold medal and gained admission to the faculty of law of the University of Warsaw despite a quota severely limiting Jewish enrolment. Although a Russian institution, the University of Warsaw served as the training grounds for much of the political elite of Poland, both Jewish and non-Jewish.[30] The ethnic and ideological divisions within the student body reflected the general political landscape of Congress Poland. As may be expected, national tensions were inflamed here, where the languages of the indigenous population were suppressed, to a greater extent than in universities in Russia proper. In the Russian interior, in contrast, Russian was not only both the imperial language and language uniting students of different ethnic backgrounds but it was also that of the general population. This made its everyday use by students less of an offence to minority nationalist sensibilities.[31]

University Years

Prylucki's university years, 1902–07, represent a period of great intellectual ferment in his life. During this time his mature political ideology began to take shape against the background of the Russian revolutionary movement and the rise of nationalist and socialist politics in Eastern Europe. His attraction to left-wing Zionism around 1905 brought him into contact with other young Jews of similar backgrounds and with similar inclinations. He joined *Kadima* (Eastward, alternately Forward), a student group that shared the Democratic Faction's affinity for Ahad Ha'am's ideals of cultural nationalism and self-reliance and opposed Herzl's emphasis on diplomacy and philanthropy within the Zionist movement. He also participated in the non-partisan Jewish student organization *Łączność* (Unity) and was elected a member of the committee of the *Tsionei tsion* (Zionists of Zion), which then led a battle within the Zionist movement against territorialism and the Uganda project to establish a Jewish colony in British East Africa as a temporary alternative to the founding of a Jewish state in Palestine. As a representative of the committee, he travelled to various cities in the Russian Empire (Warsaw, Łódź, Dvinsk, Brześć) to lecture in Russian on Zionist topics and earned a reputation as a gifted orator.

Offended by the tacit approval of antisemitism in the Polish public sphere, Prylucki helped organize a demonstration to disrupt a performance of Stanisław Dobrzański's play *Złoty cielec* (The Golden Calf) in December 1902. The play, which presented stereotypical depictions of money-hungry Jews speaking broken Polish, was warmly received by audiences. To Prylucki's dismay, Polish Jewish students in attendance did not raise their voices in objection. His obstreperous efforts to defend Jewish 'national honour' were denounced as a defilement of sacred cultural precincts by members of the *Endecja*'s Polish nationalist youth movement, on the one hand, and as chauvinism by polonized Jews, on the other. He and his colleagues succeeded, however, in removing the provocative play for several years from the theatre's repertoire. His boldness also landed him, along with other leftist Jewish students, for three weeks in Warsaw's notorious Pawiak prison. Later participation in student riots earned him a second prison term – this time, for two months – in 1904.[32]

While attending the Zionist Congress in Vilna in 1904, Noah Prylucki came under the influence of Zionist workers' groups. He began to move ideologically towards socialism, a shift generally observable among politically active Jews around 1905.[33] An interest in the specific needs and concerns of the broad Jewish masses without access to higher education in either Hebrew or Russian brought the beginnings of a reappraisal of the value of the Diaspora as a natural and culturally creative locus in Jewish life. It spurred him, with some difficulty, to adopt Yiddish as the language of his Zionist speeches. Such a reorientation was shared by a number of his peers in the Jewish nationalist movement. A fellow student at the University of Warsaw, his future rival Yitzhak Grünbaum, for example, similarly came to embrace Yiddish language culture in the Diaspora as part and parcel of his Zionist ideology.[34] He was a linguistically polonized Jew raised in a *maskilic* home in Congress Poland (his mother was a polonophile and his Yiddish-speaking father a supporter of *Hibat-tsion*). A 'Russian' rather than 'Polish' Jew, Prylucki, in contrast with his polonized Zionist colleagues, seems to have sympathized but never intimately identified with Polish culture and the Polish national cause.

By 1905 Prylucki, like many of his contemporaries, was convinced of the movement's need to become representative of all segments of the Jewish population, not just its Westernized elite. It also needed to adopt an interventionist policy in Diaspora life instead of concentrating its energies exclusively on the establishment of a Jewish state while maintaining neutrality in European politics. He therefore supported the Zionist movement's acceptance of *Gegenwartsarbeit* ('work for the present'), cultural and political work on behalf of the millions of Jews dwelling in the Diaspora prior to their resettlement in Palestine in the indefinite future. He exhorted Zionist youth to take an active role in the Russian revolutionary movement, maintaining that the Jewish question in Eastern Europe could not be solved independently of the general Russian question. At the Seventh Zionist Congress that year in Basel, he was chosen to serve as secretary of the central committee of *Dovrei ivrit* (Hebrew Speakers) societies that had multiplied throughout Europe to promote Hebrew as a spoken language. Having drawn closer to the Zionist left, he was also recognized for his facility with Yiddish and was recommended to serve as language editor for the Yiddish language paper of the recently formed socialist-Zionist party Poale Zion in 1906.[35]

Addressing a large assembly of leftist students at the University of Warsaw in 1905, Prylucki issued the demand that the Polish student body support the national rights of the Jewish people in Poland. These rights included the right to a state-funded Jewish national school in Yiddish. It is a credit to Prylucki's oratorical skill that he was reportedly received with thundering applause even though he delivered his speech in Russian (he did not adequately command Polish despite his sympathies for Polish autonomy). The meeting recognized the demand as justified and adopted a corresponding resolution.[36] Shortly afterwards, a middle school strike erupted in Warsaw, part of the wave of revolution engulfing the Russian Empire after its defeat in the Russo-Japanese War. The strike aimed at removing Russian control and coercive russification from schools in Poland, as well as implementing radical reforms in the education system.[37]

A milestone in the struggle for Polish independence since the suppressed insurrection of 1863, the strike also represents a significant event in the growing campaign for Jewish national rights. Numerous strike participants and organizers were Jews, especially members of Poale Zion and the socialist, anti-Zionist Bund. Like their Polish colleagues, Jewish nationalists and Bundists desired to see religious and other restrictions rescinded and to attain linguistic and cultural autonomy in the schools. They also protested authorities' recognition of the Jews as solely a religious group and sought the extension of the Jewish education system beyond an exclusively religious character. Prylucki himself invested much effort in the organization of the Jewish academic youth in Warsaw schools and agitated among them to support the demand for a Jewish national school with Yiddish as its language of instruction.

Along with several others, including the future Bundist leader Henryk Ehrlich, he was expelled in 1905 from the university as part of a complex of retaliatory measures employed by tsarist authorities to suppress the strike.[38] A badge of honour among revolutionary youth, the expulsion did not impede him from later resuming his legal studies in St Petersburg. That Prylucki repeatedly managed to gain admission to Russian state schools notorious for their *numerus clausus* restricting Jewish enrolment – even after his imprisonment – testifies as much to his capabilities as a student as to his father's personal connections in the capital.

Meanwhile, alongside his political activity, Prylucki continued his literary activity. He published belles lettres, poetry, and feuilletons, as well as journalistic pieces, in the Hebrew newspapers *Ha-melits* (to which he apparently contributed the beginnings of a novel in 1904),[39] *Ha-tsofe* (The Observer, St Petersburg), *Ha-tsefira* (The Dawn, Warsaw), and in the Russian *Evreiskaia Zhizn'* (Jewish Life). His career as a Hebrew writer was, like his career as a Russian novelist, however, short-lived.

He met his greatest success in the Yiddish press. It was in rapid expansion following the 1905 Revolution and in need of writers familiar with politics and current journalistic styles. The Yiddish press offered a person with Prylucki's qualifications and personal connections the largest potential readership and, consequently, the largest commercial and cultural potential. With his father's encouragement and support, he began in 1905 to contribute regularly to *Der veg* (The Way), a new Yiddish newspaper edited by Tsevi Prylucki. In *Der veg*, 'the first daily Jewish newspaper in Warsaw' (as its masthead proudly announced), Prylucki found a regular forum to polish his Yiddish style and to express his evolving ideas about Jewish culture, nationhood, and democracy.[40] The founding of *Der veg* two months before the first Russian Revolution and the subsequent liberalization of press and theatre in Warsaw marks the beginning of a new era in that city as the 'metropolis of the Yiddish press in Eastern Europe.'[41]

The Birth of Warsaw's First Yiddish Daily: *Der veg*

After the closing of Alexander Zederbaum's *Dos yudishes folksblat* (The Jewish People's Paper, 1882–90), tens of applications for concessions to found a new Yiddish newspaper in the Russian Empire were routinely rejected by the official responsible for press affairs at the Ministry of the Interior (Y. Feoktistov and later Soloviev). While no ban on the Yiddish press was made legally explicit, it was routinely explained that Russian censors were ignorant of the vernacular of the vast majority of the Empire's Jews and that applicants for concessions were politically unreliable. Since Jews were collectively suspected of revolutionary fervour, even Jewish converts to Christianity were not to be trusted as censors charged with the delicate task of detecting subversive content. For reasons that are not wholly clear (perhaps because Hebrew was considered a classical language and the potential audience for a Hebrew newspaper consisted of a relatively small and conservative elite; perhaps because propagating Yiddish conflicted with the official goal of russifying Jews), the government was far more lenient in granting permission for Hebrew publications. In any case, the legal Yiddish press ceased to exist in Russia despite the official toleration of a Hebrew one.

The need for a Yiddish-language literary and journalistic tribune among Russia's close to six million Jews, most of whom were Yiddish-speakers, was only partially met when two new newspapers began to appear outside the Russian Empire under the auspices of Warsaw publishing houses: *Der yud* (1899–1903, published by Eliezer Kaplan's 'Ahiasef') and *Yidishe folkstsaytung* (Jewish People's Newspaper, 1902–3, published by Tushia). Both newspapers were edited in Warsaw (*Der yud*'s editor Y.H. Ravnitzky first conducted his work in Odessa and later relocated to Warsaw) and their contents were sent across the border to be printed in Kraków in the Habsburg province of Galicia, where tsarist restrictions on Yiddish publishing were not in effect. Finally, the published copies were mailed back to Russia to be inspected by the imperial censor and subsequently

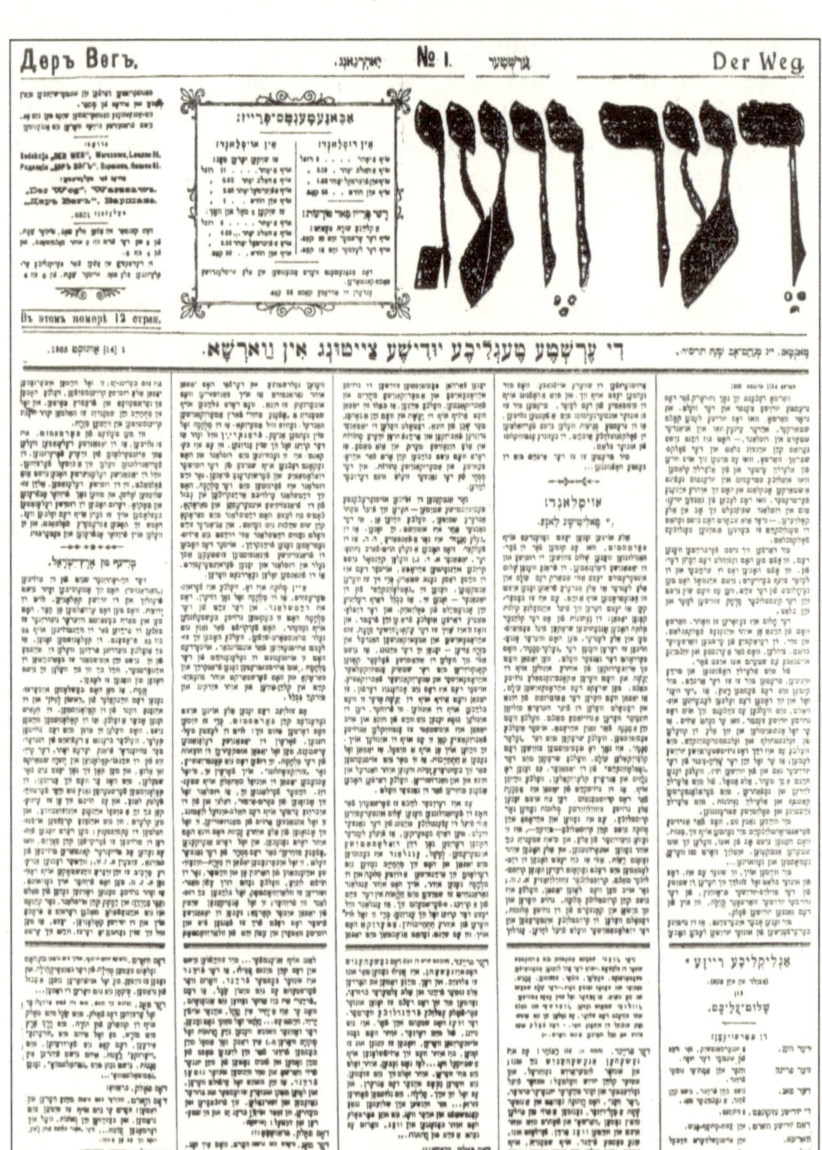

Дерь Вегь. № 1. Der Weg

דער וועג

Въ этомъ номерѣ 12 стран.

די ערשטע טעגליכע יודישע צייטונג אין ווארשא.

2.1 A page from the newspaper *Der veg*, 1905.

distributed to subscribers. Consequently, even with the least of delays, an article did not reach readers before a minimum of two weeks had elapsed since its completion. Further, these newspapers were primarily literary and theatre reviews containing little in the way of news or publicistic material. Thus, the need remained acute for a Yiddish newspaper that would react immediately to local events in the Russian Empire and respond to the pressing issues of the day.[42]

By 1902 Tsevi Prylucki already played an important role in the Russian-Jewish and Hebrew presses in St Petersburg. He entertained the same idea as other entrepreneurs who appreciated the tremendous commercial and cultural potential of a Yiddish daily. That year Rabinovich, the Pryluckis' previous editor, unsuccessfully applied for official permission to transform his *Bleter fun a togbukh* into a weekly. Despite this refusal, Minister of the Interior Viacheslav Plehve's position on Yiddish had, for reasons of political expediency, become more pliant. His interest was sufficiently piqued by the prospect of using Yiddish as an instrument to combat revolutionary activity among Jews, specifically to counter the influence of the underground Bundist press, that he requested expert information about the language.[43] Around this time Tsevi Prylucki too requested official approval to issue a newspaper in Yiddish. He was reminded by the press bureau chief of the politically suspect status of Yiddish in the eyes of the government. Undeterred, Prylucki seized upon Plehve's invitation: in a memorandum to the official he sought to dispel notions of the political unreliability of Yiddish by arguing that content, not language, determines the beneficial or harmful consequences of printed matter; further, he pointed out, no one had ever suggested banning Russian in order to prevent revolutionary newspapers from appearing in that language. Finally, he assured officials that the Russian censor for Jewish publications would be able to verify the content of a Yiddish newspaper.[44]

Perhaps swayed by Prylucki's arguments, Plehve approved 'as a test' concessions for two Yiddish and two Hebrew newspapers (in addition to the already existing *Ha-melits* and *Ha-tsefira*) but Prylucki did not learn of this decision in time. In August 1902, Sh. Rappoport (a partner in *Ha-melits*) heard of Plehve's decision from a contact in the Ministry of the Interior and obtained permission in October for *Der fraynd* (The Friend). Russia's first Yiddish daily, it ushered in a new era in the history of the Jewish press in the tsarist empire when it began publishing in January 1903 in St Petersburg (it was relocated to Warsaw in December 1909).[45] The second concession, granted to Natan Golubov, official translator of the Warsaw Provincial Polish Administration, went unused, for the general governor of the city refused to permit a Yiddish newspaper (purportedly because of Golubov's Zionist sympathies)[46]; the concession was snatched, however, by Rabinovich, who then founded *Der tog* (The Day) in St Petersburg in 1904 (it transferred in 1905 to Vilna, billing itself as the 'first Yiddish daily in the Jewish Pale'). Ben-Zion Katz received one of the Hebrew concessions for *Ha-zeman* (Time, St Petersburg) and Eliezer Eliyahu Friedman received the other for *Ha-tsofe* (Warsaw). By the time Prylucki learned of the concessions, it was too late to get hold of one.[47]

Tsevi Prylucki's fortunes changed when a wealthy Lithuanian Jew approached him for assistance in obtaining a concession for a Yiddish newspaper. The unnamed 'Litvak,' as he is identified in Noah Prylucki's recollections, was most likely an illegal resident of the capital who earned his living as an agent for members of the Russian aristocracy seeking to conceal their financial speculations. Eager for broker's fees from leasing out a newspaper concession under his own name, he explained the undertaking to his titled clients as a means to rescue himself from financial straits and received their eager backing. Despite the exceptional political connections afforded him by his clients, he needed the name and experience of the elder Prylucki, now unemployed after having left *Ha-melits* a few months earlier, in the press world. Tsevi Prylucki, he hoped, would be able to navigate the appropriate government channels and overcome the obstacle posed by Plehve, who had come to regret having permitted even a single 'jargon' newspaper.[48]

Enjoying connections to the governor-general of Moscow, P. P. Durnovo, the 'Litvak' nearly breached the wall of Plehve's obstinacy. A revolutionary's bomb, however, ended Plehve's life prematurely. Following the assassination, Tsevi Prylucki, supported by the patronage of an aristocrat (also unnamed in Noah Prylucki's memoirs but identified by the journalist Dovid Druk as Prince Obolensky), approached Prince P.D. Sviatopolk-Mirski, the new appointee to the position of minister of the interior, to request a concession. But Sviatopolk-Mirski refused Prylucki, arguing that Jews ought to abandon Yiddish and integrate into Russian-speaking society. When he offered a concession for either another Russian or Hebrew newspaper, Prylucki temporarily laid aside his goal until Sviatopolk-Mirski left his post and was replaced by Buligin. The press administrator Vyerev soon also resigned and was replaced by the Estonian vice governor Belgard. Again armed with letters of patronage, Prylucki approached him for a concession. This time his efforts were not in vain. A more favourable attitude towards Yiddish had been inspired by the government's new inclination towards 'thorough reforms' in response to the unrest of the time. Permission for *Der veg* to be printed in St Petersburg was finally granted on 17 April 1905 and the first issue appeared on 1 August of that year.[49]

Since two Yiddish newspapers, *Der fraynd* and *Der tog*, were already published in the imperial capital, far from the millions of Yiddish readers in the Pale, it was decided to have the concession transferred to Warsaw. The city with the largest Jewish population in the Empire (260,000 in 1906), it was also home to a burgeoning Jewish literary and cultural scene presided over by the writer Y.L. Peretz. A literary pilgrimage to Peretz and his critique of their writings were considered de rigueur for a generation of aspiring young writers newly arrived from the Polish province and elsewhere. David Frishman, Mordkhe Spektor, Sholem Asch, Hersh-Dovid Nomberg, and Avrom Reyzen, all of whom made names for themselves largely through the vehicle of the Yiddish press, were then residents of the city. Prior to 1905 only two long-running Jewish periodicals existed in Warsaw: the *maskilic* Hebrew *Ha-tsefira* (The Dawn, 1862, 1874–1906, weekly until 1886 and then daily) and the Assimilationist Polish-language *Izraelita* (The Israelite, 1866–1913, weekly). Both were linguistically inaccessible or ideologically foreign (if not taboo) to the vast majority of Polish Jews, who were Yiddish-speaking and traditionally religious. Many Jews did read liberal Polish newspapers, such as Stanisław Kempner's *Nowa Gazeta* (New Gazette), and many Jews, including converts to Christianity, worked in the Polish press. However, there was no mass support for *Izraelita*, which supported the integration of the Jews into Polish culture and society and was officially hostile to manifestations of Jewish 'separatism.'[50]

Transferring the concession to the Empire's third largest city also made sense from a financial standpoint. The unofficial capital of partitioned Poland, Warsaw was significantly closer to the potential readership for a Yiddish press and enjoyed commercial and cultural connections with Jewish Lithuania and Volhyn.[51] Tsevi Prylucki managed to convince Warsaw's Chancellor Jashchkovski (Jaczkowski), who was sympathetic to Prylucki's request, that 'jargon' was not a harmful tool of revolutionaries. Thanks in part to pressure exerted by the concession's holder, permission for the transfer was obtained in July from Warsaw Governor-General Maksimovich and subsequently from authorities in St Petersburg.[52]

Politicizing Warsaw Jewry

Upon arriving in Warsaw in 1905, Tsevi Prylucki encountered a Jewish community far larger and more diverse than what he had known in St

Petersburg. In St Petersburg, the roughly twenty thousand Jews made up less than 2 per cent of the population of more than one million and were almost as a rule highly acculturated whatever their degree of religious observance. In Warsaw, they composed more than a third of the population and were overwhelmingly Yiddish-speaking and Orthodox. Despite this apparent homogeneity, Warsaw Jewry was also quite economically and socially variegated, supporting rival and often mutually hostile fractions. Apart from their internal divisions, the Jews of Warsaw found themselves caught in the midst of the political and cultural struggle waged between the imperial regime and Polish society, both of which used the Jews, according to Tsevi Prylucki, as a 'whipping boy' (*kapore-hindl*).[53]

The beginnings of a politically and nationally mobilized Jewish presence in Warsaw aroused the ire of the camp of acculturated (and acculturating) Jews and their allies in the *kehila*, the Orthodox and Hasidic leaders whose at times feuding rival factions held sway over most of Polish Jewry. Assimilationists played for decades a significant role in Jewish community politics despite the Orthodox rabbinic leadership's principled opposition to them as bearers of modern and secular currents. Although a wall of mutual distance and incomprehension stood between them and the Yiddish-speaking, culturally distinct majority in their charge, the Assimilationists occupied the majority of seats in the Warsaw *kehila*-board from 1867 until the interwar period. They achieved control of the *kehila*-board through an alliance with Hasidic leaders, who relied upon the Assimilationists to counter the appointment to the position of *rav ha-kolel* of a rabbi supported by their *mitnagdic* opponents. The institution of a voting tax that granted franchise only to the financial aristocracy of Warsaw Jewry, within which the Assimilationists were strongly represented, also contributed to this 'unholy alliance.'[54] Despite tremendous cultural differences, though, the Assimilationists and the Hasidim were united in the conviction that the Jews constituted foremost a religious community. In contrast, the Bund and the general Zionist movement agreed upon a secular national definition of the Jews but diverged on most other issues, most famously the desirability of sustaining the Jewish Diaspora indefinitely. They were also received with great alarm by most Polish parties, which saw in their demands for national minority recognition a challenge to the notion of a culturally and preferably ethnically homogeneous Polish state.

To win mass support for their programs of civil and national rights in the Diaspora, twentieth-century Jewish political parties needed to cultivate both a modern political consciousness among Jews and a sense of nationhood according to secular criteria. To this end, they made vigorous use of the Jewish, above all, the Yiddish press, the most effective instrument of mass culture available at that time. Poland's largely traditional Jewish readers, accustomed to perusing religious texts at specified times, were still acquiring modern reading habits at this time, and Warsaw's Jews were little accustomed to reading Yiddish.[55] Indeed, many Jews, having received formal instruction in reading the Hebrew alphabet but not in deciphering their mother tongue, possessed only rudimentary reading and writing skills in it. The process of becoming Yiddish readers had begun in the preceding century thanks to papers like *Kol mevaser* (The Heralding Voice, 1862–71),[56] the very first Yiddish newspaper in the Russian Empire, and the widespread publication of Yiddish popular novels (such as the works of Shomer) but only become advanced in the early twentieth century. Not only were the genres of literature and news reporting, along with their specialized vocabulary and stylistic register, largely unfamiliar to readers. The secular press itself faced opposition from religious leaders for being immoral and undermining both traditional values and their own authority as Jews turned to it for guidance in daily life.[57]

Religious strictures notwithstanding, the Yiddish press drew a huge Orthodox, including Hasidic, readership as a result of the tremendous hunger for information and entertainment. Much credit in preparing the Polish Jewish readership to understand politics is due to Tsevi Prylucki. An advocate of the revival of Hebrew, about which he spoke and wrote with great passion in his youth, he also valued Yiddish greatly for its use in popular education and spreading the values of the Jewish national renaissance.[58] Apart from possessing prodigious skills as an editor and in recognizing and drawing literary talent to *Der veg*,[59] he was a master of the art of '*lezhanke-politik*.' This was a style of writing about politics in a folksy manner suited to traditional Jewish men unschooled in world affairs and accustomed to 'politics as conducted by *batlonim* [literally, 'idlers' – men who spent the entire day in synagogue available for religious functions and did not pursue paid work] on the cold winter nights by the warm oven (*lezhanke*) in the synagogue.'[60]

Affectionately known as 'the old man (*der alter*),' Tsevi Prylucki possessed, 'white little cheeks with a suspicious rosiness on the them, a soft, not too long beard with suspicious, too young blackness mixed with the snow-white greyness of an uralt man and, on top of this, a shining bald spot.'[61] Frequently described in the memoirs of contemporaries as a man averse to conflict, he deemed the preservation of his honour and the protection of his good name from scandal of paramount importance. Raised in affluence, he was, in the description of the journalist and writer Meylekh Ravitsh, a *balebatisher yid* – the embodiment of bourgeois Jewish sensibilities and aesthetic tastes that appealed to conservative readers: 'The entire world was, or ought to have been, for Tsevi Prylucki like a room in the softened light of an *abat jour*. And everyone around him is supposed to go about in slippers. There is no reason to get excited.'[62] Nonetheless, he was unwilling to compromise his principles, engaging in public debates about politics on the pages of the press and standing trial more than once upon accusations of fomenting sedition by spreading provocative and false information in his capacity as editor.[63]

As early as 1906, Shmuel Yankev Yatskan (Samuel Yackan), later the editor of popular Warsaw daily *Der haynt* and the Pryluckis' chief rival in the Yiddish newspaper world, mockingly captured the contrast between the mild-mannered, well-connected father and his firebrand son in the satiric journal *Di bin* (The Bee): 'The old one – as a person who lived several years in St Petersburg and came into contact with the highest spheres and still knows to this day the number of all 'stolonatshalnikes' [capital city officials] in all departments and their viewpoints – is eager to believe in the power of bureaucracy. Usually he does not disclose this and keeps it a secret buried deep in his heart. The young one – sulphur, tar. Sitting at Pańska 20, he calls everyone to battle ... the Russian bureaucracy, the Turk, and even his father. Both are, however, great Zionists.'[64]

Content of *Der veg*

Together with *Der veg's* printer, the engineer Y.B. Ippo (later replaced by the merchant Ginzburg when Ippo lost his enthusiasm for the enterprise), Tsevi Prylucki envisioned *Der veg* as a general encyclopaedia compiled by a team of experts with a mission to educate the Jewish public. They outfitted the newspaper's offices, which occupied an entire floor with a garden on Leszno Street in the city's centre, in grand style. Ippo believed, according to Tsevi Prylucki, that this would impress Jews and non-Jews alike and thus serve as the best means for the newspaper to draw a large circulation and advertisements.[65] While the newspaper became a tourist attraction for curious locals, the very fact that it published in Yiddish, not to mention its ideological orientation, aroused dissatisfaction in the community of Warsaw's newspaper editors. Nearly all contributors to *Der veg* were Zionists or sympathetic to Zionist aspirations, and the daily bore a populist-Zionist colouring. Despite courting

Zionist financial backing, however, it never became a party organ.[66] The paper adopted an aggressive line against the Polish Progressives who opposed the granting of national (although not civil) rights to the Jews, the antisemitic National Democratic Party (*Endecja*), and Assimilationists.[67] With the exception of *Kurjer Warszawski* (Warsaw Courier), Polish newspapers were unwilling to publish advertisements for *Der veg*.[68] Similarly, the editors of Polish newspapers, with the exceptions of the then socialist Wacław Sieroszewski and Stanisław Kempner, an Assimilationist and principled opponent of the preservation of Yiddish among Jews, were unwilling to speak with Tsevi Prylucki at a meeting convened by the tsarist censorship committee in late 1905. Prylucki was especially offended by this snubbing since he was unaccustomed to this kind of treatment by the community of editors in St Petersburg and because he had specifically begun Polish lessons in order to communicate with colleagues.[69]

Like *Der fraynd*, the model for Yiddish newspapers in this period, *Der veg* resembled a Russian newspaper in its layout and its emphasis on literature. The first sixty issues featured a constellation of the best known Jewish authors of the time, including the Yiddish classicists Mendele, Sholem Aleichem, and Y.L. Peretz, who was an especially close associate in the daily.[70] Works were also published by the young generation then making their debuts – I.M. Vaysenberg, Sholem Asch, L. Shapiro, Yente Serdatski, Moyshe Taytsh, Dovid Aynhorn, Dovid Druk, A. Kapel, and A. Orbach. In addition to Tsevi and Noah Prylucki, established literary names were hired as associates in the editorial board. Among them were Dr Eliashev (the literary critic known by his pseudnoym Ba'al Makhshoves), Hersh-Dovid Nomberg, A.L. Yakubovitsh, L. Shapiro, Dovid Druk, and a bit later, Reb Mordkhele (Khayim Tshemerinski).[71]

Still a law student residing in St Petersburg, Noah Prylucki joined the staff of *Der veg* with great trepidation despite having already published a few dozen articles and feuilletons – in Yiddish in *Bleter fun a togbukh*, in Hebrew in *Ha-melits* and *Ha-tsofe*, in Russian in *Budushchnost'* and the left-oriented *Syn otetshestva* (Son of the Fatherland). He recalls in his reminiscences (possibly to make his literary accomplishments sound all the more impressive) the inadequacy of his Yiddish then and the intimidation he keenly felt in the presence of so many established talents in the realm of Yiddish letters.[72]

As with nearly all of his endeavours, however, this initial period of hesitancy and self-doubt quickly came to an end. By his own reckoning a tried hand in Yiddish journalism after only a few months, Noah Prylucki profited from his position on the newspaper's staff to refine his political views and sharpen his writing skills in addition to making pioneering contributions as a theatre critic and engaging in polemics with Yiddish writers (the subjects will be addressed in the next chapter). A prolific writer, he occasionally penned as many as four articles a day on issues close to his heart such as the 1905 Zionist Congress in Basle, the position of Jews in university unrest, the need for chairs in the minority languages and literatures (including Yiddish) of the Russian Empire at the University of Warsaw, and the condition of Jewish youth resulting from the strike in the middle schools in 1905.[73] His publicistic articles and literary overviews were on the whole quite popular with readers, whom he sought to educate towards national awareness.[74] He also caused a sensation when, disguising himself as a railway official, he managed to gain entrance to Siedlce for a daring 'scoop' in 1906. (The city was closed to the press and all non-authorized personnel following a pogrom there conducted by Russian soldiers.) His boldness created a sensation upon his return to Warsaw, where no other paper had coverage of the events and whence the information was sent to St Petersburg and, subsequently, abroad.[75]

Noah Prylucki's Political Views

The First Duma, or Russian parliament, was convened in the wake of the 1905 Revolution but was dissolved as too radical by the imperial government after only a few months. Shortly thereafter, Prylucki issued his first independent publication in preparation for elections to the Second Duma in February 1907. A small selection of articles that first appeared in 1906 in *Der veg*, the twenty-four page brochure *Natsionalizm un demokratizm (tsayt-artiklen)* (Nationalism and Democracy) reflects the influence on him of the movement for the democratization of the Russian Empire and the campaign for Jewish national autonomy in the Diaspora. By 1905–6, these demands had been adopted as a programmatic point by nearly all Jewish parties in Russia.[76] Conceptually, the brochure, along with his other political writings published in *Der veg*, reflect his stance as a left-leaning Zionist more occupied with cultural and political questions in the Diaspora than with Palestine. In retrospect, they represent the crystallization of core political convictions that would accompany him throughout his career.

In publishing *Nationalism and Democracy*, Prylucki identified as his goal to dispel for the Jewish reading public 'the muddle that reigns among us regarding the concepts of nationalism and democracy.' In contrast with the Jewish socialist parties, he laments, the Jewish bourgeoisie fails to comprehend that the two ideologies in no way constitute irreconcilable opposites. On the contrary, nationalism may be subsumed under the ideal of democracy – the freedom to determine one's own development whether as an individual or as a group. The 'objective' nation, a cohesive group united over time by cultural and racial features, eventually gains a sense of 'subjective' nationalism. That is, it becomes aware of its unique needs and aspirations. As a social body, the nation 'has the right to free cultural, economic and political development – briefly – to free "national" development.' Once this consciousness has arisen, it is the function of the nationalist movement to galvanize those forces at its disposal to realize the right of the nation to unfettered development.[77]

While nationalism cannot exist deprived of the national ego dictating its particularistic needs and desires, the ruthless pursuit of a nation's goals without regard for the concerns of other nations constitutes militant chauvinism, the most primitive and dangerous form of nationalism. It respects brute force alone and must be combated in order to prevent its trampling upon the rights of weaker nations and the consequent perpetuation of discord:

> As long as there will be oppressed nations, there can be no true freedom. The oppressed nation will eternally strive for its freedom. The stronger will always have to shore up its positions. The constant struggle ruins both sides. Freedom must not be founded on oppression because oppression is a source of hatred and strife.
>
> The most highly developed stage of nationalism, ethical nationalism refuses to tolerate serving the interests of one nation at the expense of another. Instead, it relies upon compromise to resolve national problems.[78]

As a minority in the Diaspora, Jews are incapable of both achieving their national aims through the exercise of physical might and of defending themselves from the militant chauvinism of other nations. Their sole protection lies in the upholding of democracy. If Jewish deputies in the Duma pursue only the advancement of narrow Jewish interests and neglect the general welfare of the lands in which they dwell, they can surely expect to find no support among non-Jewish delegates for issues specifically affecting Jews. Jewish voters must therefore elect delegates to the Duma who will work to resolve the general problems of the Russian Empire along with the Jewish question.[79]

Despite his commitment to Palestine as the Jews' historic homeland,

Prylucki considers the Jews autochthonous inhabitants of Poland who can neither be expelled nor successfully assimilated. Their culturally distinct, centuries-old presence in the land entitles them to the same rights for 'national development' as the Poles. Only through cooperation between the two aspiring nations and complete democratization of the political system will the Jewish question in the Diaspora be solved to the fullest extent possible. Existence as a territorially dispersed minority in the Diaspora, however, can never fully satisfy the needs of the Jewish people. While not elaborating on the nature of a future homeland for the Jews in Palestine, Prylucki remains convinced that 'the complete solution to the Jewish question lies only in *Eretz yisrael.*'

In the absence of a Jewish national homeland, Prylucki cites the call of the Austrian Social Democrats Karl Renner and Otto Bauer, who first proposed political and cultural autonomy for national minorities in the framework of a multiethnic empire in the 1890s, as the most plausible solution to the minorities problem.[80] Yet, the two theoreticians explicitly excluded Jews from recognition among the 'nationalities' of the Austro-Hungarian Empire for lack of requisite criteria for nationhood (contiguous territory and undisputed national language).[81] Meanwhile, Prylucki fails to recognize any intellectual debt at this time to the pioneers of Jewish autonomism – the seminal historian of Eastern European Jewry Simon Dubnow, whom he would later celebrate as the 'intellectual father' of the folkist movement, and the political philosopher and early exponent of Yiddishism, Khayim Zhitlovski. Perhaps this silence is to be explained by Prylucki's lack of accord with these thinkers regarding the role of the Diaspora in Jewish national life. As demonstrated by his enduring commitment to *Eretz yisrael* as the singular locus for a 'complete' resolution of the Jewish question, Prylucki rejected the perpetuation of Jewish life in the Diaspora as a terminal goal to which the project to establish a Jewish national home in Palestine was subordinate or superfluous.

As a feuilletonist and political commentator residing in revolution-era Petersburg, Prylucki presumably watched with keen interest the formation there in 1906 of Dubnow's own short-lived Folksparty. This circle of Jewish intellectuals later served as a model for Prylucki's party of the same name in interwar Poland. Organized with the assistance of Yisroel Efroikin, Dubnow's short-lived party demanded the democratization of the political order, strict parliamentarianism, national minority rights and the creation of national minority assemblies, autonomy for the territories of the Russian Empire, and the right to use Yiddish in public life.

Although it lacked agents, funds, or the initiative to recruit supporters in the provinces, the party was not without immediate ideological significance. It influenced the Bund, for example, to place greater emphasis on national elements in its platform.[82]

In his election pieces appearing in *Der veg* during the campaign for the Second Duma, Prylucki was critical of all parties, both Jewish and Polish. His primary target was the Endeks (members of the *Endecja*) and their new-found allies in the 'National Concentration,' the Polish 'Progressives' (a splinter group of the Progressive Democrats). To his great consternation, both parties claimed support for equal rights for the Jews as individuals but not as a nation. A crucial moral distinction, he reasoned, existed however between these two parties:[83] as hostile to Jewish interests as the reactionary Endeks were, they were at least forthright in their antisemitism and did not shy away from anti-Jewish rhetoric on the pages of their organ *Goniec* (Courier); the duplicitous 'Progressives,' on the other hand, concealed their anti-Jewish sentiment behind a veil of liberalism. While ostensibly condemning antisemitism, their program failed to recognize the legitimacy of Jewish nationalism and the need for a Jewish national curia to insure proportional representation of the Jews in the Duma.[84] In Prylucki's conception, the refusal to support Jewish collective rights was tantamount to the denial of the Jews' individual rights, for the latter was the only reliable guarantee of the former.

Turning to the Jewish parties, Prylucki excoriated the Jewish Election Committee, which was under Zionist leadership, for minimizing its nationalist stance in order to draw support from the politically conservative Hasidim. More specifically, he criticized the Jewish Election Committee for insisting upon neither proportional elections nor official recognition for the Yiddish language. Foreseeing the imposition of Sunday rest laws (a reality in interwar Poland) as a tool for the economic ruination of the Jews, the young journalist further blasted the committee for not demanding that the right of Jews to close their businesses on Saturday, the Jewish Sabbath, and reopen them on Sunday be defended in the Duma.[85] Next, he attacked Assimilationists such as Henryk Nussbaum for exhorting Jews to support the 'National Concentration in order to insure that Warsaw, despite its more than one-third Jewish population, be represented only by ethnic Poles for the sake of good relations between the groups.'[86] Finally, he scolded the political and social indifference of the Jewish middle class.[87] Jewish voters, he urged, must vote for candidates irrespective of their national origins who will support the democratization of the Russian Empire, autonomy for Poland based upon democratic principles, and civil and national rights, including cultural autonomy, for the Jews.[88]

Even more hostile to the government than the First Duma, the Second Duma survived only three months before its dissolution. Prime Minister Stolypin subsequently rewrote the electoral laws to reduce Polish representation in the Duma drastically. Congress Poland's representation was cut to fourteen relatively harmless seats, two of which were reserved for new Russian curiae in the southeast and in Warsaw. Popular apathy and disillusionment were the direct results of this policy and most voters opted to refrain from exercising their franchise in the elections to the Third Duma, held in October 1907. In Warsaw, the Endeks ran without allies and faced almost no opposition in the general curia. Successful at the ballots, their leader Roman Dmowski headed a small Polish circle that found little support in the Duma. The Duma, much more Russian in its composition than previously, was permitted to complete its term and adjourned in the summer of 1912.[89]

Closing of *Der veg*

Although *Der veg's* contributors were often close to high political circles in the capital, news was seldom fresh and, the twenty-five rubles paid monthly in bribes notwithstanding, little could be published in the way of current public affairs. A rather zealous censor in Warsaw, to whom all galleys had to be brought before going to press, tended to 'read between the lines' and discover seditious content even where no such intentions were present. Nonetheless, the short-lived periodical enjoyed great popularity among Jewish readers, especially because of its high-quality literary section and because *Der fraynd* arrived from St Petersburg with a delay of two days. *Der fraynd* was also more interested in political affairs in 'exotic locales' like South Africa and America than events in Congress Poland, a reflection of a russophilic and capital-city bias that understandably did not appeal to Polish Jews.[90]

Following initial success, *Der veg*'s fortunes took a turn for the worse. Government repressions, libel and sedition suits, changes in content dictated by the preventive censor,[91] and the manifold difficulties of distribution were bad for business. In Warsaw the sale of individual newspapers was poorly organized, and vendors were reluctant to carry them since they deemed their sale for profit shameful or for fear that the conspicuous sale of a Jewish newspaper might discourage purchasers of other newspapers. It was necessary to acquire permits from Polish governors in order to sell Warsaw Yiddish newspapers in provincial bookstores. Since existing bookstores were initially reluctant to carry Yiddish newspapers, permits also had to be obtained to open new ones. The heavy cost of travelling representatives and sales agents (who often considered their work a favour to the publishers and refrained from submitting collected monies) further depleted the newspaper's already dwindling capital base. Since advertisements did not generate enough revenue for the press, subscriptions remained the primary and most reliable source of income for the two-kopek *Der veg*.[92]

After the general strike called in the wake of the October Manifesto, which held the promise of a constitutional monarchy with guarantees for civil rights for the tsar's subjects in response to revolutionary unrest, *Der veg* resumed publication after a brief hiatus, albeit with only two pages and deprived of contact with the province and normal sales. Fearful that Poland's first Yiddish daily would go under, Noah Prylucki submerged himself in the duties of both day and night editor when a number of technical associates ceased work. Despite his efforts, personal frictions between the editorial board and business management coupled with poor finances caused *Der veg* to close only three months after its founding. It was temporarily revived, though, with a smaller but more attractive format, including a new masthead, and with a reduced regular staff at the end of November 1905. The cover page of the first issue of the revived paper clearly articulated its political orientation: 'Our slogan is self-sufficiency, civil and national rights for our people, freedom, social and economic justice for the broad *folksmasn*. We deem securing and broadening our position in Palestine, our historic homeland, one of the most important tasks of Jewry.'[93]

Aside from continuing its literary section and enhancing the popularity of Yiddish drama through the introduction of theatre feuilletons, the revived *Der veg* devoted more space to current political and economic issues than previously. With censorship restrictions unclear following the October Manifesto, an atmosphere of radicalism prevailed. Even lèse-majesté was transgressed in the few months prior to the proclamation of 'temporary' press regulations.[94]

Despite increased revenue from advertising and the newspaper's popularity, especially in the time of Duma elections in 1906, financial woes and government repression again undermined the well-being of *Der veg*. When the reaction following the October Manifesto set in, censorship, briefly relaxed, tightened even more than earlier, and the individual sale of newspapers was suspended throughout Poland.[95] Criticism of public officials, the expression of what was judged excessive enthusiasm on Polish patriotic holidays, and calls by leftists to support class struggle were particularly sensitive subjects for which newspaper issues were confiscated, journals and newspapers suspended (but often immediately reappeared under new titles), and editors arrested and fined.[96] Newspaper boys and hawkers were dissuaded from carrying the paper by beatings and imprisonment.

Judging the moment inopportune for political discussions in the editorial board, Tsevi Prylucki played host in his home on Długa Street in 1906 to literary 'Friday evenings' ('fraytiktsunakhtsn') attended regularly by Y.L. Peretz, Dr Gershon Levin, Dr Meshoyrer, H.D. Nomberg, Avrom Reyzen, Sholem Asch, and other prominent Jewish writers and intellectuals. It was the custom that authors present at the meal read aloud from their newest literary works – an occasion which often resulted in sharp critiques and arguments.[97] When visiting his parents in Warsaw, Noah Prylucki joined them for a Sabbath meal of fish and wine. The student and budding journalist was undoubtedly influenced by the political, cultural, and stylistic tastes of his father's distinguished guests and newspaper colleagues. In particular, Peretz, around whose person concentrated much of the energies and activities of the modernized Jewish intelligentsia at this time, provided a model for his later cultural endeavours. The young Prylucki became acquainted at this time, as well, with a future co-founder of the Folksparty: the popular writer H.D. Nomberg (1876–1927), a former Hasid who lost his religious faith and left behind a family at age twenty-one in his native Mszczonów (Amshinov in Yiddish, Warsaw province) to seek Peretz' guidance in beginning a literary career.[98]

Attempts were made to prop up *Der veg*'s sagging financial base through the creation of an evening edition – the first of its kind in the Jewish press – and by sharing the profits made by a Hebrew sister newspaper. *Ha-yom* (The Day) was founded with the expectation that Jewish notables would contribute funds to a new Hebrew newspaper after the closing of *Ha-tsefira* left Warsaw without a Hebrew daily.

These strategies, however, proved insufficient in the face of competition from the city's first one-kopek paper, Shmuel Yatskan's sensationalist *Yidishes tageblat* (Jewish Daily Paper). The three-kopek *Der veg* closed definitively in January 1907. The impending liquidation of the paper, accompanied by frictions between the publishers, likely explains why Tsevi Prylucki, expecting to withdraw from the enterprise, founded his own short-lived daily (it survived only three months), *Di naye tsaytung*

(The New Gazette), in August 1906.[99] Even before the final closing of *Der veg*, Tsevi Prylucki began to contribute publicistic materials to *Fraytik* (Friday), Mordkhe Spektor's attempt to provide Warsaw a serious weekly newspaper and literary journal modelled on the Russian *Ponidelnik* (Friday). It too failed to survive the competition, lasting only eight issues from January to March 1907.[100]

Unzer lebn

An idea circulated among *Der veg*'s former staff to launch a new newspaper, one founded as a co-operative rather than financed by an individual. Mordkhe Spektor approached Tsevi Prylucki with a plan to draw Saul Hochberg, the publisher of *Fraytik*, as the paper's publisher. A migrant to Congress Poland from the Western Provinces at the turn of the century, Hochberg had failed to receive permission to publish a Yiddish daily in Łódź but succeeded in Warsaw.[101] Each of the men contributed fifty rubles and *Unzer lebn* (Our Life) was born on 3 March 1907. Spektor served as its 'sitting editor,' the person who would assume legal responsibility for the contents of the publication and face trial and possible imprisonment in case of legal infringements. Tsevi Prylucki accepted the duties of de facto editor.[102]

The paper was officially 'non-party,' presenting a variety of political viewpoints in order that each reader could, as Hochberg expressed it, 'find something for himself.' Nonetheless, because of the personal inclinations of its writers and editors, it expressed an essentially pro-Zionist stance. Like *Der veg*, it published discussions of the latest political events (above all, in Tsevi Prylucki's unsigned column 'Der moment') along with government news, telegrams from abroad, news from Warsaw Jewish life, reportages, feuilletons, local and provincial news, surveys of the press (Russian, Polish, and Jewish), stock quotations, and advertisements. It also published belle-lettres in instalments, including Sholem Aleichem's novel *Der mabl* (The Flood). Among its contributors, who were the best known Yiddish writers of the time, were Hillel Zeitlin and David Zagorodski.[103] Having resumed his legal studies in St Petersburg following expulsion from the University of Warsaw, Noah Prylucki served as Duma correspondent for *Unzer lebn.* He also continued to write about theatre for the newspaper, contributing original research into the history of the Yiddish theatre in the Russian Empire.[104]

Unzer lebn faced its first serious challenge in 1908 in the form of a brash new daily edited by the Pryluckis' rival of some time, Shmuel

2.2 Portrait of the founders and first editors of *Haynt* (Today), the first large-format Yiddish daily in Warsaw: editor Shmuel Yatskan; associate publishers Noah Prylucki and Nehemia Finkelstein; Avrom Goldberg, secretary of the editorial board; and Aaron Gawze. The political and commercial rivalry between the pro-Zionist *Haynt* and the Pryluckis's pro-Folkist *Moment*, the two major Yiddish dailies in Poland, was a subject of regular scandal among Warsaw Jews. (YIVO Institute, record 10241, frame 4694.01, 36085)

Yatskan, a Lithuanian yeshiva graduate and ordained rabbi turned Hebrew and Yiddish journalist. When it became apparent that his small-format *Yidishes tageblat* was too limited in scope to satisfy the political and cultural needs of the tens of thousands of readers whom he sought to attract, Yatskan launched a larger and more expensive newspaper with the financial support of the Warsaw merchants Chaim and Nehemiah Finkelstein. While initially unable to dislodge *Unzer lebn* from its perch on the newspaper market, the two-kopek *Der haynt* won great popularity with its 'suspenseful and highly interesting novels' (*shpanende un hekhst interesante romanen*), that is, formulaic potboilers, and Yatskan's fiery articles written in a frank, folksy tone. The publication of the serialized *shund* novel 'The Web of Sin' (*Di nets fun zind*) in 1910 alone reportedly expanded its circulation from 15,000 to 35,000.[105]

Apart from adding a few new literary talents to its stable of writers, *Der haynt* continued to employ much the same staff as the *Yidishes tageblat.* In contrast with *Unzer lebn,* which concentrated chiefly on events in Warsaw and the Polish provinces, *Der haynt* styled itself a newspaper for Jews in all of the tsarist empire.[106] It revolutionized the Yiddish press with its large format and innovations in the form of regular columns and thematic sections. As suggested by its title ('Today'), it gave priority to current news items, albeit in a highly sensationalized manner. Indeed, the pejorative term 'Yatskanism' entered the Polish and Yiddish lexicons to describe a penchant for journalistic scandal and sensation.[107] The paper's early popularity was also spurred on by a series entitled 'Brivelekh tsu der yidisher yugnt' (Letters to Jewish Youth) discussing non-coercive approaches to religious observance by the spiritual philosopher Hillel Zeitlin. Zeitlin's treatment of contemporary problems facing the religious Jewish youth of Poland and his explorations of moral philosophy contrasted with the otherwise boulevard tone of the paper, which strongly distinguished it from Tsevi Prylucki's 'respectable' newspaper aimed at petit bourgeois and Hasidic readers.[108]

Affiliated with the territorialist movement, *Haynt* embarked upon a crusade against its competitor *Unzer lebn,* the dominant large-size newspaper of the time.[109] In order to keep pace with *Der haynt, Unzer lebn* began printing feuilletons and pictures but it did not recognize the need to imitate *Der haynt*'s publishing of fresh news dispatches and foreign correspondence.[110] It was not long before internal frictions began to undermine *Unzer lebn.* Although it was founded as a co-operative, Hochberg transformed it into a private possession, arousing great dissatisfaction in the editorial board, administration, and print offices.[111] Disputes and financial difficulties led to the creation of a new newspaper, *Di naye velt* (The New World), by M. Spektor and Y.Kh. Zagorodski in July 1909.[112]

An advocate of the 'idealistic' Hebrew press and an avowed secularist, the writer (and son-in-law of the famed author Sholem Aleichem) Yitshak Dov Berkovitsh quipped;

> A desolate competition blazed between the newspapers. They sought to grab the reader not only with a trashy novel of the worst variety, but also with a lowly, dark tone that was supposed to destroy the progressive spirit which ruled the secular Jewish world since its first days. The newspapers

> were published in Warsaw, in the very heart of the *rebbe*-centric 'Itshe-Mayer' Hasidim, so they turned to the Warsaw and [the heavily Jewish suburb of Warsaw] Praga Hasidic prayer houses, lowered themselves to their concepts and beliefs, flattered and lied to them in an affected, excessively conservative language, with all the movements and grimaces of the Hasidic slobs ... Each newspaper strove to outdo the others with its falsely pious, religious-ecstatic language ... The most skilful of them was in those days *Haynt* ... After *Haynt*, the ignorant *Unzer lebn* danced clumsily. *Di naye velt* stood between the two confused and lost.[113]

Der moment

After completing his legal studies, Noah Prylucki returned to Warsaw in 1909 to pursue a legal career as an assistant attorney (*pomoshchnik prisiazhnogo poverennogo* – Jews were then seldom given the title of full attorney) devoted primarily to criminal cases.[114] His budding philological interests, along with continued journalistic work, were, however, a significant distraction from his practice.[115] Both under his proper name and a variety of pseudonyms (Iks, Oktava, Aleksander Ts.)[116] given him by newspaper owners,[117] he continued to write for *Unzer lebn.*

Dissatisfied with both the honoraria he personally received from *Unzer lebn* and his father's treatment by Hochberg, to whom he attributed the desire to rid the enterprise of its old partners, Noah Prylucki conceived a plan to begin his own tribune on co-operative foundations. He discussed the matter with Dovid Druk and Hillel Zeitlin. Like a number of contemporary intellectuals, the two writers were appalled by what they deemed the low quality of a Yiddish press dictated by vulgar street tastes and desired to edify the public with a newspaper free of what they deemed falsifications, scandal, and sensuality. Since the staff of *Unzer lebn* was rife with discontent, additional support for Noah Prylucki's plan was easily found.[118]

Characteristically disinclined to conflict and risk, Tsevi Prylucki, now a mature man nearing his fifties was sceptical of the plan. After a decade of experiences in the newspaper world he recognized the difficulty inherent in such an undertaking and the stiff competition a new gazette would face in a potentially saturated market. By this time, four Yiddish dailies were being published in Warsaw: *Unzer lebn, Der haynt, Der fraynd* (relocated to Warsaw in December 1909), and *Di naye velt.*[119] He chose to continue his duties under Hochberg. Although dissatisfied, he informed Spektor and Zagorodski, who sought to lure him over to *Di naye velt,* that he would continue his duties under Hochberg as long as he did not interfere with the newspaper's content.[120]

At first unable to find a financial backer willing to accept all of the typesetters and writers leaving *Unzer lebn* as partners in a new paper, Noah Prylucki collected 5,000 rubles from among the participants (including money awarded to the typesetters by a court of arbitration) to found a co-operative. Shortly afterwards, a Vilna lumber merchant agreed to serve as the paper's backer so long as the typesetters would share in the profits of the enterprise but not be made full partners. Noah Prylucki then successfully petitioned to have a concession obtained a few years earlier for a weekly entitled *Nayes* (News) that never came into being converted into one for a daily newspaper.[121] Seeking to capitalize from the popularity of Tsevi Prylucki's popular daily column in *Unzer lebn*, the new paper adopted *Der moment* as its title. The first issue of *Der moment* appeared 18 November 1910. The financial backing for a new paper now assured, the ever cautious Tsevi Prylucki agreed some time later in 1910 to assume responsibilities as editor-in-chief of *Der moment*. Eventually, a deal was struck for *Der moment* to absorb *Di naye velt*, including its printing machinery, premises at Nalewki 38, and its editorial board.[122]

Der moment was officially a non-partisan forum in which expressions of all Jewish political and cultural orientations were in principle welcome (with the exception of Assimilationism). The Yiddish actor and director Michael Weichert recalls: 'Among the article writers, each one marched to the beat of his own drummer. The Friday edition was like a tramway, where everyone sits together but each person enters at a different station and travels to a different destination. The publishers intended in this way to interest the broadest possible reading circles so that each one could find something for himself and purchase a newspaper. I could not believe that there were readers who read everything. But other contributors swore by beard and *peyes* that there are Jews who read the Friday edition from cover to cover.'[123]

Despite this seeming lack of ideological consistency, *Der moment* essentially reflected the Zionist sympathies of Tsevi Prylucki and a number of other contributors in the years prior to 1916. The elder Prylucki served as its editor-in-chief and directed the political segment of the paper. His son Noah headed its publicistic and belle-lettres portions. He also regularly stood in for his father as editor when the former was prevented from fulfilling his duties (e.g., when travelling outside Warsaw) and, along with one-time friend and colleague in the Zionist movement Yitshak Grünbaum, defended the newspaper in legal suits.[124] Magnus Krin-

2.3 The founders and staff of the Warsaw Yiddish daily *Moment* (1910–39), in which Noah and Tsevi Prylucki played a dominant role for decades, pose at a summer resort in Józefów, outside Warsaw, in August 1922. *Front row, left to right:* writer Hillel Zeitlin, editor Tsevi Prylucki, writer Shmuel Zitron; *back row:* writer Aaron Zeitlin, son of Hillel Zeitlin; writer Joseph Opatoshu; and Yitskhok Yankev Propus, secretary of the editorial board. (YIVO Institute, record 4818, frame 1318, 30381)

ski, who operated a Jewish commercial school in Warsaw (which Noah's brother Nakhmen attended and to whose parents' association Tsevi belonged), supervised the preparation of the Friday humour section and also wrote about pedagogic issues. Active primarily as a publicist, 'Reb Hillel,' as Hillel Zeitlin was respectfully known among the paper's staff for his religious piety and personal integrity,[125] continued his popular 'Letters to Jewish Youth' in *Der moment* and ardently combated the phenomenon of Assimilation. Additional materials were drawn from writers hired outside the regular editorial board.[126]

The capital raised by 'Yidishe prese' enabled *Der moment* to attain a circulation in Warsaw and the provinces of approximately 10,000 issues on weekdays and 15,000 on Friday, numbers adequate to keep the newspaper afloat but insufficient to compete with *Der haynt*. *Der moment*'s financial salvation came ironically not from the journalistic or literary endeavours of its contributors but from a gimmicky response to a pressing social problem: the Warsaw housing shortage. In 1911, *Der moment* announced that it had purchased a large plot of land near Warsaw where it would erect a garden city to remedy Jews' unhealthy alienation from nature and cramped city living. Parcels of the land, it promised, would be allotted to winners of a lottery among its readers and cheap credit would be furnished them in order to build homes and gardens. The interest of both poor Jews and affluent burghers piqued by the novel campaign, the newspaper's circulation climbed to around 20,000 issues. Although the plan was never realized, the circulation of *Der moment* only grew from then on, enabling it to remain competitive with *Der haynt* over the course of the next three decades.[127]

By 1912 *Der moment* could afford to expand its number of contributing editors, adding M. Spektor, Y.Kh. Zagorodski, B. Yeushzon, Yoysef Tunkl, Shloyme Yanovski, and others to its staff. It also began publishing serialized novels. The rivalry between 'Chłodno Street' (*Der haynt*) and the 'Nalewki' (*Der moment*), in no small measure a very personal rivalry between Shmuel Yatskan and his loyal supporters and the Pryluckis, became legendary thanks to regular mud-slinging between Warsaw's two most prominent Yiddish newspapers. More than one slander trial was convened and an honour court (in which the attorney and Zionist publicist Yitshak Grünbaum participated) was organized by community leaders as early as 1910 to save Jewish society from disgrace when mutual denunciations and insults hurled between the two 'families' made it to the attention of the Polish press. The very first scandal involving the two newspapers surrounded the figure of Hillel Zeitlin, a popular member of the *Der haynt* team prior to his 'defection' to *Der moment* in 1910. Zeitlin was spotted by a *Haynt* correspondent allegedly eating pork (he was actually eating an egg)[128] at the Brześć (or, according to some 'eyewitness' accounts, Pinsk) train station.[129] Yatskan's daily barrages discrediting the influential writer were countered by *Der moment's* feuilletonist Yeushzon with base accusations until Tsevi Prylucki, who was in Vienna at the time, put an end to the skirmish.[130] The incident is reminiscent of accusations the previous year that Zeitlin violated Sabbath prohibitions by writing his articles on Saturdays.[131]

The Litvak 'Invasion'

The Pryluckis, along with their archrival Shmuel Yatskan, Hillel Zeitlin, and scores of others active in the propagation of modern Hebrew and Yiddish culture in Warsaw, belonged to a category of Jews popularly called 'Litvaks.' Strictly speaking, the designation 'Litvak' refers exclusively to Jews from the Lithuanian and Byelorussian provinces of the Russian Empire, where Hasidism, with some notable exceptions, failed to become firmly entrenched because of the opposition of the *mitnagdim.*[132] The term came to be applied derisively to almost any Russian Jew originating beyond Congress Poland. Indeed, 'a true Warsaw chauvinist,' mocked the Polish-Yiddish translator and journalist Samuel Hirschhorn in 1906, 'calls all Jews who do not live in Warsaw Litvaks, not excluding the inhabitants of the (Warsaw) suburb of Praga.'[133]

'Litvaks' included refugees fleeing anti-Jewish excesses and oppressive measures in the Western Provinces, as well as individuals seeking economic and cultural opportunities. The pogroms of 1881, the ruinous May Laws of 1882, and the expulsion of 20,000 illegal Jewish residents from Moscow in 1891 were among the chief causes for their migration. Military service was also less arduous in Congress Poland than in the Western Provinces and rights of residence in this relatively prosperous part of the Empire were easily acquired.[134] It is estimated that between 100,000 and 250,000 Litvaks migrated to Congress Poland by the beginning of the First World War.[135]

The arrival of the Litvaks was cause for widespread dissatisfaction among both Polish Jews and ethnic Poles. Foreign to the Polish Jews in speech, dress, and habit, the Litvaks were regarded as keen competitors in the already overcrowded manufacturing and artisan sectors of the economy, as well as in the housing market. Often fleeing poverty and economic ruin, they frequently arrived without the burden of families and were satisfied with lower wages than Polish Jews. Further, they were perceived as less stringent in their religious observance and beliefs: they did not pay homage to the miracle-working Hasidic *rebbes*, pronounced Hebrew and Yiddish differently, and were suspected of walking with heads uncovered at home.

To the extent that they adopted elements of a non-Jewish culture, their orientation was a Russian and not a Polish one – a profound insult to supporters of the Polish national cause. Significantly, while frequently unfamiliar with the Polish language and local ways, they were equipped with a valuable knowledge of both the imperial language and Russian markets. As Shmarya Levin observes, 'Their language was Russian; and without any desire to help the Russian administration in its violent campaign of Russification, they became an instrument in the hands of the anti-Polish authorities.'[136] Typically more accepting of secular education than the largely Hasidic Polish Jews,[137] they were inclined to send their children to Russian-language gymnasia long before Polish Jews[138] and were blamed for the spread of subversive ideologies: 'Many local Jews regarded them as a bad influence: they adopted Russian or European fashions, and their women, independent or emancipated, were a far cry from the browbeaten Jewish women of Warsaw.'[139]

Despite varying degrees of secularization and russification, however, Litvaks did not typically espouse the abandonment of a distinctly Jewish identity. Nor did they seek to isolate themselves from broader Jewish society. To the contrary, they were identified as the primary bearers of secular nationalist ideologies, most notably Zionism and Bundism. Unlike Polish Jews, for whom secularization in the main meant polonization, Litvaks, in particular those truly originating in Lithuania and Byelorussia, originated in multiethnic regions where no local urban culture exerted such a strong attraction on them as Polish culture did on Polish Jews. Hence, there existed no dominant neighbouring culture into which integration or assimilation was desirable. While education and secularization for Litvaks often meant the adoption of the hegemonic Russian language as a vehicle for social and economic advancement, it did not imply identification with the Russian people. In general, the confrontation of deeply rooted Jewish identity and Western liberal ideas resulted in the creation of a new Jewish identity earlier among them than among Polish Jews.

Apart from providing much of the leadership of the Jewish socialist and nationalist movement in all its various shades, Litvaks included numerous scholars, teachers, and journalists prominent in the creation of the Hebrew and Yiddish presses and the movement to revive Hebrew as a spoken tongue. Writer Yitshak Dov Berkovitsh observed that around

2.4 The Russian Empire, ca. 1914. Shortly before the collapse of the tsarist empire, Jews resided in large numbers in European Russia, above all in the Pale of Settlement and Congress Poland, making for the largest concentration of Jews in the world. The imprecise 1897 census registered more than five million Jews in

1906 'among the Warsaw writers, more than a good half came from *Lite* and southern Russia. The Warsaw publishing houses and newspaper publishers were also mainly Litvaks and even the readers of the Warsaw newspapers and published books originated more often in *Lite* and the southern provinces than in Poland itself.'[140] A similar phenomenon was to be noted in Łódź, where migrants from the Western Provinces also played an important role in the founding and development of the city's Jewish press.[141]

Among these Litvaks were financially successful, university educated men like the Pryluckis who were not ashamed to speak Yiddish among themselves or in public. They provided a model for Polish Jews disillusioned with the apparent bankruptcy of Assimilationism in the face of increasingly virulent antisemitism and challenged the notion that a Jew must devote himself to Polish culture in order to become a modern European intellectual.[142]

The Yiddish Press and Polish-Jewish Relations

By 1906, five Yiddish newspapers – *Der veg, Der telegraf* (The Telegraph), *Yidishes tageblat* (Jewish Daily Paper), *Morgnblat* (Morning Paper), and *Di naye tsaytung* (The New Paper) – appeared with a combined circulation of 96,200. In contrast with the Hebrew and Polish presses, the Yiddish press was accessible to nearly all Jews, both male and female, as long as they knew the Hebrew alphabet (and most did).[143] Since each copy of a newspaper was commonly read aloud or shared by several individu-

---

the Russian Empire, about 4 percent of the overall population; the figure does not necessarily include the nearly three million Jews who left the Empire and migrated, mainly westward, from the 1870s to 1917. Thousands of Jews, making up the so called 'Litvak invasion' of Congress Poland, also relocated from the Pale of Settlement to the more economically advanced Polish provinces. In the second half of the nineteenth century, increasing numbers of Jews also settled in the Russian interior (especially in St Petersburg), both legally and illegally. During the First World War, the tsarist High Command expelled whole communities of Jews, suspected of disloyalty, from frontline areas into the Russian interior, effectively (although not legally) dismantling the Pale. (*Source: The YIVO Encyclopedia of Jews in Eastern Europe*) als, it may be assumed that the Yiddish press reached an audience much larger than this figure in Warsaw and the Polish provinces beyond.[144] The Jewish press in other languages – those in which significantly fewer Jews were literate – also grew, although hardly as dramatically: that year three daily newspapers (*Ha-yom* – The Day, *Ha-tsefira* – The Dawn, *Ha-tsofe* – The Observer) appeared in Hebrew with a combined circulation of 12,000 and one Polish-language Jewish daily also appeared (*Gazeta Nowa;* for a time called *Ludzkość* – Humanity) with a circulation of 10,000 copies.[145]

The explosive growth of the Yiddish press beginning in the tumultuous summer of 1905 educated Yiddish journalists and writers through practical work and for the first time furnished a real economic base for Jewish writers and intellectuals in Eastern Europe.[146] As a result of the russification of the education system in Russian Poland, non-Russian scholars, both Jews and Poles, had great difficulty in finding academic or other suitable posts. Generally speaking, they turned to office jobs that left them time and energy for their cultural and scholarly pursuits. The builders of Polish culture also often found patrons in the persons of wealthy Poles and polonized Jews. Jewish intellectuals, however, received little financial support from the latter group and none from the former. Nor could they find employment, like their Polish counterparts, in quasi-government posts such as the railroads. For them, the Yiddish press provided an opportunity to support themselves, if not profit, from their creative endeavours.[147] It also helped to provide a milieu and forum in which the emerging Jewish nationalist intelligentsia could gather and shape its unique values and ideas.

The familiarity with imperial press culture that the Pryluckis and other 'Litvaks' brought to Warsaw, together with their strong Jewish national consciousness and entrepreneurial instincts, were essential in navigating government channels and overcoming other obstacles to establish a Yiddish daily. Having overcome common prejudices towards the language, both father and son played important roles in popularizing the ideal of the Jewish national 'revival' via an idiom accessible to the vast majority of Jews. Without great difficulty, probably because he knew Yiddish as his literal mother tongue, Noah Prylucki quickly made the transition to writing and lecturing in the language with great aplomb. In *Der veg* and subsequent newspapers edited by his father, he found a mass audience for his evolving ideas about politics and culture. He also began to develop a notoriously vituperative public persona.

The existence of a thriving Yiddish press serving the needs of a minority composing a significant part of the population of urban centres challenged the aspirations of the Polish nationalist movement for cultural and political hegemony in a resurrected Polish state. Written in a vernacular mocked as a debased German jargon by most Poles (and many Jews too), its very language offended sensibilities and allegedly testified to the perpetual foreignness of the Jews to the Slavic cultural sphere. The very notion of a modern Jewish culture in Yiddish was simultaneously oxymoronic and menacing, an open challenge to the supremacy of the Polish language and culture on Polish soil. In the eyes of Polish nationalists, Litvaks and, by extension, all Yiddish-speaking Jews, were speakers of both a corrupt German dialect and the tongue of the tsarist oppressor. This led to paradoxical accusations that Jewish nationalists were not only Russifiers maliciously dispatched by Moscow and bent on infecting politically tractable Polish Jewry with the 'foreign' contagions of socialism and Jewish nationalism. They were Germanizers too – all this despite their support for the cause of Polish independence and their persistent refusal to identify with either of these imperial powers despised for the suppression of Polish culture and national aspirations.[148]

Noah Prylucki, for one, dismissed such charges as patently absurd and offensive to Jewish national ideals.[149] He mockingly dismissed Polish fears of a 'Litvak invasion' as unjustified as long as (the erstwhile liberal turned hostile to Jews) Aleksander 'Świętochowski still does not wear *peyes*, [and] the vaudeville theatres are not yet playing "Dos pintele yid."' His aggressive Jewish nationalist stance, elaborated on the pages of newspapers edited by his father, earned him condemnation on the pages of *Izraelita* as an arrogant chauvinist endangering Polish-Jewish relations.[150] Hoping to use the Yiddish press to dissuade its readers from Jewish nationalism in time for the Duma elections of 1912, representatives of the Assimilationist camp approached the management of *Moment* with the promise of a substantial subsidy to allow for the publication of articles written from its perspective. When this failed, an unsuccessful offer was made to purchase the newspaper.[151]

Polish-Jewish relations did indeed continue to decline in the years prior to the First World War, largely as a consequence of the especially acrimonious parliamentary elections of 1912. In elections to the Fourth (and final) Russian State Duma, an Endek-supported candidate was defeated by a Polish socialist – the only Polish candidate willing unequivocally to support equal rights for Jews – with the decisive help of Jewish votes marshalled by the Yiddish press. Anti-Jewish polemics filled the Polish nationalist press condemning the victory of the 'Jewish candidate' and the Endek newspaper *Gazeta Poranna 2 grosze* (Two Groschen Morning Gazette), which soon had the highest circulation of any Polish daily, mounted a furious economic and social boycott of the Jews under the slogan *swój do swego po swoje* ('each to his own and for his own') which did not lose its vigour until 1914.[152]

Conclusion

By the outbreak of the First World War, several Warsaw Yiddish dailies, each espousing a political orientation, boasted a combined circulation in excess of 200,000 copies.[153] The two largest circulation Yiddish dailies in Poland, the bitter rivals Shmuel Yatskan's *Haynt* and the Pryluckis' *Moment* transformed the face of Yiddish journalism and continued to dominate the Jewish press and to shape Jewish politics and culture in Poland until the outbreak of the Second World War.

As the most far-reaching instrument of mass culture among Jews, the Yiddish press laboured to combat the Assimilationist ideal, to politicize the traditionally religious Jews of Poland in the early twentieth century, to educate them about the wider world, and to transmit to them new secular ideologies intended to revolutionize Jewish society. It achieved great success in organizing Jewish public opinion in support of a nationalist position and, together with the Polish press, in contributing to the concretizing of ethno-linguistic divisions in society. More than any other factor, it prepared Polish Jewry for the campaign for national minority rights in the post–First World War era promoting the doctrine of national self-determination.

Although frequently pandering to popular tastes and indulging petty personal grudges, the press helped to elevate Yiddish's prestige in the eyes of its readers and to project an idealized image of how the high culture of a Yiddish-speaking society should look through its publication of literature and reviews of theatre and art. Once a Zionist firmly committed to Hebrew and Russian, Noah Prylucki came to see Yiddish and Jewish life in Eastern Europe in a decidedly more positive light through his work in the press and his political engagement. His diverse and manifold contributions to the creation of modern Yiddish language and culture – often achieved with the assistance of his *Moment* colleagues and protégés – will be explored in the next chapter.

chapter three

Creating Modern Yiddish Culture

To the consternation of his Zionist colleagues, Noah Prylucki grew increasingly distant from formal activity and membership in the Zionist movement in the oppressive wake of the 1905 Russian Revolution. Despite continuing to espouse many Zionist tenets in his articles, he formally left the socialist Zionist party Poale Zion and rejected identification with even the more Diaspora- and culture-oriented wings of the Zionist movement.[1] Like many Jewish nationalists frustrated by the tenacity of the tsarist autocracy, Prylucki turned to scholarship and cultural activity as an auxiliary to and, increasingly, a surrogate for political activity.[2]

While not part of the founding generation of Yiddishists, such as the writer Peretz or the philosopher Khayim Zhitlovski, who first articulated and agitated on behalf of the ideology in the closing decades of the nineteenth century, Prylucki began contributing to the creation of a modern culture in Yiddish in his adolescence. He was already its principled champion by the time of the Czernowitz Yiddish language conference in 1908.[3] Exuding confidence and determination on behalf of his cause, he unfurled an array of nation-building cultural activities characteristic of contemporary nationalist movements in Central and Eastern Europe.[4]

Prylucki was, of course, not alone in his desire to reconcile European culture with Jewish identity via – rather than through the rejection of – the Yiddish language and a 'modernized' Ashkenazic culture. In moving beyond a strong affective bond to the language and utilitarian recognition of its communicative value to adopting an ideology that venerated and promoted it as a value in itself, he was joined by a cohort of writers, artists, and intellectuals who drew upon the cultural and intellectual perambulations of the preceding generation. By the late nineteenth century, this generation had laid the foundations of Yiddishism as a cultural ideology and established Warsaw as Yiddish culture's largest centre.

Among contributors to the daily Yiddish press, especially those grouped around *Der moment*, he found kindred spirits who shared his idealism and aspirations as well as enthusiastic collaborators, if not assistants, for his creative endeavours. What chiefly distinguishes Prylucki from others active in the nascent Yiddishist movement is neither the originality of his ideas nor the aesthetic merits of his endeavours, but rather their sheer range and the leadership role that he arrogated to himself at a relatively young age. His profuse writings from 1908 to 1915 span the disciplines of poetry and literary criticism, folklore and ethnography, linguistics and philology, as well as art and theatre criticism, albeit with uneven success. All bear equally, though, the imprint of his nationalist ideology.

The promotion of the Yiddish language and the development of a modern European culture expressed in it became sacred, indeed obsessive causes for which he worked indefatigably and through which he aimed to transform the Jewish people into a secularized nation. They occupied the focus of his cultural and political activity, especially from 1908 on, the year of the landmark First Yiddish Language Conference. This chapter will explore Prylucki's growing commitment to Yiddish and to Yiddishism as the only legitimate expressions of Jewish identity in the years preceding the First World War. Expressed in prolific writings, this ideology would accompany him for decades to come and serve as the foundation for renewed political engagement during the First World War.

Politicization of the Language Question

The cultural wings of the Jewish nationalist movement, like analogous movements among other peoples in Europe, placed great emphasis on language as the 'soul' of a people. Language represented the most perfect expression of the 'national genius' that, according to Romantic thought, distinguishes one nation from another and guides the nation in the fulfilment of its unique historic mission for the benefit of all humanity. For the Jews, like other stateless and 'non-historic' peoples (i.e., lacking a tradition of statehood) dwelling within multinational empires, the development of a national language along with art, music, literature, theatre, and scholarship in it was to serve as a surrogate, temporary or permanent depending upon one's long-term political views, for a national territory. Yet, among themselves, Jewish nationalists in Eastern Europe could hardly agree as to which language embodied this romantic ideal and what should be its appropriate relationship to the other languages commonly in use in Jewish life.

The synthesis of nationalist and populist ideas adopted from the Eastern European milieu, Yiddishism glorified the language of the Jewish masses and sought through it to fashion a modern, secular culture for the Jews on the basis of nearly a thousand years of European life – the time, roughly, during which Yiddish was the spoken language of the largest part of European Jewry. Not only would Yiddish serve, however, as the medium for the expression of a modern sensibility among Jews. The very language itself was to replace religion as the force binding the Jewish people as a collective.

Like other forms of European populism, Yiddishism reproached intellectuals with betrayal and abandonment of the loyal *folk* (the Yiddish parallel to the German concept of *Volk*), the idealized guardians of the national soul and identity, through the adoption of foreign tongues and cultures. Taking inspiration from the Russian *narodniki*, these wayward sons and daughters were exhorted to return to their people, to help awaken in them a secular national consciousness, and to educate and modernize them in their own language. In return, the alienated intellectuals were to be inspired with and reinvigorated by the unreflective naturalness of the *folksmentsh*'s (the simple person of the masses) assumedly uncomplicated and unembarrassed identity. Yiddish was to undergo a process akin to that by which other European vernaculars were transformed into standardized, national languages in the eighteenth and nineteenth centuries (if not earlier) and reliance upon both Latin and 'foreign' languages was shed among educated classes. It was to be carefully cultivated, modernized, and its use expanded into domains of life such as mass politics, secular education, and modern scholarship from which it had been previously absent or excluded. Eventually, it would become the primary vehicle of both high and low culture.

Positing language as a supreme value from which all others flow, Yiddishism represented essentially a form of cultural nationalism and reflected the democratizing trend in the Russian Empire in general and in Jewish society in particular.[5] It was *not* intrinsically incompatible with either Bundism or Zionism, which emphasized, respectively, socialism and the establishment of a national homeland as solutions to the problems of contemporary Jewry. Left-wing Zionists championed the cause of Yiddish in the Diaspora and in some cases (e.g., Poale Zion-Left) in Palestine too. Despite common misperceptions, not all Yiddishists were hostile to Hebrew and Hebraism, although many in fact were. Hebraism – the movement to enthrone Modern Hebrew as the national language of the Jews and make it their vernacular wherever possible – was, of course, as much a product of the secularization of the Jews as was Yiddishism. Zionists generally favoured Hebrew as *the* national language of the Jews and wished this to become the spoken language in Palestine, although this did not deter them from making use of Yiddish in their work, especially after 1905, in the Diaspora. Indeed, Zionists such as Yosef Luria, Yitshak Grünbaum, and Nahum Syrkin desired to allot a special place to Yiddish in Zionist thought and culture. Most Zionists, like the rest of the Jewish intelligentsia, tended, though, to use Russian (or Polish) at home; few were willing to make it the language of their daily lives or believed in its revival outside Palestine.[6] Traditional Jews rejected outright both nationalist ideologies as dangerous fetishism and continued to emphasize religious observance as the sine qua non of Jewish self-definition. The intended disruption of the complementary relationship between Hebrew and Yiddish (diglossia), sanctified by centuries of practice, represented in itself a heresy to them.

Yiddish in the late nineteenth and early twentieth centuries possessed few conscious literary norms: decisions concerning spelling and punctuation were within the authority of the individual writer or editor; questions of standard grammar and gender to bridge dialectal variation had scarcely been formulated yet in a scholarly fashion. On the whole, an image prevailed of Yiddish as ugly and impoverished, incapable of expressing lofty and nuanced ideas, and devoid of an internal logic and stable lexicon. It was the language of the uneducated and impoverished while the 'better classes' appropriated more 'sophisticated' non-Jewish tongues. It was a language without a modern dictionary and a written grammar, then the hallmarks of national pride in language in Europe, and, it was commonly assumed, would never possess these because of some inherent defect. Even among those Jewish writers who recognized the irrational flaws in this critique and sought to cultivate Yiddish as a literary language, *maskilic* notions of the 'purity' of German compared with the 'mongrel' nature of Yiddish, in addition to the general prestige accorded German as a language of high culture in Eastern Europe, commonly resulted in the conscious patterning of Yiddish spelling, vocabulary, and syntax according to German literary norms – a phenomenon known derisively as *daytshmerish.*

It was precisely to elevate the prestige of Yiddish within and without Jewish society and to draw up plans to resolve an array of cultural and linguistic problems that the First Yiddish Language Conference was convened in 1908 in Czernowitz, capital of the Austro-Hungarian province of the Bukovina.[7] The conference, organized by the then Diaspora nationalist Nathan Birnbaum, drew delegates from political parties, most notably the Bund and Poale Zion (both of whose ideologies assigned an important role to Yiddish), along with some of the foremost writers and theoreticians active in the 'national renaissance' in Eastern Europe and even the United States. Among those present were the writers Y.L. Peretz, Sholem Asch, H.D. Nomberg, Avrom Reyzen, and Noah Prylucki, as well as Khayim Zhitlovski and a promising young linguist from Galicia, Matthias Mieses.

The conference aimed at no less than a sociolinguistic revolution within Eastern European Jewish society, one which would democratize Jewish life by giving primacy to the vernacular of the masses in areas of both high and low culture. Carried to its logical end, this would mean the displacement of both the traditional Hebrew-educated religious elite and the newer Polish- and Russian-speaking secular elites. A significant shift in the language's political and social status would require concomitant work to codify Yiddish and elaborate its vocabulary (corpus planning) both as a means to justify this change in status and in order to equip the language for new functions. Much time intended for the discussion of practical matters, such as the standardization of orthography and the creation of an authoritative dictionary, however, was lost to heated debates concerning the relationship between Hebrew and Yiddish. In fact, the issue of the status of Yiddish within Jewish society alone was debated to the exclusion of any discussion of its desired recognition by non-Jewish authorities. Out of personal respect for Hebrew and for fear of alienating much of the Jewish world, few participants were willing to accept the radical motion demanded by the Bundist Esther Frumkin relegating Hebrew to the past as a clerical relic. Instead, a seven-person committee, in which Prylucki took part, agreed upon a compromise formula proposed by Nomberg to recognize Yiddish in the name of the conference as *a* national language of the Jewish people. Each individual was left free to determine his personal stance towards Hebrew.

While the contemporary Jewish press attributed little significance to the Czernowitz Conference, Prylucki was certain that its meaning would not be lost on future historians. They would recognize it as a conference not merely for the Yiddish language but for the entire 'Jewish national-cultural present.' In the Diaspora, he noted, the Jewish people has lived more with its historic past and future dreams than with its present. The

3.1 Portraits of Hillel Zeitlin (1872–1942), a Hebrew-Yiddish writer and religious national philosopher who was among the founders of the Folkparty and the Yiddish daily *Moment*, and Nathan Birnbaum (1864–1937), writer and sometime Zionist, Yiddishist and Diaspora Nationalist, and, ultimately, Orthodox leader. Birnbaum, a Viennese Jew who located Jewish cultural authenticity and national integrity in the Jews of Eastern Europe, was the chief convener of the landmark 1908 Czernowitz Yiddish conference, in which Zeitlin took an active part. (YIVO Institute, record 12641, frame 6864.01, 9640, 39641, 39642)

3.2 Leading Jewish writers Sholem Asch (*left*) and Y.L. Peretz (*centre*), Peretz's son Lucjan (*right*), and writer and journalist Hersh-Dovid Nomberg (1876–1927), a founder of the Folkist party and briefly member of the Polish parliament. Asch, Y.L. Peretz, and Nomberg all participated in the First Yiddish Language Conference, held in Czernowitz in 1908. (YIVO Institute, record 12637, frame 6847, 39630, 39631)

conference, however, was proof of awakened Jewish self-awareness and commitment to self-help as a means to a better future; it served as evidence that the Jewish people was still alive, if a bit anaemic. Czernowitz, he continued, united rival political groupings to lay the ideological foundations of an organized movement on behalf of Yiddish, the tongue that served as the Jews' contemporary national language alongside their historical one. Both the Bund and the Zionists have been forced to confront the present and therefore created, respectively, programs embracing cultural autonomy in the Diaspora and a plan of *Gegenwartsarbeit.*[8] These plans would necessarily make extensive use of Yiddish and struggle for its official recognition, for 'the national recognition of the Jewish people depends upon the recognition of the Yiddish language.'[9]

Like Prylucki, Nomberg comprehended instinctively the need to draw the intelligentsia to Yiddish and to make an independent cultural value of the language in order for its cultivation to be effective. For this reason, following the Czernowitz Conference he chided those 'friends' of Yiddish who supported the language's development and codification, yet stopped short of recognizing it as a national language:

> If we say, 'Yiddish is a national language of the Jewish people,' that means that we believe that the future Jewish national life will be cast in the form of our mother tongue; that is, among us must cease the division between 'intelligentsia' and 'folk,' that the former must become *folkstimlekh* and have the same language for its own use as the folk has; that is, the language must become a cult, a self-sufficient value, etc., and only then do we come to the conclusion that it needs a grammar, an orthography, etc. ... A language that does not become a cult for the people is truly no more than a 'jargon' and can do without a grammar and an orthography.[10]

Prylucki's understanding of Yiddish as the quintessence of Jewish identity – a fundamentally secular, nationalist view borrowed from the European context – was not necessarily shared by all active on behalf of Yiddish, even those who deemed it of the greatest importance for Jewish life. His very public joy in contemplating the Czernowitz Conference and his sense of the dawning of a new era in Jewish life were lambasted by none other than his newspaper colleague, the future Folkist Hillel Zeitlin.

Zeitlin proclaimed the event 'not a holiday for *mame-loshn*' but one for the ignoramuses who gathered in Czernowitz: '*Jargon* is not a national language because all our spiritual treasures are in *loshn-koydesh* and only in *loshn-koydesh. Jargon* is the day; *loshn-koydesh* – eternity.'[11] Zeitlin was hardly an opponent of the cultivation of Yiddish as a literary language and its expanded use in Jewish life. He remained all his life an ardent supporter of traditional diglossia and was loath to contemplate a future in which Yiddish-speaking children would not read religious texts in their original language. He attributed great value to the preservation and cultivation of Yiddish, which had been sanctified by generations of use, but refused to concede it status equal to that of sacrosanct Hebrew, much less agree to see it supplant Hebrew. By Hebrew he understood *loshn-koydesh,* the historically layered language of Jewish liturgy and rabbinic literature. Least of all was Zeitlin willing to countenance modern spoken Hebrew with Sephardic pronunciation as propagated by Palestinocentric Hebraists; this he denigrated as an irredeemably artificial dialect and, still worse, a debasement of *loshn-koydesh.*[12] While Zeitlin wrote on pressing social issues of the day in Yiddish, he pondered the eternal and expounded upon mysticism and religious philosophy chiefly in *loshn-koydesh.* This bilingualism reflected not merely Zeitlin's separation of realms of endeavour between the mundane and the spiritual but was characteristic of the Jewish literary world in Poland prior to the First World War as a whole – a dichotomy which Yiddishism sought to undo.[13] Characteristically, Prylucki attacked this conservatism and accused Zeitlin of seeking to 'invalidate all that others approach with creative purposes' because of his own lack of will or ability to contribute to the building of a new culture.[14]

In Defence of Yiddish: A Response to 'Kosher Assimilationists,' 'Polish Antisemites,' and 'Jews Who Call Themselves Poles'

Although the Czernowitz Conference avoided a definitive pronouncement displacing Hebrew from paramount status in Jewish life, the significance it accorded Yiddish resulted in the heightening of tensions and the formal drawing of battle lines between the so-called Yiddishists and Hebraists, proponents of rival linguistic and cultural visions for the future of the Jewish people. Prior to 1905, when Jewish nationalist parties began to include official recognition for Yiddish as part of their programs for national and cultural autonomy in the Diaspora, language represented more a secondary factor, an instrument for educating and indoctrinating the Jewish public, than a value or goal in itself. Despite the penchant of some ideological Yiddishists to locate progenitors of the movement as early as the medieval period in order to emphasize its popular roots, the relationship between Hebrew and Yiddish in Eastern European Jewish society was simply not widely politicized. Even the Bund, after 1905 a chiefly Yiddish-speaking and -writing organization which became associated with hostility towards Hebrew, failed to condemn Hebrew cultural work in its first resolution excoriating Zionism as bourgeois and reactionary at its third party conference in 1901.[15]

The gains made by Yiddish since 1905 put Hebraists on the defensive: Hebrew book sales were already on the decline in the first decade of the twentieth century, publishing houses were failing, and potential readers were opting for other languages. Scandalized and threatened by the convening of an upstart 'jargon' conference in 1908, Hebraists felt compelled to call their own conference the following year in Berlin to reaffirm the dominance of Hebrew (and to denigrate the proponents of Yiddish) in Jewish life and to prepare the convening of a full-fledged congress to coordinate and support Hebraist activity worldwide.[16] Nonetheless, most writers continued to write in both Hebrew and Yiddish until the First World War, even if they publicly expressed distaste for one or the other language or pessimism with regard to its future.

Persistent attacks on Yiddish by prominent Hebraists, notably Ahad Ha'am and the literary critic and historian Yosef Klausner, impelled Prylucki to formulate a public stance regarding the respective roles of Hebrew and Yiddish in contemporary Jewish life. In tirades that went without response, he accused these men of wilfully ignoring reality for the sake of an impossible dream, the revival of Hebrew as a spoken language. Inadvertently, they encouraged the Jews' 'assimilation' through the implementation of their misguided language ideology. These arguments reflect his conviction, expressed with ever increasing belligerence, that the Jews were condemned to disappearance as a people if they did not maintain Yiddish as their primary language and adapt it to the needs of a secular future.

Ahad Ha'am erred, Prylucki claimed, in describing Yiddishism as merely a product of romanticism among intellectuals estranged from traditional Jewish life. Nor was Yiddish bound to disappear within two to three generations as the Jews' level of general education and exposure to the non-Jewish world increased. It was the very mundaneness of Yiddish, the fact that the masses employed it without question while Hebrew lacked most everyday functions, Prylucki argued, which was the source of its strength and guaranteed its future.[17] That the language was called by such names as *yidish* (meaning Jewish) and *mame-loshn* (mother tongue) testified to the people's attachment to it.[18] Only the linguistically assimilated Jewish intelligentsia was ignorant of Yiddish, and those in its ranks who had become nationally conscious were hastily endeavouring to master the same tongue they formerly held in such low esteem as an essential step towards *rapprochement* with their people.[19]

In making such an argument, Prylucki failed to acknowledge the extent to which Ahad Ha'am was correct in his analysis. Much of the intellectual leadership of the Yiddishist movement, the so-called *folks-inteligentn* (people's intellectuals), at this time consisted precisely of national 'penitents.' Men like Peretz, Zhitlovski, and the writer and ethnographer Sh. An-ski (Shloyme Zaynvil Rapoport), as well as the Bundist Vladimir Medem (born into a converted Jewish family), and founder of Poale Zion Ber Borokhov (raised from birth as a Russian-speaker because his father, a Hebrew teacher, and family desired that its children not speak a Russian recognizably influenced by Yiddish),[20] were motivated in part by both antisemitism and nostalgia to 'return' to their now idealized people and adopt Yiddish as their primary language. And he himself, while active in nationalist circles from a relatively young age, was by his own, albeit exaggerated, confession a non-native (and hence, in his own eyes, not wholly authentic) speaker of Yiddish. Moreover, he regularly chided Yiddish readers – supposedly not indifferent to their mother tongue – in his articles for their lack of attachment and appreciation for the language, sacrificing their heritage for the sake of fashion and socio-economic advancement. Clearly, the habit of speaking and reading Yiddish, even among those claiming affective bonds to their beloved mother tongue, did not necessarily make for its valorization.

Prylucki further faulted Ahad Ha'am for arguing that a national literature, one of enduring worth, could be created only in Hebrew. Even if Yiddish were to decline eventually as a spoken language, its literature would neither be forgotten nor read exclusively in Hebrew translation. Rather, it would be preserved in the original just as were works written in Aramaic, long the vernacular of the Jews once Hebrew ceased to be widely spoken.[21] Years of participation in the movement to revive Hebrew as a spoken idiom as a member of *Safa brura* convinced Prylucki that, regardless of the admirable idealism exhibited by youth who spoke Hebrew among themselves, the resuscitation of Hebrew in the Diaspora was an utter impossibility. Quotidian interaction with other Jews required that Hebrew enthusiasts resort to other languages, especially Yiddish, no matter how strong their desire to resist this fact of Diaspora life. To insist upon Hebrew and nothing else, as did the fanatical Ya'akov Rabinovitz, a Hebrew journalist and writer, was to deny Diaspora Jewry its primary source of intellectual sustenance and to condemn it consequently to disappearance.[22] Moreover, the improbable revival of Hebrew as a spoken language could be achieved only in *Eretz yisrael,* where Jews from all over the world would gather and the ancient tongue-turned-book language of the Jews function as a common idiom. Even there, however, the strength of Yiddish could not be ignored: a mass immigration of Eastern European Jews would make legal recognition for Yiddish a necessity there too.[23]

Contrary to popular Hebraist libels, Prylucki continued, there was scarcely a principled opponent of Hebrew to be found among the 'jargonists.' The importance of Hebrew to Jewish life as an historical and national language is indisputable and all Jews are consequently obliged to study it. Because Yiddish displays the indelible mark of Hebrew upon both its lexicon and its syntax, an active command of it actually facilitates the learning of Hebrew.[24] In fact, at the Czernowitz Conference, Prylucki attributed what he saw as the poor quality of much contemporary Yiddish literature to the dire economic straits of writers and the decreasing knowledge of Hebrew, which enriches Yiddish, among the new generation of writers who were not always drawn like previous generations from the educationally privileged *yeshiva* elite and therefore lacked a solid grounding in the classic Jewish tongue.[25] He thereby affirmed an indispensable yet fundamentally auxiliary role for Hebrew in Jewish education.

Prylucki was quite adamant, however, about the dangers posed by a Hebraist education. Not only did the use of a foreign language for primary education slow a child's intellectual acquisition according to contemporary pedagogical theory, but the emphasis placed on language and the Bible in the Hebraist *heder metukan* (the 'reformed kheyder,' which pioneered the technique of Hebrew immersion) to the exclusion of practical subjects actually made the child ill-equipped for higher education. In any case, the pupil must obtain a higher education in another language, for no Hebrew high schools and universities existed. By the time he completed a Russian-language gymnasium, the graduate of the *heder metukan* could seldom read a Hebrew newspaper with comprehension since he had forgotten so much of the language following years of disuse. Ultimately, the product of an exclusively Hebraist education was an individual ineligible for most forms of employment.[26] Curiously, in his anti-Hebraist fervour, Prylucki discounted the educational experience of thousands of Jewish intellectuals, including himself, educated in 'foreign' tongues without detriment to their intellectual abilities. He also neglected to consider that, just as there existed no opportunities for a formal higher education in Hebrew, there also existed none in Yiddish.

Ahad Ha'am disingenuously protested, according to Prylucki, that he bore a neutral position towards Yiddish as a folk language. He insisted that there is no reason to proscribe it as a medium for the education of those with access to no other language as long as no pretence were made to its status as a national language and no energy wasted in its cultivation as a literary language.[27] Such a position was no different from wilfully denying Yiddish (and with it, Prylucki implied, the Jewish people) a future. The likes of Dr Klausner, on the other hand, unwittingly aided and abetted the cause of the Jews' national dissolution by fanatically waging a campaign for the eradication of Yiddish in public life. Blinded by their undoubtedly well-intentioned nationalist fervour, these 'Kosher Assimilationists' played directly into the hands of genuine Assimilationists and antisemites: they banned Yiddish from national assemblies while welcoming all other tongues.[28] The demands 'Russian or Hebrew!' or 'Polish or Hebrew!' heard at conferences mean effectively that only non-Jewish languages are spoken (and often poorly) at Jewish national conferences, for even among Hebrew writers few are capable of actually speaking Hebrew. Such rhetoric is to be expected not from the camp of Jewish nationalists but from its opponents. After all, the enemies of Jewish nationalism venerate Hebrew as a classical language and support its use among Jews precisely because they are aware that, unlike Yiddish, it is a weak opponent, a language known by few and spoken by virtually none.[29]

It is absolutely true, as the rapacious 'devourers of jargon' (*zhargon-freser*) gleefully point out, that not only does much of the Jewish intelligentsia use non-Jewish languages in daily life, but that a segment of the Jewish youth and lower classes are also ashamed to speak Yiddish in public. Their imperfect mastery of non-Jewish languages is reflected in 'a caricature of a broken dialect' and should be no cause for rejoicing among Jewish nationalists. Wherever Yiddish disappears from Jewish life, assimilation is sure to creep quietly, almost unnoticed into its place; on the contrary, the spread of the Yiddish printed word, the work of agitators on behalf of Yiddish, and the popularity of Yiddish lectures and of even *shund* theatre are all factors which contribute to the strengthening of Jewish national feeling and to reversing the tide of assimilation. It is therefore essential that Jews exclusively employ Yiddish with one another in all situations and for all purposes. The anxiety-inducing expectation must be shattered among the Jewish masses that one must address a Jewish professional in clumsy Polish or Russian rather than comfortable *mame-loshn.*[30] Thus, Jewish nationalist newspapers must be printed in Yiddish and no other language,[31] the minutes and reports of Jewish societies must be kept in Yiddish,[32] merchants and doctors must hang only Yiddish signs, business cards must be printed in Yiddish, wedding announcements must appear in correct Yiddish (and not with a cosmetic admixture of *daytshmerish*, e.g., *ferlobte*, from the German *Verlobte* for fiancée), and even household utensils bearing initials, such as salt and pepper shakers, must bear Yiddish and not Latin or Cyrillic letters: 'And again, don't say that these are trifles. From such "trifles" (*narishkeytn*) begins assimilation. At first, Kopel becomes Filaret, Zangvel – Zenzwi, Efraym – Franciszek and Sore – Solomea. After the Jewish names, the Jewish books, the Jewish heart, the Jewish soul are driven out of the house.'[33]

While repeatedly expressing an appreciation of Polish culture in articles about art and literature, Prylucki furiously rejected demands for the polonization of the Jews, considering it a form of national suicide. In the past, that is, prior to the *Haskalah*, the average Pole never dreamed of the Jews' assimilation but rather viewed their distinct cultural life, including their *szwargot* (gibberish), as a natural, albeit comical phenomenon. The Assimilationists, however, decry as abnormal the Jews' desire to make use of their native tongue. They spread the canard that Jewish nationalism, of which the Litvaks are purportedly the standard bearers, is inherently hostile to *Polskość* (Polishness). In this way, the Assimilationists contribute to the antisemites' already well-stocked arsenal of anti-Jewish rhetoric.[34]

Prylucki hyperbolically declared that 'Jews who call themselves Poles' and 'Jewish Jews' (*yidishe yidn*, a term usually meaning traditionally religious Jews but here meant as a reference to nationalist, Yiddish-speaking Jews), constituted two separate nations.[35] He faulted the younger generation of Assimilationists for, in contrast with their fathers, not maintaining even the slightest connection with Jewish life and failing to contribute to Jewish philanthropy (apparently his opposition to the Assimilationists did not extend to their money).[36] He also demanded that Poles cease regarding Jews as 'foreigners' despite centuries of residence in Poland and instead both treat them as equals and recognize their Yiddish language and culture. Rejecting claims of Jewish 'separatism' hurled by the same Polish leaders who took pride in Polish national and cultural sentiment among Polish émigrés in the United States, Prylucki presented the heroism of Colonel Berek Joselowicz (1764–1809), organizer of a Jewish unit in the 1794 Kościuszko insurrection against imperial Russia, as justification for the Jews' right to dwell in Poland. For Prylucki, Joselowicz fulfilled the same function as Kazimierz Pułaski, the Polish nobleman whose sacrifice for the colonies' cause in the American War of Independence purportedly provided the moral basis for Polish settlement in the

United States.[37] In equating Joselowicz with Pułaski, Prylucki indirectly gave voice to his support for the cause of an independent Poland despite being a product of Russian imperial culture.

His general antagonism towards polonized Jews was at times, however, tinged with a shade of pity. Those individuals raised in Assimilationist homes or who adopt Assimilationist ideology of their own volition were for him misguided souls, sufferers of an acute sense of embarrassment which motivated them to distance themselves socially from what they condescendingly viewed as the uncultured Jewish masses. Their shame, which at times extended to self-loathing, was rooted in woeful ignorance of the proud language and culture of their people. Trapped in a hopeless delusion, the Jewish proponents of Assimilation identified with a nation that would never truly accept them into its bosom despite the sincerity of their longing to unite with it. Regrettably, their personal anguish all too frequently translated into an adversarial position towards Jewish culture and the Jewish nationalist cause, a stance that for Prylucki was tantamount to antisemitism – the refusal to allow Jews to exist qua Jews. Interestingly, Prylucki failed to draw the parallel between his own *maskilic* upbringing, which imparted to him a certain condescension towards Yiddish as the speech of the uncouth lower classes, and the attitudes of Assimilationists. Nor did he question whether so many of his cultural endeavours were not, apart from their language, of a specifically Jewish dimension or coloration.

On the other hand, Assimilationists posed a direct threat to the Jewish nation, for they paternalistically interfered in internal Jewish affairs and attempted to use their wealth and influence to impose their conception of Jewishness as an exclusively religious category on the whole of the Jewish people. Craven 'enemies of Judaism,' the Assimilationist leadership of the *kehila* combatted Jewish cultural organs and neglected legitimate Jewish economic, political, and educational interests in order to curry favour with its antisemitic Polish masters.[38] Orthodox members of the Warsaw *kehila*-board who cooperated with them were likened to the biblical Esau for 'selling their birthright to those who seek the destruction of the nation' from within.[39]

Ever a liberal, Prylucki in principle accepted acculturation and/or the dissolution of a Jewish identity as an option for individuals. Yet he castigated Assimilationists for treacherously abandoning their nation and, inevitably, leading their children to the baptismal font and the lethal embrace of antisemitism. No matter how great the contributions to Polish culture and industry of men like the economist and *Nowa Gazeta* editor

Stanisław Kempner and the mathematician Szmuel Dickstein, the Assimilationist could be accepted as a Pole only when he had converted and proved himself an inveterate antisemite. The neophyte was not merely a traitor to his native people. He also forever remained suspect in the eyes of his adoptive nation, his renegade character and motivations for conversion distasteful even to those who theoretically welcomed him into their fold.[40] Thus, while affirming the rights of the individual to identify as he wished, Prylucki rejected embracing a Polish identity as not merely delusional but necessarily dangerous to the national collective – the fundamental social unit in his conception. Needless to say, Jewish and Polish cultural and national identities could in no way be reconciled.

Poet or Pornographer?

Consistently on the attack, Prylucki was himself put on the defensive by reviews of a book of sensual poetry entitled *Farn mizbeyekh* (Before the Altar) which he published in early 1908.[41] The headstrong twenty-seven year-old dedicated the collection to his bride, the Polish-language poet Paula R. (Rozental, neé Edelsztein). While she spoke little Yiddish at the time of their marriage, Paula shared his interest in Yiddish literature and theatre, an interest which he encouraged over the years of their marriage. Raised in an affluent 'assimilated' family in Warsaw, Paula married the dentist Adam Rozental at age seventeen but this marriage ended in divorce. Prior to the dissolution of the marriage, she played host from 1903 to 1905 to a literary salon in their home drawing leading Polish writers and, eventually, Yiddish writers too. Among them was the charismatic philosopher, literary critic, and dramatist Stanisław Przybyszewski. He was an 'uncompromising Bohemian,' a champion of art for art's sake and of individualism who 'became a cult figure in the circle of young writers and poets who shaped the movement known in Polish literary history as 'Młoda Polska' (Young Poland)' – the first Polish literary movement as a whole to draw Jewish writers.[42] Under the influence of the Yiddish-Polish writer and dramaturge Mark Arnstein, a disciple of Przybyszewski, Paula and her husband became active in the Yiddish theatre world. There she became acquainted with Esther Rokhl Kaminska, who later performed in the Yiddish dramas she wrote under Prylucki's influence.[43] Since she was some six years his elder and had been married to a man whom Noah Prylucki's parents held in disrepute, their marriage in late November 1908 was itself cause for family scandal.[44]

Tortured by what he judged the poverty of forms in Yiddish literature, Prylucki not only preached the exploration of new literary themes and styles in his newspaper and magazine articles, but also attempted to demonstrate how to write 'well-rhyming, rhythmic-sounding, and multiform verse' in Yiddish. His interest in introducing greater eroticism into Yiddish literature was consonant with a 'generation-wide search for new values and beliefs' among Russian intellectuals of this time, including a surge in pornography following the relaxation of censorship laws in 1906.[45] Bearing a red cover, presumably in consonance with its fiery content, the slim edition aimed to drive 'prayer-house modesty and bashfulness' from Yiddish literature and to introduce into it sexual passion and sensuality as found in contemporary Russian and other European literatures.[46] Typical of his verse is the poem titled 'Embrace':

Embrace my ailing body
With the golden rays of snakes!
I yearn for you, mild, slim woman!
Press my ailing body
To the silkiness of the stalks!

My tender face,
Far from you, grows ever paler!
The yellow light barely flickers …
My withering face thirsts
For the fresh water of kisses …

Reveal your white breast to me!
Stretch out your cherry lips to me!
In the garden that is empty
I want to sup hot, sweet spices
From your bosom of roses.

Show your teeth of pearl
And braid your locks of fire!
I want to bite your ivory feet
With my wolf's teeth,
Drink the wild honey juices …

I long for you, my heavenly dream!
I yearn for your silky limbs,
And I perish like foam

Far from you, my heavenly dream,
Far from your eyes of song.[47]

Although retrospectively deemed naïve and modest by memoirists in comparison with the more daring Yiddish poetry of the interwar period, *Farn mizbeyekh* was then considered the very last word in pornography and dissoluteness. As Zeitlin's son Elkhonen, a child at the time, recalled, critics 'argued about every poem, interpreted ambiguously every word, laughed, made fun, got angry, cursed the author – repeated from memory verses from *Farn mizbeyekh.*'[48]

Perhaps in anticipation of accusations that his poetry was indecent, Prylucki published an article that year in defence of the erotic as a legitimate literary genre in the first issue of a new illustrated journal, *Teater-velt* (Theatre World).[49] He began his discussion of 'Art and Pornography' with a denunciation of what he considered the Russian press's hypocritical condemnation of the writer Artsybashchev, then on trial for charges of pornography, while applauding the worst *shund* on the stage. The bourgeoisie in Russia, he dismayed, delights in indecent French farces and operas such as *The Merry Widow* that conceal disgraceful talk and conduct behind a façade of beautiful music and coquettish humour. At the same time, it feigns shock upon hearing the names of serious artists who treat the 'sexual question' in their works. True pornography – naked photographs, postcards, and brochures clandestinely produced in cellars by 'specialists' or racy limericks anonymously penned for singing in taverns – recognizes itself as such and its purveyors therefore deliberately conceal their identities. To brand indiscriminately any work treating sexual subjects as pornography merely constitutes an assault on the freedom of the artist and deprives him of a valid subject: 'Why should art ignore sex, the axis of the organic world, the power that hangs over human psychology? What other area of life is so full of secrets and beauty? Since art draws most of its themes from psychology, normal and abnormal, why should abnormal sexual phenomena – homosexuality and lesbianism not be depicted in art? Why should the woman's body be forbidden to art?'[50]

In support of his claim, he pointed to the 'pornography' of the ancient Greeks, who appreciated such elements in epic poetry as part of their national lore without it arousing prurient interest. Similarly, sexual themes pervade the Hebrew Bible, yet fail to corrupt pious Jews, for whom its every word is sacred.[51] Prylucki failed to acknowledge, however, that this is largely the achievement of the Jewish interpretative tradition, which routinely seeks to spiritualize or otherwise explain away blatantly sexual content.

The sensation of the day, Prylucki's verse earned him the mocking epithet 'the breast-poet,'[52] a reference to the many paeans dedicated to his beloved's bosom such as:

Closer! Closer! Closer
Embrace me, sister!
Press my desirous lips to your breasts –
To the twinned white roses!
Needs churn in my breast
Like the storm in the wide sea!
I yearn for the nectar of young flowers![53]

Above all, he was accused of impiety towards God and the debasement of Yiddish through his use of immodest language.[54] Reviewers also deplored his 'rigmarole' (*ployderay*) and the clumsy use of rhyme reliant upon the haphazard mixing of dialects (e.g., southern Yiddish *shu* 'hour' and Lithuanian-Yiddish *ru* 'rest').[55] The most damaging criticism, however, categorically denied him any literary talent and even refused him recognition as a pornographer, for 'the pornographer goes directly for his goal, knows what he wants, does not use poetry. Prylucki seeks to be a poet and is not even capable of pornography. Prylucki's impudence is a surrogate for his desire for boldness. He who is bold need not talk about his boldness.' His approach to eroticism was deemed lewd and cynical: if he truly meant his roaring sexual invocations, he would neither need to be so explicit nor have recourse to so many exclamation points as to render his words utterly meaningless. The poet infuses even the most subjectively prosaic or base subject with holiness and thereby elevates its essence. Prylucki succeeds, the influential literary critic Shmuel Niger bemoaned on the pages of *Der fraynd*, in the contrary: he desecrates the holy and makes it instead quotidian.[56] In a similar tone, the reviewer Izidor Lazar complained in *Roman-tsaytung* (Novel Gazette) that Prylucki failed even while freely adapting the works of Russian poets Fedor Sulogub, Valery Bryusov, and Konstantin Bal'mont. They know how to distinguish between the language of passion and that of simple vulgarity. Prylucki, in contrast, is utterly incapable of expressing erotic ecstasy, offering at the very best a course in human physiology.[57]

Prylucki defended himself and his views on contemporary Yiddish literature with customary vigour in an ensuing polemic with Shmuel

Niger.[58] He seems, however, to have been discouraged from publishing any further collections of his own poetry by the humiliating reception *Farn mizbeyekh* received. Still, his love for literature remained undiminished and he published a Yiddish translation of the Russian author Leonid Andreev's popular novella *Seven Who Were Hanged* ('Rasskaz o semi poveshennykh,' 1908) about political terrorism.[59] With the exception of the occasional poem dedicated to Paula R. or to nature, however, he now channelled this passion primarily into cultivating the unpolished talents of others, whom he charged with the sacred mission of creating a national body of literature.

Warsaw Yiddish Literary Salons

After returning to Warsaw in 1909, Prylucki enthusiastically opened his home to readings and critique of the work of aspiring writers. In addition to his, two other literary salons were also active: that of another relative newcomer to the world of letters, Hillel Zeitlin, and the long-standing one hosted by Y.L. Peretz, which was active from 1880 on. With the piety of Hasidim making a pilgrimage to their *rebbe*, many an aspiring writer left behind his native *shtetl* or smaller city in the Polish provinces with unpolished manuscripts held in trembling hands to seek the guidance and approval of the man whom they deemed the ultimate arbiter of literary taste. The most fortunate became regular members of Peretz's literary coterie, elated that the great writer had recognized their artistic potential.[60] While they did not enjoy the cachet of the Y.L. Peretz's legendary Cegałno Street salon, acceptance into which held a promise of literary success, the homes of Hillel Zeitlin and Noah Prylucki proved an attractive gathering place for dozens of writers and intellectuals after 1908.

In the main, the two salons, especially Prylucki's, attracted those writers who lacked the courage to stand the challenge of Peretz's legendarily acerbic critique or who refused to be discouraged despite having already been branded deficient in talent by the *eminence grise* of Warsaw Jewish letters. These writers were joined by others who simply desired to sample the atmosphere of other circles or bask in their own glory once Peretz had already conferred upon them citizenship in the Yiddish literary republic.[61]

While there was free movement among writers and intellectuals between the three Warsaw salons, each literary circle possessed a distinct character and purpose reflecting the interests and talents of its central figure and founder. To Hillel Zeitlin's home at Śliska 60 flocked religious and philosophically minded youth from Warsaw and the provinces who were inspired by his Hebrew writings and, above all, his 'Letters to Jewish Youth.' Not all, however, who were drawn to the physically impressive presence of the tall, blue-eyed, copper-bearded mystic aspired to be writers, either in Hebrew or in Yiddish; many came simply to hear his forays into religious and ethical matters or to become acquainted with other Jewish writers.[62] In contrast with Peretz, who had prescribed hours of visitation, Zeitlin received his guests without appointments and in a free and informal manner. The roster reads were like a 'Who's Who' of the Warsaw newspaper and literary world prior to the First World War. Zeitlin's patriarchal figure presided over impassioned discussions among Jewish Warsaw's intellectual elite, as well as over the singing of folksongs and Hasidic melodies and the exchange of jokes and anecdotes – a practice shared by Peretz's circle in Warsaw and Hebrew-Yiddish writer Mendele's (Sholem Yankev Abramovitsh) in Odessa.[63]

By the time Hillel Zeitlin (1872–1942) arrived in Warsaw in 1907 expressly to work in the Yiddish press, he already possessed an established name in Jewish journalism in Poland. His early biography is in many respects typical of his generation of Jewish intellectuals. The son of a wealthy merchant and disciple of Habad Hasidism, he enjoyed a traditional education in rabbinic sources in his native *shtetl* Korma (Mohilev province, Byelorussia) and in various Lithuanian *yeshivot.* Recognized as an *ilui,* or Talmudic prodigy, by his eleventh birthday, he experienced the wavering of his religious convictions under the impact of *Haskalah* literature in Hebrew and their erosion by a course of intense, autodidactic study in the natural sciences and philosophy that he pursued after his father's death.[64]

Throughout his life Zeitlin refused allegiance to a single party but expressed sympathy for more than one. After initial support for the Zionist movement, he came to embrace territorialism as the solution to Jewish economic misery and rightlessness. Under the influence of the poet Avrom Reyzen, he began to write in Yiddish, which he initially viewed as merely an instrument to enlighten the masses, and published his first work in that language in 1906 in Yaakov Luria's *Dos yidishe folk* (The Jewish People).[65] While himself not strictly observant of Jewish law at this time, he combated 'assimilationist' and anti-religious currents in his articles in the Yiddish press and sought to make modern ideas comprehensible to religious readers in terms they understood.[66] He attacked not only the Jewish left, which he blamed for misleading the Jews and undermining their unity as a people, but also secular Yiddishism and its prophet, Y.L. Peretz. 'Peretz has a heaven,' he wrote, 'but in this heaven there is no God.'[67]

By the end of first decade of the twentieth century, the secular-territorial phase in Zeitlin's ideology had begun to yield to the beginnings of a religious return. Like the Zionist movement as whole, which he had only recently left, he began to turn his thoughts to the spiritual facets of national revival. He identified in religion the source of the cultural uniqueness of the Jewish people and called for a comprehensive religious renaissance separate from the needs of material existence and of a collective territory.[68] In *Der haynt* in late 1908, he began publishing his enormously popular 'Letters to Jewish Youth.' He also contributed literary criticism and articles popularizing the great ideas of Jewish religious philosophy, especially those of Hasidism, in *Di naye tsayt* (The New Era), a Yiddish quarterly that he published with his close friend David Frishman.[69]

In contrast to this imposing religious leader, young 'Noyekh,' as the writers and folklorists who gathered at his home affectionately called him, was considered a comrade and peer despite an air of stiffness and formality which he took pains to project.[70] Recently arrived from the imperial capital, he and his wife Paula settled on affluent Świętokrzyska Street[71] and 'brought with them true Russian generosity and refined squandering': 'Always in a freshly pressed Russian attorney's frock with stiff, white worsted wool, with an elegantly brushed little black beard that surrounded his tender face, Prylucki looked more like some sort of foreign diplomat than a Yiddish writer for a newspaper in the very *Nalewki* [a primary street in the heart of Jewish Warsaw]. Even Paula R., with broad, dressed lamb fur, with diamond rings on her hands, with the strangely decorated hairstyle, looked more like a grande dame, like an aristocratic Russian baroness.'[72]

Unlike Peretz, whose notorious mood swings and devastating, laconic critique terrified callow writers, Prylucki was extremely encouraging in his reviews of literature and theatre. His literary daring, as demonstrated in the scandal surrounding *Farn mizbeyekh,* was one of those qualities that drew writers into his sphere and he exercised his influence to help those in whom he recognized artistic potential to be published in magazines and the daily press, including those edited by his father.[73] He offered a tribute to poets and belletristic writers including Yoyne Rozenfeld, Yoyel Mastnboym, Moyshe Taytsh, Moyshe Stavski, Shloyme Gilbert, Yehoshue Perle, and I.M. Vaysenberg on the pages of the literary anthologies *Der yunger gayst* (The Young Spirit) and *Goldene funken* (Golden Sparks), which he published and edited in 1909.[74] These collections also included works by his wife, whom he was helping to master Yiddish, and his own poems (which appeared on the first page of the collections) and critical essays treating the works of his protégés and others.[75] In particular, he polemicized in a lengthy article ('Dos bisl yidishe shriftn,' The Paucity of Yiddish Writing) in *Goldene funken* with the unswerving Hebraist Yosef Klausner's pronouncements denying the viability and quality of Yiddish literature.

While pundits mocked Prylucki's poetry, the literary and cultural value of these anthologies, which were suffused with enthusiasm and youthful hope for the future, was duly recognized. Prylucki's merits as a publisher and editor were also recognized in no small way because he paid writers honoraria.[76] He also distinguished himself with his unparalleled skills as a public speaker at literary evenings, silencing his hecklers and winning female hearts with his well-modulated voice despite a noticeable nervous tic.[77]

As evidenced by the repetition of names among the frequenters of the Warsaw literary salons, there was much going back and forth between them despite moments of heightened personal and political antagonism between individual Jewish intellectuals. While certain personalities harboured abiding resentment for each other, on the whole 'between various literary circles extended ties of love, mutual interest, and temporary misunderstandings, although they were aware that they were contributing to the enterprise of Yiddish culture.'[78] Thus, for example, despite his public derision of the literary abilities of Prylucki and contributors to the Friday literary supplement to *Der veg*,[79] Hillel Zeitlin did not hesitate to publish his 'Di inerlekhe velt' (The Inner World) alongside their works in Prylucki's *Goldene funken*. Both Pryluckis, father and son, were also regular guests in Zeitlin's home. Moreover, it was the younger Prylucki who managed to convince Zeitlin, whom he had criticized in *Der veg*, to join the staff of *Der moment* in 1910 when his father's entreaties failed.[80]

Yiddish Folklore

In return for his services as a literary patron and mentor, Noah Prylucki requested that writers collect folklore – songs, *tkhines* (prayer composed in Yiddish addressing women's concerns), stories, and jokes – for him and even offered remuneration for both collectors and informants. The writer Avrom Zak recalls Prylucki 'exploiting' everyone he knew for ma-

3.3 Collectors of Jewish folklore on the occasion of a literary evening. *Standing, right to left:* Y.H. Skatnicki, Kh. A. Viner, Pinkhes Graubard, L. Skutnitski, M. Rosental, V. Rosenberg, F. Volrat; *sitting, right to left:* Noah Prylucki, Yoysef Rosenfeld, Prylucki's wife Paula Rozental. (YIVO Institute, record 9168, frame 3571, 33493, 33494, 33495)

terial: 'both the young writers, who used to come to him for literary advice, and simply Jewish men and women from Warsaw and the provinces who came to him in the capacity of a lawyer for legal counsel. Prylucki used to draw them into extraneous chats and obtain from them certain proverbs and turns of phrase for his collections.'[81] Very quickly, his interest in literature, apart from its value as a nationalist tool, became subordinate to that in folklore and philology.

Ironically, the first wave of interest in the folklore of the Jews in Poland arose in the 1880s among Polish scholars and polonized, 'progressive'

Jews under their tutelage. Most Jewish intellectuals in the late nineteenth century, whether under the influence of the *Haskalah* or Assimilationist movements, were at best ambivalent towards the enterprise of collecting and preserving Yiddish folklore. They viewed with distaste cultural mores, practices, and elements of material culture not grounded in what they deemed legitimate religious tenets or in consonance with middle-class European norms and saw the disappearance of Yiddish and its folk culture as part of the juggernaut of rational 'progress.'[82]

The Polish collector Oskar Kolberg, seeking to glorify the beauty of Polish village life in pursuit of a nationalist agenda, included in his publication in the 1880s Yiddish folksongs learned from Jewish coachmen during his ethnographic expeditions. More significantly, the publisher of the respected folklore journal *Wisła* (Vistula, founded in 1889), Jan Karlowicz, convinced a number of young researchers – several Jews and one Polish woman – to form a circle devoted to the collection and publication of Jewish folklore in the 1890s. The first significant theoretician of Polish folklore and ethnographer of world renown, the positivist Karlowicz desired not to idealize folk life but rather to elevate the masses by emphasizing the most positive traits, such as music, dance, and dress, of their culture and by assuming, like the *maskilim*, a critical position regarding superstitions such as folk medicine.[83] Collectors of folklore among Jews wished to demonstrate the Jews' humanity through the beauty of folk creation and to familiarize Polish readers with the difficult material conditions of their everyday life in order to dispel harmful myths and prejudices about them. In this way, they hoped to justify the suitability of the Jews for emancipation and social integration. With the exception of the Viennese *Urquell* (Fountainhead), journals published Yiddish materials in the language of the land.[84]

Inspired by the accomplishments of Polish ethnographers, by the first decade of the twentieth century, a positive nationalist attitude towards folklore had gained acceptance in Jewish intellectual circles. In contrast with Zionists, who were chiefly interested in folkloric elements in the ancient Jewish literary tradition, Peretz venerated the oral production of the contemporary Jewish people, included its unlettered segments. Apart from early publishers of Yiddish folksongs and proverbs, the historian Dubnow also contributed to making folklore acceptable by recognizing ethnography and folklore, along with literature and philology, as ancillary disciplines of historiography and tools in the creation of a secular Jewish identity.[85] For Dubnow, in contrast with Peretz, it was historical consciousness, not language and the 'golden chain' of the Jewish literary tradition, which would provide the basis for a modernized Jewish identity.

A major breakthrough occurred with the publication in 1901 of *Evreiskie Narodnye Pesni v Rossi* (Jewish Folksongs in Russia), a collection of 376 folksongs by the historians Shaul Ginzburg and Peysekh Marek which celebrated the rise of Yiddish poetry and the struggle for the recognition of Yiddish alongside Hebrew. The authors penned their scholarly commentary in Russian, but the songs themselves appeared in Yiddish with Russian transliteration. In publishing the second, enlarged edition of his collection of Yiddish proverbs and sayings in 1908,[86] the *Hovev-tsion* and scholar of proverbs Ignatz Bernstein similarly provided annotations and transliterations to Yiddish entries in another language, choosing German for this purpose.

As a collector and publisher of folklore materials, Noah Prylucki rode in on the second, stronger wave of interest in the discipline between the years 1908 and 1914.[87] From earliest youth, he possessed an abiding interest in the colourful language and rich treasury of folklore possessed by more traditional Jews in his immediate surroundings that conflicted with the *maskilic* attitudes towards language imparted to him. In an interview published in 1931 in honour of the thirtieth anniversary of his literary activity, he recalled learning Yiddish folktales from the Jewish children of Kremenets who gathered in the evenings in front of his grandfather's house. Already familiar with the Russian folktales of Afanasyev, at age nine he first encountered Yiddish stories of kings, princesses, witches, golden apples, and the like from a tailor's apprentice 'from the backstreets' of Kremenets and began to record them, characteristically, in Russian.[88]

According to his own reckoning, he began to collect Yiddish proverbs, figures of speech, witticisms, riddles, and exorcism incantations in 1900 and folksongs, of which he claimed having gathered two thousand in less than a year's time, in February 1910.[89] His interest in ethnography is evident as early as 1908, when he praised Sholem Aleichem for describing perfectly 'the transformation that has occurred in Jewish intellectual and material culture in the last forty years of the nineteenth century' through the speech, manners, customs, food, and clothing of his vivid characters.[90] He published a portion of this enormous treasury in several volumes between 1910 and 1917, the years during which he was most active as a folklore collector and scholar. This was, however, not the work of one man alone; Prylucki's collection was significantly augmented by the contributions of young amateurs to whom he served as a mentor, as well as those of hobbyists throughout Poland from whom he elicited materials both personally and in printed appeals.

From 1909 to 1912, an informal folklore circle of relative novices to the discipline gathered regularly in his home. The group includes names that went on to be recognized as some of the most accomplished folklorists and ethnographers of Polish Jewry: A. Almi (1892–1968), Shmuel Lehman (1886–1941), and Pinkhes Graubard (1892–1952). Little is known about the origins and workings of Prylucki's group apart from that which can be gleaned from the memoirs of its members, especially A. Almi. In the estimation of folklore scholar Itzik Gottesman, the circle yielded remarkable results over the course of only a few years and rapidly developed the field of Yiddish folklore, 'expanding previous definitions such as that of "folk," "folksong," and "folklore" to include larger and larger segments of the population, as well as more and more previously excluded oral genres.'[91] For the lower classes, the eagerness of Prylucki and his circle to purchase their songs and stories was primarily cause for bewilderment. At times, it was perceived as a hostile intrusion into their lives. Almi recalls of the members of this coterie: 'In truth, most of us collectors had no precise idea of the value of folklore and also no special love of it (with the exception perhaps of P. Graubart and later Shmuel Lehman). But Noah assured us that it was extremely important for Yiddish culture. We believed and worked like bees. He had a strong influence on us and we were thankful.'[92]

At times Prylucki's collectors even placed their own lives in danger to satisfy his seemingly insatiable hunger for folklore, visiting the Jewish underworld for folklore material once friends, relatives, and neighbours had been exhausted as sources. Affectionately recalling his mentor, Almi tells, for example, of being held captive for hours while a naïve adolescent by the angry management of a bordello because one of his informants communicated in song to him how she had been coerced into prostitution.[93]

In 1911 Prylucki published the first volume, 'Religious and Holiday Songs' of his two-volume *Yidishe folkslider* (Jewish Folksongs),[94] the largest collection of Yiddish folksongs since Marek and Ginzburg's seminal collection first appeared in 1901. More significantly, Prylucki's work distinguished itself as the first scholarly collection of folklore to be printed entirely in Yiddish, the language of his informants, and not in Latin or Cyrillic transliteration with commentary written in a recognized academic language (such as German, Polish, or Russian). In printing the volume entirely in Yiddish, like all of his subsequent scholarly works save one (it was printed in Hebrew),[95] he pursued a twofold goal: to include the broad Jewish population of all social classes within his audience and to assert Yiddish as a suitable language for scholarly use. The style of his academic prose, however, does not differ appreciably from those of his feuilletons and he does not set out to fashion a specific vocabulary for the field in Yiddish. Indeed, despite a growing penchant for linguistic purism, he borrows ingenuously from German when necessary such terms as *zilbe* (German *Silbe*, syllable).

He attributes the volume of this collection, assembled in a very brief period, to the sheer wealth of songs created by the Jewish people and asks in his preface, 'Has any nation in the world such a fortune of folksongs as the Jewish one?'[96] While the question was attacked by reviewers as naïve and statistically unsubstantiated,[97] it is to be understood as a reflection of Prylucki's sheer enthusiasm for this endeavour and within the context of the era. By emphasizing the multi-thematic nature of Jewish folksongs and the varied emotions and experiences to which they give voice, Prylucki celebrated the wealth of folk creation and sought to counter among Yiddish-speaking readers, both the intellectuals and the uneducated workers, the perception that the masses were culturally uncreative, one-dimensional, and alienated from romantic sentiment. To demonstrate the dissemination and diversity of folk creativity, he also included multiple variants (including songs previously published in Grünwald's *Mitteilungen*). In disagreement with other collectors, his understanding of folksongs included songs written by *badkhonim* (wedding jesters), troubadours, and published poets that had become widespread and popular enough to be assimilated and modified by the folk without recognition of their original authorship.[98] Just as his idealized conception of the Jewish people included all classes (as long as they spoke Yiddish), he included the anonymous compositions of the religious elite, to whom he attributed most religious songs, as folksongs as long as they existed only in oral tradition and had become deeply rooted among the masses. This more comprehensive definition of the folk paved the way for Prylucki's disciples Lehman and Graubard to embrace undesirable elements – revolutionaries, criminals, prostitutes, and pimps – as valid sources for folklore.[99]

Prylucki invites the reader in his preface to recognize in folksongs the reflection of the 'soul' of the Jewish people and the imprint of the historical processes that have shaped it: 'The entire *Innerlichkeit* – the Weltanschauungs, ideals, thoughts, and feelings; the entire cut of the Jewish street – the conditions of life, the lifestyle, the course of life – everything is reflected in our folksongs with the greatest comprehensiveness, precision, and depth. A distinct signature of our historical fate lies, therefore, in the themes, motives, and language (above all this last one) of the Yiddish folksongs when we consider everything together, one next to the other.'[100] Despite expressing an anticlerical stance that became increasingly pronounced over time, Prylucki believed religious songs at this time to be the only original folk creations.[101] In keeping with the conventions of the time, he did not provide musical notation for the songs he collected, treating them exclusively as texts. Curiously, music is perhaps the one major art form about which he never wrote throughout his career.

In seeking insights into the 'folks psyche,' Prylucki was interested not merely in the content of folksongs, but above all in their language, the defining feature of nationhood in contemporary thought. In particular, he was concerned with pronunciation, which he describes as a 'complicated product of the most diverse factors – geographical, anthropological, cultural.'[102] He saw in variegated pronunciation and dialectal diversity evidence of the underlying cultural and ethnic unity of Yiddish-speaking Jewry. While general awareness existed among Russian Jews, he maintained, as to the most easily recognizable features of Warsaw Yiddish speech, Jews knew very little about their language since the discipline of Yiddish philology remained in its infancy. Prylucki vowed that this condition would not endure and dedicated the remainder of his life to this cause.[103] For this purpose, he procured for himself necessary scholarly literature in the field of German linguistics and philology and began to amass what was to become one of the richest collections in Europe of old Yiddish prints.[104]

While Peretz and the celebrated writer and ethnographer Sh. An-ski sought poetic inspiration in religious life and reworked folkloric themes and customs in a highly stylized manner for use in their secular artistic works, such as Peretz' *Folkstimlekhe geshikhtn* ('Stories in a Folk Vein), and An-ski's play *The Dybbuk*, Prylucki mined folklore primarily for linguistic data. Local dialects, scorned by most other collectors who felt their particularities obscured the beauty of folk poetry, were in Prylucki's conception to provide a source of enrichment for the developing literary language. The songs, drawn overwhelmingly from Congress Poland, were intended to come to use in describing the lexical and grammatical features of Polish Yiddish.[105]

Following the example of Krauss' *Urquell* and Leo Wiener's contributions to *Mitteilungen*, Prylucki attached utmost importance to the phonetically accurate transcription of dialects. Unlike these Western collectors, who lived at a social and geographical distance from their informants, he did so not merely for the sake of scholarly accuracy. Rather, like Ber Borokhov, the ideological father of Labour Zionism whose 'The Tasks of the Yiddish Philologist' undoubtedly influenced him,[106] he viewed philology together with ethnography and literary history as 'national' disciplines that derive their vitality from a living people. He invited 'all who understand the meaning of the cause'[107] to collect and send him songs, stories, proverbs, riddles, and *purim-shpiln* (Purim plays) in phonetic transcription.

The publisher of *Yidishe folkslider* failed to see the benefit of dialect transcriptions and argued that they would be unintelligible to readers. As a compromise, Prylucki agreed to print a portion of the songs in dialect and the remainder in the emerging standard then known as literary Yiddish.[108] Rather than follow the example of his predecessors and employ Latin characters in his transcriptions (a technique which would significantly reduce ambiguity in rendering speech on paper in comparison with the prevalent Yiddish orthography of the day),[109] he was motivated by ideological zeal to elaborate over the coming years a private system for this purpose that would permit him to avoid recourse to non-Hebrew symbols. This attention to pronunciation was almost universally judged excessive and distracting by reviewers, who argued that his unexplained system of transcription 'ruins the good impression made by the songs.'[110]

The following year brought the publication by Prylucki's very own publishing house, 'Nayer farlag' (New Press),[111] of a collection dedicated to three of the nation-building academic disciplines that he endeavoured to promote. The first volume of *Noyekh prilutskis zamelbikher far yidishn folklor, filologye un kulturgeshikhte* ('Noah Prylucki's Anthologies of Yiddish Folklore, Philology and Cultural History') was published in collaboration with his disciple Lehman, with whom he authored the first collection in the volume, *Yidishe shprikhverter, glaykhvertlekh, redensarten un tsunemenishen vegen lender, gegenden, shtedt un shtetlekh* ('Yiddish Proverbs, Aphorisms, Expressions, and Nicknames about Countries, Regions, Cities, and *Shtetlekh*').

This second folklore publication by Prylucki speaks in more sober, less romantic tones than the first. Its approach is more academic and oriented towards recording the remnants of a way of life in decline as a result of urbanization, immigration, and secularization rather than singing the praise of Jewish 'national genius.' The forword to the collection begins by immediately proclaiming long overdue the publication of a special organ for Jewish ethnography in the language of the material researched. Hoping to collect as much and as diverse data as possible, Prylucki calls for contributions from readers, above all from youth and teachers 'who stand near to the unmediated life of the folk' in remote Jewish cities and in *shtetlekh* where 'the old-fashioned prayer books and customs, the patriarchal atmosphere, and the old-time material culture' have not yet disappeared. The over 400 geographical nicknames he collected with Lehman, he advances, reveal the particularity and characteristic traits of each community as a 'social-societal organism.' Together they contribute to the crystallization of a *Gestalt* of the socioeconomic conditions of Jewish life.[112]

In addition to the section on toponymics, Prylucki contributed to the volume the first annotated collection of *purim-shpiln* ever printed in Yiddish, an article concerning the distribution of grammatical gender in Yiddish, philological miscellanies and notices, and a polemic against An-ski in response to his review of Prylucki's *Yidishe folkslider*. The linguist Mordkhe Veynger, later to become a prominent Soviet scholar of Yiddish, authored an article about Yiddish dialectology.[113] Assuming a lack of familiarity with the field of linguistics on the part of his readers, Prylucki explains that dialectology constitutes 'a branch of linguistics that deals with dialects, pronunciations of a certain language.' This limited definition notwithstanding, Prylucki undertook in his article to shed light on the phenomenon of the 'huge difference that exists between Polish, Galician, Volhynian and southern Russian Yiddish, on the one hand, and Lithuanian, on the other, in the matter of the gender of nouns.' The discussion, which constitutes Prylucki's first linguistically grounded defence of Yiddish as a language, explains that a lack of agreement concerning gender among dialects is not evidence of linguistic chaos, as frequently argued by the opponents of Yiddish. It reflects a stage shared by all gendered languages in their developmental path from dialects to a literary, that is, standardized, language. Prylucki also claims to be the first to have noted the lack of a neuter gender in Lithuanian Yiddish, although he cannot yet account for this.[114]

Ber Borokhov, himself a nationalist philologist, inveighed against Prylucki in a review in his volume *Der pinkes* (The Ledger, 1913). While acknowledging Prylucki as 'one of our energetic folklorists' and praising his good intentions, he took him to task for hastily preparing the volume, applying an idiosyncratic transcription system and a shoddy scholarly apparatus. Relying upon folk sayings for some of his sharpest barbs, he assailed Prylucki for failing to distinguish between true folklore, that is, widespread sayings, and local, narrow, possibly even idiosyncratic sayings associated with the geography of the Yiddish-speaking world:

> He presents about a thousand sayings such as 'Odrzywół peasants (odzshiviler poyern), Ulaszewo goats (ulashnover tsign), Ozorków pigs (ozyerkover khazeyrim), Izbica geese (izshbitser gendz), Ochota thieves (okhoter ganovim), Mszczonów scabs (amatshiner parkhes), Ostrowiec buffoons (ostrovtser naronim), Opoczno corpses (opotshiner pgorim), Bibrka moon (bobrker levone), Bialobrzegi fools (byalobzshiner leytsim)' and the like. This is what you call 'folklore'? Is then every saying that a Jew uttered somewhere an element of folk creation? Where does Prylucki have evidence that everything he recorded here is actually a folk saying? ... It's an old axiom that a Jew doesn't lack, thank goodness, pointed words. What does a Jew say about his own agile tongue? 'In ten waters you cannot wash yourself clean of Jewish talk.' Having not read the relevant scholarly literature, Prylucki offers linguistic observations about Lithuanian Yiddish made a decade ago by scholars.

'Additionally,' Borokhov argued, 'he frequently fails to note the provenance of proverbs and explains widely known toponymic-based sayings and sobriquets while ignoring hundreds of obscure items':

> Just as various stories are thrown together in Prylucki's work with no criticism, no objective commentary, the rare explanations of sayings that he brings are similarly inconsistent. Where the usual reader does not need commentary, Prylucki enters into precise investigations: for example, does the saying 'Odessa is a small Paris' or 'Odessa connivers' – I ask you – require an interpretation? Certainly not. Immediately afterwards we have a saying 'he's playing with the Odessa moon!' Its meaning is so clear to the reader and also to the collector himself that he refrains here from superfluous explanations.

'Moreover,' Borkhov continued, 'Prylucki attacks An-ski in a rebuttal to the folklorist and dramaturge's critique of his collection of folksongs ("Polemic – a Reply to a Reviewer") with a virulence and degree of personal antagonism entirely unbefitting a scholar,' although commonplace, Borokhov failed to note, in the Yiddish press, where invective was the order of the day.[115] Finally, he is so narcissistic as to launch the very first Yiddish-language organ for philology, folklore, and cultural history

– a desideratum among all involved, as An-ski expressed it, in the quest for the 'education of the people toward nationhood'[116] – under his own name: 'You see the people is quite correct when it says, "it is not fitting to praise yourself but it doesn't hurt either." Sometimes it does hurt.'[117]

The following year, 1913, Prylucki published a second volume of folk-songs containing two sections, 'Songs and Tales of Death' and 'Ballads and Legends with or without a Moral.' Its scant preface, three paragraphs in length, merely describes its contents and requests that readers submit any additional variants of the published songs. The collection received a positive review in *Vokhenblatt* (Weekly Paper)[118] for its inclusion of unpublished materials and so many Polish-Yiddish songs but was faulted by the Vienna-based Yiddish linguist and folklorist Alfred Landau for at times inaccurate transcriptions and the inclusion of songs sung by Jews but which are, according to language and motif, of German origin.[119]

For all its productivity, Prylucki's folklore circle disintegrated, according to Almi, over the issue of transcriptions in 1912. He, a Volhynian Jew, insisted that he knew better how Polish Jews speak than his Polish collectors – Almi, Lehman, and Graubard, none of whom was particularly interested in phonetic transcription. While he was likely right, Prylucki's egotism and obstinacy contributed to the disruption of this working relationship. Nonetheless, the men maintained friendly relations, supported each other's work and research, and even occasionally collaborated for decades to come.[120]

Orthography

Because Prylucki was intent upon demonstrating the independence and self-sufficiency of Yiddish as a language and attached tremendous significance to the phonetically accurate representation of the spoken word, it comes as no surprise that he took a strong interest in language standardization. He demanded that Yiddish spelling be unencumbered of superfluous letters and pronunciations reflecting the conscious imitation of German norms. The issue of normative Yiddish spelling figured on the agenda of the Czernowitz Conference but was never addressed. While he conformed in his work as a journalist to the conservative orthography of the daily press, Prylucki experimented in his personal correspondence and, later, his philological work with a system that would reflect his own Volhynian pronunciation.[121]

In a 1909 article entitled 'Materials for Yiddish Grammar and Orthography,' he issued a call for language planning and concrete measures to extirpate undesirable grafts from contemporary German. During the *Haskalah,* Yiddish orthography became encumbered with superfluous letters in an attempt to ennoble (if not supplant) the language by modelling its usage and even spelling (despite different alphabets) on that of contemporary German. The Germanization of Yiddish orthography was executed rather inconsistently and unsystematically, however, allowing many peculiarities of traditional Yiddish orthography to remain. Nonetheless, even those works by *maskilim* written in non-Germanized, popular (*folkstimlekh*) Yiddish, as well as traditional religious and devotional literature (e.g., biblical translations, edifying literature, and Hasidic texts), generally followed these new conventions.[122] Germanization tendencies were intensified as a result of the influence of German socialists and anarchists on the Jewish labour movement towards the turn of the century.[123] Borrowings from literary German were at times pragmatic, filling lexical gaps in Yiddish; other times, they served solely the purpose of stylistic nuance or sheer ornamentation. In particular, much modern vocabulary, especially in the realm of political life, was borrowed from German, as were a small number of grammatical and morphological features.

Likening Yiddish to a river overflowing its banks, Prylucki identified in 'Materials for Yiddish Grammar and Orthography' the need for an academy to expound scientifically its spelling and grammar. Among the most pressing tasks of such an institution he counted the publication of an adequate grammar (the lack of a published grammar was then taken by many as evidence that Yiddish lacks grammatical rules and therefore legitimacy as a language) and the production of an historical dictionary that would facilitate the scholar's understanding of Yiddish morphology (and presumably help in creating new words). Because an adequate and widely understood vocabulary for use in linguistic discussions did not yet exist in Yiddish, Prylucki relied upon Russian glosses for Latin and German grammatical terms.

Although Prylucki took both at this time and later a more charitable position towards German loan words than many of his linguist colleagues (indeed, his own language was fraught throughout his career with words which qualify as *daytshmerish* according to the standards he later expounded),[124] he objected to non-useful borrowings, that is, ones that do not fill lexical gaps and in fact do undue harm to the language by forcing out traditional elements. As illustrations of the lexicographic, orthographic, and morphological *daytshmerizmen* which corrupt Yiddish, he pointed to the use of the word *antvort* (German *Antwort*, answer) instead of Yiddish *entfer*, the appearance of the letter *hey* in mimicry of German silent h (e.g., *thun*), and the use of the verbal suffix – *end* to create participles instead of Yiddish – *dik* (as in the frequent description of *shund* novels as *shpanende* instead of *shpanendike romanen*, suspenseful novels). In this last case, *hinkend* both means 'while limping' and serves as the adjective 'limping' in German. Yiddish contrasts in this respect because it natively possesses *hinkendik* to convey the former meaning and *hinke(v)dik*, containing the productive adjectival suffix *e(v)dik*, to convey the latter.[125]

He charged journalists, writers, and actors with a moral responsibility to serve as linguistic models for those elements of the Jewish intelligentsia which, because either they lack adequate knowledge of Polish or Russian or because their 'national conscience' forbids the use of a foreign tongue, converse in a 'strange *daytshmerish* language' in everyday life. Little aware of the popular foundations of Yiddish, the Jewish bourgeoisie prides itself on the use of foreign words and speaks a language lacking the harmony of organic growth and gradual development. In seeking to convey the clumsy Germanized speech of this class in his novels, Sholem Asch, whom Prylucki once described as 'the most ignorant of all Yiddish writers and a boor' but possessing innate talent,[126] may succeed in a realistic depiction of the speech of this class. He ultimately fails Yiddish literature and the reader, however, by not helping to provide the Jewish intelligentsia with 'its own Yiddish language,' a cultured register free of *daytshmerish.* Sholem Asch, Prylucki argues, ought to follow the model of the three giants of Russian literature – Gribyedov, Pushkin, and Lermantov – who, rather than depict the reality of a French-speaking upper class that was ashamed of Russian, implanted in its mouth a cultured, literary Russian (one using many lexical and phraseological calques from French, he neglects, though, to mention) of each author's own design but befitting the social station.[127] From these masters, Prylucki contends, the Russian upper class learned its own language and their works have become classics. The works of insignificant writers who included many conversations in French have long passed into oblivion. 'From writers who have faith in the future of *mame-loshn,*' he concludes his reproach of Asch, 'we have a right to demand a more serious attitude towards their task.'[128]

Employing a botanic metaphor, Prylucki likens Yiddish to a forest in need of cultivation and proper grooming. Not the Hebrew, Germanic, and Slavic elements that his generation inherited from its grandparents are to be uprooted, but the 'weeds – the laughable Russicisms, Polonisms, and *daytshmerisms* of the recent period.' That is, those elements that have historically developed within the system of the language over the course of centuries are to be cherished while borrowings from European literary languages since the nineteenth century are to be expunged. Once this process of extirpation is completed, 'only the old stems will remain, those nurtured by the Jewish soul and raised with the strength of Jewish thought.'[129] In keeping with his profound devotion to 'authentic' Yiddish, he lauded the pioneering Yiddishist Nathan Birnbaum, a native German speaker raised in Vienna and the organizer of the Czernowitz Conference. Birnbaum had come to Yiddish only in his forties through his nationalist engagement but had adopted the folksy dialect of the Bukovina, where he resided for a time, and eschewed *daytshmerizmen* and the 'artificial intellectual speech in which foreign words are mixed.' His preference for forms and phrases culled from the rabble (*hamoyn)* over putatively sophisticated borrowings, particularly from German, make his style exemplary:

> He understands that a language is not a wanton thing. He grasps that a writer may not be blind in his style. A language is a living body that develops according to its own laws. He who uses it is obliged to know its soul.
>
> ... Innovations are welcome but they must not contradict the foundations. Frivolous accomplishments harm the language, destroy its harmony.

An illustration of this last point is Birnbaum's naturalization of commonly used (and presumably acceptable in Prylucki's eyes) borrowings from German by replacing the German prefix *er-* (e.g., *erziehen*) with its Yiddish cognate morpheme, *der* (thus, Yiddish *dertsien* formed by analogy with the correspondence between such German words as *erschlagen* and *ersehen* and Yiddish *dershlogn* and *derzen* despite differences in meaning).[130]

Prylucki himself practised what he preached. He became famous for a 'juicy' language permeated with proverbs and charming localisms even if it was at times difficult to grasp. Some critics, such as *Der moment's* satirist 'Der tunkeler' ('The Dark One,' Yoysef Tunkel), satirized what they considered an overzealous drive to emphasize the specificity of Yiddish and to naturalize foreign elements already integrated into the language by making them sound absurd. His overly precise spelling system (whose nuances escaped the average person) along with his tendency to add the suffix *–ish* to adjectives that are internationalisms (e.g., *populerish, genialish*), for example, was prime fodder for mockery.[131]

Art

Prior to 1910, Prylucki was still very much under the influence of cultural Zionism, which reasoned that every nation develops an art of its own and that 'full-fledged Jewish art,' a prerequisite to Jewish statehood, was 'possible only on Jewish soil.'[132] Nineteenth- and early-twentieth century scholars and thinkers, both Jewish and Gentile, generally concurred that the Jews were historically deficient in the visual arts as a consequence of the biblical prohibition of graven images. It was debated, however, whether alleged Jewish aniconism constituted an ethnic virtue, evidence of Judaism's moral self-restraint and renunciation of the libidinal instinct in contrast with the carnal, ancient pagan cultures that so highly prized art; or, as antisemites argued, proof of Jewish inferiority and the Jews' inability to contemplate beauty because of their preoccupation with the practical rather than the spiritual world. Sensitive to antisemitic barbs, acculturating Jews stepped up their procurement of European artworks to demonstrate their aesthetic sensibility. They argued that, rather than create a specifically Jewish 'look' in art, Jewish artists throughout time always drew on the stylistic repertoire of the lands in which they dwelled. Taking precisely the opposite viewpoint, cultural Zionists sought evidence of Jewish art in the work of contemporary Jewish artists, as well as 'ransacking' the distant past in order to re-establish and justify the idea of a distinctive Jewish national art.[133]

Despite an ever-growing commitment to the Diaspora and its culture, Prylucki's attachment to Palestine is evident as late as 1911 in pronouncements describing *Eretz-yisrael* as the 'cradle of Jewish civilization'[134] and the 'only piece of earth about which we can say it is ours and no one will deny this.'[135] He bemoaned Jews' lack of interest in Palestinian archaeology, whose uncovering by non-Jewish European scholars and tourists confirmed the existence of an ancient Jewish tradition of plastic arts. Materials found in *Eretz-yisrael*, he proudly proclaimed, testify to the existence of both a unique Jewish style and to the harmonious fusion of native and Greco-Roman styles in ancient Palestine – a phenomenon akin to what he hoped to achieve for Yiddish culture.[136]

Prylucki held up as a model for the creation of a Jewish national art the accomplishments of the Bezalel Academy of Arts and Design, a school for Jewish art and crafts founded in 1906 in Jerusalem by the Lithuanian-born painter and sculptor Boris Schatz (1867–1932). The example of Schatz, who, according to Prylucki, abandoned his position at the Warsaw Art School because of its 'assimilationist tendencies,'[137] illustrates perfectly what Prylucki considered the plight of the Jewish artist who can find no place in the Diaspora. Reviewing an exhibit of works in Warsaw created by the academy, Prylucki speaks of the beneficial effect of the 'blessed *Eretz-yisrael*' air upon artists who feel instinctively the 'national Jewish form, the national Jewish line, the national Jewish colour, the national Jewish tone.' Their work produces a 'colossal synthesis of biblical poetry with the fantastic mood of modern European art.'[138]

While Prylucki never mentions the common allegation by antisemites that the Jews are insensitive to art, he nonetheless makes similar reproaches of his readers, charging them with an underdeveloped appreciation of the plastic arts. Polish Jews, with the exception of Assimilationist circles (perhaps his only kind words for them), are preoccupied exclusively with everyday concerns and lack an appreciation for the visual medium. Characteristically, affluent Jews pay a fortune to decorate the homes of their soon-to-be married children, but purchase only the cheapest oleographs for the walls. The lack of Jewish consumers and patrons of the graphic arts forces talented young artists to 'sell their souls' and abandon Jewish themes in their work in order to find the support of wealthy Poles and Assimilationists.[139] To remedy this dire situation, he recommends the creation of a Jewish national art fund to prevent the estrangement of artists from the Jewish milieu and urges Jews to become consumers of art. By visiting exhibitions such as at the Bezalel School, the aesthetic sensibilities of Jews will be sharpened, helping to create the necessary commercial demand for Jewish art.[140] To this end, he regularly reviewed art exhibits, the work of both Jewish and non-Jewish artists, in *Moment*. In particular, he celebrated the works of Jewish artists, such as Jósef Gabowicz, Jakob Weinles, and Maurycy Trębacz, who 'returned' to their people by choosing Jewish themes, although with mixed success attributable to years of estrangement from the Jewish milieu.[141] More than the works of any other artist, he delighted in those of Maurycy Minkowski, a deaf painter whose innate talent and 'hot Jewish heart' enabled him to overcome the obstacles of deaf-muteness and a family distanced from Jewish culture to depict Polish-Jewish life with unparalleled warmth, affection, and attention to ethnographic detail.[142]

Theatre Criticism

From the early nineteenth century on theatre found an appreciative audience among Jews in Warsaw notwithstanding the dire spiritual warnings, menaces, and jeers of rabbis who condemned it as a vulgar and immoral squandering of time.[143] Especially following the 1883 formal ban on Yiddish theatre, which had begun to grow popular under the influence of its 'father' Avrom Goldfaden in the 1870s, the Polish theatre – one of the few public domains in which the Polish language was officially tolerated by tsarist officials – served as an important source of entertainment for Jews of all social classes. While the lifting of the ban in 1905 did not spell an end to the Russian censor and various forms of extortion and harassment, it did mean the opportunity to create for the first time an open, stable theatre in Yiddish. Actors no longer needed to dodge the police or disguise their performances as German or, more accurately, *daytshmerish* passing for German to avoid arrest. A serious interest in Yiddish theatre among the masses, as well as Yiddish-speaking intellectuals, was the immediate result.

In the years 1905 to 1914 numerous professional and amateur troops were formed in Warsaw and Łódź and throughout the Polish provinces. By 1910 perhaps as many as 360 such groups existed in the province, in addition to those in Warsaw, which became the most important theatre centre in Russian Poland.[144] Organized Jewish workers' groups, cultural organizations, and writers all invested their energies in their creation of a theatre that would rise above the melodrama and low comedic *shund* of early playwrights such as Lateiner, Shomer, and Goldfaden.[145] Nonetheless, vaudeville plays, often imported from the American Yiddish theatre, and crippled versions of the dramas of Jacob Gordon, Yiddish theatre's first 'high art' playwright, dominated the Warsaw stage.

For nationalist intellectuals, 'conditioned by the East-Central European explosive linkage of culture and nationalism,' the cultivation of a sophisticated Yiddish theatre became a cornerstone of the Jewish renaissance. Yiddishist intellectuals attributed to the stage a sacred mission as both a vehicle for the promotion of high culture among the Jewish masses and a powerful instrument for the awakening and reinforcement of national consciousness.[146] Literary clubs sponsored lectures, and evening courses about both Yiddish and non-Jewish theatre and periodicals with such titles as *Teater* (Theatre), *Kunst un teater* (Art and Theatre), and *Yidishe drame* (Jewish Drama) appeared. All newspapers introduced theatre feuilletons, and literati like Peretz, Nomberg, and Asch, displeased by what they saw on stages, began to compose their own plays for performance, as well as write their own theatre criticism.

While others wrote occasional feuilletons about plays without discussing the performances and style of individual actors, Prylucki engaged in explicit critiques of the artists independent of the plays in which they performed. He is widely credited with being the first to apply the techniques of European theatre criticism to the Yiddish stage, and his literary criticism and Russian-style theatre reviews were invaluable in the aesthetic education of readers, writers, performers, and theatregoers. He learned the genre most likely from reading the daily Russian press and attending plays in St Petersburg, where theatre-going was something of a mania among students and all forms of art and academics were inseparable from politics.[147] His theatre reviews, generally deploring the state of the Yiddish stage despite what he felt the legitimate talents of the actors, aroused a storm of letters to the editor from directors and artists.[148]

Typical of Yiddishist intellectuals, Prylucki severely upbraided the Jewish intelligentsia for its wilful ignorance and denigration of the Yiddish stage. This condescension, he argued, has contributed, along with official persecution, to retarding the development of the Yiddish stage from primitive forms reflecting the taste of the uneducated masses to high art on a European scale. As with all facets of the 'national revival,' the intelligentsia bears a responsibility for the cultivation of Jewish theatre and imparting to it the aesthetic traditions of general European culture. In contrast with other theatre activists, however, he took a rather benevolent view of the vagabond Yiddish actor and his *shund* repertoire. Despite his desire to transcend *shund*, which he acknowledged panders to vulgar tastes and stunts the abilities of actors, he saw in it the expression of the vitality of the masses in the face of serious obstacles and a certain degree of primitive moral value. Moreover, he argued, the works of Goldfaden and his successors brought the first seeds of secular culture to the most isolated classes of the Jewish people. Since *shund* theatre draws broad audiences, including the 'fanatical' Orthodox, it will help to create the necessary economic basis for the future growth and improvement of the theatre.[149] While recognizing Prylucki as the 'first, more or less, true theatre critic,' his rival theatre critic Dr Alexander Mukdoni, newly arrived from Vilna in 1910 and chief collaborator in Spektor's *Di naye velt* (The New World), reproached him precisely with this sentimentality and his indulgence of actors. Mukdoyni, who consciously avoided Prylucki in the streets of Warsaw, likened him to a 'trembling mother who constantly exorcises an evil eye.'[150]

Prylucki reproached the intelligentsia for demanding unreasonable standards of a theatre not even permitted to speak its own language until recently.[151] What the Yiddish theatre needed now most, he claimed, was financial support and systematic, constructive criticism, not morally out-

3.4 Portraits of Dr Alexander Mukdoni (Aleksander Kapel) and a young Noah Prylucki. Leading theatre critics for the Jewish press in pre–First World War Warsaw, the two were bitter rivals who played important roles in the development of modern Yiddish culture. (YIVO Institute, RG 121 #123)

raged attacks on actors and playwrights.[152] He regularly penned encouraging reviews of actors and expressed great hope for translations from the European theatre repertoire and the works of new dramaturges, above all Jacob Gordin, whose death in 1908 he mourned as a tragic event orphaning the Yiddish theatre. His defence of the view, especially in connection with Gordin's plays, that theatre was an autonomous world independent of the standards of literature (i.e., a first class literary work in dramatic form may be wholly unsuited for the stage while a worthless work may succeed) was bitterly attacked as heretical in Warsaw.[153] Upon Ester Rokhl Kaminska's troupe he lavished especial praise for travelling from city to city to 'awaken the Jewish soul with the beauty of its national cultural creativity,' and he advocated the establishment of a special union to raise money to support what he deemed the 'premier Yiddish dramatic troupe.'[154] Apart from being the first regular theatre critic in the Yiddish press, he was also the first to recognize Sholem Aleichem as a playwright.[155]

Rupture with Zionism

At the same time that he threw himself into the Yiddishist cause, Prylucki also grew increasingly distant from the ideals of political Zionism and, eventually, the Zionist movement entirely. As a correspondent for *Der moment* to the Tenth Zionist Congress in Basel in 1911, Noah Prylucki publicly reflected upon the nature of his own changed relationship with Zionism. While he waxed emotional at the sight of the 'ingathering of the exiles' – the assembly of Jews of differing linguistic and cultural backgrounds on behalf of a common goal – present at the congress, the former 'zealous party activist,' as he describes himself, claimed to have lost interest in political Zionism as the definitive solution to Jewish rightlessness and pauperization: 'I have stood in the last six years apart from official Zionism. Everything that is done and occurs in *Eretz-yisrael* interested me intensely. The remaining issues, over which the Zionist organization is in turmoil, did not concern me at all. And now I am, one can say, entirely indifferent to them.'[156]

Prylucki dismissed the Zionism of Leo Pinsker and Herzl as ill-conceived responses to personal desperation and existential agony. In the movement to obtain a charter for an internationally recognized national homeland for the Jews in Palestine he saw the pained reaction of Assimilationists spurned by the non-Jewish host societies in whose arms they had longed to find solace and acceptance. Ignoring the day-to-day reality of Jewish life in the Diaspora, political Zionism in no way constituted a natural outgrowth of the internal needs of the Jewish people.[157]

In repudiating involvement in political Zionism, which he felt ignored the day-to-day reality of Jewish life in the Diaspora, Prylucki embraced a modified form of Ahad Ha'am's spiritual Zionism. He enthusiastically posited *Eretz-yisrael* as the cultural and spiritual centre of world Jewry but vehemently rejected the influential theoretician's exultation of Hebrew culture at the expense of Yiddish and Diaspora creativity.[158] He seated upon the throne of his pantheon of Jewish nationalist heroes Moses Hess, the nineteenth-century German journalist philosopher who was the first to fuse socialism and Jewish nationalism in his *Rome and Jerusalem* (1862).[159]

Prylucki ecstatically lauded Hess, whom he proclaimed a modern prophet, for philosophically transcending Karl Marx by recognizing the priority of what Hess terms 'racial struggle' (*Rassenkampf*) over class struggle. In contrast to his contemporary, the pioneering Jewish historian Graetz, Hess grasped that Jewish national life had continued to develop for two thousand years in the Diaspora. During this time, religion served as 'armour' to safeguard the Jews' national individuality once they were bereft of a national socioeconomic structure, tongue, and soil. Even before the advent of Ahad Ha'am's 'spiritual Zionism,' Hess correctly framed the Jewish question as above all a national-cultural rather than territorial one. Nonetheless, only when the Jews are returned to their own land and religion no longer needs to function as a protective shield will they be able to develop freely and to create new intellectual and cultural values. Their spiritual centre in *Eretz-yisrael* will illuminate Jewish life elsewhere and cause the Gentile nations to recognize an equal in the Jewish people, who will set an example for the world through its fulfilment of the ideals of the biblical prophets for social, political, and economic justice.[160] Despite embracing the ethical teachings of the Hebrew prophets and employing religious imagery in his rhetoric, Prylucki made no clear statement regarding the future place of religion in Jewish life.

Despite his deviations from the dominant Zionist currents dictating the supremacy of Hebrew culture, Prylucki continued to preach at this time some of the major tenets of Zionism regarding the need to heal the purportedly enfeebled Jewish national body and to restore the Jews' dignity both as an end in itself and as a means to win the respect of the gentile nations. Over the course of centuries, he argued, the Jews have been shaped into a biological nation with a particular physiognomy and cultural forms. While the experience of two thousand years of Diaspora has not stripped them of their fundamental character, the Jewish nation had forfeited much of its vitality and creative energy.

Himself a member of the Jewish intelligentsia whose weapon was the pen rather than sword, Prylucki expressed profound admiration for Theodore Herzl's lieutenant Max Nordau, whose 'Semitic nose' and forceful voice made him the embodiment of Prylucki's ideal of the Jewish aristocrat.[161] In particular, Nordau's ideal of 'Muskeljudentum' (Jewry of Muscle), the corporal regeneration of the putatively weak and effeminate Diaspora Jew through physical labour, was attractive to him, although he seems to have paid little attention to it in his personal life. He thus rejoiced in rounds of beer swilling accompanied by demonstrations of physical prowess by Jewish nationalist students in Basel and praised their activities as 'healthy gentilification' (*goyizatsye*), the synthesis of body and spirit, of Jewish *Innerlichkeit* and Gentile *Äusserlichkeit.*[162] Jews must put an end to passive resistance and martyrdom and assume an active stance, not only in politics, but in matters of self-defence. He therefore praised the self-sacrificing heroism of Yekhezkel Nisanov, a young Jew from the Caucasus who forfeited his life as a member of *Hashomer*, the defence brigade for Jewish settlements in Palestine, when a Bedouin marauder attempted to pilfer one of his donkeys.[163]

Despite this idealization of physical might and romantic sacrifice, Prylucki did not ignore the accomplishments of the scholar, poet, and artist for the national cause. On the contrary, it was cultural work that he prized above all other activity directed at strengthening national consciousness. The historian Pinkhes Rabinovitsh and the Białystok physician Dr Yosef Khazanovitsh, for whom the creation of a Jewish national library in Jerusalem was the goal of a life's work, figure prominently among his heroes at this time.[164] All who contributed to the Jewish national awakening and the strengthening of Jewish culture, whether in *Eretz-yisrael* or in the Diaspora, such as the pioneering Yiddishist and Diaspora nationalist Nathan Birnbaum,[165] were worthy of praise in his eyes.

Conclusion

Noah Prylucki joined his voice to calls for a 'Jewish national renaissance,' a slogan popular in Jewish nationalist circles of the time, to reinvigorate the Jewish people both physically and intellectually in a secular context. As an avid consumer and keen student of European, especially Russian, literature and culture, he intuitively understood the processes by which national movements had transformed folk languages in the eighteenth and nineteenth centuries into standardized languages and fashioned impressive literary canons. Taking the history of Russian, German, and French cultures as his models, he sought to telescope cultural transformations that unfolded over decades among other peoples into a single generation among the Jews in order to transform them into a modern, secularized European nation.

By 1910 he had distinguished himself as an autodidact scholar of Yiddish language and culture and made important contributions to the establishment of Yiddish linguistics, literary criticism, and folklore as independent fields of academic inquiry rather than a mere subset of German philology. In current linguistic terms, Prylucki exhibited an inclination for *Ausbau*[166] – the fostering of a language through corpus planning in order to increase the apparent differences between it and a stronger, socially more secure language to which it is structurally similar – vis-à-vis German. He was also active as a political commentator and popularizer of his own scholarly research, through which he aimed to legitimize the creation of a Yiddish secular culture rooted in folk traditions, as well as mentor to a number of budding writers and ethnographers. In the evaluation of Yiddish linguist Yudl Mark, he was 'a one man centre for folklore and dialectological research in Warsaw.'[167] In the absence of funded institutions to support independent research and the arts in Yiddish, he accomplished this at great personal expense and by relying upon his virtually unfettered access to *Der moment* and upon the assistance of a circle of colleagues and protégés.

Evaluations of Prylucki's prolific literary and scholarly undertakings varied little. His attempts at poetry were roundly dismissed, although his role as literary mentor and patron was welcome. Reviewers of his more scholarly work praised his unbridled enthusiasm and commitment to the Yiddishist cause as well as the sheer volume of data he collected. They argued, however, that these data were often indiscriminately selected, prepared in haphazard ways, and subjected to inadequate or methodologically flawed analysis. Genuinely valuable material, observations, and insights were mixed in with much that was deemed confusing or even valueless. Moreover, the aggressiveness and egocentrism he expressed in the journalistic realm extended also to the 'gentlemanly' domain of the scholar, where he savagely responded to critiques of his work. Those same qualities – self-confidence verging on arrogance, stubborn commitment, and impulsive passion – that made Prylucki an inspiring mentor, also made him a difficult task master and, as will be seen, an inflexible political leader.

Having left the Zionist movement, Noah Prylucki converted his pro-Yiddish convictions into political activity with the advent of the First World War, during which occupying German troops brought increased freedom for cultural and political life. More than any other issue, the issue of a Yiddish secular school, prior to 1915 primarily a theoretical issue because of its illegality in the Russian Empire, served as a catalyst for the formation of a new political party. The type of education Jewish children would receive in a future independent Poland, it was agreed by leaders across the political and cultural spectrum, would determine the cultural orientation and political loyalties of a new generation of Jews. Formed upon the initiative of Prylucki and his colleagues Zeitlin and Nomberg, along with a handful of others associated with *Moment,* the Folksparty arose, above all, to assure the right of Polish Jewry to a modern political, economic, and cultural life – all in Yiddish.

chapter four

Cultural Politics in Action: The Birth of Folkism

Noah Prylucki was travelling abroad when the First World War broke out in August 1914. The subject of a hostile power, he was detained in Germany for several weeks before being permitted to return to Poland via a circuitous route through Sweden and Russia.[1] Upon his arrival in Warsaw in October that year, Prylucki found his legal expertise in acute demand among an urban population swollen with hungry, ailing, and homeless war sufferers from both nearby towns and the provinces.

The experience of the war was not wholly negative for the population of Poland, however.[2] Despite the tremendous hardship suffered by the civilian population, the chaos and displacement brought by war and occupation ultimately opened Polish society to significant new opportunities for political and cultural expression. The general atmosphere of liberalization during the German occupation of Congress Poland and Lithuania afforded educators and political activists, Polish and Jewish alike, the opportunity to transform many of their cultural postulates into reality. The popularity Prylucki enjoyed among Warsaw Jews in recognition of his accomplishments as an indefatigable defender of their rights, both as an attorney and a journalist, during the war would prove directly convertible into substantial support for a new political party formed in the summer of 1916. The Folksparty, whose chief organizers relied largely upon their employment in *Der moment* to diffuse their ideas, came into being above all to champion the rights of Yiddish as the foundation of Jewish social, political, and economic life.

Together with Prylucki, founding members of the Folksparty such as H.D. Nomberg, Hillel Zeitlin, Samuel Hirschhorn, Lazar Kahan, and Saul Stupnicki were public figures active in shaping the very culture that stood at the foundation of its political program. This chapter will describe the origins and program of the Folksparty in the context of German policy in occupied Poland in order to explain the party's origins and how it distinguished itself from other Jewish nationalist and Yiddishist political parties. It focuses on debates concerning the language of instruction in Jewish schools and the emergence of the first legal network of Yiddish secular schools. The Yiddish secular school, the foundation of the Folkists' vision of Jewish national autonomy in Poland, represents the party's most conspicuous cause and, arguably, its most significant concrete achievement. A major vehicle for imparting political and cultural ideology during this period, the Yiddish school is also a prism through which to view fundamental ideological differences between Prylucki and other Folkists concerning the very importance of Yiddish for Jewish identity and survival.

Jewish Life under German Occupation: Congress Poland during the First World War

The military operations of the German and Russian combatants wreaked havoc upon the daily lives of the civilian population and brought about the economic ruin of Congress Poland, through much of whose territory ran the front line. Industrial concerns were evacuated to deep in the Russian interior and factory personal were often given no choice other than to accompany them. Military requisitions, together with the general paralysis of commerce and handicrafts, deprived tens of thousands of the means to support themselves.[3]

Desperate for deliverance from arbitrary Russian rule, many Jews openly welcomed the advance of the German and Austro-Hungarian forces into Poland and Lithuania. The joint armies were eager to gain the confidence and assistance of the Jews, in whose hands lay much of Poland's commerce and whose active resistance to the Russians they sought to enlist. They issued an official proclamation in 1914 promising the unconditional emancipation the Jews had long hoped to be granted by the tsar. This proclamation served only to intensify Russian suspicion of Jewish loyalty, without yielding any immediate benefits. Accused of hostility, treachery, and treason, more than half a million Jews were driven from their homes in front-line areas after January 1915 into the Russian interior, effectively dismantling the Pale of Settlement.[4] Homeless and hungry refugees flooded such Jewish centres as Warsaw, Vilna, Łódź, and Kraków as well. In Warsaw alone 30,000 Jewish refugees were to be found at the beginning of 1915.[5] In 1914 the Jewish population of Warsaw counted some 337,000 souls, making up 38.1 per cent of the city's population.[6] By 1917 a 7 per cent increase in the absolute number of Jews alongside a temporary wartime decline in the Christian, predominantly Polish Catholic, population, resulted in the Jews accounting for roughly half of the city's inhabitants.[7] According to the estimate of a German Zionist visiting Poland in 1916, of the roughly 400,000 Jews present in Warsaw in 1916, 200,000 were proletarians and over half of them paupers.[8]

In response to its material plight, East European Jewry rapidly arrayed a diverse network of charitable and relief institutions – soup kitchens and poor-houses, co-operative stores selling food at heavily discounted prices, as well as rent assistance programs and societies for the free distribution of food, clothing, and fuel. Hospitals and asylums cared for the infirm and aged, along with the large number of children orphaned by the war or whose impoverished parents were unable to provide for them. Tea houses, legal aid societies, and organizations for the care of the wives of soldiers away at war also abounded.[9] Membership in the Jewish Artisans' Club in Warsaw increased greatly for the simple reason that free bread was available there.[10] Funding for relief work came largely from the St Petersburg–based *EKOPO* (*Evreiskii komitet pomoshchi zhertvam voiny*, Central Jewish Committee for the Relief of Victims of War) and Jewish funding from abroad, above all from the large Eastern European immigrant community in the United States. Local welfare institutions were mostly independent or only loosely affiliated with existing political parties and organizations.[11] The Warsaw Municipal Relief Committee refused Jews representation on its executive body and denied them assistance, claiming that they already received adequate help from Jewish organizations.[12]

Early in the war, the heads of the Warsaw *kehila* assembled a commission of lawyers to furnish legal advice to Jewish war sufferers. Although it was initially intended that the commission's duties would be limited to the submission of various petitions for legal redress to the authorities, such as requests for the payment of pensions to the wives of soldiers and appeals for school enrolment, its members soon found themselves hard at work documenting instances of physical abuse at the hands of Russian military and civilian authorities. Materials were collected and made ready by the commission for presentation by the liberal Cadet Party in the Duma or for publication abroad in the aim of attracting global attention to Russian atrocities. The *kehila* administration could not countenance under its own roof, however, organized activity casting doubts on the Jews' patriotism at the time of the Russian army's heroic defence of the fatherland. Tsarist officials similarly sought to conceal reprisals against the Jews for fear of imperilling their relations with their liberal democratic, Western allies. Under these circumstances, a number of commission members opted to take up their work elsewhere.

Prylucki's private residence at Świętokrzyzska 48 was already the address to which many turned for legal assistance and free defence from accusations of collaboration with the enemy.[13] It soon became the headquarters, as well, of this semi-conspiratorial project, which continued until the Germans captured Warsaw in August 1915.[14] Materials gathered by the team – minutes of meetings, originals and copies of secret military staff circulars testifying to abuses of Jewish civilians and soldiers, along with antisemitic announcements – were clandestinely dispatched from Prylucki's home to a Jewish communal activist in the imperial capital whose function was to insure that they reach their intended audience.[15] Prylucki even risked his own personal safety to insure the delivery of documents.[16]

On 6 December 1914 German forces captured Łódź, and between May and September 1915 the Russian army was forced to withdraw from several towns and cities, including Warsaw, with substantial Jewish populations. By September 1915 nearly half of the Jews of the vast Russian Empire were living in the German occupation zones *General-Gouvernement* (corresponding roughly to Congress Poland) and *Ober-Ost* (which included the Russian provinces of Grodno, Vilna, Suwałki, Kovno, and Courland). Although humane and unprejudiced in its official attitude towards Polish Jewry, the German military proved oppressive and corrupt at the level of individual soldiers and bureaucrats. Hard-pressed by the Allied blockade, the occupant proved himself more ruthless than the tsarist regime in expropriating food, raw materials, machinery, and industrial apparatus from the region. Much of Poland's material resources were shipped back to Germany, as were part of its human resources in the form of forced labourers.[17] The extreme deprivation engendered by the war intensified the economic rivalry between Jews and Poles.

Because the German policy of suppressing Polish national consciousness in Poznań (the region of partitioned Poland annexed by Prussia in the late eighteenth century) was notorious in Congress Poland, little sympathy existed among Poles for the invading German troops and their promises of liberation from autocratic Russian rule. The open joy with which Jews greeted the invaders and the intervention by Germans on the behalf of individual Jews, including help by soldiers to Jews mistreated by Poles and the placement of Jews in positions of authority alongside or even over Poles, all contributed to reinforce the thesis that the Germanophilic Jews sought to betray Poland. One Polish observer remembers the impression made on Poles by some Jews' reaction to the German entry into Warsaw: 'In general, however, the Warsaw public behaved decently, showing calm, cold blood – only our beloved Jews very warmly and ostentatiously greeted the Germans, which everyone expected anyway.'[18]

Even following the partial flight of Endek politicians with the retreat of the Russians, enough Endeks remained in Poland to revive their antisemitic press, which had been banned together with other newspapers by the Russians at the outbreak of the war, under the averted gaze of the German occupier. With the fear of starvation and economic demise no longer the pseudo-menace from which the pre-war Endek boycott drew its vitality, the party's anti-Jewish rhetoric gained new meaning and popularity. The *Gazeta Warszawska* and *Gazeta Poranna 2 Grosze* called at Easter 1915 for the resumption of the boycott after it had been significantly undermined by the disorder of war.[19]

On the whole, the German occupying regime expressed little affection or understanding for the peculiarities of the traditional Eastern European Jewish lifestyle. Even measures intended to promote public health, such as greatly needed sanitary relief work, were typically effected with great severity. While a minority of German soldiers were impressed by the cultural achievements and profoundly spiritual lifestyle of Eastern European Jewry, most were offended by the sight of filthy, impoverished, and at times demoralized masses among which prostitution, black market speculation, and smuggling had become blatant because of their desperate situation. For many soldiers, both Jews and non-Jews alike, the encounter only confirmed stereotypes carried with them from Germany of a morally and physically degenerate Eastern European Jewry.[20]

This aversion notwithstanding, the Germans largely kept their promise of equality for the Jews by easing most of the antisemitic restrictions imposed by the tsarist regime. In an atmosphere of unprecedented, albeit carefully monitored intellectual and literary freedom, the institutions of secular Yiddish and Hebrew culture flourished. Not only were educational restrictions abrogated, such as the *numerus clausus* limiting Jewish admission to schools and universities, but secular elementary education regardless of race or creed was made compulsory by the Germans. Evening classes were organized, often by political parties, for the purpose of educating workers who were illiterate or had been denied a primary school education in their childhood. Jewish libraries, clubs, and sports organizations were organized in hundreds of communities where they had previously been forbidden. The Yiddish theatre drew audiences of both indigenous Jews and curious, entertainment-starved German soldiers. No less significant than this cultural liberalization was the legalization of political parties and of the trade union movement, allowing socialists much more latitude to operate. An explosion of Zionist sentiment also occurred at the time, as reflected in the enormous growth of the number of local Zionist groups chiefly engaged in cultural activities.[21] Elections to the Warsaw City Council, the first free elections in Poland since the partitions, were called for the summer of 1916.

The German army lifted the ban on Hebrew and Yiddish publishing issued by the tsar at the beginning of the war and even founded Yiddish and Polish dailies through its agents in Warsaw, Łódź, and Vilna. A major factor in Jewish life, the Yiddish press lost much of its regional character and gained a more respected status, even if cut off from areas still under Russian rule. Especially in Warsaw, Yiddish newspapers were eagerly read by individual purchasers, as well as by frequenters of Jewish coffee halls and soup kitchens. Journalists of generally high intellectual calibre wrote for the Hebrew and Yiddish presses and not infrequently for both. Inclined towards Jewish nationalism, they were at times more outspoken in their demands for Jewish rights than the only recently legalized Jewish political parties. The Jewish press, above all the Yiddish press by virtue of its mass readership, continued to play the crucial role it had assumed prior to the war in the secular education and politicization of the Jewish masses, as well as in the shaping of public opinion.[22] To keep abreast of political currents among the Jews, German government offices carefully monitored responses to official decrees and coverage of local and world events.[23]

Taking a cue from the growth of unions and cultural associations under the German occupation, Jewish writers and journalists in Warsaw founded their own association in March 1916 to protect their economic interests and to assure themselves an appropriate place in the political and societal life then unfolding. The premises of the *Fareyn fun yidishe literatn un zhurnalistn in varshe* (Warsaw Jewish Writers' and Journalists' Association) at Tłomackie 11 (from 1918 on, Tłomackie 13) also served as a gathering point for Hebrew and Yiddish writers to socialize and discuss literature and current events. The Yiddish novelist Yankev Dinezon was elected its chairman and treasurer, and the Hebrew writer Ben-Avigdor served as its vice-chairman. H.D. Nomberg and Samuel Hirschhorn were also among the members of the organization's first administration.[24]

In May 1915, German Press Chief von Cleinow launched *Dos lodzer folksblat* (Łódź People's Paper), a Yiddish daily espousing a nationalist position, as a counterweight to Polish national aspirations and hopes for independence tied to a Russian victory.[25] Appointed as its editor was Lazar Kahan, an experienced editor of Yiddish periodicals. Interest existed early in the war among the Germans, above all the military, in the possible annexation of parts of the *General-Gouvernement* for strategic and economic reasons and in the creation of a pro-German buffer state in Congress Poland. An independent Polish state, it was hoped, would nurture close ties with Germany, especially economically, and serve under its influence as a guard against Russian aggression. Certain concessions to Polish national sentiment were made, such as the granting of permission to open Polish language schools and the transfer of lower courts and local self-government into Polish hands. The Germans, however, were careful not to make any definitive pronouncements about the future of Poland. At least officially, the occupier endeavoured not to favour one element of the population over another but merely to maintain order and further German interests.[26]

Kahan (1885–1946) was soon brought to Warsaw to head a second German-financed Yiddish daily, *Dos varshever tageblat* (Warsaw Daily Paper), which began publishing in October 1915. Although raised in the highly Germanized Jewish milieu of Courland (Latvia), Kahan received a traditional religious education in a local *kheyder* and yeshivas and acquired a general education in his adolescence. An enthusiastic supporter and participant in the new Yiddish culture then taking shape, he was married to a Yiddish actress and attended the Czernowitz Conference in 1908 as a representative of the Yiddish dramatics association *Dramatishe kunst* (Dramatic Art). A supporter of the *Tsionei tsion*, Kahan began his journalistic career in Tsevi Prylucki's *Der veg* and *Unzer lebn*. He also wrote for Hillel Zeitlin and Shmuel Yatskan's *Yidishes vokhnblat* before becoming the editor of Poland's first provincial newspaper, *Lodzer nakhrikhtn* (Łódź News), in 1907. He shared his responsibilities as general editor of *Dos varshever tageblat* with its literary editor, H.D. Nomberg.[27]

Kahan and Nomberg were joined on the staff of *Dos varshever tageblat* by, among others, Samuel Hirschhorn and Saul Stupnicki. Hirschhorn (1876–1942) was born in Slonim, Grodno province, but migrated to Warsaw at age thirteen, where he graduated from a commerce school in addition to receiving a religious education. He began his journalistic career in the progressive Polish press. With the strengthening of the Jewish national movement, he authored *Co to jest syonizm?* ('What is Zionism?'

Warsaw, 1903), the first brochure about Zionism in Polish. He became a frequent contributor to the Polish-Jewish press, where he specialized in Jewish-Polish relations and the translation of Yiddish poetry. He did not become active in the Yiddish press, though, until 1915, when the German administration closed *Opinja Żydowska* (Jewish Opinion), the weekly he had founded under Russian rule to combat Polish antisemitism.[28]

From 1908 Saul Stupnicki (1876–1942) was a contributing editor for *Der haynt*, for which he penned philosophical arguments in favour of national rights and Jewish autonomy. Born and raised in Belsk, Grodno province, he was a respected expert in rabbinic literature who had attended traditional yeshivas in Eastern Europe followed by a modern rabbinical seminary in Prague. He also studied history, philosophy, and Near Eastern languages at the University of Bern. There he became active in Zionist and socialist circles before returning to Poland in 1901 to take up activity on behalf of, first, the Polska Partia Socjalistyczna (PPS) and, later, Poale Zion and the Yidishe teritorialistishe organizatsye (Jewish Territorialist Organization or ITO).[29]

Like the *Lodzer tageblat*, the *Varshever tageblat* received a fixed budget from the German government and stood under its complete political scrutiny.[30] Although created to serve primarily as a mouthpiece for German policy in occupied Poland, the paper expressed a Jewish nationalist-populist position.[31] Official sponsorship of the *Varshaver tageblat* was likely tantamount in the eyes of Prylucki, Nomberg, and their colleagues to a German endorsement of autonomist strivings. German press policy at this time seems to have been directed by the conviction that if granted freedom of national and cultural development, the Jews, especially their numerically significant merchant and artisan classes, could be relied upon in the future to support German interests in Slavic Eastern Europe.[32] Moreover, it is probable that the Germans desired a Jewish newspaper to publicize before the West reports of Russian atrocities committed against Jewish civilians in order to help counter Russian accounts of German atrocities.[33] Apart from serving as the newspaper's literary editor, Nomberg continued to write for *Der haynt* until 1916.

Prylucki also remained on the staff of *Der moment*, as did Hirschhorn, in addition to pursuing his profession as a lawyer and his scholarly avocation. He took full advantage of daily visits from war sufferers from *shtetlekh* near and far to augment his collections of proverbs, folklore, and linguistic data. His dialect observations were immeasurably enriched by contact with multiple informants from the same locales.[34] In 1917, at the height of the war, he published a second volume of his *Zamlbikher far yidishn folk-*

lor, filologye un kulturgeshikhte, and a collection of his political and cultural essays from 1905 on (*Barg-aroyf*) in addition to three linguistic studies.[35]

The Jewish School Movement

The atmosphere of relative political liberalization and the presence of thousands of refugee children in the city in need of schooling also provided Jewish nationalist and socialist educators the opportunity to create the first mass kindergartens and elementary schools with Hebrew or Yiddish as their language of instruction. Since secular education in Yiddish (or, for that matter, Polish) was prohibited by Russian law, work on behalf of a Yiddish school was, with the exception of a few illegal initiatives, purely theoretical until now.[36] Long a plank in Yiddishist and socialist platforms, a secular school in the mother tongue of the vast majority of Jewish children suddenly became a reality.[37] The creation of a Jewish school system under the supervision of a Jewish school board was universally viewed by Jewish nationalist parties as the first practical step towards the achievement of national cultural autonomy.

Responding to the dire material needs of nearly 60,000 children of homeless parents, a number of nurseries (*kinderheymen*) were created in the first months of the war in Warsaw and other cities.[38] According to the provisions of the Napoleonic Code, which was introduced in Congress Poland in the early nineteenth century, nurseries could be opened in the mother tongue of the children. However, only the religious *kheyder* and the Russian elementary school were permitted by Russian law to provide primary education to Jewish children. Educational activity for older children in Yiddish was necessarily clandestine in the nurseries, many of which came to offer the first few years of a primary school education.

Legal prohibitions, however, were not the only obstacles impeding the development of a Yiddishist school movement: attitudes towards Yiddish as the language of secular instruction in Jewish society ranged from widespread apathy to public condemnation by the ideological opponents of Yiddishism. Apart from extreme Hebraist and Assimilationist perspectives, these attitudes stemmed largely from long-standing views of Yiddish as subordinate to Hebrew in traditional Ashkenazic society. For the stringently observant, Yiddish was a fact of life and the customary language of Jewish education in the *kheyder* and yeshiva. They attached, at least ostensibly, little or no ideological significance to its use other than the maintenance of tradition or resistance to change and foreign ways. Education in Yiddish was also judged impractical for advancement in general, non-Jewish society among more affluent bourgeois elements with social and economic aspirations. The Yiddishist movement was thus confronted with the task of changing attitudes towards Yiddish among its critics, who were not infrequently identical with its speakers. Further, it needed to combat the deeply ingrained notion that an education without an emphasis on *loshn-koydesh* and sacred literature was not a Jewish education at all.

Organized opposition to any type of a purely secular school for Jewish children – whether in Yiddish, Hebrew, or Polish – was directed by the *Freie Vereinigung für die Interessen des orthodoxen Judentums* (Free Association for the Interests of Orthodox Jewry, FVIOJ), an organization representing the most conservative wing of German Orthodoxy. The FVIOJ received permission to establish a permanent representation in Warsaw in order to serve as advisers to the German authorities and to act as a liaison authority with the Orthodox, who represented the largest part of Polish Jewry. While not officially a part of the German administration, the FVIOJ also stood to further German interests through its vehement opposition to the radicalization, both socialist and nationalist, of Polish Jewry, which had been on the rise since the lifting of Russian restrictions. Viewing the Jews strictly as a religious community, the FVIOJ opposed the activity of Jewish nationalists and desired that Polish Jews become equal citizens in a postwar Polish state, as well as Germany's chief supporters in the East. Its representatives formed close relationships with a number of *tsadikim* heading various sects of the intensely religious, anti-secular nationalist Hasidim (especially the influential Gerer *rebbe*) and sought to influence them to accept the model of German Orthodoxy combining strict religious observance and the mastery of traditional sources with elements of a secular education. With the support of Polish rabbis, who desired to preserve the traditional educational system, the representatives of the FVIOJ helped to keep German interference in the *khadorim* to a minimum and also erected a number of yeshivas in order to strengthen Jewish education. Significantly, they also convened assemblies to politicize the religious Jewish masses. In mid-March 1916, the *Agudat ha-Ortodoksim* (Orthodox Union) – the precursor of the powerful interwar *Agudat Yisrael* (Union of Israel) party – was founded to unite religious Jews and to end their dependence upon non-religious representatives in public office. It soon counted 23,000 members.[39]

In contrast with the largely non-partisan relief work, the secular educational movement clearly reflected the ideologies of the parties and cultural organizations behind it. The majority of its institutions were founded and maintained by Jewish proletarian parties, such as the Bund, Poale Zion, and the 'Fareynikte' (the 'United,' a Jewish socialist-territorialist party), or by individuals and organizations close to them in spirit. They were thus reliant upon a combination of party funds and subsidies provided by the St Petersburg–based *Hevra Mefitsei Haskala* (Society for the Promotion of Enlightenment among Jews), the Society for the Preservation of Jewish Health, economic co-operatives, and labour unions. Some were also established independently by organized community and bourgeois elements – the so-called Jewish democracy. The journalist Osher Perelman, for example, helped the administration of the Jewish Artisans' Association (formerly the Jewish Artisans' Club until the Russians left Poland) to recruit educators trained in the pedagogical system of German educator Friedrich Fröbel (1782–1852), founder of the kindergarten, for its own nursery.[40] Characteristically, these instructors spoke Yiddish with a Polish accent since no teachers' seminary yet existed for Yiddish teachers and trained nursery school teachers often came from polonized families at this time.[41]

Yiddishist educators were convinced of the rectitude of contemporary pedagogical theories, holding that children learn best in their mother tongue. Through Yiddish, they contended, the bond between the individual and her or his people could best be strengthened, 'the separation between educated and uneducated eliminated and the education of a national community made possible.' Out of their own love for the language and conviction that it merited the legal recognition enjoyed by other languages of high culture, those active in the Yiddish schools strove to impart to pupils a love and respect for the beauty and purity of the language. In contrast with the religious *kheyder*, the secular elementary school aimed at the symmetrical development of all facets of the child – intellectual, physical, and spiritual. Frequently themselves the product of Orthodox homes, teachers imbued with socialism and theories of Jewish productivization sought to combat the traditional taboo against physical labour as undignified among Jews and thereby 'lead the Jewish child to artisanry and physical work in general and tear it away from unproductive professions.'[42]

Meanwhile, Zionists in Warsaw opened their own Hebrew-language kindergartens for homeless children and Assimilationists created Polish-language institutions. With the notable exception of Poale Zion, Zionists pressed for the Hebraization of Jewish schools on the model of the new Jewish schools in Palestine, where Hebrew was taught according to the so-called natural method through the medium of spoken Hebrew. While the Assimilationist schools were supported with *kehila* monies, Yiddishists and Hebraists competed within various St Petersburg Jewish organizations for financial support for their institutions. Eventually a compromise in the language quarrel was reached whereby Yiddish would be the primary language of nursery activities but time would be devoted also to Hebrew songs and games in schools funded by the *Hevra Mefitsei Haskala*.[43]

Once contacts with St Petersburg were severed by the German occupation, Jewish schools and relief institutions in Poland became reliant upon monies collected by the German-Jewish *Hilfsverein* and, above all, upon the contributions of American Jewish organizations. Uncertain of what position the Germans would take with regard to Jewish schools, educators hurried to create additional nurseries (they were commonly then transformed into schools) despite their financial straits. In all, seventeen Yiddish secular schools were founded in Poland in 1916; an additional five were opened the following year.[44]

The retreat of the tsar's armies in 1915 meant an end to the obligatory use of Russian in schools. Almost immediately, Polish officials seized control of the schools and eagerly began work towards the creation of a national school system. All schools in Poland were soon placed, though, under the supervision of the German administration, which refused the request of Assimilationists in the *kehila* board and Poles to introduce Polish as the universal language of *kehila*-run nurseries and schools. Only where this was already the case or where the children's mother tongue was not Yiddish could Polish be used. The German administration simply failed to consider schools in Polish the sincere desire of the broad masses of Jewish parents.[45] Nor did it favour the children's polonization, which would make a future Polish state, whatever shape it would take, more linguistically homogeneous. The preservation of ethno-linguistic divisions was especially a concern where the protection of the distinctiveness of local Germans was at stake, such as in Łódź. German interests would best be served by maintaining a multinational, multicultural composition to the city as a counterbalance to Polish political and cultural aspirations.[46]

The central organizational figure in Yiddish school work in Poland, the writer Yankev Dinezon, appealed desperately in the American Yiddish daily *Der forverts* (The Forward) to raise money for the operation of Yiddish nurseries free from Hebraist activity.[47] When $20,000 approved at a relief conference in New York in 1915 for the support of secular Yiddishist nurseries never reached their destination, H.D. Nomberg published a sharp letter of protest in the 25 February edition of the *Varshever tageblat.* In it, he accused Assimilationist and Hebraist elements of misappropriating funds specifically earmarked for nurseries of the 'Dinezon type' (i.e., Yiddishist). The funds had been forwarded via the *Hilfsverein* to the Warsaw Jewish Relief Committee, the main Jewish relief body in Poland that had been organized prior to the German occupation by the Warsaw *kehila* board. Presided over by the Assimilationist Dr Stanisław Natanson, the relief committee consisted mainly of Assimilationists with a minority of Zionist, pro-Zionist, and Orthodox members. No representatives of the Bund or of any other labour or Yiddishist groups sat on the committee.[48]

The committee, Nomberg alleged, had intentionally concealed the matter from both Dinezon and the public and distributed the funds among all of Warsaw's Jewish children, from the *Talmud Torahs* to the orphanages, for use for food and clothing, but not education. When Dinezon went to implore the Zionist Heshl Farbstein, who had been notified by the *Hilfsverein* that the money was expressly intended for schools of the Dinezon type, for financial assistance, Farbstein failed even to mention that money had arrived from the United States for the Yiddishist institutions.[49] To avoid the further diversion of monies collected specifically for these schools, the People's Relief Committee, an American relief organization formed by various labour organizations (it joined the Joint Distribution Committee in late November 1915), undertook independently to send funds directly to a committee under the names of Dinezon, the Bundist leader Vladimir Medem, and the Poale Zion activist Y. Raykhman.[50] Gradually, the committee developed from a body for the simple distribution of relief monies into the Central Dinezon School Committee, the core of the interwar *Tsisho* (*Tsentrale yidishe shul-organizatsye,* Central Jewish School Organization) system.

With the expansion of the Jewish school system, the idea arose of uniting independently functioning Yiddish schools of various political and cultural orientations. A number of pedagogical issues, such as the pressing need for standardizing grammar and orthography,[51] were discussed at a series of conferences but ideological divisions prevented a unified school front. Members of the Bund, Poale Zion, the Fareynikte, and non-party Yiddishists agreed only on language and secularism and diverged concerning pedagogical methods, educational goals and ideals, and their attitude towards Hebrew and *Eretz-yisrael.*

Early in the German occupation an attempt was made by supporters of the Yiddish secular school to find common ground with other elements in Jewish society who did not support Yiddish as the language of instruction in Jewish schools. Approximately three hundred representatives of teachers' groups, professional and cultural associations, community and party leaders, as well as writers of different orientations, assembled in Warsaw in August 1915 on the premises of the newly founded Jewish Teachers' Association to discuss the question of the Jewish elementary school, which was materially ignored by the Warsaw Citizens Committee. A passionate debate erupted concerning the language of instruction, pitting nearly equal forces of Hebraists and Yiddishists against each other. The former opposed a public declaration on the language issue and were satisfied with the general formula of Jewish schools while the latter demanded nothing less than official recognition for Yiddish in the schools. In a 44–35 vote, a resolution was passed in favour of the Yiddishist stance argued by Bundist leader Vladimir Medem in the name of the labour unions. His pronouncement represented the first public declaration concerning the Yiddish language in the Jewish elementary school during the German occupation and the beginning of political agitation on an organized societal, rather than individual, basis on behalf of the Yiddish school. The resolution presented the Polish public for the first time with the demand of an autonomous organ to organize and administer a Jewish school maintained at the expense of the municipal treasury. It was published in *Der haynt* and *Der moment* without its concluding clauses calling for Yiddish as the language of instruction in Jewish schools. The efforts of Hillel Zeitlin and Noah Prylucki, by this time both outspoken supporters of the Yiddish school, to convince their Zionist editors, who were uncomfortable with a pronouncement championing Yiddish alone, to publish the resolution in full were to no avail. Only later was it printed in its entirety in the *Varshever tageblat*, in which Prylucki and Nomberg were active.[52]

When the German administration intervened upon its own initiative in school policy in late 1915, a number of Yiddishist schools and nurseries were already in operation throughout Poland. Yiddishist educational activity in Congress Poland was chiefly directed by the *Shul- un folksbildung-fareyn* (School and Public Education Association), an organization dedicated to the creation of a Yiddish model elementary school and the coordination of adult education programs. Although founded in 1915, the School Association was not legally recognized by German authorities until March 1916. The School Association's administration comprised Bundists, Poale Zionists, and non-party elements, including Saul Stupnicki and Noah Prylucki, who served as its president.[53] In mid-September 1915 German officials unexpectedly extended to the Polish occupation zone an ordinance already in effect for several months in the Lithuanian occupation (*Ober-Ost*) zone. The ordinance declared that, since the German administration had no desire to suppress national particularity, education in the occupied zones would be conducted in the mother tongue of the children: Polish for Polish children, German for both German and Jewish children. The choice of German for Jewish schools was motivated by attitudes viewing Yiddish not as an independent cultural language (*Kultursprache*) fit for schooling, but rather a German folk dialect bound to evolve into Standard German after a generation or two under the proper influences. German was forcibly introduced into the curriculum of a number of Jewish schools, very often as the language of instruction, especially in *Ober-Ost*, where German annexation remained a possibility until late in the war. An insufficient number of German-speaking educators, however, made continued instruction in Yiddish a necessity. Nonetheless, such measures enraged Polish and Jewish nationalists in Poland alike. While many Poles saw in the German proclamation confirmation of what they alleged were Jewish separatist and pro-German sentiments, Jewish nationalists and socialists rejected the implication that Eastern European Jewry was a cultural stepchild of Germany and now feared the Germanization of their schools after having stubbornly combated their Polonization and Russification.[54]

The School Language Debate

The issue of the language of Jewish schools sparked a rancorous debate that pitted supporters of Yiddish, Hebrew, German, and Polish against one other to determine the cultural orientation of a new generation of Polish Jews. A torrent of articles appeared in the Polish, Jewish, and German presses between 1916 and 1918 – the peak years of the campaign for Jewish national recognition in Poland – along with a number of partisan books and treatises proposing solutions to the school question in a time of inflamed national tensions. Each participant in the debate claimed to speak legitimately in the name of Polish Jewry or on behalf of its interests.

In their attacks on Yiddish and Jewish cultural autonomy, Polish nationalists, including antisemites, did not fail to capitalize on negative attitudes towards Yiddish expressed by Assimilationists. Moreover, apart from bringing the usual aesthetic and practical arguments portraying Yiddish as an ugly jargon and an obstacle to the rapprochement of Poles and Jews, Polish opponents of Jewish cultural autonomy seized upon the undeniable linguistic kinship between German and Yiddish as evidence of Jewish disloyalty to Poland and collaboration with the German occupier. Propaganda spread by the *Kommitee für den Osten* (KfdO, Committee for the East), an unofficial Jewish non-party committee led by German Zionists with close contacts to the German government, strengthened such claims. Little did it matter that the nationalist leaders of Polish Jewry adamantly insisted on the cultural distinctiveness of Eastern European Jewry and outright rejected the notion of the Jews as representatives of German culture and interests among the Slavs. The KfdO emphasized, somewhat paradoxically, cultural and linguistic affinities between Germans and Yiddish-speaking Jews as a means to win German support for Jewish cultural autonomy in Poland at the same time that it sought to gain the sympathy of the Jews in Poland and in neutral countries for the Central Powers.[55] Such accusations, which had actually first emerged with the rise of the Yiddish press in Warsaw in 1905, were dismissed with characteristic indignity by Noah Prylucki in 1911 when he declared:

'Just as no means, whether good or bad, will manage to convince us to commit national suicide and help the Polish stomach to swallow us up, so will the future rulers of the land – if it is truly ordained that the Prussians will capture Warsaw – not for any price purchase our souls, which can be free even in the greatest servitude. We will not change our "impoverished," "impure," "jargon" into the rich man's tidy German language just as we haven't exchanged it for the rich, flowery Polish language.'[56]

Prylucki joined the language war in November 1915 with an article entitled 'What is Yiddish?' The strength of the article lies not in its linguistic analysis but in its discussion of Old Yiddish literature, an area in which Prylucki made a number of ground-breaking discoveries, and in its framing of Yiddish as an independent field of inquiry. He ingenuously locates himself in a long line of diversely and ideologically motivated Yiddish researchers, helping to establish a pedigree for the field and tracing a trajectory culminating in its Eastern European nationalist phase.

Beginning with sixteenth-century German Humanists and continuing with merchants, missionaries, and policemen into the eighteenth century, gentile scholars learned and analysed the language for a variety of reasons: they believed its proximity to German would hasten the mastery of Hebrew thanks to the large number of 'deformed' Hebrew lexica and forms integrated into it; they sought in it means to facilitate commerce with Jews or to explain the meaning of obscure words in German thieves' cant (*Gaunersprache*), a notorious professional jargon that absorbed elements of Yiddish and other 'secret' tongues; they hoped a mastery of the Jews' language would render more successful the preaching of Christianity to them. By the nineteenth century, however, Yiddish scholarship was no longer the private domain of gentile researchers distant from Jewish life. *Wissenschaft* scholars, Germanized Jews who were typically negatively disposed towards Yiddish on ideological and aesthetic grounds, viewed it as relic of medieval German that had been corrupted over the course of generations of ghettoization and distance from the broader German cultural milieu. At best, it was a linguistic curiosity, a subject worthy of doctoral dissertations. In contrast with these Jewish researchers, who frequently wished to confine Yiddish to a shameful chapter in pre-emancipation Jewish history, a new generation of Eastern European-born and -raised scholars had arisen. Inspired by the Jewish nationalist movement, these scholars insisted upon the independence of Yiddish as a full-fledged language. Echoing Ber Borokhov, whose 'The Tasks of Yiddish Philology' helped define the goals of this generation, they insisted not only upon its preservation, but its cultivation as a tool for national fulfilment.[57]

Mustering knowledge gained from a decade of amateur philological study, Prylucki offers a scientifically grounded defence of Yiddish as a language but adds no new linguistic arguments to the arsenal already deftly wielded by Yiddish scholars such as Matisyahu Mieses before him.[58] The exception is his significant insight that while Yiddish shares many features with German dialects, it does not entirely correspond in its features to any single one. This observation further undermined claims that Yiddish had arisen from a specific regional variant of German and somehow gone 'awry' rather than followed its own organic path of development.

The polemic takes to task the philologically ignorant opponents of Yiddish who reject it as unsuitable as the medium of instruction in Jewish schools because 'it is not a language' but a grammarless jargon or, at best, a dialect of German. Taking the example of Standard German, a literary dialect lent super-regional prestige by its use in Martin Luther's sixteenth-century translation of the Bible, Prylucki explains the meaninglessness of such designations as language and dialect when no clear scientific distinction exists between them. The division of speech into related dialects, he asserts, is but an artificial means employed by scholars to facilitate research. National languages are essentially no more than socially privileged dialects whose prestige confers upon them normative status. Dutch, to cite but one example, is often considered a dialect of Low German yet it is recognized as the national language of the Netherlands. Thus, two geographically distant subdialects (*mundartn*, a borrowing from German, in his terminology) of a certain language, for example, Mandarin and Cantonese, may even be less similar than two geographically close subdialects of two different languages, for example, the mutually comprehensible Low German dialects spoken on both sides of the Dutch-German border.

The regularity of 'deformations' in pronunciation and flexion vis-à-vis Yiddish's source languages, to which denigrators commonly point, is evidence of the existence of internal laws governing the language as an integral whole regardless of the provenance of its elements. In support of this claim, Prylucki traces the parallel development of Yiddish vowels in each of the language's three main components and stresses the influence of Slavic phonetics. Yiddish, he asserts, recast Slavic, German, and Hebrew materials into a new and independent entity through a 'chemical fusion' in order satisfy the exigencies of 'our national psyche.' Hebraists are mistaken when they characteristically speak of Yiddish as a corrupt foreign dialect and ignore the important role played by Hebrew in making the language distinctly Jewish. Sharing a precocious insight into the nature of Western Yiddish, the idiom widely spoken by pre-*Haskalah* Jews in Western Europe and the German lands, he notes that the Hebrew component of Yiddish even differs according to region and dialect. Most notably, Western dialects are without the unique source of Hebrew-component enrichment offered by the Hasidic movement, which did not make significant inroads into Western Yiddish speech territory.

Prylucki points to the existence of fourteenth-century Hebrew-Yiddish dictionaries in the Vatican and early modern Yiddish manuscripts in German libraries, as well as enumerates several eighteenth- and early nineteenth-century writers of Yiddish (including the physician Moshe Markuze, whose popular medical guide *Seyfer-refues* he discovered and first analysed) to support the thesis that Yiddish is a language possessing a venerable and distinguished literary tradition.[59] He stresses that this is a literature of secular, as well as religious, character and encompasses all domains of human endeavour – religion, science, mores and social life, politics, and so on. It is the language of a full-blooded nation, not merely a religious community. 'A dialect with a past and with a present, with a role in the life of an entire people and with a literature,' he proclaims, 'ceases to be a dialect. It becomes, it is already a national language.'[60]

Finally, the article entered the growing body of debates on Yiddish language planning, a subject that gained in importance and urgency thanks to the movements on behalf of the Yiddish school and national cultural autonomy. Running perhaps counter to his primary interest in dialectology, Prylucki announced the need for an orthoepy (a standard pronunciation) or 'general Yiddish' (*algemeyn yidish*), as he calls it, to be taught in the Jewish national elementary school. This would promote the formation of a standard spoken dialect, which he understood as a necessity for any self-respecting nation and prerequisite to further cultural development.

The German School Language Ordinance ignited an immediate protest movement among both Jewish nationalists and Assimilationists in Poland. Left-wing Jewish activists clamoured for Yiddish schools in Łódź in September 1915 and some 30,000 Jews signed a petition to this effect.[61] Assimilationists, fearing the Germanization of the Jews of Congress Poland and the strengthening of 'separatist tendencies,' initiated a petition campaign in Łódź in October demanding the institution of Polish as the language of Jewish schools. Similar campaigns occurred in Warsaw and Sosnowiec.[62] The Yiddishists retaliated shortly afterwards, organizing a counter-campaign that same month. Approximately one thousand participants, predominantly members of the Jewish working class, assembled at a concert hall in that city to demonstrate their support for the Yiddish schools at a protest meeting convened by the *Shul- un folksbildung-fareyn.*[63] The following month, a petition with more than twenty thousand adult signatures in favour of Yiddish as the language of instruction for all Jewish children was submitted to German authorities.[64]

A similar petition, this time with 32,645 signatures, was submitted to the German administration in Warsaw in February 1916.[65] The first signature on the 756-sheet petition is that of Noah Prylucki, followed by those of Vladimir Medem, Sh. Zusman (active in the Fareynikte and later secretary of the Bundist organization *Undzer shul*, Our School), M. Birnboym (pioneer of Yiddish children's literature, long-time teacher, and author of textbooks in Yiddish), and the educator Sh. Gilinski. The signatures of the managing committees of forty Jewish labour unions followed.

The petition begins by identifying the deleterious effect of education in a foreign tongue on the elementary school student. It continues with a philological and partly juridical defence of Yiddish as a fully developed literary idiom spoken, composed (although unsigned) by Prylucki. It points to contemporary support for recognition of Yiddish as the language of Jewish schools in the Russian Duma, as well as its use, along with other Eastern European languages, by the occupying authority in official proclamations in *Ober-Ost.*[66] The comprehensive apologia further demands that the Jewish people cease to be used as a tool for political-assimilatory purposes and instead be permitted to realize its own cultural needs. Schools under the authority of the Jewish community, it asserts, employ Polish and firmly resist all attempts to introduce Yiddish; meanwhile the *khadorim*, in which Yiddish is the language of instruction, are grossly unsuited to provide a modern education. The petition concludes with demands for the official recognition of Yiddish as the language of instruction in Jewish schools, a network of Yiddish schools at city and Jewish community expense, and the creation of a democratically elected Jewish School Council to administer these schools parallel to the Polish education department of the Warsaw Citizens Committee.[67]

A widespread campaign was subsequently undertaken by the Bund to awaken the Jewish masses to the dangers of German as the language of Jewish schools and to organize popular support in favour of the Yiddish school. Petitions similar in content to the one described above were submitted to German authorities in a number of cities where Yiddishist educators were active.

Prylucki also hurried to publish by mid-January 1917 *Der yidisher konsonantizm* (Yiddish Consonantism), his first major study devoted exclusively to linguistics and an attempt at spelling reform, in order to furnish scholarly material for use in the campaign on behalf of the Yiddish language and its rights.[68] He was delayed, however, by technical difficulties and his subsequent involvement in City Council elections in the summer of 1916.[69]

In any event, Polish allegations of Jewish Germanophilia had no real basis in the conduct of German occupation troops or in the behaviour of German Jewry as a whole towards Eastern European Jewry. Although some German officials expressed interest early in the war for the KfdO's advocacy of Jewish autonomy and the possible Germanization of Eastern European Jewry, the KfdO's plans were never seriously entertained by the German Foreign Office.[70] From 1916 on German authorities, certain that an independent Polish state would necessarily emerge from the war, lost interest in cultivating Jewish support as a counterweight to Polish national aspirations and increasingly favoured Polish over Jewish national interests. Moreover, German-Jewish theses of a community of German and Eastern European Jewish interests were quite often undisguisedly linked to the desire to improve conditions for Eastern European Jews on their native territory as a strategy to discourage their immigration into Germany. A postwar influx of kaftan-clad Polish Jews, many German Jews feared, would interfere with their hard-won progress towards full emancipation, integration, and social acceptance by their countrymen.[71]

The Germans viewed the rejection of the language of *Dichter und Denker* as an offence to their national pride and arrested a number of Jewish leaders for their work on behalf of Yiddish schools and cultural activities. The sheer impracticality of the Language Ordinance, coupled with the extensive protest movement, however, succeeded in eventually compelling the Germans to relax the regulation concerning Jewish schools. Rather than revoke the law prescribing German in Jewish schools, though, the Germans begrudgingly tolerated Yiddish for some time as a German dialect and permitted its continued use in schools in order not to disturb them. Only in October 1916 was the requirement to use German definitively revoked in the *General-Gouvernement.*[72]

Desiring to promote political and social stability in the occupied zones, the Germans accommodated Jewish nationalists by establishing continuing education courses in Hebrew and Yiddish, as well as Polish, for elementary school teachers in Warsaw. Instructors for the Yiddish courses included Hillel Zeitlin, Noah Prylucki, and Sh. Gilinski. The Germans also fostered the opening of new schools with Yiddish as the language of instruction and forbade any reduction in the number of Yiddish schools already in existence. Such measures were the result of practical considerations and not a demonstration of support for the Jewish national cause or Yiddish. Indeed, when the pedagogical delegation entrusted with conducting the German-sponsored courses refused to assume its duties until the term 'Jargon' had been replaced with 'Yiddish' on the instructional program, the Germans threatened to arrest the instructors. Only Yiddishist intractability eventually persuaded them to yield on this point.[73]

It is important to recall that not all supporters of Yiddish in the schools considered themselves ideological Yiddishists even if they were intensely active in and on behalf of Yiddish. Accused by Nomberg and others in the *Varshever tageblat* of referring to Yiddish as 'zhargon' during his lessons, Zeitlin expressed regret if his tongue had inadvertently slipped and referred to his extensive cultural activity as testimony to his commitment to Yiddish. However, he maintained his fundamental opposition to 'fanatical' Yiddishism: 'In the end, the so-called Yiddishists cause much damage. Their claims about the Yiddish language, which they purportedly defend with their affected fanaticism and laughable reproaches, manage only to prevent anyone from taking "Yiddishism" seriously. The idol of Yiddishism is laughable and brings about its own downfall.'[74]

Warsaw City Council Elections

On 1 July 1915 the Germans called for the convening of City Councils based upon the Prussian model to replace the system of Citizens Committees put in place under Russian rule. Since the entire governing mechanism of German-occupied Poland was by appointment, the popularly elected City Councils represented the single democratic organ in Poland until the end of the war. Despite their authority being limited mainly to decisions concerning the municipal budget and city management, the councils served as an arena for open political debate. In particular, the Warsaw City Council, whose composition reflected the political landscape of the unofficial Polish capital, was widely viewed as the embryonic parliament of a future Polish state. While news of events in the Łódź City Council seldom reached beyond the limits of the city, the decisions and debates of the Warsaw council were discussed daily in the Warsaw press, which was widely read in the provinces as well. Active in it were those same political forces that would govern independent Poland after 1918.[75]

Elections to the Warsaw City Council were scheduled for July 1916. Although the new self-administration organs were meant to represent all segments of the population, a curial system divided the electorate according to wealth, education, and profession and accorded disproportionate influence to the wealthier classes. Since Jews carried much weight in these classes – the Germans did not permit any restrictions on the number of Jewish voters – the antisemitic Polish press, above all the *Gazeta Poranna 2 Grosze*, agitated against the Jewish candidates. With the exception of a few, but not all, adherents of assimilation, Jewish candidates were denounced as incapable of serving Polish interests. Only the 'pious' Orthodox candidates, it was claimed, could be relied upon not to mix in politics and to remember always that Poland 'is Polish and not Polish-Jewish land.'[76] Of the six curiae slated to send fifteen representatives to the City Council, only the sixth was allotted to the general population – labourers, petty bourgeois elements, and the *Lumpenproletariat*.[77]

The Socialist Bloc, which was supported by the Jewish left, had no expectations of wielding real power. The Bund had difficulty assembling a list due to the requirement that candidates be aged at least thirty years and command the Polish tongue. It used the opportunity provided by the elections, however, to expound a program denouncing nationalism and antisemitism, which it considered a tool exploited by bourgeois Jewish nationalists to defend their class interests. The bloc also demanded

Jewish cultural rights and called upon the government to recognize Yiddish-language schools, to issue public notices in Yiddish, and to grant petitioners the right to address the government and receive replies in this language. The platform made no specific mention of permission for Jewish workers to rest on Saturday with impunity since this was deemed insufficiently important to the Jewish proletariat. It also failed to include national cultural autonomy as this was considered implicit in the demand for Yiddish schools.[78]

Conforming to the Polish desire to present a unified front before the Germans as a symbol of commitment to an independent Polish state, the United Jewish Election Committee (UJEC, formed 16 June 1916) entered a coalition with the 'Revolutionary Fraction' of the Polish Socialist Party (PPS-Frakcja) and the Polish National Workers' Committee (a coalition of Christian Democrats and Endeks).[79] With much difficulty a platform was worked out to unite the non-socialist Jewish groupings in order to prevent any one Jewish party from running its own list and thereby destroying the Polish-Jewish bloc. Judging the climax of Poland's struggle for national independence an inopportune moment to champion minority rights, the Zionists in the UJEC chose not to emphasize national demands for the time being and consented to a number of representatives (15) disproportionately small relative to the large number of Jewish voters in Warsaw (36,679 out of 78,567, or 44% of the total electorate). Along with the Orthodox, including Hasidic groups, and the 'Neo-Assimilationists' (a term, to be explained more fully below, designating polonized Jews who nonetheless rejected the contention that all Jews must 'assimilate'), they were content with the formula of civic equality and religious rights for the Jews of Poland. The Polish-Jewish consolidation ran a single slate of candidates in the first five curiae (with the exception of the third curia, which belonged to intellectuals and Germans), making an election in all but the sixth curia unnecessary. Three of the total fifteen mandates allotted to the UJEC in its agreement with the Poles were to be awarded to each grouping – the Zionists, the Orthodox, the Neo-Assimilationists, moderate Hasidim, and unaffiliated merchants.[80] The Jewish press in Warsaw, including *Der haynt* and *Der moment*, expressed satisfaction with this consolidation, seeing in it a major achievement: for the first time, Jews were recognized as political partners.[81]

Jewish socialists were, however, not the only Jewish group to oppose the UJEC. Some extreme Assimilationists implored Jews in press appeals to vote not according to religious or ethnic loyalties, but in support of those Polish parties that best conformed to their economic and political views. They saw the formation of a separate Jewish committee as a contradiction of liberalism and feared that it would only perpetuate Jewish separateness in Poland.[82] The 'Neo-Assimilationists,' a grouping that emerged during the war out of dissatisfaction with the tenets of 'official' Assimilationism ('Old Assimilationism'), were willing, in contrast, to join the Jewish voting bloc. Although committed to Polish culture in their own lives, they viewed assimilation as a process subject to the decreasing will of the Poles to absorb Jews into their midst. Further, they rejected the demonstration of what they considered excessive patriotism and toadying to the Poles by old-style Assimilationists when Jewish civil rights had been violated. Despairing of the slow pace of polonization, they saw assimilation as the solution for the problems of individuals but not for the Jewish masses, which they recognized as separated by an unbridgeable chasm from the 'Old Assimilationists.' Some Neo-Assimilationists even began to show interest in Yiddish and Hebrew culture and to sympathize with Jewish nationalism. No crystallized ideology, however, united them.[83]

Non-party democratic elements, including artisans, teachers, intellectuals, and writers were also dissatisfied with the UJEC, but for quite opposite reasons. Those elements of the Jewish petite bourgeoisie and intellectual middle class who were strongly attached to Yiddish culture and the Diaspora felt that they could not depend upon the Palestinocentric Zionists to secure their future in Poland. Although Jewish socialist parties could be counted upon to present national demands in the cultural sphere, they were by definition unable to represent the bourgeoisie and refused cooperation with it in elections.[84]

Several meetings were held in the second half of June on the premises of the Jewish Teachers' Association with the intention of forming a Jewish School Committee to represent the Yiddish secular school in the future City Council. Participants in the meetings believed that the existence of a School Committee supported by all pro-Yiddish elements in time for the convening of the Warsaw City Council would oblige the municipality to subsidize Yiddish schools with public monies. Moreover, it was feared that, considering the composition of the UJEC, the issue of recognition and support for the Yiddish schools would likely not even be discussed in the City Council. These meetings, however, yielded no practical results due to the failure of certain groups to cooperate – the parties of the Jewish left in one instance, and Jewish artisan unions in another. Articles published by Nomberg and Prylucki in *Der moment* and

Dos varshever tageblat denouncing the anti-national character of the UJEC served to rouse members of Jewish unions somewhat from their political lethargy but none was yet willing to sign a petition to form a new election committee.[85] The use of the Yiddish press, specifically *Der moment* and *Dos varshever tageblat*, helped to prepare the Jewish public for the creation of a democratic bourgeois nationalist party.[86]

At an assembly of the Writers' and Journalists' Association, a resolution was passed in late June calling upon the UJEC to (1) select delegates who will defend Jewish national, as well as civil and religious, rights in the City Council; any Assimilationists elected must not apply forced assimilation (this term is not explained but assumedly means that Polish will not be made the language of Jewish schools, nor will any coercive means be employed to promote the use of Polish among Jews at the expense of Yiddish); and (2) grant a place on its candidate list to a member of the Association, specifically its president Noah Prylucki. A delegation consisting of Ben Avigdor, Hillel Zeitlin, Saul Stupnicki, H.D. Nomberg, and Samuel Hirschhorn delivered the memorandum. Negotiations with the UJEC yielded, however, no compromise.[87] With the combined support of the Teachers' Association, the Artisans' Association, and the Writers' and Journalists' Association, a Jewish Democratic Election Committee was organized to run with a clear nationalist program.[88] On 28 June 1916 official permission was requested from the German authorities to form a *Folks-komitet* (FK, People's Committee) to participate in the elections. It presented its list of candidates the following day – Noah Prylucki, Samuel Hirschhorn, Professor Volfovitsh, the Zionists Engineer B. Efron and the writer Ben Avigdor, Hershlikovitsh, Sh. B. Ronani, and the artisan representative Chaim Rasner – that was soon approved by the authorities.[89]

Ten unions joined the FK, which appealed for support from diverse segments of Jewish society, including merchants, Hasidic youth, students, women, and the elderly, with articles in *Der moment* and *Dos varshever tageblat* addressed to all 'democratic' elements in the Jewish community. The party also relied for popular support on the numerous cultural and professional associations (youth clubs, student associations, sports clubs, continuing education programs, school associations, etc.) that had emerged during the war.[90] Meetings were held on the premises of the Artisans' Association and the Writers' Association, which Hirschhorn, Prylucki, and other prominent writers joined.[91] A party platform was adopted calling for civil equality for the Jews, the right to observe the Sabbath and work Sundays, a state-supported Jewish School Council, and the right to use Yiddish in communications with authorities.[92] Like the Bund, the FK argued that UJEC was fundamentally undemocratic, had issued no list of candidates, and that it had sealed a treasonous pact sacrificing Jewish national interests without ever consulting the Jewish public.[93]

Negotiations were attempted again with the UJEC, during which the *Folks-komitet* offered not to run a separate list if it were granted a portion of the Jewish mandates and if the UJEC would offer a proclamation principally opposing forced 'assimilation.'[94] A proclamation was made by the Neo-Assimilationist Julian Muttermilch, who declared that 'it is against national dignity to apply coercion for assimilation,' but the UJEC remained intransigent on the issue of mandates. Rather than break the Polish-Jewish bloc, the FK chose to run only in the sixth curia, where no election pacts had been made.[95] In early July 1916, the FK published in the *Varshever tageblat* an appeal urging voters in the sixth curia to support it rather than the Assimilationists in collaboration with the Orthodox and Zionists to betray vital Jewish interests in return for an illusory vision of peace with the Poles.[96] Similar appeals also appeared in *Der moment.*

The political division in the Jewish community provided an excuse for a renewed eruption of hostilities between *Der haynt* and *Der moment.* Since the beginning of the war, the two papers had not engaged in any serious conflicts, although personal attacks did not abate. Both espoused general Jewish nationalist, non-partisan positions welcoming all orientations except the Assimilationist one. While he did not eagerly support the Polish-Jewish consolidation, *Der haynt* editor Shmuel Yatskan seized the opportunity to launch a new assault on his chief competitor.[97] *Der moment* not only vigorously supported the FK despite Tsevi Prylucki's Zionist leanings but its leading writers – Noah Prylucki, Hillel Zeitlin, H.D. Nomberg, and Samuel Hirschhorn – were among its primary organizers and occupied its chief positions. To dissuade voters from supporting the FK, Yatskan sought to refute its claims to be the sole body pledged to the defence of Jewish rights and to denigrate its candidates, above all Prylucki.

In the days preceding the City Council elections, Prylucki was consistently denounced on the pages of *Der haynt* as an opportunist and liar. His personal ambition checked after failing to secure a place on the UJEC list, he crusaded to 'save the honour' of the Jewish people from the 'treacherous' bloc composed of respected Jewish nationalists and religious leaders without any extreme Assimilationists.[98] The allotment of votes to the Jews, Yatskan further argued, is just since the City Council is to be a representative body for all of Poland and Jews represent a much smaller proportion of the total Polish population than of the Warsaw population.[99] To break the Jewish bloc, *Der haynt* warned, would not only justify Dmowski's charge that the Jews desire to impede the Poles at this historic moment, but it will also vindicate before the world claims that Jewish nationalists represent but an insignificant, separationist group of 'Litvaks' with no influence among the mass of Jews in Poland (a curious claim considering that he, the editor of the tremendously influential daily, was himself a Litvak and a Jewish nationalist).[100]

To cast doubt on Prylucki's moral character, readers were reminded of his 'pornographic' poetry, which was subjected to all manner of mocking interpretations. It was claimed that he demanded fees from Jewish merchants seeking legal aid in regaining their arbitrarily confiscated market stalls. Further, the same 'man with a clear Jewish program' whom Nomberg now champions, it was pointed out, was not so long ago mocked by him (in *Ha-boker*, No. 17, 1907) as a vulgar, scandalous, and talentless writer with an insatiable appetite for controversy.[101]

Prylucki was not the only target for character assassination. The former *Der haynt* staff member Zeitlin was labelled a sanctimonious hypocrite who sells tickets to his lectures on the Sabbath and a demagogue who disgraces himself with invectives and polemics.[102] (The irony of the charges, like those he made about Litvaks, seems to have been lost on their author.) Yatskan also likened his business rival Tsevi Prylucki to a father exceedingly eager to marry off his son and alleged that the elder Prylucki had vowed to destroy the UJEC with the aid of his newspaper if *his* Noyekh were not made a candidate.[103]

Not surprisingly, *Der moment* denied all charges against the FK and explained the UJEC's continued existence as motivated solely by the vindictive desire to wage a war against Noah Prylucki. The 'Assimilationists and their helpers' in the UJEC, it warned, will neither protect the Yiddish elementary school nor fight for Jews' equal treatment by the city administration, an important provider of jobs for tens of thousands in tramways, gas facilities, electricity, gardens, bridges, and so on.[104] If the UJEC includes a commitment to a free Poland in its platform, it must also include the matter of the Jews' place in a future state and therefore demand guarantees for the rights of national minorities.[105]

Among Polish-language newspapers, the liberal *Nowa Gazeta* welcomed the Polish-Jewish consolidation as a symbol of the union of citizens of different religions and the beginning of lasting harmony between them after the Jewish question had become so enflamed in recent years. The *Dwa Grosze*, on the other hand, failed even to make mention of the union with the Jews.[106]

Attacks on the FK, including the accusation of mandate bargaining, did not harm the FK in the least. Even some members of the UJEC – the liberal rabbi Dr Sh. Poznański, the Neo-Assimilationist Dr Goldflam, and the Orthodox candidates Leizer Priwes, and Lejb Dawidsohn – came out in support of it.[107] The results of the Warsaw City Council elections of 13–14 July 1916 brought a surprise victory for the FK over the UJEC, demonstrating mass Jewish support for a Jewish nationalist alternative to Zionism and/or to Prylucki's popularity as a public figure.[108] The FK received 8,611 votes and sent four delegates – Prylucki, Hirschhorn, the painter Avrom Ayznberg, and Efron – to the City Council. The 1,924 votes garnered by the UJEC in the sixth curia, in contrast, gained it no seats. Many Jewish votes also went to the socialist list, which captured four mandates. The largest number of mandates (7) in the sixth curia went to a coalition of Endeks and Christian Democrats.[109] In total, nineteen Jewish deputies (4 FK, 15 UJEC) were dispatched to the ninety-seat City Council.[110]

On 16 July, two days after the elections, *Der moment* cheered the victory of the FK while the Zionist *Ha-tsefira* criticized Noah Prylucki as a parvenu who stubbornly refused to submit to 'those who have always assumed communal work.'[111] Prylucki himself attributed his bloc's success to its energetic agitation in synagogues and to the work of the Jewish press in the preceding ten years to politicize the Jews and strengthen national consciousness. Employing the allegory of Mendele's satiric novel *Di kliatshe* (*The Nag*), he likened the Jewish electorate to a nag that has finally hurled its oppressors from its back and forced them to recognize its human face and soul.[112]

The victory of the *Folks-komitet* was a fiasco for *Der haynt*, which had relentlessly attacked Prylucki in the preceding weeks and now censured its voters for their gullibility in electing him. *Der haynt* had already lost a part of its readership to *Der moment* when its best literary talents fled to Russia before the occupation. The victory of the FK, which was closely associated in popular opinion with the person of Noah Prylucki, dealt it a further blow, and attacks on Prylucki only resulted in further harm to its circulation.[113] Even after the election, *Der haynt* continued for several days to rail against Prylucki and the FK with accusations of all manner of impiety and the misuse of American relief monies to finance its campaign.[114]

At the opening of the Warsaw City Council on 25 July 1916, representatives of all Jewish parties present expressed solidarity with a declaration made by Polish parties on behalf of an independent Poland that would grant civic equality to all of its citizens. Sensitive to their election loss, yet not wishing to antagonize their Polish allies, the Zionists issued a written statement registering confidence that a free Poland would guarantee equal civil and national rights to the Jews. Speaking on behalf of the Polish and Jewish proletariats, a PPS delegate allied with the Bund denounced the City Council as a bastion of political and social Reaction and demanded an end to anti-Jewish discrimination in the administration in addition to national cultural autonomy for minorities. In particular, he emphasized the need for schools with Yiddish as their language of instruction (a demand which overstepped the authority of the City Council) and the right to address the state and receive responses in Yiddish. Samuel Hirschhorn, speaking for the Folkists, recognized the 'Polish character of the land' but also demanded recognition for Yiddish in the schools and issued a series of political demands: proportional taxation according to income and wealth, the placing of all social institutions under the authority of the city administration, equal access for unemployed Jews and non-Jews to municipal jobs, the convening of a publicly funded Jewish School Council to supervise Yiddish schools, and exemption of Jews from mandatory Sunday rest. He concluded by expressing confidence that Poland, which had recognized Jewish national-cultural particularity in its best times - an allusion to pre-partition Jewish autonomy – would again recognize the Jews' due right to this. The *Gazeta Poranna* reminded councilmen that agitation in the realm of higher politics, including wide-ranging declarations, was not within in the purview of the council – a reproach to the Jewish parties for seeking to settle the issue of Jewish rights before a state had even been declared.[115]

The Warsaw City Council

Jewish-Polish relations were an issue of tremendous tension in the daily affairs of the City Council. The longer the war dragged on and the more aggressively the Germans courted Polish support as an ally against Russia, the more resolute Polish will became to refuse concessions to the Jews. Over the course of 1916 the policy of the German regime vis-à-vis Poland changed from annexation to the erection of an independent Poland under the aegis of the German and Austro-Hungarian empires. In early November, the Germans demonstrated unambiguous support for the Poles by promising a Polish state and issuing a decree concerning the creation of a parliament and national council. The German proclamation also decided the fate of the Jews in conformity with Polish wishes by rejecting national minority status and instead granting the Jews only civic equality and religious autonomy. Hoping to secure German support for recognition of Jewish national rights in a future Polish state, the Folkists privately approached Ludwig Haas, the Advisor for Jewish Matters in the general German administration in Warsaw, with a plan to recruit Polish Jews to serve in a Jewish-commanded legion on Germany's side. The plan, initially conceived by the KfdO and adopted by Prylucki, was quickly discarded by Haas, a non-nationalist Jew, after initial enthusiasm. He recognized the staunch opposition it would arouse in Polish nationalist (and, of course, Assimilationist) circles, thereby undermining German efforts to gain Polish support.[116] The favouring of Polish interests over those of Jewish nationalists meant that organized Polish Jewry would need to seek an accommodation with the Poles rather than rely on German aid in repressing antisemitism and championing Jewish national rights.[117]

The *Varshever tageblat* abruptly ceased publication on 30 January 1917 after sixteen months of operation when its funding was withdrawn from the Germans 'in order to cede place to another newspaper.'[118] The following day *Dos yidishe vort* (The Jewish Word) debuted, the first Orthodox daily newspaper in Poland. The legal publishers of this new daily were the German rabbis Pinchas Kohn and Emmanuel Carlebach of the FVIOJ, who technically leased the existing *Tageblat* from the German government with the money of wealthy German Orthodox Jews. The paper maintained close contacts with German authorities and devoted more attention to the interests of high political circles than to the daily concerns of Warsaw's Orthodox masses. The rather clumsy closing and opening of newspapers unambiguously marked a shift in German sympathies from Jewish autonomist, specifically Folkist, elements to Orthodox leaders, whose lack of national demands and hold over the largest part of the Jewish population promised the least friction in Jewish-Polish relations.[119] The paper was viewed by both Poles and Jews as a thinly veiled German organ and poorly received by Orthodox readers.[120]

Jewish deputies in the City Council combated a number of anti-Jewish measures and regulations tolerated by the Germans despite an official policy of civic equality for the Jews that was ostensibly supported by all Poles, as well. This further polarized the Jewish camp between Jewish nationalists and Assimilationists. The latter group generally preached co-operation with the Poles and blamed a legacy of divisive Russian policy for the failure of Jews to acculturate to Polish norms. It downplayed the anti-Jewish boycott along with anti-Jewish menaces directed at it together with Jewish nationalists by the Endeks.[121]

Folkist activity in the City Council was coordinated by a *Folksrat* (People's Council), which collected statistics on Jewish commerce and artisanry and directed the party's deputies in the Council.[122] The Folkists were also active in protesting a number of other abuses that persisted into the postwar period, further embittering Polish-Jewish relations: police harassment of Jewish pedlars in Christian neighbourhoods; discrimination in hiring for municipal jobs and exclusion from, as well as harassment by, the city militia; enforced Sunday rest; the preservation of a special tax on the Jewish community for Jewish patients in city hospitals in addition to a tax on Jewish hospitals (this amounted to double taxation since non-Jewish patients treated in Jewish hospitals were not required to pay an additional tax); the attempt by Polish officials to avoid paying pensions to the wives of Jewish soldiers fighting in the Russian army on the ground that marriage certificates issued by the Jewish community were invalid. While they received the support of other Jewish parties on most issues, this was not the case for their demands for a state-supported Yiddish school under the authority of a Jewish school board – a proposal not supported by the Zionists or the Orthodox, although it received some support from Polish socialists.[123] The party was also excluded from the Assembly of Elders, an internal organization in the City Council not mandated by law, for allegedly not supporting the Polish cause.[124]

Noah Prylucki distinguished himself as the most active among the Jewish deputies, speaking frequently on general and, more commonly, Jewish issues. His party's extreme nationalist position was a provocation in the eyes of many Poles.[125] No other delegate was so often cautioned, mocked, and derided by his political opponents as Prylucki.[126] His incessant agitation on behalf of Jewish rights and call for a world power to guarantee Jewish rights in Poland at a future peace conference earned his party the description in the socialist paper *Robotnik* (The Worker) as 'żydowska endecja' (Jewish Endecja), equating it with the zealously nationalist Endecja.[127] He effortlessly inspired the opprobrium of the Endeks, whose deputy Ilski decried the Folkists as insular separatists seeking to harm the Polish cause abroad by incessantly decrying alleged injustices and promoting Jewish welfare at the expense of Poland as a whole.[128]

Since he was generally blocked from bringing Jewish issues directly to the daily agenda by various parliamentary strategies, Prylucki regularly took the floor on budget discussions in order to argue his points. He pointed to the preservation of anti-Jewish legislation enacted under the

Russians despite promises of full civic equality for the Jews. Among the anti-Jewish measures against which he led campaigns was the segregation of Jewish merchants upon the request of their Christian competitors in the recently renovated *Gościnny Dwór* market. The Jews' obstreperous manner, racial solidarity, and use of 'jargon' among themselves, it was alleged, granted them an unfair advantage over Christian merchants. Despite the protests of Prylucki and others, the City Council did not abolish this 'market ghetto.'[129] He was more successful in his efforts to annul an ordinance dating from the Russian period that refused entry into a number of public parks and gardens to Jews dressed in traditional garb. In contrast with the Fareynikte, which quietly appealed to the municipality's sense of dignity and civilization, Prylucki was temporarily suspended from the City Council for his vehement denunciation of park signs refusing admission to those not in 'clean, orderly and European dress.' He characterized the kaftan, which was denounced by its opponents as dark and unhygienic (due to infrequent washings), as the 'national costume of the significant majority of the Jews in Poland' and pointed to the long Polish folk dress as similarly 'unEuropean.' The parks issue united Jews of all orientations, including Assimilationists, and the sign's wording was eventually changed to discriminate only against the 'slovenly' dressed.[130]

The Folkist Platform

In its first year of activity, the *Folkskomitet,* which soon adopted the name *Folksgrupe* (People's Group) after the elections, strove for good relations with other Jewish parties and to justify its continued existence despite a large degree of programmatic similarity to the Zionists. An attempt was even made in late 1916 to form a Jewish National Club, an interparty organ to coordinate joint practical work between the two parties. It failed when the Folkists objected to the defection of one of their councilmen, the artist Ayznberg, to the Zionists and refused to accept an unequal number of representatives of each party on the committee.[131] The Folkist position remained nebulous on many issues in its early years.[132] The Zionist and Folkist parties diverged most significantly on the role of the Diaspora and value of Yiddish culture in Jewish life, as well as in their degree of assertiveness in demanding national rights for the Jews.

At the heart of the Folkist platform was the doctrine of autonomism, which was adopted in some form by most Jewish parties, including the Bund and the Zionists,[133] by 1905–6. Autonomism applied to the Eastern European Jewish context a solution first proposed to resolve tensions between socialism and nationalism at the Brünn party conference of the Austrian Social Democrats in 1899 and elaborated by party theorist Otto Bauer in his *Die Nationalitätenfrage und die Sozialdemokratie* (Vienna, 1907). This principle dictates that the constituent nationalities within multinational states, such as the Russian and Austro-Hungarian Empires, be organized – in part or entirely – on a non-territorial basis and that certain basic functions of government be placed in the hands of these nationalities. The territorially dispersed Jewish minority within these empires would constitute a corporate body recognized by the state and be entrusted with democratic elections to its own legislative and executive bodies, as well as granted its own state budget. Like all other nationalities, the Jews would enjoy the right to use their national language in public and to administer to their own education and cultural needs. In all other domains where the collective of nationalities shared common interests, such as defence of the state and in the administration of justice, they would be subject to the same rights and responsibilities as all other citizens.[134]

Prylucki endorsed this concept in his writings as early as 1907, crediting it to the Austrian Social Democrats Karl Renner and Otto Bauer despite that they excluded Jews from recognition among the 'nationalities' of the Austro-Hungarian Empire for lack of requisite criteria for nationhood (contiguous territory and undisputed national language).[135] He neglected then to recognize any intellectual debt to the pioneers of Jewish autonomism – the seminal historian of Eastern European Jewry Simon Dubnow and the political philosopher and early exponent of Yiddishism Khayim Zhitlovski.

In contrast with those who saw centuries of life in the Diaspora as an aberration, even if a culturally creative one, in the historical development of the Jewish people, Dubnow deemed Diaspora living a positive experience: it had transformed the Jews from a primitive, territorial nation into a 'spiritual nation,' the most advanced stage of national development. In articles appearing between 1897 and 1903 on the pages of the leading Russian-Jewish journal *Voskhod* (Sunrise; the articles were published in book form in 1906 under the title *Letters on Old and New Judaism*) he postulated a philosophy of history in support of Jewish national-cultural (rather than political or territorial) autonomy based upon the unrestricted use by Jews of their languages in the lands of their residence.

According to his views, the *kehila* had historically served as a surrogate for statehood in the Diaspora. It had been, however, both voluntarily abandoned by Jews as the organizing point for their social and cultural lives and been abolished as an autonomous entity by the modern centralized state in the era of emancipation. The *kehila* was to be revived not as a religious-based organization but in a modern, democratic, and secularized form as the basic unit of national cultural autonomy. Zhitlovski, also from the Russian Empire but active after the turn of the century in America, arrived at a similar formula at approximately the same time. He emphasized, however, socialism more than nationalism and was also more occupied with championing Yiddish literature and culture than with political issues. In contrast with Dubnow, whose philosophy accorded equal place to Hebrew and Russian alongside Yiddish as the media through which Jewish culture be transmitted, Zhitlovski, like Prylucki, was a principled exponent of Yiddish as the exclusive language of contemporary Jewish life.[136] Now, during the First World War, Prylucki had come to fully identify as a Diaspora nationalist and celebrated Dubnow as the 'intellectual father' of the Folkist movement.

Despite its attempt to appeal to diverse Jewish groups, the *Folksgrupe* appealed mainly to the same mass of voters as the Zionists, the Jewish petite bourgeoisie – petty merchants, shopkeepers, brokers, and artisans who occasionally took on other employment. Mostly but not all poor, both religiously observant and distanced from the traditional way of life, the members of this class did not form a monolithic group. Their attitudes towards Zionism ranged from wholly negative to extremely supportive. They were united, though, by economic independence and a bourgeois rather than proletarian-socialist outlook.[137] The party's theoretician Stupnicki argued against socialism as dangerous to the interests of the Jewish people because it promotes class conflict within the traditionally petty bourgeois nation. He saw the Jews' further proletarization as neither desirable nor possible: lacking their own economy in the Diaspora, the Jews are reliant upon free competition for survival and will only suffer a diminishment of national wealth through the transfer of capital into the hands of a non-Jewish government. The Jewish artisan and petty merchant must be helped to remain competitive with large-scale industry in order that the Jews become a uniformly middle-class people.[138]

The doctrine of Folkism was elaborated primarily on the pages of *Der moment* and the party organ *Dos folk*, which began publication as a weekly in February 1917 under the editorship of Lazar Kahan. It saw itself as the 'intellectual inheritor' of the *Varshever tageblat* and declared itself 'committed to serving Jewish national interests, to battling uninvited benefactors and Assimilationist usurpers.'[139] Apart from political and ideological discussions and Jewish and Polish press overviews, the weekly featured much cultural material: selections from Yiddish and European belle-lettres in translation, historical essays by the original political ideologist of Folkism Simon Dubnow, literary criticism, articles on the need to encourage the appreciation of the arts among Jews, tributes to the heroes of Yiddish culture and Folkism (above all Peretz, who was considered one of the intellectual fathers of Folkism as a cultural movement), sports reports, and a chess column. Readers were exhorted to support the party financially through the purchase of a 'Folksgroshn' ('People's Penny') presumably modelled on the example of the Zionist 'shekel.'[140]

Folkism viewed itself as a present-oriented phenomenon called into existence not by individuals or ideals, but by the exigencies of daily life in the Diaspora. According to the Folkist organ, it represents the culmination of Jewish nationalist thought achieved through the fusion of positive aspects of both spiritual Zionism and territorialism. For the Folkists, the Diaspora was not only the locus of the ethnogenesis of Ashkenazic Jewry and the thousand-year home of a 'long golden tradition' of culture and spirituality, but also destined to be the future site of its national flourishing. They rejected the Zionist slogan of the 'negation of the Diaspora' – the effacement of 'unhealthy' mental and physical traits and behaviours allegedly conditioned by the crippling abnormality of Diasporic living – as fundamentally pessimistic, the reaction to an exaggerated fear of the disappearance of the Jews as a people through a combination of complete assimilation and economic extinction. From Ahad Ha'am's doctrine of Spiritual Zionism, Folkism embraced the mission of practical work as a means to reinvigorate Judaism and to satisfy the intellectual and cultural, as well as the physical, needs of Jews. However, it opposed on principle the construction of a new-old spiritual and intellectual centre in Palestine for a small Hebrew-speaking elite while the daily interests of the masses remaining in the Diaspora, including the satisfaction of their cultural needs in Yiddish, were ignored or accorded secondary importance. Although it endorsed Territorialism's embracing of the Diaspora, Folkism rejected the conviction that the Jews need a territory of their own in order to be free of hindrances to their proletarization or their adoption of productive labour. As explained by Stupnicki, 'Jews are citizens of the lands where they live and not guests. The task of Jewry is to strive with the best part of humanity for a better and more just future [and], at the same time, to strengthen Jewish positions in the intellectual and economic realm and to struggle for national rights. Folkism grew beyond Zionism and Territorialism, [and] is a legitimate child of Jewish optimism.'[141]

While Folkism lacks a political history beyond Dubnow's short-lived Folksparty in Russia, its origins can be traced to the Czernowitz Conference and the person of Y.L. Peretz. More importantly, its ideological underpinnings were rooted deep within the living people and supported by a diverse and lively Yiddish literary tradition: 'What is Mendele's desire to make the people healthier, more suited for life in its struggle against the powerful if not Folkism?' Zionism, by way of contrast, was an abstract, romantic nationalism fixated on a 'classical era' in hoary antiquity and on a utopian vision of the future in which a reformed Jewish people would dwell in Palestine; it was deemed insufficiently willing to confront the Jewish present and to improve and repair its native structures in situ.[142]

The Folksparty (the name was fixed at an 11 March 1917 meeting) aspired to be, in Hillel Zeitlin's words, 'the expression of the people [*folk*] itself' – a political umbrella organization welcoming supporters of all Jewish orientations united in support of national and civil rights for the Jews in Poland.[143] Like the Zionist organization, which included a multitude of parties of varied political and cultural shadings, there was, at least theoretically, room for diversity within the Folksparty as along as all members shared the conviction that national demands in the Diaspora must take priority over all other goals.[144]

The official party line was sympathetic to colonization in *Eretz-yisrael*, which it honoured as the Jews' unforgettable historical homeland. It opposed, however, efforts to channel mass immigration there as both a devaluation of Diaspora existence and as an unrealizable solution to the difficulties of Jewish life in Poland and Russia since the land already possessed a sizable Arab population and could accommodate at most a fraction of the rapidly growing Jewish population of Europe. Zionism's very nature as a global organization uniting Jews living under a number of different regimes in pursuit of a common goal, it was argued, made it woefully unsuited for involvement in local politics. Were the Helsinfors program for *Gegenwartsarbeit* – work on behalf of the Diaspora – to be taken seriously by Zionists, as demonstrated to the contrary by the performance of Polish Zionists in the Warsaw City Council elections and their opposition to Yiddish schools, the need for the Folksparty would not have been so acute.[145]

The most sympathetic to Zionism among the Folkists was Hillel Zeitlin, whose religious sensibilities and lack of enthusiasm for 'extreme' Yiddishism guarded him from outright rejection of the Zionist enterprise. He likened these rival strains of Jewish nationalism to two sides of a coin, inseparable and complementary:

> Zionism is concerned with abstract Israel, with abiding values of Israel and its holy land, the eternal. Folkism is concerned with concrete Israel and its real needs in the Diaspora, the ephemeral ... Zionism cannot replace Folkism, cannot care for Diaspora needs. How can it create and build in the Diaspora when it views all of the Diaspora as a great misfortune? ... Folkism, from its side, can, however, also not take the place of Zionism because then it will remain detached from the eternal ground from which the people derives its sustenance. It will then be transformed into merely a smallish democratic opposition without any higher internal content and no justification for its existence.[146]

The official program of the party was first issued in October 1917 (*Dos folk* 32) but left certain divisive issues to be resolved at a future party conference, namely, its positions on emigration, immigration, colonization in Palestine, and its relationship to other Jewish parties and forms of Jewish cultural expression other than in Yiddish. Apart from general principles calling for a democratic and independent Poland with equal protection before the law for all citizens, progressive taxation, and social welfare measures, it sets forth a series of demands predicated on the recognition of the Jews as an 'independent national entity.' All Jewish citizens no younger than twenty years of age were eligible to vote for the Jewish People's Council, the official state-funded representative of the Jewish people in Poland whose competence embraces '(a) the entire system of Jewish schools and popular education; (b) the concern for the development of Jewish culture; (c) the concern for teaching professions and trades, the organization of low term credit, mutual insurance, consumer unions, producers' co-operatives, etc.; (d) the concern for the health of the people; (e) the compilation of Jewish statistics.'[147]

At the local level, Jewish life was to be regulated by the *kehila*, the democratically elected body to which all Jews living within the boundaries of a municipality belonged. The activities of the *kehilot* within a district (or several districts) with less than twenty-five thousand Jews were to be supervised by a similarly elected district council; larger *kehilot* were subordinate directly to the *Folksrat.* The details of the *kehila* organization, as well the relationships between the *kehila* council, district council, and the *Folksrat,* were to be determined by a Jewish Constituent Convention.[148]

Yiddish was to be the official language of the Jewish people in Poland and could be used in general government institutions, in courts, and in administrative and municipal institutions in municipalities wherever Jews compose no less than 25 per cent of the overall population. It was to be the language of state-supported Jewish primary schools, although Jewish private schools with other languages of instruction could be founded. Should a law be instituted recognizing Sunday as the official day of rest from commerce and labour, Sabbath-observant Jews were to be be excluded from this provision.[149]

Specific points of the program were adumbrated in subsequent issues of *Dos folk*. The formation of a Jewish national curia, without whose consent no law affecting the interests of a national minority was to be confirmed, was intended to insure proportional representation in the Polish government and support for Yiddish as *the* national language of the Jews. The program presupposed the existence of the Jews as a 'national cultural unity' indigenous to Poland after centuries of residence but conceded the insufficiency of an anthropological or cultural-historical definition of Jewishness. To satisfy the need to define membership in the Jewish nation, the non-*Halachic* axiom, 'He who rejects idolatry is a Jew' (*kol ha-kofer be-avoda zara nikra yehudi*, Babylonian Talmud, Tractate Megilah 16a) was set forth with the elaboration that 'to the Jewish people belongs every Jew as long as he has not declared through a public act (i.e., conversion) that he is leaving the collective.'[150] The question of children born to non-Jewish mothers and Jewish fathers was never discussed in the Folkist press, presumably because Jewish-Polish intermarriage was not a relevant concern in this period (without civil marriage) of high Jewish endogamy.

Seeking to appeal to religious Jews for whom the idea of secular nationalism was unpalatable, Zeitlin argued in *Moment* that the Jews existed as a nation in Egypt even prior to divine revelation and that their cultural, historical, and biological, as well as religious, particularity had been shaped by a tradition of 'national separation.'[151] Further, he sought to reassure them that, contrary to the reports of *Dos yidishe vort*, the organ of the Agudah, Jewish nationalists are not hostile to the Jewish religion even if personally non-observant.[152] On the contrary, he warned Hasidic voters that they were being misled by leaders who collaborated with the Assimilationists. The Assimilationists were wholly alienated from Judaism and dedicated to its eradication, argued Zeitlin, as evidenced by their opposition to Jewish schools and the disparaging remarks made by certain Assimilationist leaders at the expense of the Talmud and traditional Jewish dress.[153] The Agudah sinned against God by seeking to separate Orthodox Jews from all other Jews and serving as the tool of the Assimilationist *kehila* leadership.[154] Prylucki went even further to condemn the existence of a specifically religious party (although not of religious leaders as members of general parties), for it meant, he maintained, to assert the hegemony of the clergy over the masses: 'Clergy does not have the right to speak for the people other than in religious matters, not on social, economic, and general political questions.'[155]

In practical terms, language served in Folkist theory as the most salient marker of national belonging despite the recognition that language is not a genetically transferable trait but must be transmitted and cultivated through education and society. Membership in the Jewish nation was to be determined by a language registry (*metrike*), allowing an individual to choose his or her national affiliation by choosing his or her (preferred) language. Ideally, this would permit 'true' Jewish leaders to wrest control of the *kehila* from the hands of the Polish-speaking Assimilationists, who would necessarily be excluded from the *kehila*.[156]

The Yiddish-language school, the cornerstone of national-cultural autonomy, would be funded with allocations from the government budget entrusted into the hands a Jewish School Board. The school would assure the future of the language at the same time that it educated children in the language most natural to the vast majority of them. Hence, for the Folkists, the Yiddish language was a value in itself and not merely an instrument to a political or economic end, as in the philosophy of the Zionists and Bund. Hebrew, the Jews' historical national language, could not aid in attaining Jewish national recognition because it was not a living element of Jewish life; it could only endanger the Jewish national cause to claim Hebrew as the national language in a public forum when only Yiddish (assuming the widespread nationalist formula of the day 'one people, one language' and, by implication, 'multiple languages, multiple peoples') was recognized by the state. The Folksparty did not discourage the study and dissemination of Hebrew, however, which it honoured as playing an important role in Jewish religious life and as the language of vast Jewish cultural treasures. Its use and cultivation was an internal Jewish matter whose discussion was to be excluded from the general political arena.[157]

The Folkists clung to the third paragraph of the German Ordinance of November 1916, according to which the *kehila* was to be responsible for the education of Jewish youth and philanthropic work. Although the ordinance specifically failed to recognize the Jews as a national body in Poland, the Folkists believed that these two areas of activity could be expanded and exploited beyond the fulfilment of purely religious needs. Even before the attainment of autonomy, all Jewish educational and cultural institutions were to pass into the hands of the *kehila*, which would open a network of kindergartens, elementary, middle, and advanced, and vocational schools in addition to adult education programs, popular universities, libraries, theatres, and museums – all in Yiddish. The *kehila* would also assist in the development of Jewish arts and science. All existing synagogues and *khadorim* were to fall under its purview and to be kept in conformity with established hygienic and aesthetic standards. Similarly, all charitable and public health institutions, including soup kitchens, hospitals, homes for deprived children and for the handicapped, bathhouses and *mikves*, were to be centralized under its authority and regulated. Under its roof would also be housed programs to improve Jewish economic conditions: an association of Jewish merchants and artisans, credit unions, co-operative and professional guidance, and an employment bureau.

Since the *kehila* was meant to function essentially as a government in miniature, the party, like the Zionists, placed a premium on 'conquering' the *kehila* in upcoming elections. Its popularly elected managing board was to cease functioning as the private domain of a handful of aristocratically entitled Assimilationists and their Orthodox cronies and to become truly accountable to the Jewish masses. The party campaigned heavily in 1918 and possessed the support of much of the Warsaw Artisans' Association, which did not create its own list for the democratic *kehila* elections scheduled for late 1918.[158] The elections were, in any case, postponed over the protests by Jewish nationalist parties until 1920, thereby permitting the pre-war *kehila* board to preserve its office.[159]

The pro-Zionist *Der haynt* mocked the Folkists, men who had until recently identified as Zionists and were careful to criticize Zionist leaders but not ideals, for arrogating the title of exclusive bourgeois champions of Jewish national rights as if they had themselves invented the doctrine of national cultural autonomy. It countered Folkist accusations that the Zionist movement was in principle hostile to national cultural autonomy in the Diaspora and to Yiddish (although this may be, it conceded, the position of individual Zionists) by asserting the role of Zionism in the development of Yiddish language and literature (e.g., the pioneering Yiddish periodical *Der yud*, the Jew).[160] *Der haynt* attributed the Folkists' victory to an 'accidentally unnatural and sadly confused situation that arose in the last electoral campaign' and sought to convince readers that Folkist political and cultural demands were meaningless when the Jews still lacked officially recognized institutions of self-government. Of primary importance to the Folkists, it commented, was a language question that could be actualized only in the case of an obligatory elementary school. Yet, no public, only private Hebrew and Yiddish schools existed, and the struggle for a Jewish School Board was yet to be won. (The only public schools in Jewish hands were those under the authority of the *kehila.*) Moreover, the entire language question – Yiddish, Hebrew, or Polish – was an internal Jewish matter that could not be resolved in the City Council. To use mother tongue or vernacular as the criterion of national belonging was considered to be a great error, for it would necessarily exclude many from membership in the Jewish nation, including some prominent Folkists – likely a reference to Hirschhorn, who commonly gave party talks in Polish.[161]

On the whole, the Zionists sought to convey the impression that the Folksparty represented merely a defection from Zionism, one fraught with contradictions, impotent, and fatally incapable of bringing any new ideas to the public. With the announcement in November 1917 of the British-issued Balfour Declaration recognizing the Jews' right to a 'national homeland in Palestine,' the Zionist movement gained an important degree of credibility among Polish Jews. Yatskan solemnly affirmed his Zionist loyalty in *Der haynt* and the paper became an independent Zionist organ.[162]

The Bundist *Lebnsfragn,* which first became legal during the German occupation, regarded the emergence and crystallization process of the Folksparty with curious amusement. It was ultimately sceptical, though, of the party's chances to draw a mass following and to represent a real force in Jewish politics. It likened the Folkists to generals in search of an army and recognized the debt owed in its victory to Prylucki's personal ambitions and popularity, as well as to the tactical error made by the Zionists in the City Council elections. Characteristic of the Folkists, it claimed, was that their organization was launched by the Writers' and Journalists' Association, an 'association of ineffectual intellectuals' (*nebekhdike inteligentishe gezelshaft*). Its founders, all Zionists (Prylucki, it reminded readers, was formally aligned with the left wing of proletarian Zionism), were loath to attack the ideals of Zionism, which they still revered, and contradicted each other in their justifications of the party's existence after having fulfilled the original goal of 'saving Jewish honour' in the elections. They also, it was argued, portrayed themselves as progressive radical democrats although they venerated Jewish religion and tradition. In short, the Bund reproached the Folksparty with a vague platform and reluctance to take a clear oppositional stance vis-à-vis other Jewish parties: 'A young party must be convinced of its rectitude and that it alone is correct; otherwise, voters will ask why it needed to be formed.'

It mockingly characterized the party's hesitance to alienate any segment of the population as a reflection of the Jewish bourgeoisie's discomfort with conflict.[163]

The Folkists, in turn, condemned the Bund for refusing to cooperate with bourgeois democratic parties, even on the issue of the secular Yiddish school, where much room existed for collaboration. Meanwhile, from Polish socialists, Hirschhorn argued, even those infected with chauvinism and antisemitism to a lesser degree than the Polish bourgeoisie, no support could be expected for 'Jewish interests.' Neither would the acculturated Jewish middle and *grande bourgeoisie* (whose economic interests were tied to markets in Russia and Germany) nor a large part of the Jewish intelligentsia sympathize with Jewish nationalism. Thus, the entire struggle for national and cultural rights was effectively left in the hands of the poor classes – the petite bourgeoisie and the proletariat – between which the Bund promoted struggle.[164]

Culture Congress

In a demonstration of initiative and purpose, the Folkists convened in March 1917 'the first Jewish Culture Congress.' Its purpose was to 'formulate our cultural ideals' and 'to provide leadership and orientation to various independent cultural efforts and to provide material support for the struggle' on behalf of Yiddish culture in the German-occupied zone. Officially, the three-day conference was non-partisan and its organizers requested that all cultural organizations positively inclined towards Yiddish and Jewish nationalism – libraries, educational associations, school committees, choirs, art associations, and so on – in Warsaw and the provinces send three delegates each.[165] The conference was, however, hastily announced in *Der moment.* Cultural organizations were given twenty-four hours to register their willingness to attend and no travel funds were available from the organizers. Further, elected conference officers were almost exclusively Folkists: Noah Prylucki (chairman), H.D. Nomberg (vice-chairman), Sh. Stupnicki (vice-chairman), Lazar Kahan (secretary), plus some provincial delegates. Representatives of left-oriented organizations, including the Warsaw Teachers' Association, protested the hurried convening of the conference and that no invitations had been sent specifically to either the Bund or the Zionists, making the event essentially a Folkist party congress. Delegates of the Poale Zion–founded Workers' Homes and the Educational Association for Jewish Workers left the Congress or refused to recognize it as more than a 'pre-conference' because it was not considered representative of all nationalist orientations in Polish Jewry.[166]

The Congress was held on the premises of the Warsaw Association of Travelling Salesmen. The Congress decorations themselves testified to the ideological pedigrees and inclinations of those present, who had often only recently left other parties. An honour guard was provided by the Jewish National Students Organization, and the speakers' podium was decorated in blue and white, the Jewish national colours associated with Zionism. Upon the podium hung a garlanded picture of Y.L. Peretz (who had died in 1915), the idol of the Folkist movement despite onetime socialist sympathies. The first session of the conference was opened on 26 March 1917 with a speech by Noah Prylucki emphasizing the need for future-directed cultural work precisely in a time of such great misery and material want: 'Culture is very important for us. It replaces a land and other national possessions of other peoples. Culture is our most distinguishing mark, the strongest wall that protects us from downfall. It is our most powerful means for struggle in this sad time.'[167]

About 150 delegates representing largely pro-Folkist organizations – such as the Writers' and Journalists' Association, *Ha-zomir*, the *Folkshoyz* (People's House, the Folkist youth centre), the Artisan Club, and various educational and artistic societies – heard addresses by Prylucki, Nomberg, the *Haynt* writer Nosn Shvalbe, Efron, Kahan, and others. The chief subject of debate was the issue of the Yiddish school, although resolutions were also adopted concerning the need to foster Yiddish culture in general, both organizationally and materially, through the creation of committees for Yiddish theatre, literature, popular publishing, folklore and folk-music collection, and provincial libraries. The need was also recognized to treat Yiddish-language research and the popularization of its results as a 'national task' and to establish both a Yiddish dramatics academy and a national museum of European Jewish antiquities. Delegates variously indicated the need to correct the widespread notion that an individual who speaks only Yiddish cannot be an intellectual and to draw the Jewish intelligentsia to read Yiddish literature in order to bring it closer to the masses – a strategy that had achieved a degree of success among Russian-Jewish intellectuals.

Councilman Efron delivered a speech emphasizing the need to include Jewish traditions and the Hebrew language in the Yiddish school's curriculum. In the debates following Efron's address, Nomberg bemoaned the Jews' lack of preparation for national cultural autonomy as evidenced by the absence of accord concerning the nature and content of the proposed Jewish national school. He objected to the partisan nature of Jewish education, reflected in the existence of three school organizations, and insisted upon the importance of vocational education, the Hebrew language, and the Jewish religion in a future unified school curriculum. His sentiments were echoed by the artisan leader Chaim Rasner and others. In keeping with his previously enunciated position, Zeitlin called for the reform, although not the abandonment, of the *kheyder* and the necessity of Torah and *loshn-koydesh* as the foundations of a Jewish education. He deplored the condition of Hebrew literacy and writing ability in Poland in comparison with his native *Lite*, a region renowned for its Jewish scholarly tradition.

A resolution was adopted almost unanimously foreseeing the establishment of a democratically elected Jewish school board to create and administer Yiddish elementary schools, Fröbel courses, a teachers' seminary, vocational instruction, and a school organization for all of Poland. Although a majority supported the position that Hebrew instruction be obligatory in the schools, it was decided to entrust a special commission with details of the school except the matter of Hebrew.[168]

Despite continuing its jibes at Noah Prylucki and the Folksparty, *Der haynt* took the conference seriously enough to cover its daily activity.[169] It foresaw no practical results arising from its proceedings because of what it described as the preponderance of young, intellectually immature cultural activists mainly from Warsaw and its suburb Praga upon whom the proposed cultural work was dependent.[170] Rather than simply denounce the conference organizers as heretics, the ultraorthodox *Dos yidishe vort* (No. 48, 1917), whose editors were former members of the staff of *Der haynt*, echoed Yatskan's criticism of the Congress as a meeting of a small Yiddishist party to which were not invited representatives of respected workers' cultural institutions.[171] The Bund was not represented at the Congress but its leading figure Vladimir Medem attended as a reporter and deplored the haste with which the Congress had been convened and the poverty of ideas expressed by many of its speakers. Although he dismissed it as a narrow party conference and hardly the historical moment which the title 'First Jewish Culture Congress' implies, he recognized that the Folkists could play an important role in the 'Jewish Renaissance': 'Only they can bring a new life to the petit bourgeois mass.'[172]

In response to detractors, Prylucki defended the Congress at a party meeting the following month: rapid organization without squandering precious time on all manner of pre-conferences was necessary in order to demonstrate interest in Yiddish culture and to assert the claim for

Jewish national cultural autonomy in the future Poland at a crucial juncture when the opponents of Jewish nationalism refused to accept Jewish nationhood because of the alleged non-existence of a Yiddish language and literature. In contrast with the Poles who, led by their elders, had been laying the cultural groundwork for their national independence (in the form of schools, books, etc.) since the beginning of the war, the Jews had to rely on their youth to build their culture since the older generation was not active in Yiddish cultural work. The conference, he maintained, had successfully identified the Jews' cultural needs in order that they may be fulfilled.[173]

Individual Folkists continued to flesh out their at times divergent positions, above all on cultural issues, following the conference. Hillel Zeitlin, much of whose popular appeal lay in his fusion of traditional religiosity and secular nationalism, deplored the disappearance of 'ordinary Jews' (*stam yidn*) in Warsaw – Jews who identify simply as Jews – and the province's imitation of the city in all matters, including atomization into mutually hostile political factions. He saw Yiddish schools where *loshn-koydesh* and, more importantly, Torah were taught as the only viable means to combat 'assimilation' and the decline in morals and religious textual knowledge among children. Moreover, teaching children in any language other than Yiddish was a sure way to alienate them from their home environment, to make them linguistically and culturally estranged like the upper bourgeoisie.[174]

He cautioned that a *kheyder* and *yeshiva* made Polish 'in language and in spirit' would necessarily close eventually: neither are the *melamdim* equipped to teach Jewish subjects in Polish, nor does Polish possess the specialized vocabulary for Jewish study which Yiddish has forged over generations.[175] While defending Yiddishists from accusations that they are principled opponents of Polish, Hebrew, and *khadorim*, he made clear, however, that he did not belong ideologically to their camp: 'I am not a Yiddishist and hate all "isms" but do not want to see my brethren deprived of civil and national rights and their children estranged. Therefore, I support the "Folksgrupe" and side with the Yiddishists even though I disagree with them as to the quantity and purpose of teaching *loshn-koydesh.*'[176] Zeitlin identified sufficiently with ill-defined (at least in the matter of Hebrew) Yiddishist ideology, though, to collaborate with journalistic colleagues on behalf of Yiddishist goals, such as work to standardize the language and to expand the range of Yiddish secular and educational publications. Thus, together with Stupnicki, he co-edited in 1917 *The First Yiddish Encyclopaedic Dictionary*, a one-volume work compiled by a team of *Moment* writers. The reference work, which the publisher describes as a national necessity for all European peoples,[177] was intended both to familiarize Yiddish speakers with concepts from various disciplines in science and the humanities and, in Zeitlin's words, 'as an attempt to create a degree of uniformity and wholeness in the sense of enriching and expanding the Yiddish language.'[178]

His colleague Samuel Hirschhorn, himself the product of a Polish-language education who did not begin his literary activity in Yiddish until 1916, assumed a very different stance. Unlike Prylucki or Zeitlin, who were incapable of conceiving of a viable Jewish future in Polish, he advocated a more flexible position on the school language issue as a result of his more nuanced understanding of 'assimilation.' Accustomed to lecturing and writing in Polish, he was both unwilling to exclude polonized Jews from the Jewish nation for their linguistic peccadillo and more positively inclined towards Modern Hebrew. Instead, he urged the gradual 'nationalization' of acculturated Jews:

> It is wrong to separate Jews into Assimilationists and nationalist Jews in practical life. Few are the Jews with one foot in the church, waiting for a 'fanatical' rich grandmother to bequeath money. Most 'Assimilationists' disagree with nationalists in points or are simply poorly informed about the essence of Jewish nationalism.
>
> Most 'Assimilationists' may oppose Hebrew or Yiddish as the language of instruction or find too much Hebrew or Judaic Studies in the curriculum but usually want the child to know Jewish history, have some education in Hebrew language, and to be raised in a religious spirit, although without excess fanaticism. Nationalization of the half-assimilated cannot be accomplished at once or they will not return and we will lose them entirely.

Hirschhorn understood, although he did not sympathize with, the concern that motivated the Polish-speaking Jewish intelligentsia to send its children to privately funded Polish schools devoid of Jewish content rather than to Polish-Jewish schools. It believed that its children would learn more there and be preserved from the danger of learning Polish inadequately or of acquiring a socially stigmatizing Yiddish accent. He cast the lion's share of responsibility for this situation on Jewish mothers, to whom Hirschhorn attributes the greatest authority in educational decisions and whom he bitterly blames for valuing fads and foreign ways over Jewish culture. The popularity of Polish schools among Jewish parents must be combated by popularizing Jewish-Polish schools financed by the *kehila* in ever broader circles of parents. The future *kehila,* it was argued, was going to need to operate three types of schools: Polish-language schools for the children of 'half-assimilated' classes, Hebrew- or Yiddish-language schools for the children of the 'fully national' (in the form of currently existing institutions), and secondary schools with either Hebrew or Yiddish as the language of instruction.[179]

To celebrate the founding of the *Shul- un folksbildung-fareyn,* Noah Prylucki publicized in *Moment* the statutes and mission of the organization, describing it as a surrogate for a Jewish state in matters of education. He foresaw an economic struggle for the Jews in independent Poland, one in which education would be 'one of the most powerful means in the struggle for existence,' and called upon Jews to exploit their influence in cities where they controlled the majority of the City Council to open additional schools at municipal expense. Elsewhere Jews would have to use their own monies to open as many schools, teachers' seminaries, courses for adults, textbook publishing houses, etc. as possible.[180]

In opposition to his colleagues Zeitlin and Hirschhorn, who emphasized educational content and attributed to language a secondary, albeit essential, role, Prylucki made all other elements of the school subordinate to the language question. Instruction in the national language, he argued, necessarily imparts the 'national spirit' and renders superfluous much national content in the curriculum. Not only did he oppose any other language as the primary language of Jewish schools, but he warned that education in the 'national spirit' but in a 'foreign tongue' would likely yield the undesirable by-product of national chauvinism.[181] Still worse, without a national school of uniform curriculum, the Jewish elite would follow the example of the Ukrainians, whose most creative talents, he claimed, adopted Russian, German, or Polish.[182] Interestingly, despite his public disparagement of the use of Polish among Jews, together with H.D. Nomberg, he did not shy away from the practical task of agitating in the Polish-language, general Jewish nationalist paper *Głos Żydowski,* which published from 1917 until the end of the First World War.[183]

The very nature of the Folksparty and whose interests it represented remained a subject of contention among its members in its first two years of activity. By early February 1918, it was recognized that internal differences would likely soon result in a party split between 'more religious and conservative' and 'more democratic and folks-socialist' elements.

While Hillel Zeitlin sought to make the party open to as wide an audience as possible, Lazar Kahan argued the opposite position: Jewish workers were organized and represented by socialist parties but not enough political parties existed to represent the Jewish middle class, which made up as much as 80 per cent of Polish Jewry and was in great measure politically apathetic. The Folksparty existed for the benefit of the petite bourgeoisie and all who subscribed to its platform, although collaboration with other parties was possible through inter-party commissions.[184]

The Zionist N. Shvalbe, on the contrary, protested Stupnicki's disparagement of socialism and Prylucki's allegiance to exclusively petit bourgeois interests after he had promised to defend the interests of the working masses too during his City Council campaign. Shvalbe expressed admiration for the socialist elements active in the Folksparty that had formed early that year in Russia, where, he argued, the petite bourgeoisie was inclined to socialism thanks to the revolutionary climate of the time.[185]

The significance of religion for the Jewish nation was also a source of division. No position was taken on religious observance, leaving it, as the Bund and Zionists did, a matter of personal concern.[186] Zeitlin's insistence upon the Jewish religion as the basis of Jewish nationalism was assailed by Karlinius (the *Moment* writer Ber Karlinsky), who rejected religious dogma as an essential component of nationalism and defended the works of atheistic and secular Jewish artists as important contributions to Jewish culture.[187] Zeitlin's position was provided ideological backing by Stupnicki and Hirschhorn, although neither was a traditionally observant Jew. Stupnicki likened Jewish nationalism (for which he uses the Modern Hebrew neologism *leumiyut*) and religion (*dat*) to body and soul, describing them as elements that grow together and are incapable of independent existence. He deemed religion, however, the more powerful force and asserted that without the influence of Jewish scripture, Jews will eventually cease to exist as a collective. Instead, individuals will look elsewhere to satisfy their spiritual needs. From a practical standpoint, however, he recognized the impossibility of an objective definition of Jewishness (*Yidishkeyt*) and viewed conversion as the only clear rupture with the Jewish people.[188]

Hirschhorn similarly viewed the Jewish religion as thoroughly 'national' and sufficient in itself to earn the Jews recognition as a people; indeed, religion is the only element of the manifold criteria (language, land, culture, etc.) defining a nation that is shared by all Jews. While a Jew can theoretically exist as a Jew without religion, the other national traits are not sufficiently strong to preserve his Jewish identity in the long run. Conversion or a declaration of *Konfessionslosigkeit* (i.e., formal withdrawal from a religious community), he submitted, in actuality would lead to the severing of bonds with Jewish life. By the same token, he maintained, it is impossible to be religious and not a nationalist – a critique of the position of the Agudah.[189]

Poland Resurrected

As a concrete step towards Polish independence, the German and Austrian emperors established a conservative, three-man Council of Regency in September 1917. The Council created both an executive branch and in February 1918 a legislative organ, the Council of State, which consisted partly of members elected by municipalities and district assemblies and partly by direct appointments by the Council of Regency. Since the eleven Polish councilmen representing the sixth curia in the Warsaw City Council refused to participate in selecting a member of an undemocratically elected Council of State, the remaining Jewish councilmen had complete power to choose a representative. Expressing reservations regarding the unrepresentative nature of the Council of State, Prylucki accepted the mandate with the full support of the other City Councilmen, including the Zionist Ayznberg. He was joined by an Assimilationist sent by another Warsaw curia and a Zionist elected by the municipality of Łódź. The Council of Regency directly appointed two members of the Agudah and two Assimilationists in addition to an *ex officio* member of the Council of State to represent the rabbinate, Rabbi Abraham Zwi Perlmutter of Warsaw.[190]

The Council of State, which solemnly opened on 22 June 1918, was short-lived; it adjourned for recess on 31 July and never reconvened since the end of the war was at hand. During its brief existence, Prylucki justified his participation as necessary to hinder representatives who were not popularly elected from speaking on behalf of Polish Jewry. He also called upon the Council of State as a first and final act to convene elections for a democratic constituent assembly for all of Poland before dissolving itself. Since this call went unheeded, he put his education as a lawyer to good stead by continuing to combat discriminatory measures against Jews in addition to championing the ideal of national-cultural autonomy and participating in general economic discussions. Again, he was most active on the subject of schooling, arguing vociferously against both Polish and Jewish opponents of Yiddish as the language of Jewish schools and, implicitly, Jewish national recognition.[191]

Although the political efforts of Prylucki and his Folkist colleagues on behalf of the Yiddish school – the party's chief concrete issue – met with little success in organs of the nascent Polish state from 1916 to 1918, the value of their organizational and propaganda work on behalf of the Yiddish secular school is not to be underestimated. Working together with the Bund, Poale Zion, and the Fareynikte, they played the leading role in establishing a legal, material, and organizational basis for an interwar network of schools – one of the few domains of cooperation between Jewish socialists and the 'democratic intelligentsia.' By the close of 1917 twelve Yiddish elementary schools and kindergartens were active in Warsaw: four schools run by various institutions under the supervision of the Central Dinezon School Committee, five belonging to Prylucki and Nomberg's *Yidishe shul- un folksbildung fareyn* and affiliated with the Dinezon schools, one Bundist kindergarten, and two additional schools with kindergartens established by the Poale Zionist *Arbeter-heym.*[192]

While the party's activity was centred in Warsaw, Folkist candidates were elected by 1917 to city councils in Będzin, Kaluszyn, Węgrów, Rawa, and elsewhere. Folkist groups were also organized throughout the cities of the Polish province.[193] The party drew the support primarily of artisans and petty merchants, whose allegiance the Zionists also endeavoured to win, with its uncompromising and provocative defence of Jewish rights and through its energetic work to organize and politicize these elements. Its surprising success forced the Zionists to re-evaluate their strategy of cooperation with 'anti-national' elements. It also made clear to Zionists, many of whose older cadres feared the recognition of Yiddish would legitimize the Diaspora, the necessity of widely employing Yiddish in party activities in order to assume a leading role in Polish-Jewish life.[194]

Conclusion

Owing its birth to the unique conditions of the First World War, the Folksparty distinguished itself from other Yiddishist parties, such as the Bund and Poale Zion, chiefly through its resolute rejection of socialism and championing of the economic interests of the Jewish petite bourgeoisie. Further, as nationalists, the Folkists viewed the nation as a living organism, the desirability of whose preservation was unquestioned. They emphatically rejected the Bund's theoretical neutrality to Jewish acculturation and assimilation as long as it was not coerced. Folkism attempted to appeal mainly to the same mass of voters as did its chief rivals, the General Zionists – the petty merchants, shopkeepers, brokers, and artisans who composed the largest part of Polish Jewry. As Diaspora nationalists and Yiddishists, the Folkists naturally distanced themselves from Zionism and Hebraism through their refusal to regard mass Jewish settlement in Palestine and the establishment of a Jewish state there with Hebrew, a language spoken by a tiny minority of Jews worldwide, as its official language as anything other than a utopian dream born of the frustrations of discrimination and unfulfilled national aspirations in the Diaspora.

United by their official commitment to the party platform, however, individual Folkists were not necessarily in accord about these fundamental issues or even how to define the party's purpose and constituency. Further, while all Folkists championed Yiddish as the primary language of Jewish schooling and everyday life, their motivations and attitudes towards this and other languages were often quite disparate. This divergence is best illustrated by contrasting the personalities and perspectives of Hillel Zeitlin and Noah Prylucki, the two party activists articulating the most radical positions on language and education. Apart from their positions – one on behalf of aggressive monolingualism and a linguistic definition of membership in the Jewish nation, the other on behalf of an updated form of traditional diglossia along with religious practice – stood Samuel Hirschhorn, who was comfortable with the reality of a multilingual Jewish society and saw in religion the strongest element of Jewish identity despite his own personal lack of observance.

Regardless of these differences, Folkists in Poland exuded confidence in their future as a, if not the, leading party in Jewish political life. They cheered the formation of a party of identical name and similar platform in both Ukraine and Russia, to which it had no formal connection, as confirmation of the rectitude of Folkism in meeting the exigencies of contemporary life. The national-cultural autonomy granted Jews, Russians, Poles, and Ukrainians in neighbouring Ukraine – extremely short-lived and exceedingly difficult to implement in retrospect – was welcomed by the Folksparty in 1918 as a model for future political developments in Poland.[195]

Moreover, the Polish Folksparty's leader was virtually a celebrity. Although vilified by his political opponents, Noah Prylucki was tremendously popular among Warsaw Jews for his personal intercessions on their behalf before the government.[196] His name regularly appeared in the German-language *Warschauer Zeitung*'s coverage of affairs in the Warsaw City Council and the Council of State and his Polish-language oratory skills were respected by Jews and non-Jews alike. If we are to believe one of his admirers, some Poles, apparently not all too familiar with the name Piłsudksi, even joined popular cheering of the future leader of Poland in late 1918 with shouts of 'Prylucki, Prylucki.'[197]

The long-anticipated emergence of a new Polish state in November 1918 sounded the end of Jewish nationalists' dress rehearsal for the struggle for national-cultural autonomy. Noah Prylucki, the 'most popular Jew in Poland' at the time according to a contemporary observer,[198] was well positioned for leadership in what was eagerly anticipated as a new era in Polish-Jewish politics and culture.

chapter five

From Avant- to Arrière-garde: The Folksparty in Interwar Poland

Almost immediately following the outbreak of the German Revolution on 9 November 1918 and the subsequent disarming of German troops in Poland, a sovereign Poland was declared, with Marshall Józef Piłsudski as its provisional head of state and commander-in-chief. Primarily rural with a largely illiterate peasant majority, the reborn state was weighed down with the legacy of its eighteenth-century partitioning. Political, economic, cultural, and legal differences impeded the shaping of a unified country with a modernized economy and stable currency. Its leaders were for the most part fervent nationalists experienced in the struggle for Polish independence but little accustomed to the day-to-day affairs of managing a sovereign state with a substantial population of national minorities possessing their own nationalist hopes and ambitions. Throughout the interwar period, the problem of Poland's national minorities was both intensely resented and dreaded by much of the state's political leadership, who saw in it a dangerous challenge to the integrity of the infant state and to its identity as a nation-state. The question of the state's relations to its minorities remained a major issue in interwar politics distinct from, although frequently linked with, the host of internal problems and external menaces that befell the Second Polish Republic.[1]

Of the 21,176,717 individuals registered in the 1921 census, more than a third were not ethnically Polish. Ukrainians formed the largest minority group, followed by Jews, Byelorussians, and Germans. Concentrated in the *kresy*, the Slavic minorities, particularly the Ukrainians in East Galicia, possessed their own aspirations for autonomy or political independence and it was feared that they would look to the Ukrainian and Byelorussian Soviet republics for aid and inspiration. Similarly, the Germans of the western regions were suspected of conspiring to restore German rule. Poland's definitive borders in the interwar period were not

5.1 The Polish Republic in the Interwar Period, ca. 1930s. After two unsuccessful uprisings against Russian rule in the nineteenth century and more than a century after its territory was divided between neighbouring empires, Poland re-emerged as a sovereign state following the First World War. Interwar Poland was home to, in addition to a majority of ethnic Poles, a number of groups (above all Ukrainians, Byelorussians, Jews, and Germans) guaranteed collective rights for the maintenance of their cultures by the 1919 National Minorities Treaty. Its Jewish population was roughly three million (about 10% of the total population but usually a much larger proportion of urban populations), made it the largest Jewish community in non-communist Europe. A remarkable diversity of competing religious, linguistic, political, and economic ideologies characterized Jewish life in Poland in this period, and this diversity was reflected in the vast array of political parties and cultural institutions, both modern and traditional. (*Source: The YIVO Encyclopedia of Jews in Eastern Europe*)

settled until 1923 following extensive diplomatic manoeuvres and much bloodshed. In contrast with the Slavic and German minorities, the community of nearly three million Jews (as determined by religion) making up 10.5 per cent of the 1921 population lacked an ethnic homeland outside Poland to protect its interests.[2] Jewish nationalists looked eagerly to negotiations with the new state and the Paris Peace Conference of 1919 as an opportunity to secure guarantees for the protection of the Jews in Poland as a national minority.

During the war, the Yiddish language had made tremendous concrete gains, becoming a language of mass, supra-regional culture via the press, schools, theatre, and political parties. The Yiddishist movement seemed to be ascendant: Yiddishists had struggled for official recognition for Yiddish as a legitimate language and felt this had been achieved during the German occupation of Poland; now, they hoped to see this recognition implicitly extended into the international sphere and enshrined in the constitution of a sovereign Polish state. Further, a publicly funded Yiddish school system, the cornerstone of the Folkists' vision of national cultural autonomy, would provide the ideal opportunity for the implementation and diffusion of the kind of language reforms that Noah Prylucki and other Yiddishists had long contemplated.

Riding the crest of his popularity among the Jews of Warsaw, Prylucki ran twice successfully for a seat in the parliament of interwar Poland. The Folksparty's early electoral success, largely the result of the chaotic circumstances engendered by the war and its leader's charismatic appeal, would now be tested in new conditions. This chapter will survey Prylucki's activity in both the explicitly political realm and in the closely related areas of cultural and relief work as the conditions of life everywhere grew increasingly inhospitable to his ideals. While not intended as an exhaustive party history from 1918 to 1926, it seeks to account for the Folksparty's rapid decline following such an auspicious start. As will be seen, Prylucki's own uncompromising personality and zealous pursuit of the Folkist program – assets winning him support previously – now became liabilities contributing to the party's ultimate undoing. An analysis of the Folksparty's accomplishments and failings also reveals much about interwar Polish Jewry's changing cultural profile and concerns for the very future of Yiddish.

The 1919 Sejm Elections

Eager to secure the support of all segments of the population even prior to assuming his role as head of state, Piłsudski invited Jewish political leaders to confer with him regarding the responsibilities of Poland towards its Jewish citizens. Greatly alarmed by the widespread outburst of anti-Jewish violence (to be discussed below) accompanying the emergence of the new state, Jewish leaders could not have accorded greater urgency to such a meeting. Only the Bund boycotted it, refusing cooperation with a bourgeois government.

The Zionist position was expressed by Yitshak Grünbaum, who had recently returned from Russia, where he spent the war years, and assumed leadership of the Polish Zionist Federation in 1918. An accomplished journalist in Hebrew, Yiddish, Polish, and Russian, as well as a mesmerizing public speaker, he quickly proved a fitting adversary to his erstwhile colleague in the Zionist movement, Noah Prylucki.[3] Uncompromising in his pursuit of national demands in the Diaspora as well as favourably inclined towards Yiddish, Grünbaum recognized the error in his party's ways under Farbstein's leadership during the 1916 Warsaw City Council elections. Apart from asserting the Jews' loyalty to a free, united, and democratic Poland whose constitution would be established by a constituent parliament (Sejm), he seized the moment to make maximum demands for constitutionally guaranteed legal autonomy for the Jewish national minority under the authority of a government-recognized Secretariat for Jewish Affairs. Cultural autonomy would be administered by a Jewish National Council with representatives from all Jewish parties. Grünbaum's position was echoed in separate declarations by Noah Prylucki on behalf of the Folkists and also by the Poale Zion representative. The Agudah spoke of equal civil, although not national, rights for the Jews and emphasized the opportunity for unrestricted cultural and religious development. Piłsudski left the meeting with an accurate impression of internal Jewish division.[4]

Jewish parties could not arrive at a unified list in preparation for elections to Poland's inaugural or Constituent Sejm, whose purpose was to work out a constitution for the country, and viciously attacked each other in election propaganda. In Warsaw, where twenty-one electoral lists with a combined 268 candidates competed for sixteen Sejm mandates, nine distinct Jewish lists ran a total of seventy-seven candidates in elections held in late January 1919. The Folkists were particularly sensitive to an election law granting the right to vote exclusively to (a) those born in any of the Polish partitions included within Polish borders at the time of elections; (b) those born outside of Poland but of 'Polish nationality,' that is, ethnic Poles; (c) the wives of Polish citizens. The law effectively excluded all 'Litvaks,' including the party's Volhynian-born leader

Prylucki, and was consequently protested by Folkist, Zionist, and Orthodox leaders in separate memoranda until the government granted that no inhabitant of Poland, regardless of place of birth, would be denied the right to vote or run for office provided that his inclusion in voter lists was not protested by Polish citizens.[5] While satisfactory to Jewish parties for the time being, this clarification of the law would later be used against the Folkists.

Poor Jewish election turn-out and electoral gerrymandering to favour Polish candidates notwithstanding, the Folkists capitalized on their large popularity base in Warsaw to win 38.1 per cent of the Jewish vote there and two mandates to the Sejm. They also benefited from the Bund's boycott of the elections in Warsaw as Bundists preferred to support the Folkists over other Jewish Workers' parties as a strategy to weaken the Zionists. A self-proclaimed Temporary National Jewish Council consisting of pro-Zionist representatives from various cities and *shtetlekh* came in second place among Jewish voters, polling 24.8 per cent of Jewish votes and gaining one mandate in that city. It was followed by the Agudah with 17.8 per cent of the vote and no mandates. The Merchants' Organization, the Poles of Mosaic Confession, the Independents (Neo-Assimilationists), Poale Zion, and the Democratic List (a Folkist splinter group headed by Dr Y.H. Davidzon) each won less than 10 per cent of Jewish votes and received no mandates.[6]

The Folkists ran exclusively in formerly Russian areas of Poland and were unsuccessful in Łódź, where they polled only 4.1 per cent of Jewish voters, and elsewhere – evidence that popular support for them was limited to Warsaw, where their leadership and activity were concentrated. The Zionists picked up three additional mandates in Łódź, Będzin, and Kraków. The Agudah won seats in Łódź and Lublin, and a final Jewish mandate went to Poale Zion in Chełmno. Only forty-six of seventy voting districts participated in the elections because of a state of ongoing war or because political borders had not yet been fixed in the *kresy*. To preserve their neutrality in the conflict between the Poles and the Ukrainians, who struggled to prevent the Polish military from crushing the independent Ukrainian republic declared in East Galicia in 1918, Jewish parties abstained from elections in that region. Elections held somewhat later brought two additional Zionist victories in Białystok and Biała Podlaska. The final results of the Sejm elections yielded six mandates for the Temporary National Jewish Council (Grünbaum, Apolinary Hartglas, Dr Shloyme Weinzieher, Dr Ozjasz (Yehoshua) Thon, Dr Jerzy Rosenblatt, and Heshl Farbstein), two for the Agudah (Rabbis Perlmutter and Halperin), two for the Folkists (Noah Prylucki and Samuel Hirschhorn), and one for Poale Zion (the historian Ignacy [Yitshok] Schipper). Two Galician Jewish deputies (Dr Natan Loewenstein and Dr Steinhaus) were co-opted from the former Austrian Reichsrat without elections, thereby introducing the only Assimilationists in the Sejm. The Assimilationists excluded, the eleven popularly elected Jewish deputies made up 3 per cent of the Sejm despite that the Jews represented roughly 11 per cent of Poland's population according to the 1921 census.[7]

All in all, the Zionist-dominated Temporary National Jewish Council showed the greatest returns at the ballots, with 51.3 per cent of the vote going to Jewish parties. The Agudah followed in the distance with 21.4 per cent, the Folkists with 13 per cent, and Poale Zion with 6 per cent. A secular, nationalist Polish state favoured secular, nationalist parties among the Jews, too, for they were better equipped to utilize political institutions and the press than religious parties. To develop a mass following, the Orthodox needed to learn to imitate the tactics of secular politicians and achieved a great deal of success at this during the interwar period despite an inherent distaste for politics. The Agudah generally proved a distant second in strength to the Zionists with some exceptions, for example, Warsaw, where the Folkists were popular.[8] The Bund's meagre 3.7 per cent of the vote reflects the party's disorganized state at this time and the greater nationalist than socialist sympathies among conservative Polish Jews. The election results also effectively demonstrated the Assimilationists' lack of a power base and their political demise in the new democratic regime.[9]

Folkist strength was concentrated exclusively in the Polish capital and at the parliamentary but not the local level, where everyday concerns, often connected with religious life (to which Folkists were generally indifferent), were treated. In contrast, the Bund, together with Poale Zion, fared better in City Council elections, which were held at approximately the same time. The Agudah also proved far more successful in city and local *kehila* elections than at the Sejm level. Nonetheless, with the exception of Warsaw, where an alliance of the Agudah with the Central Organization of Jewish Merchants captured the largest proportion of Jewish votes (24.6%), the bourgeois Zionists generally captured pluralities, if not majorities. The Folkists (14.7% of Jewish votes) trailed slightly behind the Zionists (16.1%) and the Bund (17.1%) in Warsaw. In Łódź, the Zionists obtained 31.5 per cent of the Jewish vote, the Bund 25 per cent, the Orthodox and merchants 19.4 per cent, Poale Zion 14.3 per cent, and the Folkists a distant 4 per cent.[10] According to a poll covering

5.2 Jewish representatives in the first Sejm or Polish Parliament (1919). They include members of the Orthodox Agudat Yisrael (Agudah), Folkist, and Zionist parties: Rabbi Moyshe Eliyahu Halpern (Agudah), Noah Prylucki (Folksparty), Rabbi Avraham Tsevi Perlmutter (Agudah), Dr Salomon (Shloyme) Weinzieher, Yitshak Grünbaum (Zionist), Ozjasz (Yehoshua) Thon (Zionist), Dr Jerzy (Uri) Rosenblatt (Zionist), and Ignacy (Yitshok) Schipper (Poale Zion). (YIVO Institute, record 4063, frame 4320.01, 27852)

ninety-seven cities in 1920, there were 735 Jewish city councilmen, of whom 194 were Zionist, 78 Mizrachi, 68 Poale Zion, 64 Bund, 95 Agudah, and 12 Folkist.[11]

The Question of Jewish National Rights

In retrospect, the tone for negotiations concerning Jewish national rights in the Sejm was foreshadowed in a meeting about Polish-Jewish relations held on 20 February 1919 between the Prime Minister Ignacy Paderewski, a member of the Endecja, and the leaders of Jewish parliamentary factions. Prylucki presented a maximalist program: he demanded recognition of the Jews as a nation in Poland, the introduction of a Jewish curia in elections for all representative institutions, a guaranteed percentage of Jews participating in all state and communal offices, and the creation of state schools with Yiddish as their language of instruction. Grünbaum, whose demands were slightly more modest, sought national, and not merely religious, communal bodies for Jews and the fulfilment of national cultural autonomy. Paderewski rejected these demands on the grounds that the majority of Jews were Orthodox and therefore did not support Jewish nationalist aims. He also refused to recognize Yiddish as a language, stating that 'there is no Jewish language, rather a German jargon.' He made even clearer his opposition to these positions by menacingly announcing that were a Pole in America to speak from the podium as Prylucki had, that Pole would not escape with his life. The taunt underlined, of course, that Jews were not Poles in his eyes. Nor were they to be recognized as a nation either. 'The Jewish question,' he concluded, 'must be resolved in the spirit of the great Western democracies and America, that is, on the basis of equal rights for citizens ... no Polish government will agree to the Jewish nationalist program.'[12]

Similar attitudes were commonly voiced in the Constituent Sejm. Representatives of the Polish right openly hostile to the Jews predominated slightly alongside slightly lesser numbers of centre and left deputies. Apart from the three Jewish factions – the Temporary Jewish National Council (seven deputies), the Folkists (two deputies), and the Agudah (two deputies) – seven representatives of the German population, who joined the Sejm somewhat later, were the only voices present to speak in the name of the national minorities.

Despite intense electoral competition, the Agudah joined the Folkists and Zionists in the non-programmatic 'Free Union of Deputies of Jewish

Nationality,' which was recognized as one bloc according to the regulations of the Sejm. At the opening session on 24 February 1919, deputies of each of the ten parliamentary blocs proclaimed their loyalty to the state. At the first 'Jewish day' (day devoted to the discussion of issues affecting the Jews) the following week, both Prylucki and Grünbaum denounced anti-Jewish violence and called for recognition of the Jews as a national minority entitled to cultural autonomy and not merely as a religious group as made explicit by the wartime German ordinance still in effect. Grünbaum added to his remarks a call for the recognition of Jewish aspirations in Palestine whereas Prylucki emphasized cultural expression in the form of Yiddish schools. Rabbi Perlmutter, under the influence of the radical slogans of Jewish nationalists, issued an appeal uncharacteristic of the Agudah for not merely religious autonomy, but also for cultural autonomy with state subsidies for Jewish social and cultural institutions. Considering anathema the notion of a secularized *kehila* as championed by Jewish nationalists and socialists, Perlmutter also insisted upon the need for a state-supervised *kehila* built upon religious tradition. The Galician Assimilationist Loewenstein struck a conciliatory tone in his words and, as may be expected, opposed Jewish nationalist demands as re-enforcing the separation between Polish Christians and Jews. Not indifferent to the grave situation facing Jews, however, he did not fail to evoke murderous violence and the failure of the state to recognize the sacrifices of its Jewish citizens on its behalf as factors weakening the Assimilationist ideal among Jews. The Polish right, hostile to Poland becoming what it denounced as a minority 'nationalities' state' instead of a Polish 'nation-state,' was unwilling to regard the Jews as a national minority meriting autonomy, especially when they possessed no such status in Western lands. Polish socialists outright rejected minority rights for groups not concentrated upon their own territory and were disinclined to recognize Yiddish as a language, much less so a national language.[13]

The Activity of Jewish Parties in the Constituent Sejm: An Overview

Despite the declaration of equal political and civil rights for all citizens regardless of descent, religion, or nationality at the founding of the Polish state, many restrictions remained on Jews from the partition period. Polish legal scholars and politicians necessarily coped with the unification of four distinct legal traditions, a task so difficult that it still was not completed by 1939.[14] While most restrictions were lifted in the former

German and Austrian lands (with the exception of the ban on the use of Hebrew or Yiddish on official documents in Galicia), a number of legal handicaps remained in effect in former Russian territory: for example, residence and property-owning restrictions, impairments in the fulfilment of certain functions in local government, and the ban on the use of Yiddish and Hebrew in legal documents. Jews also experienced systematic discrimination in hiring for civil service and government jobs and in promotion to officer ranks in the army. They suffered economic discrimination in the form of mandatory Sunday rest and preference granted to Poles in obtaining various government concessions, such as those for alcohol and tobacco.[15] As autonomous institutions, universities also had their own policies to reduce the number of Jewish students despite that no *numerus clausus* formally existed.[16]

Because the Sejm was willing to recognize only one member of the Jewish bloc to speak in its name on a given issue – a strategy that Prylucki identified as meant to restrict Jewish participation and which he used to buttress his claim that only a Jewish national curia could put an end to discrimination of the Jews[17] – conflicts frequently occurred even within the same Jewish fraction as to which topics would be discussed and by whom. The Jews, along with the Germans, were also effectively excluded from the influential Assembly of Elders, in which it was decided after election results had already been registered to limit membership to blocs with a minimum of twelve deputies – a number the Jews could not muster. The Assembly of Elders exceeded all other Sejm councils in importance because it determined the Sejm's activity. Jewish deputies were additionally hampered by a regulation requiring a minimum of fifteen signatures for any proposal to be discussed on the Sejm floor, making them generally reliant upon the support (or at least sympathy) of the Polish left in order to bring any specifically Jewish issue to the floor.[18]

In general, Jewish nationalists sided with the Polish left, a strategy which actually furnished the Endecja ammunition against the left and caused progressive Poles to distance themselves from the Jews for fear of losing popular support among voters inclined towards antisemitic feelings.[19] An alliance between Jewish parties and Polish socialists was also not entirely comfortable because Jewish parties were in the main not inclined towards socialism and Polish socialists generally had little interest in specifically Jewish issues.[20]

In contrast with the secular Jewish nationalists, the Agudah pursued an independent course and preferred a policy of accommodation and traditional *shtadlanut*, or intercessory politics based upon the strength of individual personalities and interpersonal relationships, to the 'new Jewish politics' of confrontation and militant defence of Jewish rights advocated by their political rivals. Agudah deputies were not always fluent in Polish and were generally overshadowed in their oratorical talents by the more acculturated and better educated secular nationalists. However, the Agudah also did not face the same opposition from the government as the Zionists and Folkists because it demanded less and chiefly concerned itself with religious interests.[21]

Their vehement denunciations of *shtadlanut* as craven and undignified notwithstanding, Zionists and Folkists alike resorted to intercessory politics on an almost daily basis too. They did so without ceasing to condemn the Agudah's minimalist and moderate stance.[22] Prylucki even 'apologized' to *Moment's* readers for personally intervening on behalf of falsely accused Jewish arrestees rather than pursuing a parliamentary route to clear them of guilt. He explained that interpellations, proposals, and newspaper articles were generally ineffectual, especially in urgent cases of life and death. Jewish deputies, he regretted, could scarcely agree among themselves, let alone muster the support of other parties to obtain the requisite number of signatures (30 for an urgent proposal, 15 for an interpellation) to bring motions to parliamentary discussion. 'The man of the people [*folksmentsh*] will cease going to the Jewish politician who does not employ *shtadlanut*,' he observed, because he does not believe him capable of accomplishing anything otherwise.[23]

Jewish deputies made their support for each government conditional on its relationship to the Jews and entered the parliamentary opposition whenever dissatisfied with the new premier's attention – or lack thereof – to Jewish concerns.[24] Their activity in the Constituent Sejm was headed by the Temporary National Jewish Council, whose offices throughout the country collected and published documentary material, as well as conducted interviews with civilians and officials, to assist its deputies in combating offences against Jews. The much younger and less established Folksparty employed similar methods, although on a smaller scale.

To circumvent the censor, which frequently confiscated newspapers for printing materials deemed counter to the interests of the state, Jewish deputies more than any other deputies availed themselves of interpellations as an opportunity to exploit parliamentary immunity to read aloud banned articles. Because parliamentary proceedings were published verbatim in the press, this technique enabled sensitive information to escape censorship. Members of the Jewish bloc were regularly shouted down and most of their interpellations received no response, however.[25] Defence against insults and allegations – often of disloyalty to the state and of efforts to undermine it domestically and abroad – made by the Polish right against Jewish deputies (and Jews in general) took much time and yielded meagre results. Prylucki and Grünbaum, in particular, drew attacks. Jewish deputies found their opportunities to protest personal affronts and to bring attention to social and individual concerns restricted by the closing of speakers' lists to them. Already in the second session of the Sejm, for example, Prylucki and Grünbaum were prevented from expressing themselves concerning a pogrom in Dąbrowic Górnicza and Hirschhorn from addressing the question of universal military service.[26]

The greatest number of interpellations was brought by Jewish deputies reacting to the wave of anti-Jewish violence immediately following declarations of independence in Poland and, to a lesser extent, throughout Eastern Europe.[27] Demands for national minority rights only exacerbated Polish suspicions of disloyalty already heightened by anti-Bolshevik furor as Poland fought to maintain its independence and for control of disputed territories on its eastern border in the Polish–Soviet War of 1919–21. The proclamations of Jewish deputies hailing an independent Poland were of no use in dispelling this fear. The first major pogrom occurred in Lwów in November 1918, when the city was captured from the Ukrainians, and it was followed by brutalities in a number of cities in Galicia and elsewhere, including Kielce and Chrzanów. Anti-Jewish excesses were routinely downplayed or denied by Poles, who were angered by the negative international attention drawn to Poland by Jewish reports abroad. The Endeks even alleged that the Jews had themselves instigated them with acts of violence directed against the Polish military.[28] Claiming that Jews had consistently betrayed Poland throughout its history, the Endek daily *Gazeta Warszawska* quipped, 'Bismarck, sneeringly discussing the weaknesses of Poland's position, said, "Pourquoi Dieu aurait-il créé des Juifs polonais, si ce n'est pour server d'espions."'[29]

Grünbaum and Prylucki, in particular, distinguished themselves with efforts to exonerate Jews accused of collaboration with the Partitioning Powers during the First World War or of siding with the Ukrainians in the Polish-Ukrainian conflict. Prylucki intervened personally in his capacity as a lawyer on several occasions to defend Jews charged with acts of treason and violence against the Polish military.[30] He also served as secretary of a Sejm commission, which included also Grünbaum, that was dispatched for nine days to Pińsk to investigate the summary execution there by the Polish military in April 1919 of thirty-five Jews suspected of being Bolsheviks. The Jews, who were known Zionists, Bundists, and members of anti-Bolshevik organizations, had lawfully assembled for the purpose of dividing food and American relief.[31]

The vast majority of Polish Jews – both Orthodox and secular nationalists – were fervently opposed to communism, but they were collectively identified with the Soviet Union, which invaded Poland in 1920, and with Bolshevism in general because of the prominence of Jews in the socialist and communist parties and because of the intervention of the Polish left in the Sejm on the behalf of civil rights for minorities. In a gruesome repetition of events during the First World War, Jews were forced out of border areas in preparation for a Polish counter-offensive against the Soviets. The passage through Jewish-inhabited areas of counter-revolutionary Russian-Byelorussian divisions under the direction of General Bulak-Balakhovitch and of the Ukrainian soldiers of Ataman Petliura brought a torrent of massacres, rapes, and pillaging to unarmed Jews. Because some Jews had participated in local organs created by the occupying Soviet army, collective responsibility was applied to the entirety of the Jewish population in these parts.[32] Only in Vilna, which the Poles wrested from the Lithuanians, was there some truth to accusations that the Jews, who usually strove to remain impartial in territorial disputes, supported the enemy as a collective.[33]

Prylucki's Exclusion from the Sejm

Prylucki's intransigence on Jewish national issues and his zealous challenging of those speakers in whose words he suspected even the slightest hint of anti-Jewish animus did little to endear him to his fellow deputies, especially the Polish ones. While perhaps of little consequence in affecting state policy, his speeches furnished the opponents of Jewish rights the basis to attribute limitless demands to all Jewish parties.[34] More than once he was excluded from Sejm sessions for interjections deemed offensive, and he was even once assaulted – in 1924 – by other deputies. One of his unrepentant assailants, the Endek Ludwik Dobiją, remarked of the incident, 'Now Jews, like Communists, know that there is a definite limit to their insolence in the Sejm.'[35]

Prylucki sparked something of a cause célèbre in late February 1919 when he assailed as antisemitic a proposal calling on the Sejm to prefer 'Polish' artisans and trade unions in assigning military contracts. He was accused by Endek leader Korfanty of not considering himself a Pole and wilfully misinterpreting the statement, which presumably meant to include all citizens of Poland, to exclude specifically Jews. He was heckled ('A Litvak cannot be a Pole') as a foreign provocateur bent on defaming Poland before the world when he took the floor in his own defence. Rabbi Halpern's subsequent speech distancing himself from what he regretted as a 'tactless' – albeit understandable due to the pressures of recent anti-Jewish violence – utterance by his colleague served only to underscore divisions between the Jewish factions. The incident won Prylucki censure for his belligerent tactics in both the Polish and Yiddish presses with the exception of *Der moment*.[36] The first denunciation of one Jewish deputy by another on the Sejm floor, Halpern's utterance meanwhile earned him condemnation by Jewish society, including the Orthodox leaders Eliasz Kirszbraun and Rabbi Abraham Perlmutter.[37]

Prylucki alone among Jewish deputies rejected a proposal brought by the Endeks to establish a fifteen-member parliamentary commission to research the 'Jewish question' and to make concrete proposals for its resolution. He recognized in it a ploy to prevent Jewish issues from coming to discussion before the Sejm plenum or being included in the constitution while such an approach was taken in relation to no other national minority. Despite his protests and changes proposed by Grünbaum, the proposal was approved and the short-lived commission, which existed only until the Paris Peace Conference of 1919, succeeded in evading any direct discussions of Jewish issues.[38]

Irritated by a regular barrage of remarks that they vociferously denounced as provocative and inimical to the Polish state, Prylucki's parliamentary adversaries succeeded in employing the previously contested election laws to bring a premature end to his first term of office. On 24 May 1919, scarcely three months after the Sejm had gone into session, Prylucki was stripped of his mandate on the ground that he had been born outside Poland and was therefore not a citizen.[39]

Rising to his defence, Jewish delegates pointed out that no explicit citizenship law yet existed. The second Folkist representative in the Sejm, Samuel Hirschhorn, questioned how Poland could protest the violation of the civil rights of ethnic Poles in the Ukraine and Russia in good faith when it itself denied citizenship to non-Poles who were long-time residents of Poland and yet even made such demands of them as military service. No Polish nationality was legally recognized in the tsarist empire, he continued, and registration books were not fastidiously kept because the police wished to avoid bureaucratic formalities when subjects changed location and because municipalities were reluctant to recognize declines in population for fear of seeing corresponding reductions in state monies.[40]

In a speech which he could not conclude due to a five-minute constraint (but which appeared in its entirety in the Jewish press), Prylucki cited his biography as evidence of his deep attachment to Poland. 'Who dares tell me that I do not possess Polish citizenship?' he challenged. For generations his family had resided in Kremeniec, a city with a large Polish population and where his grandfather received honorary citizenship in 1852 for his services to its economy; he had studied in Sandomierz and Warsaw; he was also active as a lawyer for nine years in Warsaw and had refused to evacuate it with retreating Russian armies in 1915; finally, he had participated in the Warsaw City Council and Council of State during the First World War.[41] The High Court nonetheless branded him a foreigner, arguing that his place of birth (Berdichev) was not found within any of the Sejm voting districts; neither was he registered in the book of permanent residents of Congress Poland dating from the tsarist period.[42]

After Prylucki's exclusion from the Sejm, he was replaced by Nomberg, who even managed to secure a seat in the influential Education Commission. Nomberg resigned his mandate in 1920, however, to pursue writing full-time and was, in turn, replaced by the artisan representative Chaim Rasner. Meanwhile, Prylucki was required to apply for Polish citizenship through the same bureaucratic process as any other foreign national while ethnic Poles born abroad were deemed to be citizens.

Leading the Folkist delegation (Rasner spoke only twice in the Sejm), Hirschhorn contributed a number of interpellations in defence of Jewish rights including protests against allegations of Jewish disloyalty to Poland and the unjustified physical abuse of Jews by soldiers.[43] Like other Jewish national deputies, the Folkists also interceded on behalf of other minorities, for example, to protest the closing of Ukrainian schools and the arrest of a delegation demanding redress for the persecution of Ukrainians in the *kresy*.[44] Meanwhile, Jewish deputies together devoted much energy to combating the citizenship law, which effectively deprived thousands of Jews of Polish citizenship, on the grounds that it lacked a legal basis and in fact violated the National Minorities Treaty issued by the Paris Peace Conference.[45]

Paris Peace Conference

Demands for national autonomy were presented by Jewish leaders at the Paris Peace Conference, which opened in January 1919. The organized Jewish presence at the Conference consisted mainly of prominent Jewish leaders from the United States but also included a Polish delegation dominated by Zionists. It sought to persuade the victorious powers and Polish politicians alike of the need for an international agreement on national and religious minorities. The Great Powers were more easily convinced than the Poles, whose deputies at the conference – the Endeks Roman Dmowski, Ignacy Paderewski, and Władisław Grabski – agreed to civil rights only for the Jews, arguing that to speak of national rights was inappropriate when the Jews could not even agree upon a national language and were not recognized as a nationality by Western democracies. On the whole, the Endek delegates to the conference resented what was perceived as a double standard and the imposition of humiliating guarantees of Jewish civil and national rights upon them by an international forum at the request of a lobbying group representing financially powerful world Jewry.

Two articles of the National Minorities Treaty signed on 28 June 1919 between representatives of the Five Powers – the United States, Great Britain, France, Italy, Japan – and Poland. specifically mentioned Jews, who were formally recognized as a national minority in Eastern Europe (the Polish Constitution later drafted, in contrast, promised citizens the right to maintain their nationality and to cultivate their language and national attributes but did not specify whether Jews constitute a nationality – a problem which returned in all discussions concerning Jews).[46] The treaty allowed for the existence of state-supported Jewish schools under the supervision of Jewish authorities and the right to use Yiddish in public institutions, as well as forbade the government from compelling Jews to violate the Sabbath except in cases of a state emergency. Beyond these provisions, there was no special accommodation of Jewish requests, such as a regulation concerning the status of the *kehila*, the creation of a Jewish curia, or the appointment of a minister for Jewish affairs in the government.

Despite the Sejm's initial rejection of the paragraph insuring national minority rights as an offence to Polish honour and the tradition of Polish tolerance, the treaty was eventually ratified by a 287–41 vote. It could not permit itself the luxury of not heeding the Great Powers, to whom Poland owed its independence and territorial acquisitions at Germany's expense, and whose good will and assistance would be necessary to establish the new state on firm footing. The other states of East Central Europe soon followed suit despite similar objections.

Of the Jewish delegates, only Poale Zion delegate Schipper shared the Polish left's objection on the ground that the treaty had been dictated by victorious capitalist powers. The Minorities Treaty was welcomed by the other Jewish Sejm deputies as the juridical basis for their expanded political and cultural activity while a constitution guaranteeing their rights was pending. The treaty legitimized extending to a mass audience the variety of secular cultural work previously limited to small, intellectual circles. Sensitive to a tremendous public outcry against the treaty despite efforts in the Sejm to portray it as beneficial to Poland, the government refrained from publishing the Minorities Treaty in its official organ until December 1920 – an action tantamount to denying its binding nature.[47]

The state's reluctance to implement the treaty in full did not discourage Prylucki. He was confident that the wars fought over border areas with mixed populations, such as western Ukraine, would convince world leaders of the rectitude of the doctrine of national personal autonomy as the only adequate solution to national conflicts. Of the Jewish parties in Poland, only the Folksparty and the Bund, he proudly pointed out, included the rights of Yiddish in their platforms. He also did not demur in attributing to himself a large share of the credit for popularizing the doctrine among the Jewish masses of Poland with his articles in the Yiddish press and for familiarizing the Polish non-Jewish population with it through his tireless efforts in the Warsaw City Council.[48] Although principally opposed to the spread of Polish among Jews at the expense of Yiddish, he published the Polish-language originals of his Warsaw City Council speeches, presumably in order to spark interest in his ideas among Polish-speaking Jews and familiarize Poles with them.[49] Most likely, he considered this de rigueur for a figure of his stature, especially since his rival Grünbaum had already published collections of his speeches and articles.[50]

Cultural Activity: Publications, Schools, and Language Reform

Following his dismissal from the Sejm in 1919, Prylucki had more time to devote to his journalistic and academic, especially linguistic, pursuits. To measure by number of publications alone, 1920–21 was a highly productive time for him as a scholar and cultural critic. In 1920 he published a collection of articles from the press about the works and literary language of Sholem Yankev Abramovitsh, the writer better known by his pen name Mendele Moykher Sforim, in addition a second volume of his *Yidishe dialektologishe forshungen* (Yiddish Dialectical Investigations), this time devoted to vowels.[51] He also provided a simple and elegant solution to the problem of distinguishing Yiddish dialects based upon the pronunciation of a single diphthong that remains, despite later refinements and additions, the foundation of the contemporary division of Yiddish dialects by scholars.[52] The following year was marked by the appearance of collections of his early publicistic and theatre essays and new volumes in his series of dialect and folklore studies.[53]

Without a doubt, though, it is in the area of schools and language reform that Prylucki, together with his Folkist colleagues, had his broadest impact in the cultural sphere. Founding members of the Folksparty such as H.D. Nomberg, Hillel Zeitlin, Samuel Hirshhorn, Lazar Kahan, and Saul Stupnicki were public figures active in shaping the very culture that stood at the foundation of its political program. The Yiddish secular school, the foundation of the Folkists' vision of Jewish national autonomy in Poland, represents the party's most conspicuous cause and, arguably, its most significant concrete achievement.

Folkists attached tremendous importance to the creation of a network of publicly funded Yiddish schools as a basis for the propagation of a new secular culture among the growing generation of Jews in Poland. The role of the Yiddish school was not merely to educate youth for productive lives in the Diaspora but to impart to them a love of their native language and to make of it the primary vehicle for the self-conscious expression of Jewish identity. To popularize the school issue, which he regarded as 'the most burning, the most current' question facing Jewish society in Poland, Lazar Kahan published in 1918 a short book surveying the comparative history and development of public education among the Jews and other European peoples.[54] By 1920 the Folkist *Shul- un folks-bildung fareyn* maintained three of a total of fourteen Yiddish secular schools with a combined enrolment of some two thousand children in the former Congress Poland.[55]

Always leftist in his leanings, Nomberg focused more on the practical than the ideological value of a Yiddish education. He argued that not every Jew could become the ideal of a 'bourgeois doctor or lawyer' and that a high school (*gimnazye*) education in Latin and Hebrew was superfluous for most. Instead, what the average child of lower middle-class parents direly needed was a primary education in Yiddish in order to prepare him for the economic struggle awaiting him. Implicit in this assertion, of course, was the assumption that the economic niche occupied by the lower middle class in commerce and artisanry would remain overwhelmingly a Yiddish-speaking one. At odds with the official Folkist stance opposing emigration, Nomberg felt that the problems of Jews could not be remedied entirely on Polish soil and saw departure to Western democracies, for which he urged a coordinated movement, as a necessary means to alleviate economic misery.[56]

To strengthen vocational training among Jewish youth, Kahan prepared a brochure on the history of artisanry among Jews that called for the organizational reform of artisan associations and their methods of handicrafts education.[57] Similarly, even prior to the formation of the Folksparty, Prylucki acknowledged in *Der moment* the inferiority of Jewish craftsmen and artisans, for which he blamed inadequate training. He called for the creation of a systematic, well-organized vocational education in the mother tongue in order to counter the economic decline of the Jews. He also urged the cultivation of co-operatives and self-help organizations among Jewish artisans (Jewish artisans traditionally discussed professional matters in *kloyzn*, synagogues organized along occupational lines), who were almost completely excluded from Polish guilds, in order to forestall their complete displacement by the rising class of Christian artisans.[58] Likely because they were intellectuals lacking first-hand experience with manual labour, leading Folkists were themselves little active in vocational training. Instead, they focused their energies more on questions of language in the schools. Given Prylucki's proclivities, the question of language standardization was naturally a subject about which he had much to say from both practical and ideological standpoints.

With the expansion of the Jewish school system the idea arose of uniting independently functioning Yiddish schools of various political and cultural orientations. A number of pedagogical issues, such as the pressing need for the standardization of grammar and spelling,[59] were discussed at a series of conferences between 1915 and 1920 but ideological divisions prevented a unified school front. Members of the Bund, Poale Zion, the Fareynikte, and the Folksparty, and non-party Yiddishists agreed only on language and secularism. They diverged on pedagogical methods, educational goals and ideals, and their attitude towards traditional Jewish texts, Hebrew, and Palestine. Party representatives and educators nonetheless cooperated on a number of practical matters. Nomberg, for example, and especially Prylucki, a dialectologist and foremost expert on Polish Yiddish, were active in commissions to develop terminologies for instruction in the sciences and mathematics and participated in committees to establish and implement a unified system of Yiddish spelling. In 1921 *Tsisho* (an acronym for the *Tsentrale yidishe shul organizatsye*), the Central Jewish School Organization, was formed as an umbrella organization encompassing 130 Yiddish secular elementary schools and forty-seven kindergartens of all political orientations.[60]

Teachers complained that the peculiarities of Yiddish spelling and the abundance of competing systems unnecessarily burdened pupils first learning to read.[61] The creation of a phonetically precise, unified system of spelling was taken up with great urgency by pedagogues, writers, language planners, and other interested individuals in the countries of the former Russian Empire and the United States. Familiarity with linguistics, much less formal study in the field, was hardly a precondition for participation in passionate debates. The orthographic reform movement was lent additional impetus by the atmosphere of iconoclasm and radical political change in Eastern Europe and by spelling reforms in co-territorial languages. Most significant among them was the reform of Russian first proposed in 1904 and finally effected after the Bolshevik Revolution.[62]

During the discussion of orthography at a 1919 teachers' conference, Prylucki repudiated reforms 'made groping the walls' and called for a disciplined academic approach to the problem in order to produce a supra-dialectal system for the entire Yiddish speech community.[63] He also supported the 'naturalization,' that is, the phonetic spelling, of Hebrew-Aramaic elements in the language. Naturalization would eliminate the visual distinctiveness of the Semitic component of the language by making all components of the language (Germanic, Semitic, and Slavic) follow the same spelling conventions.

In traditional spelling schemes, Yiddish generally maintains Hebrew and Aramaic practices of denoting only consonants and not vowels; in contrast, it denotes both consonants and vowels in words (and parts of words) of all other provenance. Naturalization plans were conceived by Jewish language planners across the ideological spectrum as a means to 'rationalize' spelling for greater facility in reading and to reflect the harmonious integration of all of the language's components. Such a democratic system eschewed particularistic, non-phonetic spellings of Hebrew-Aramaic words, which, it was contended, had to be laboriously mastered by students decreasingly familiar with Hebrew. Orthographic naturalization did not necessarily imply, though, the conscious denuding of the language of its Semitic vocabulary, even among the notoriously anti-religious and anti-Hebrew Soviets.[64] Prylucki, for one, was hardly the rabid enemy of Hebrew depicted by Hebraists and certainly appreciated the language despite rejecting it as the basis of contemporary Jewish life.[65] While he saw naturalization as a progressive and historical trend in Yiddish, he was also quite fond of Hebraisms in his writings, including more recondite ones. He in fact took issue with Stupnicki, who argued that individuals would do better to avoid Hebraisms in their writing than misspell or naturalize their difficult spellings. For Prylucki, Hebraisms were an organic part of the language and indispensable without resort to 'ignorant *daytshmerisms* and provincial Slavisicms.'[66]

Naturalization was judged premature by conference participants, as no concrete proposal had yet been made for such a reform, not even by the Soviets, who began to implement naturalization inconsistently (e.g., the same word was spelled differently in Minsk and Ukraine) in the press immediately after the Revolution.[67] Further, it was acknowledged that conservative societal opinion would likely react negatively to such a radical alteration of the traditional, time-honoured face of the language. Prylucki and Nomberg represented the Folkists on a subsequent commission formed to work out a definitive plan for a new orthography based upon the more progressive system used elsewhere in the former tsarist empire and which would also naturalize the spelling of Hebrew-Aramaic elements.[68]

Far less interested in the technical aspects of spelling reform than Prylucki, Nomberg astutely interpreted the controversy as essentially reflecting the conflict of ideologies and the contest for dominance within the Yiddishist camp. He endeavoured to clarify for *Der moment*'s readers the reasons behind the excitement and polemics generated by the obscure subject of orthography in intellectual circles and to dispel the popular notion that 'writers are simply looking for something about which to write.' For him spelling was not primarily a scientific question to be solved rationally by a team of experts but a social problem and symptom of political fragmentation. A perfectly accurate system capable of reflecting the myriad nuances of speech, he posited, is impossible for any but an artificially engineered language without recourse to an unwieldy system of hieroglyphic-like diacritic signs unsuited for the ordinary reader. Moreover, the premise is untenable, he protested, that literate adults mechanically sound out words syllable by syllable like novice child readers. Rather, the adult eye recognizes words as indivisible wholes, which, in turn, elicit corresponding concepts in the reader's mind.

In Russia and Ukraine, he continued, new elements influenced by the revolutionary atmosphere are presently directing cultural activity among Jews and Yiddish literacy is on the rise. But reform is executed in a most extreme fashion to correct a system that, albeit imperfect and haphazardly developed over generations, has the great advantage of habit and being readily comprehended by readers. With the shuffling of borders three rival Yiddish orthographic systems exist in Poland, each reflecting a specific ideology more than a scientific approach to resolving orthographic difficulties – the Bolshevik, which naturalizes Hebrew-Aramaic words; the Menshevik, centred in Ukraine and less radical than the Bolshevik system; and the bourgeois system employed in the Warsaw press.[69] What must be avoided among Yiddishists, it was argued, was the stubborn tendency of each party, cultural institution, or individual, whether Ber Borokhov or Noah Prylucki, to introduce its own system and, thereby, augment disunity and chaos. To summarize his position, Nomberg wrote, 'Better one unified orthography that it is not phonetically correct than ten correct ones' and warned against the damage that would be wrought in the schools by factions clinging to uncompromising positions.[70]

Zionist Reactions

The Folksparty, *Der haynt* jibed, had 'lost its whole dowry – its few supports and its bit of prestige' and was desperate for allies in its battle against Zionism. Having failed to win the support of workers' parties, whose cooperation was obtainable only in the matter of correcting the orthography to be taught by 'Yiddishist *kheyder* teachers (*dardeke melamdim*),' the Folkists allegedly court the Orthodox by adding their voice to the Agudah's protest of discriminatory citizenship laws independent of the entire Jewish Sejm fraction. Even when the Folkists joined other Jewish deputies, though, to condemn Rabbi Perlmutter for failing to support Grünbaum's amendment to the proposed citizenship law,[71] this action was dismissed as a meaningless and misleading gesture. Nor was it taken into account that the Agudah criticized both the Folkists and the Zionists for supporting the Polish left, which had on other occasions not supported vital Jewish concerns such as the vote on amendments to the Sunday rest law.[72] Ever scornful of Jewish factiousness, Hillel Zeitlin proclaimed Jewish politics to be the monopoly of no single party and blamed Jewish nationalists, both Folkists and Zionists, for exploiting Perlmutter's unfortunate and inexcusable error (for which he subsequently apologized) as a means to settle accounts with the Orthodox.[73]

That *Der haynt*, which became an unswervingly Zionist paper under the title *Der nayer haynt* (New Today) after combining with Grünbaum's *Dos yidishe folk* in 1920,[74] invested much energy in defaming Prylucki and the Folksparty even after his exclusion from the Sejm belied, however, its contentions by January 1920 that the Folksparty was no longer a serious challenger for hegemony in Jewish national politics. In the more moderate evaluation of the German-Zionist organ *Jüdische Rundschau*, which continued to follow Jewish politics in Poland closely after the end of the First World War, the Folksparty's political influence was decidedly on the wane in 1920, but not yet irrelevant. Due to the 'poverty of its leadership,' it claimed, the party was wholly dependent upon the tremendous popularity of Prylucki, 'a talented and energetic tribune for the folk.' Since the Zionists under Grünbaum's leadership had repudiated Farbstein's radical rejection of Yiddish and adopted Diaspora politics as a goal in itself, it reasoned, few differences now existed between the parties' programs apart from their relationship to Palestine and Hebrew. Thus, the Folksparty had relinquished its claims as sole defender of Jewish rights and honour among the bourgeoisie. While it had previously courted the Bund in order to weaken the Zionists, it now contradicted its own ideological foundations in order to win the support of the Orthodox. Poor attendance at its last conference of councilmen, *Jüdische Rundschau* maintained, confirmed its declining strength.[75]

In the contest for the Jewish bourgeois electorate, it continued, 'the fate of the Folkists will depend, as paradoxical as it may sound, on the extent and tempo of the realization of the Palestine question.'[76] That is, the greater Zionist progress in encouraging Jewish settlement towards the creation a Jewish state in Palestine while conditions in Poland steadily worsened, the less appeal the Folkist focus on the Diaspora was expected to hold among the mass of Jews in Poland. As immigration to the Western Hemisphere, particularly the United States, was increasingly restricted in the 1920s, the prospect of *aliyah* – immigration to Palestine – became correspondingly popular even if it was reduced to only a trickle by English policy and could not be financed for more than a fraction of Polish Jewry by the World Zionist Organization.

Charitable and Relief Work

Prylucki continued to write regularly on politics in the daily press and commanded his party to stay its course of pursuit of Jewish national-cultural autonomy independent of the Jewish socialists and Zionists. He rejected Zeitlin's notion of the Folksparty as a party open to all nationalist Jews and as a fusion of the best elements of folkism, Zionism, and socialism. He also spurned Nomberg's sympathy for the Bund. Instead, he argued that just as no absolute unity or absolutely peaceful coexistence is to be found in nature, so, too, is no absolute political unity possible within a nation since parties represent class interests. Complete cooperation is impossible with those who desire national suicide, that is, the Assimilationists, or who deny Yiddish as the essential basis of Jewish life, that is, the Zionists. Cooperation is necessary and possible, though, among Jewish parties in the vital spheres of relief work and the removal of discriminatory measures.[77]

Yet even the realm of charitable work was highly contested among Eastern European Jews. Here, too, Prylucki met with fierce resistance from his Jewish opponents, who were characteristically most vocal in the Zionist camp. Indeed, since relief and charitable work were among the most potent means to win popular support, competition here was no less than other domains of party activity. The arena for a contest of hyperbolic calumnies and mutual denigration was again furnished by the daily press, where political conflict heightened the long acute competition for readers between the rivals *Der haynt*, now an organ of the Zionist party co-edited by Grünbaum, and Tsevi Prylucki's *Der moment*, which was officially non-partisan but continued to carry several Folkists on its staff of writers. Both Prylucki and Grünbaum were accused of opportunism, financial malfeasance, and general neglect of the needs of the Jewish electorate.[78] While as a Zionist he rued his beloved son's departure from that camp, Tsevi Prylucki did not cease idolizing his son as a Jewish national hero – as a 'second Herzl' in the observation of fellow Folkist Elkhonen Zeitlin – and was typically indulgent of his anti-Zionist philippics.[79]

The near complete political disunity within Polish Jewry as a whole was a tremendous obstacle to American Jewish relief efforts both during and after the war. Not only did the Folkists and Zionists refuse to cooperate because of their ideological differences, so did the Bund with bourgeois elements. Even within the labour movement there existed division, as well. Representatives of the New York–based Joint Distribution Committee (JDC) frequently complained that in Poland and other Eastern European lands 'the only active social force was politics ... Each political group did its utmost to play as important a part as possible in the distribution of funds. This gave them prestige, the possibility to hand out employment and to get in touch with the population. Incidentally, the funds enabled them to cover the deficits in their administration expenses.'[80]

Boris Bogen, the director of the JDC's operations in Poland, decried the practice of various factions among Polish Jewry competing to promote their own political capital and interests at the expense of the poor and needy.[81] In his memoirs, he recalls being led by a ragged Jewish guide in 1919 Warsaw to Prylucki's home: 'Prelutzki! This was the man against whom the Zionists in Paris had warned me. I must avoid Prelutzki, they had said. I must give no prominence to the leadership of Prelutzki, for whom they had little use ... He was despised by the government and reviled by a section of Jewry which had saved its dissensions though it had lost nearly all of its other possessions, and which lived in a divided house though wolves of anti-Semitism howled menacingly at its door.'[82]

JDC funds administered by the Warsaw Committee organized on the basis of political and factional representation (including Assimilationists) were spent in large amounts on purely cultural activities, which, while of intrinsic value, diverted monies needed for the relief of actual poverty and brought divisive issues to the fore. Those in need of dire material assistance, he lamented, were widely disregarded amid a constant volley of accusations and counter-accusations of injustice and discrimination hurled between rival local parties present on the distributing committee.[83]

Quite undeniably, Prylucki was extremely active in the legal defence and material aid for Jews discriminated against and otherwise the victims of abuse at the hands of the Polish military. The meteoric rise in popularity that he experienced largely thanks to such efforts illustrates the intimate relationship between relief work and Jewish leadership in Poland.[84] Anti-Jewish violence reached its apex during the Soviet invasion in 1920, when antisemitism was fanned by the army and the state news agency. Negotiations between the government and Jewish deputies, including Prylucki, to arrive at peaceable relations and a promise from the government to halt antisemitic excesses yielded only conciliatory words in private and no practical results. Fearful of losing its parliamentary majority, the government was hesitant to alienate antisemites in the Sejm and military.[85]

Jews suffered the rampages of the Polish army and its allies and were summarily tried and executed by military courts in areas liberated from the Soviet army. In August 1920 the Ministry of War ordered the separation of all Jewish volunteers and front soldiers, especially intellectuals, from Polish troops. They were interned in concentration camps in, most prominently, Jabłonna near Warsaw and in Wszków, Piotrków, Szczakowa, Dąbie, and Tuchola. The internment was justified as a preventive measure against 'increasingly frequent cases that demonstrate the harmful activity of the Jewish element' and not lifted until Soviet troops had been repulsed.[86] The internees were deprived of adequate food and accommodations and subjected to humiliating treatment at the hands of guards of the Posen divisions notorious for their antisemitism. News of this action reached the editors of *Der moment*, which printed an appeal for food and beds for the thousands of Jewish soldiers arbitrarily imprisoned. When camp guards refused entry to outsiders, Prylucki loaded donated foodstuffs, mattresses, and sleeping bags into a truck and exploited his considerable personal influence as a former Sejm deputy to obtain permission from the camp commander to deliver them. Eventually, the efforts of Jewish Sejm deputies, including the Folkists, succeeded in having legal proceedings against nearly all arrestees ended.[87]

At this time Prylucki was himself arrested briefly after coming to the aid of several young women suspected as Bolsheviks for bringing supplies taken from Prylucki's personal collection for Jabłonna internees to Jewish soldiers imprisoned in Warsaw. He was promptly released when word reached Piłsudski of his arrest and the confined soldiers, with the exception of one whose family did not provide the necessary documents in time for his defence, were found innocent following an investigation.[88]

Prylucki in America

Prylucki's exclusion from the Sejm permitted him greater freedom to travel for extended periods in the pursuit of relief work. Accompanied by his wife, Noah Prylucki left Poland on 20 July 1921 for a visit to the United States in the name of the Central Relief Committee for War-Suffering Emigrants and Re-emigrants of Ukraine and Russia, an organization that he founded in 1920 to assist the mass of Jewish victims of pogroms and expulsions in Ukraine and Russia who had taken refuge in Poland.[89] As vice-president of this Folkist-dominated organization, he boasted in *Der moment* in the summer of 1921 that the Central Ukrainian Committee (as it was more commonly known) had obtained residence rights certificates, certificates of good character, and letters for passports and recommendations to various consulates for tens of thousands of homeless and emigrants. It also cared for their feeding, clothing, and shelter and rendered medical and sanitary assistance in addition to providing nursery schools for children orphaned by the pogroms. And, most importantly for the injured pride of Polish Jewry, the organization worked almost exclusively with local monies collected in Warsaw, thereby helping to weaken the city's image as a beggar (*shnorer*).

Prylucki was loath to see Eastern European Jewry reliant on foreign relief but acknowledged the necessity of foreign, above all American Jewish, aid to assist Polish Jewry in rebuilding its ruined economic life following the war. He was therefore eager to see that the 'true representatives' of Polish Jewry – a reference essentially to members of all segments of Polish-Jewish society apart from the Assimilationists – themselves determine the distribution of monies and cease being the object of foreign 'guardianship.' He also underscored the need for vocational and self-help agencies such as credit and loan institutions.[90]

In an interview with a reporter for the New York daily *Morgn-zhurnal*, Prylucki expressed his confidence that the Polish government, under attack by antisemitic parties, sought to bring order to the land and that 'Poland, in the end, will remain a permanent home for the Jewish people.' Yet, while his party was a principled opponent of immigration as a solution to the plight of Polish Jewry, he believed that for the Ukrainian refugees 'the greatest help is emigration' to democratic lands and not return to the Soviet Union or settlement in Poland.[91] Heightened nativist sentiment coupled with the Red Scare made immigration to the United States increasingly difficult, though, for Eastern Europe Jews, Slavs, Italians, and Asians following the war. Newcomers were frequently viewed as socialists or, worse, as Bolsheviks. This was especially true of Jews, who were commonly perceived as subversive radicals associated with or sympathizing with the Russian Revolution. The immigration law of 19 May 1921, which was passed by the U.S. Congress within the brief span of four hours, established immigration quotas at 3 per cent of a country's nationals residing in the United States in 1910. The law effectively discriminated against southern and southeastern Europeans and more than halved immigration from 800,000 in 1920 to slightly more than 300,000 in 1922.[92]

Apart from his official goal of raising funds for rehabilitation work and imploring American officials to ease immigration restrictions, Prylucki saw his visit to the largest Yiddish-speaking community outside of Eastern Europe also as an opportunity to canvas for funds for Yiddish cultural work in Poland and to familiarize world Jewry with the struggle of Polish Jews for civil equality and national personal autonomy in fulfilment of the National Minorities Treaty. The visit was also intended to acquaint him with American Jewry, which he considered a colony of Eastern European Jewry and with which he hoped to establish cultural, organizational, and perhaps even political contacts in the atmosphere of greater closeness engendered by the war. With more than 1.5 million Jews, New York City possessed the largest concentration of Jews in the world and was home to four Yiddish dailies in addition to a myriad of other Yiddish publications and cultural activities.[93] Among the matters he hoped to discuss with American Jewish cultural leaders were the convening of two conferences – one for the purpose of standardizing orthography and one for the benefit of Yiddish writers and journalists – and the exploration of possibilities to coordinate publishing activity.[94]

The JDC, which respected the Ukrainian Committee's legal work, objected to strife between it and the Emigration Bureau of the Zionist-dominated Temporary National Jewish Council. The result was that 'both sides are engaged in publishing contradictory and misleading articles in the press' to discredit one another while unable to bring accurate statistics in support of their biased claims.[95] In November of that year a representative of the JDC in Poland criticized to his superiors the Zionists for a lack of interest in the refugee problem apart from solving it according to the 'requirements of Palestine Zionism.' While expressing dissatisfaction with the Zionists, he positively evaluated the efforts of the Ukrainian Committee: 'All parties, with the exception of the labour and Zionist, are represented in this Committee, the most important being of course the "Volkist" party. According to the information obtained, and my personal impression, the work of the committee is relatively good, but still very unsystematic. Aspirations regarding extension are naturally very strong, and a certain caution towards the Ukrainian Committee must always be observed. Systematic productive work, which the political-judicial work unconditionally necessitates, is, any way, only possible in the closest reciprocal working with the Ukrainian Committee.'[96]

Goals of Prylucki's Trip to America

Prylucki outlined three primary goals for his trip to the United States. The first was to inform Jewish society in Europe and the United States about the crisis affecting Russian and Ukrainian Jewry resulting from pogroms and economic ruin. The second was to explore possibilities for Jewish immigration, especially prospects that authorities in the United States could be persuaded to ease immigration restrictions out of humanitarian considerations. The gates of all lands are closed to Jews, he lamented, because of the misconceptions that refugees fleeing communism and grave personal danger are actually Bolsheviks or because of the baseless fear that their physical and mental wounds will render them permanently unfit for labour and consequently a burden to the state. Unable to return to their home communities without risking life and limb, the refugees are welcome to recuperate in Poland only so long as they are cared for by others and represent neither a burden to the state nor an economic competitor to the native population. Finally, his third goal was to raise funds to rehabilitate the estimated 40,000 emigrants in

Poland from Ukraine and Byelorussia who would be unable to leave in the near future through constructive assistance, such as workshops and production co-operatives for artisans.

Along his route to New York, Prylucki stopped in Berlin. A number of Eastern European Jewish intellectuals had taken up residence there following the war, turning aside from political activity and devoting themselves to cultural work out of disillusionment with the Soviet revolution and the failure of the experiment in Jewish national autonomy in Ukraine.[97] In the German capital Prylucki met with representatives of the *Hilfsverein*, which pledged to take an interest in the work of the Central Ukrainian Committee. He and Nomberg, who took to extensive travel following his early retirement from parliamentary activity, represented the Polish Folksparty at an 'international conference' of Jewish Folkists held from 29–30 July. The small meeting was attended also Dr Tsemakh Shabad, a representative of the Folkist Jewish Democratic Party in Vilna, Latski-Bertholdi of Berlin, and Y. Efroikin of Paris, who was active in Dubnow's original Folksparty. The latter two individuals were among the organizers of a new incarnation of the Folksparty in Kiev in 1918 during the short-lived Ukrainian Republic, which promised autonomy for its Jewish minority (Latski-Bertholdi served briefly as minister for Jewish affairs).[98] It was decided to open a secretariat in Berlin to coordinate efforts by Folkist parties in various lands and to convene a conference for the purpose of creating a united program. Additional bureaus were to be opened by Efroikin in Paris, by Prylucki and Efroikin in London, and by Prylucki alone in New York.[99] Nothing, however, seems to have come of these plans for Folkist branches outside Eastern Europe.

While in the United States from 18 September 1921 until January 1922, Prylucki planned to travel across the land to speak at mass meetings and meet with representatives of Ukrainian *Landsmanshaftn* (hometown organizations for immigrants) in New York, Detroit, Chicago, St Louis, Kansas City, and San Francisco. He also expected to visit Canada.[100] In New York he solicited funds for the Jewish homeless from the Federation of Ukrainian Jews in America and other organizations, as well as attempted to persuade the various bodies to coordinate efforts to remedy the current situation whereby each society contributed money only to victims from its own city or *shtetl.* His itinerary also included visits to American Jewish notables Louis Marshall and Felix Warburg, a meeting with the Hebrew Immigration Aid Society (HIAS), and, most significantly, audiences with the State Department and President Harding.[101]

Results of His Visit to the United States

On the whole, Prylucki's trip to America was not the success for which he had hoped. Not only was he unable to persuade U.S. officials to ease immigration policy. He also found America uncongenial territory for his political and cultural ideology. Most significantly, he was unable to return to Poland with tangible results – financial, cultural, humanitarian, or otherwise – of which to boast in order to help boost the flagging popularity of the Folksparty.

Prylucki offered to withdraw from the collection of funds in North America and to participate in the JDC's fundraising drive if his request were granted for the JDC to provide him a lump sum payment of $200,000, enough for his organization to establish forty-seven workshops providing preliminary craft instruction.[102] The subject of several international cables between JDC representatives in New York and Europe, the request was politely but firmly denied. While wishing to avoid the duplicate collection of relief monies, in its internal correspondence the JDC judged that the Ukrainian Committee 'can not and does not do reconstruction work ... Prelutzki's committee is only competent to carry on legal work for refugees.' Much more worrisome, it feared, a political scandal arising from the competition to aid the homeless between the Folkist-dominated Ukrainian Committee and the Temporary Jewish National Council would result in 'chaos and untold harm caused [to] refugees.'[103] With Prylucki in America on behalf of the Ukrainian Committee, Moyshe Leyzerovitsh, a member of the Temporary National Jewish Council's Emigration Bureau, published three long articles in *Der haynt*, 'The Strength of Lies.' The series accused the Committee of misrepresentation in order to gain access in American-Jewish circles.[104] The charges were of course dismissed and answered with a counter-accusation by a Folkist writer in *Der moment.*[105]

The JDC representative in Berlin, the social worker and previous director of the *Hilfsverein* Dr Bernard Kahn, urged extreme caution in relations with Prylucki. He described Prylucki as a wily politician seeking to bolster his own personal and his party's fallen political standing through relief work. Kahn was willing, however, to accept cooperation with the Ukrainian Committee as long as it was not given preference over other relief organizations and would be willing to cooperate in constructive work with 'a local polish jewish committee [*sic*] composed of all parties including Prilutzki.'[106] Moreover, Kahn warned that a settlement was preferable to an open rupture with Prylucki because he 'wields immense influence' in Poland and 'possesses great ability energy resourcefulness and hold on masses.'[107] A HIAS representative in Warsaw similarly appraised the situation, complaining of the bitter rivalry between relief organizations and the difficulty of persuading the Ukrainian Committee to account for its use of requested monies. 'It is therefore of utmost importance,' his report concluded, 'that all the organizations interested in this work should be informed about the situation and of the existing necessity so that occurrences similar to those which have taken place in Kovel, where the Ukraine Committee and the National Rat [Temporary National Jewish Council] have vied with each other in renting a home and thus increased the price very much, should not take place again.'[108]

In its formal letter to Prylucki, who resided at the luxury Brozteil Hotel on East 27th Street while in New York, JDC secretary Albert Lucas explained that there existed no need for any special solicitation of funds by the Ukrainian Committee since the JDC pledged to allot $12,000 per month for a year to support all constructive refugee work in Poland. Lucas also expressed his expectation that Prylucki 'will undertake no further activities anywhere in the United States or Canada, seeking to raise funds for the refugees in Poland, independently of the J.D.C. or its constituent committees' campaigns.'[109] Prylucki protested that his was 'not an organization of a political character' and that it 'represents all classes, parties, professional organizations, every field of life of the Jewry in Poland, and, therefore, this Central Committee may be regarded as representing the *United Local Jewish Forces in Poland.*' He objected that to coordinate its activity with 'minor organizations that are of a political character and who to date have accomplished nothing in this field' will only delay the distribution of assistance to those in urgent need. He requested six direct monthly payments by the JDC to the Ukrainian Committee.[110]

It appears that Prylucki's request was never honoured since in May 1922 James Rosenberg, chairman of the European Executive Council of the JDC, expressed concern that Prylucki had been denied a clear answer after months of waiting and felt slighted. The Ukrainian Committee had received no money even after Prylucki had agreed to halt his fundraising drive in the United States in return for what he deemed friendly assurances of assistance from the JDC. Rosenberg asked for guidance on the matter since he believed that Prylucki 'is the sort of man ... where if we do not actually help his organization we are going to have him as a foe.'[111]

It is unclear how this matter was ultimately resolved. The Ukrainian Committee ceased to be a subject of scandal in the daily Yiddish press in Poland and no further mention of negotiations around this affair appear in JDC archives. The episode sheds light on the declining position of Prylucki and his Folksparty on the Jewish political scene, as well as on Prylucki's character, shortly before elections to the first regular Sejm in 1922. Representatives of the JDC, which was officially neutral towards Jewish nationalism and even expressed a preference for cooperation with the Ukrainian Committee over the Zionist-led Temporary Jewish National Council, viewed Prylucki as a dynamic and industrious, if vengeful and potentially dangerous, individual who still commanded much popular support in Poland. They also cautioned, however, that his interest in facilitating the rehabilitation, repatriation, and immigration of refugees was not above party politics. Rather, it was being cynically manipulated to counter the Folksparty's waning popularity.

Meeting with President Harding and Impressions of America

Prylucki delayed his return to Europe, scheduled for 13 December 1921, when he received last minute notice that he had been granted audiences, most likely through the agency of Louis Marshall,[112] with the State Department and President Harding in Washington, DC. He was eager to dismiss the rumour that all of Eastern European Jewry sought to immigrate to the United States, explaining that several destinations (including Argentina, South Africa, Canada, and Palestine) were attractive to the fraction of Jews who desired to emigrate. He urged the State Department, which promised to take a position on the refugee issue, to make an exception to normal immigration policy and to permit greater numbers of Ukrainian Jews to enter the United States out of humanitarian considerations.[113] Speaking to the U.S. President, Prylucki told of an American citizen whose parents and brothers were burned during a pogrom and who could not bring his one surviving sister to America.[114]

During their thirty-five-minute meeting, President Harding expressed sympathy with the refugees' plight and recognized them as a desirable element, but stated that he must uphold an immigration law that affected not only Jews, but other groups, as well. When Prylucki appealed to the president's sense of mercy, pointing out that the homeless in Ukraine and Byelorussia had neither possessions nor relatives to whom they could return, Harding reportedly responded that it was an error for certain nationalities, such as the Jews and the French, to concentrate in densely populated cities. Rather, they ought to settle in the countryside and smaller cities, where racial and religious animosities were weaker and societal integration correspondingly easier. Finally, after Prylucki explained the sociological reasons behind Jewish urban settlement and the movement to promote agriculture among Jews, the President commented on the need for Jews to demonstrate perseverance in working the land. Presumably having fully expressed himself on the issue, he then shifted the discussion to other topics.[115]

Unable to persuade the President, Prylucki was left with the overall impression that Harding possessed great 'simplicity, compassion, interest in all things human.' Still, he lacked the sharp intellect of either Roosevelt or Wilson, whom Prylucki admired as a driving force behind the thesis of national self-determination.[116]

Prylucki's experiences left him with unfavourable impressions about the nature of American democracy and the prospects for Yiddish culture there. While expressing no overt bitterness, Prylucki, the consummate European as well as Jewish nationalist, described America in his travelogues and special reports in *Der moment* with an air of condescension. He conceived of it as a young and naïve land, a plutocracy where equality is chiefly to be found in the purposefulness and industry with which work is pursued by all regardless of social station and economic class. The Americans are technologically advanced, but socially unsophisticated, as reflected in their two-party political system and their lack of gallantry towards women. Despite their flouting of European conventions of dress and manners, their tremendous degree of conformity is evident in their rigid adherence to a fixed work schedule and the visible surprise with which they greet deviance from accepted social and sartorial norms.[117]

Prylucki recognized that Jewish political life as it was known in Eastern Europe could not exist in a land where all citizens theoretically possessed equal rights as individuals and no rights as collectives. The postulates of national cultural autonomy and the 'new' Jewish politics of confrontations and militant defence of Jewish rights in the Sejm were completely without context in a land where Jews were recent immigrants and rapidly integrating into general society in a way impossible in Poland, where social and ethnic barriers were centuries old. In his estimation, a man like Louis Marshall, for whom he expressed a deep respect, was more an intercessor (*shtadlan*) than a popular leader (*folksfirer*). Marshall's use of connections in the financial and political spheres along with his personal qualities to intervene on the behalf of European Jewry smacked precisely of the sort of custodianship from which he wished to free Polish Jewry.[118]

It is, of course, ironic that Prylucki expressed such a view. A self-proclaimed democrat, he, like his political rivals, was reluctant to give other parties a say in the distribution and use of relief monies. In rejecting the alleged paternalism of American Jewry, he offered his own in its stead and, by his own admission, he engaged in *shtadlanut* to achieve results in the Sejm.

In summary, Prylucki's cursory tour of the United States impressed upon him that in American democracy lurked a negative side – the levelling of cultural and political distinctions. The Jews were no exception: while the American Yiddish press was richer in literature because of the presence of so many immigrant writers and relatively cheaper than its Polish counterpart, Jews there were on the whole more 'assimilated' than in Poland.[119] He engaged in little explicit commentary on the state of the Yiddish language, literature, and cultural institutions. He did so perhaps out of condescension towards America – a phenomenon common among Eastern European Jewish intellectuals[120] – or pessimism for the prospects of developing an independent Jewish cultural life there in Yiddish. Or, perhaps like his colleague Nomberg and other Yiddishists,[121] he withheld remarks out of disappointment with the level of Yiddish culture which he found there. Quite uncharacteristic of one so attuned to language – or perhaps out of discomfort with it – he passed over in silence the remoulding of the American Yiddish lexicon and idiom by the local vernacular, a phenomenon deplored by other Yiddishists as reaching a far greater extent than in Eastern Europe.[122] No less enthusiastic than upon his departure from Poland, he headed back in time for elections to a new Sejm.

A One-Man Parliamentary Faction: The Sejm Elections in 1922

While Prylucki, now a Polish citizen, was personally successful in obtaining a mandate, the elections confirmed what observers and critics of the Folksparty had already begun to note with some satisfaction in 1920 – the declining influence of the party among the Jewish electorate. The years 1922–26 in the party's history were chequered with public scandal and in general marked by growing disaffection within party ranks and by marginalization in the increasingly inflexible, socialist-dominated Yiddishist camp.

In the elections to the first Ordinary Sejm and Senate scheduled for autumn 1922, minority nationalities found themselves at a distinct disadvantage in the face of an electoral ordinance admittedly engineered by the Polish right to favour large parties and maximize the number of Polish deputies. The country, whose borders were now fixed and included

Vilna, the remainder of the *kresy*, and East Galicia, was divided into sixty-four districts electing a total of 372 Sejm deputies and seventeen districts electing ninety-three senators. The size and number of votes needed to secure a seat in each district varied greatly, with 52,000–65,000 votes necessary for a mandate in predominantly Polish districts and 70,000–80,000 votes necessary in mixed districts.[123]

The idea of a bloc of national minorities to redress electoral injustices was apparently the brainchild of the German Sejm deputy Edwin Hasbach, although pursued and realized by Grünbaum. The visceral scorn demonstrated by Polish parties for Jewish nationalist demands and the failure in 1920 of negotiations between Jewish politicians and the Polish government to arrive at a compromise for peaceable relations made the concept of a nationalities bloc extremely attractive at this time to the Jews.[124] The Polish right judged the bloc a real danger to the concept of a Polish nation-state and denounced it as the union of anti-state elements, while the Polish left, which had hoped to draw minority votes, argued that 'It is better to "lose" together with the whole of Polish democracy than to "win" with the aid of the money of German "Hakatists" and of the Jewish bourgeoisie.'[125] Hakatists, the popular name for members of the *Deutscher Ostmark Verein*, pressed for the suppression of Polish culture and the colonization and germanization of Polish territory that was incorporated into Prussia.

Prylucki was initially very enthusiastic about the proposed bloc and, as a secret report sent by the German embassy in Poland to the German Foreign Ministry reveals, served as a liaison in early discussions with the German embassy in Warsaw.[126] As late as mid-August 1922 he praised it in *Der moment* as the opportunity to redeem the minorities from their mutual isolation and to satisfy their legitimate national demands denied in violation of international treaty and the very liberal 1921 state constitution. He was also enthusiastic about the participation of Ukrainian and Byelorussian peasants in the bloc, whom he hoped would draw closer to the Jews despite the work of antisemitic agitators among them.[127]

The idea lost most of its appeal, however, once it became clear in the course of negotiations that only a tactical and not a principal bloc was possible. That is, the bloc was engineered to minimize the effects of gerrymandering in non-Polish regions through united election lists but was not based upon a common political or social program uniting the nationalities and was to be non-binding once the Sejm was in session. To make matters worse, the Folksparty would not receive the number of mandates to which it felt entitled.[128] Formerly enthusiastic about

5.3 'M'dreyt fun ale zaytn' (They spin from all sides). This image, published in the 22 October 1922 issue of the weekly Yiddish humour and satire journal *Der Maszchis,* shows Folkist Noah Prylucki and his political rival, the Zionist Yitshak Grünbaum, literally at each other's throats during the campaign for the 1922 parliamentary elections in Poland. The title plays on the two meanings of the verb *dreyen* – to twist and to deceive. The caption above the cartoon reads: 'The situation on the election front according to *Nasz Kurier* and *Folk.* Want to know what *Haynt* says – turn over *Der Maszchis.*' Then, in upside down type below the cartoon: 'The situation on the election front according to *Haynt.*'

prospects for cooperation with the Slavic minorities, Prylucki protested an alliance with anti-state elements supportive of Petliura and of Bulak Balakhovitch (who directed counter-revolutionary Russian-Belorussian divisions). Not only do these groups harbour irredentist aspirations for independent Ukrainian and Byelorussian states carved from Poland, he warned, but they include clerics, Russian monarchists, and other reactionary elements who will not commit to support essential elements of the Jewish nationalist platform, such as an end to the mandatory Sunday rest law and the equality of Jewish schools before the law.[129] An alliance with the other minorities, he argued, threatened to strengthen suspicions of Jewish disloyalty to the state and was in any case counterproductive from a purely numerical standpoint: he pointed out that, contrary to the miscalculations offered by Grünbaum, who maintained that only three to five mandates were possible without the bloc and sixteen with it (thereby freeing Jewish deputies from the need to rely upon the support of the left for an interpellation), the Jews could actually win seventeen mandates without recourse to the bloc through a unified Jewish list. Prylucki also changed his tune with regard to peasant support for the Jews, expressing doubt that peasants 'who have imbibed antisemitism with their mothers' milk' could be relied upon to support lists including Slavic intellectuals and Jews when their national heroes were busy creating their own ethnic lists. Nor can the Jews, he advanced, be counted on to vote for non-Jewish candidates. Finally, Prylucki noted the opposition of many prominent *rebbes* to such an arrangement, a public position that would undermine the bloc among Hasidim. He urged Jewish voters to support an exclusively Jewish list, the Jewish democratic *Folksblok* that included him and his Warsaw Folkist colleagues Hirschhorn and Rasner, as well as the popular Vilna physician and community activist Tsemakh Szabad.[130]

The Bundist *Folkstsaytung* accused the Folkists of relying upon chauvinistic baiting to withdraw from the National Minorities Bloc in order to assure themselves a few seats in the Sejm when no real difference existed between them and the Zionists. Betraying their democratic pretences, they called on Jews to support 'purely Jewish' election lists and unsuccessfully attempted to steer the Agudah away from Grünbaum. In the Bund's appraisal, the Folkists did not represent a social class or clear social group. Rather, their support came from the few Jews 'coincidentally connected with the Folkist and not the Zionist *shtibl*. Artisan groups or merchant groups who have happened to fall under the personal influence of this or that Folkist leader.'[131]

№ 39 דער משחית. 4

פערבלאנדזשעט...

פרילוצקי (ביים שייד-וועג): — וואו בין איך? אפשר האב איך
געהאט א טעות: ווער ווייסט צי די דאזיגע וועגען פיהרען צום סיים? איך
כ'האב מורא אז מ'וועט מוזען איבערדרעהען דעם דישעל...

א ביסעל עניוות'דיגע
רעקלאמע פון „מאמענט".

ווער האט איבערגעפאטשט א שייגעץ אויפ'ן באזאר?
נח פרילוצקי!
ווער האט אומגעווארפען א קאזארמע אין מאקאטאוו?
נח פרילוצקי!
ווער האט ענטדעקט דעם נארד-פאל?
נח פרילוצקי!
ווער האט ליב שטשאַוו־באַרשט מיט קעז?
נח פרילוצקי!
ווער טוישט אלע וואך וועש?
נח פרילוצקי!
ווער בעקעמפט די וואנצען?
נח פרילוצקי!
וועמען האבען אלע יודען צו פער־דאנקען זייער לעבען?
נח פרילוצקי!

פעסימיסט.

קאמוניקאט פון „מאמענט".

דאס קאלעגיום פון „מאמענט" איז צווישען זיך דורכגעקומען אויף אזא אופן: מען זאל דרוקען מעלדונגען אין [illegible] פון ביידע בלאקען. אויב עס ווערט גע־דרוקט א פערלאבונג פון א פאלקיסט, דארף ווערען געדרוקט אויך א פערלא־בונג פון א בלאקיסט־ציוניסט. דעסגליי־כען ווען מען דרוקט א נעקראלאג פון א ציוניסט, דארף ווערען כנגד געדרוקט א נעקראלאג פון א פאלקיסט.

מאטקע.

5.4 This cartoon in *Der Maszchis* (no. 39, 3 November 1922) shows Noah Prylucki seated upon a donkey labelled 'Folkism.' The donkey stands at a crossroads leading in the directions *Nasz Kurier*, 'Intrigues against the National Bloc,' and '[Folkist] List Number 20.' The caption below the cartoon reads: *Prylucki:* 'Where am I? Perhaps I was mistaken: who knows whether these paths lead to the Sejm? I'm afraid I'll have to turn around ...'

(Next to the cartoon) 'A bit of modesty. Advertisement from "Moment":
Who slapped an impudent man at a bazaar? / Noah Prylucki!
Who overturned a barracks in *Mokotów*? / Noah Prylucki!
Who discovered the North Pole? / Noah Prylucki!
Who likes sorrel borsht with cheese? / Noah Prylucki!
Who changes his underwear every week? / Noah Prylucki!
Who combats bedbugs? / Noah Prylucki!
To whom do all Jews owe their life? / Noah Prylucki!

– Pessimist'

'Announcement from *Moment*
The *Moment* executive has decided the following: we will print announcements from both blocs. If praise for a Folkist is printed, we ought to print praise for a member of the Zionist-led National bloc. The same goes if we print an obituary for a Zionist – we ought to print the obituary of Folkist.
Motke'

The Zionists accused Prylucki once again of opportunism, claiming that he had abandoned the National Minorities Bloc only because he was dissatisfied with the four mandates allotted to his party. The self-proclaimed champion of the national rights of Polish Jewry, scoffed Grünbaum, now employs the same arguments against impairing Polish-Jewish relations offered by the Assimilationists.[132] Without the support of the Ukrainians and Byelorussians, whose antisemitic camps actually opposed the bloc, he argued, Jews could win mandates exclusively in Warsaw and Łódź. The Folksparty alone, he submitted, could certainly win no more than one mandate since its popularity, almost entirely restricted to Warsaw, had been on the decline since the last Sejm elections. Folkist agitation against the bloc would result only in the loss of Jewish votes for naught.[133] To further discredit the great champion of Yiddish, *Der haynt* reported that Prylucki beat a hasty retreat from hecklers while delivering a speech at the Jewish Academic Home in Warsaw upon the Polish exhortations of his exasperated wife.[134]

The tenor of mutual denunciations between the Folkists and Zionists reached such a fever pitch that a committee was founded to reduce tensions.[135] A coalition of Folkists and Bundists rose to the defence of Samuel Hirschhorn, who was sharply censured and temporarily excluded by the Jewish Writers' and Journalists' Association, following a 42–20 vote, for his inflammatory articles attacking the bloc in the Polish-language, Jewish nationalist paper *Nasz Kurier* (Our Courier), to which he was a chief contributor. The articles were judged a dishonour to the association, an endangerment of Jewish national interests, and a source of material for the antisemitic *Dwa Grosze.*[136] *Der moment* refused to support Prylucki's anti-bloc stance despite Prylucki's considerable influence on its editor and the daily's popular writer Yeushzon added his voice to the bloc's defenders.[137] Prylucki's position was also publicly criticized by Dubnow, who considered it irresponsible to break a unified Jewish front.[138]

Characteristically, Hillel Zeitlin deplored the mutual allegations between parties and condemned the negative influence of a 'political education' on youth who would do better to spend their time on pursuits necessary for the building of their future rather than preoccupied with the insincere rhetoric, gossip, and slander which were the staple of Jewish politics.[139] While expressing an aversion for the 'tasteless jokes' and message of radical democratization found in *Nasz Kurier,* the only paper besides the Folkist organ *Dos folk* to denounce the bloc, he urged an end to the persecution of Hirschhorn, whom he deemed a sincere and proven activist for Jewish rights.[140]

The Folkists were joined in their opposition to the National Minorities-Bloc by all Jewish socialist parties on class grounds and by the Galician Zionists, who expressed doubts about the bloc's effectiveness and ran their own lists. The Jewish National Bloc (Central Merchants' Association, the Agudah, and Congress Poland and *Kresy* Zionists) joined with all other national minorities, which individually composed unified national blocs, to achieve a success far beyond expectations. Thirty-five Jewish deputies, making up 7.9 per cent of the Sejm, were elected: seventeen on the list of the National Minorities Bloc, two West Galician Zionists, fifteen East Galician Zionists (an unexpected victory resulting from the abstention of the Ukrainians from the elections), and one Folkist. Thanks to the bloc the Ukrainians dispatched twenty deputies to the Sejm, the Germans seventeen, the pro-Russian Byelorussians one, and the pro-Polish Ukrainians five (the Ukrainians in East Galicia boycotted the elections as a demonstration of their refusal to recognize Poland's annexation of this territory). The Jews won eight seats thanks to the Minorities Bloc in the Senate plus four from a separate list presented in East Galicia. In all, the national minorities won eighty-nine seats (20%) in the Sejm, of which sixty-six were elected on the list of the Minorities Bloc, and twenty-seven (24%) in the Senate, of which twenty-three were from the bloc. Among the Polish blocs, the right captured 29 per cent of the vote, the centre 24 per cent, and the left 25 per cent, while the minorities, including all nine lists, obtained 22 per cent of the popular vote. Jewish representation in the two houses of parliament nearly equalled the Jews' percentage in the total population of Poland.[141]

The victory of the National Minorities Bloc was hailed in the Jewish press as a great victory for Grünbaum and the Zionists, who sent fifteen of the thirty-five Jewish deputies to the Sejm and five of the twelve Jewish senators to the Senate. The bloc captured 80 to 95 per cent of Jewish votes throughout Poland and 55 per cent in Warsaw. The failure of the Folkists to win more than one mandate, which went quite naturally to Prylucki, confirmed the party's decline in popularity since 1919. Most of the Folkist votes came from Warsaw, the party's only real base of support, and a few thousand isolated votes were registered in Łódź, Luck, Vilna, and Lublin, along with scattered votes elsewhere. Neither the Jewish workers' parties nor the Assimilationists received enough votes to obtain a single mandate.[142]

Prior to 1922 Jewish deputies blamed their impotence and failures in the Sejm on a tiny representation that rendered almost all initiative impossible without the support of the Polish Socialist Party (PPS) and

German deputies. The government, nonetheless, served as an address to which they could turn for redress even if it proved too weak or afraid of public opinion to intercede on behalf of Jewish rights and demands. Now the Jews had three times as large a representation in the new Sejm as previously, one that amounted to a serious force in conjunction with the other national minorities.[143] On 2 December 1922 the 'Jewish Koło in the Sejm and Senate of the Polish Republic' was created with the co-operation of nearly all Jewish deputies and senators, who organized into four clubs representing the National Council, the Deputies and Senators of East Galicia, the Agudah, and the Central Merchants' Association. Preferring to preserve his freedom of action and surely indignant after the elections, Prylucki alone among the Jewish deputies refused to join. Instead he formed a faction of his own, the Club of the Folksparty.[144] Prylucki's exclusion from the Jewish Koło denied him the opportunity to participate in the work of commissions. He was unable to address the Sejm forum except during sessions when discussion was not limited and the list of speakers was not closed. He took frequent advantage of the one opportunity available to him, submitting many interpellations signed by socialist, Byelorussian, Ukrainian, and German but not Jewish deputies.[145]

A Single-Minded Pursuit: Prylucki's Activity for Yiddish in the Second Sejm

In contrast with other Jewish parties, who demonstrated a greater willingness to negotiate with other national minorities and to seek compromises with the government, Prylucki held fast to his fierce independence and belligerent parliamentary tactics. Alone in the Sejm, Prylucki maintained the militant Yiddishist and Jewish nationalist stance that had become the hallmark of his political activity. Although he joined the Jewish Koło in protesting Jewish disabilities and discrimination in all spheres, his activity focused above all on the rights of Yiddish and the Yiddish school. His interpellations, such as one in 1923 condemning the refusal of the state telegraph agency to permit Roman-letter telegrams in Yiddish but not in other non-Polish languages, generally received the support of the Jewish Koło (and sometimes of other minorities and the Polish left) as a matter of principle in defence of civil rights. Petitions he brought to stop the persecution of Yiddish schools most frequently did not reach the Sejm floor for discussion or were rejected by parliamentary commissions.[146]

Prylucki's intransigence in the Jewish language debate deprived him of the support of the Koło when he refused Zionist requests to change the wording of resolutions he proposed during a budget discussion in December 1924. The resolutions called for payment from the state budget of the deficit incurred by Yiddish schools for the year 1924–25 and for the promulgation of a law concerning a state-funded school system with Yiddish as its language of instruction.[147] An amendment proposed by the Koło to include all Jewish and not merely Yiddish schools was subsequently defeated in the Sejm. Grünbaum, who emphasized that the Zionists never excluded Yiddish from their petitions, denounced Prylucki's position as a form of Yiddishist terror against Hebraists and as a crushing blow to a united Jewish front vis-à-vis the external world. Another Koło member, the Mizrachi deputy Szymon Feldman, protested that even Orthodox deputies in the Koło voted on behalf of Yiddish schools in a show of Jewish unity despite the schools' lack of Jewish tradition and religious instruction. The school question, he insisted, must remain an internal Jewish matter and not one to be resolved among unsympathetic Polish parties.[148] In his defence, Prylucki insisted upon the necessity of express mention of Yiddish in the resolution because of the government's demonstrated hostility to Yiddish schools. He argued that, rather than fight his proposal, the Koło ought to have brought an additional resolution of its own in favour of Hebrew schools and thereby avoided this embarrassing situation.[149] The incident earned Grünbaum the Bund's denunciation as a traitor to Jewish interests and provoked a fist fight when a group of Yiddishists came to protest a speech he was scheduled to hold at the Writers' and Journalists' Association.[150]

Simon Dubnow, the father of Jewish autonomism whose public approbation both the Zionists and Folkists eagerly sought,[151] criticized the Koło for not voting for the 'lesser evil' or abstaining and later pursuing an additional proposal for Hebrew. Paraphrasing a Jewish idiom alluding to malicious behaviour, Dubnow censored the Koło in *Jüdische Rundschau* for acting out of 'hatred for Haman' (the genocidal villain of the Purim story; here, Prylucki) rather than sincere conviction. In doing so, the Koło had broadcast the message that the majority of Jews opposes its own vernacular, which forms one of the foundations of as yet unrealized autonomy. The famous scholar was not satisfied with criticizing the Koło, though. He castigated Prylucki, as well, for what he deemed irresponsible conduct in the Sejm and expressed general disapproval for the decisions taken at its 1925 Folksparty conference in Warsaw as hostile to Jewish settlement in Palestine and contradicting the program of his own pre-revolutionary Folksparty in St Petersburg. He criticized both extreme Hebraists and extreme Yiddishists for seeking to undermine each other's chosen language, both of which, he argued, were integral parts of Jewish life. The Agudah was also not spared his criticism since he considered it an equally divisive force despite its name ('Union of Israel').[152] In a private letter to Prylucki, who demanded an explanation of these remarks, Dubnow regretted that the entire Folksparty stands alone as if excommunicated from the Jewish parliamentary camp. 'You will likely understand my pain when I have lived to see that precisely our own – from the Folksparty – have destroyed this organization and the unified Jewish national front vis-à-vis the outside world.'[153]

Kehila Elections and the Ugoda

Although notorious for its drastic economic and fiscal policies that weighed especially heavily on the Jewish lower middle class, the government of Władisław Grabski (1923–5) at times extended a conciliatory hand to the Jews when in need of their support to preserve its fragile parliamentary majority. One such initiative was the organization in 1924 of the first democratic *kehila* elections in former Congress Poland, whose results serve as a more accurate barometer of internal Jewish political forces than the Sejm elections. According to a government decree of February 1919, the *kehila* and its council retained legal status under the authority of the Ministry of Religion and Education and bore responsibility for religious affairs, education, and charity. Universal male, secret, proportional elections replaced the old curial system, which democratic Jewish parties had long protested. Apart from the Orthodox and Assimilationists, Jewish parties sought to widen the *kehila*'s competence and transform it into a secularly based, national organ. The Zionists accused the Agudah of hypocrisy in excluding its Orthodox foes, including the Mizrachi and the Hasidic opponents of the Gerer rebbe, from its list while the Folkists denounced the Agudah's insistence on the purely religious nature of the *kehilot*.[154] Citing the vote of Agudah and Mizrachi deputies against permitting a special vow for soldiers who professed religions unrecognized in Poland, Prylucki called on voters to oppose clericalism and religious coercion, although not religion itself.[155] He also protested the anti-democratic voting regulations excluding women, which he saw as numerically weakening Jewish national life.[156]

Defamatory attacks abounded in campaign propaganda between all parties vying to remake the *kehila* according to their own vision. The

Folkists, for example, charged that the Zionists would levy a 'contribution' for extra-*kehila* needs – an allusion to support for settlement in Palestine. The Zionists accused Prylucki of misappropriating funds entrusted to him by the Jewish Historical-Ethnographic Society in New York for the publication of a folklore and linguistics quarterly in Warsaw in memory of An-ski. It was claimed that Prylucki used the $150 entrusted to him for initial expenses to finance the publication of *Filologishe shriftn* (Philological Writings), the long dreamed of linguistics journal that he launched in 1924 with his future colleagues in the Philological Section of YIVO (*Yidisher visnshaftlekher institut,* Jewish Scientific Institute, founded in Vilna in 1925) Max Weinreich and Zalmen Reyzen.[157] The charges were proved false but this was to no avail.[158] The Folksparty registered feeble support in elections also as a result of the poor voter turn-out in Warsaw (only 25,000 of 57,551 or 43% of those eligible voted), where few substantive changes in the administration of *kehila* affairs were expected. The Democratic bloc (Folkist list), which included pro-Folkist artisans and merchants associations, gained the support of only 5.5 per cent of the voters and three of fifty seats in Warsaw. The Agudah, in comparison, gained seventeen seats and the Zionists fourteen. In Łódź the Folkists won one of thirty-five mandates whereas the Agudah took thirteen mandates and the Zionists nine. Returns from ninety-nine *kehilot* (of which only a handful were outside Congress Poland) reveal that more than half of the total 816 mandates went to the Agudah (292) and the Zionists (192). The Folkists gained no ground outside Poland's two largest cities. The Mizrachi, the Bund, Poale Zion, and artisan groups all captured far fewer mandates than either the Agudah or the Zionists, although their tallies still far exceeded those of the Folkists. The *kehila* thus became primarily an arena for the contest between the Zionists, who were the leading force in Polish Jewish Sejm politics (but not at the community level), and the Orthodox, who provided the largest number of *kehila* members in the interwar period.[159]

Recognizing that Poland's poor relations with the Jews earned it a poor reputation in the international realm, the Grabski government also approached Jewish representatives in mid-1925 to renew direct negotiations, which had failed in 1920. A compromise with the Jewish Koło was sought to secure for Poland a large foreign loan, League of Nations recognition of Poland's borders, and parliamentary support necessary to keep the current government in power. In return for the Jews' unconditional support of the government and approval of the state budget, vague promises were made to alleviate measures threatening the Jews with economic ruination and to make certain concessions in the cultural realm. These included making uniform the *kehila* statute throughout the land, granting permission to use Hebrew and Yiddish in public assemblies and *kehila* meetings, and the opening of *szabasówki* (state elementary schools closed on Saturday) in cities with large Jewish populations.

Eager to launch a new era of cooperation between Jews and the state, the Galician Zionists and Orthodox, as well as most of the Jewish press, supported an accord. Following secret negotiations, the *Ugoda* (compromise) was ratified by the Koło on 30 June 1925. The *Ugoda* fell far short, however, of the demands for national cultural autonomy common to Jewish nationalists and socialists. Thus, it was bitterly opposed by both Grünbaum and Prylucki, who concurred in rejecting a special declaration of loyalty to the state demanded only for the Jews and the relinquishment of their fundamental democratic right of opposition in return for some concessions in the realm of civic rights that ought to be constitutionally guaranteed. Other national minorities similarly condemned the *Ugoda*'s Jewish supporters for surrendering their political autonomy and collaborating with a hostile government in return for a pittance of illusory promises. In the end, the anti-*Ugoda* voices proved correct. Although ratified by the government, the accord was never implemented and its most important points never printed by the Polish Telegraph Agency. The Koło consequently reneged on its side of the agreement and passed into the opposition camp of the Grabski government in October 1925.[160]

The Problem of Yiddish Secular Schooling

In contravention of the Minorities Treaty, financially strapped Yiddish and Hebrew secular schools received almost no state support and necessarily remained in private hands.[161] In compliance with the treaty, hundreds of public elementary schools were opened with Ukrainian, German, and other languages as the languages of instruction.[162] To be sure, the opening of these schools was dependent upon numerous formalities, such as population requirements and teacher qualifications that were manipulated by the state to reduce their number and encourage the polonization of Slavic minorities through the medium of an increasing number of bilingual schools.[163] Similarly, state policy, including educational policy, aimed at pressuring the German minority to emigrate or polonize by denying the use of its language in numerous spheres.[164]

Not a single Hebrew or Yiddish public school, however, needed to be shut down by the state, because none had been established. Of Jewish schools, the central government looked favourably only upon religious ones while both Hebrew- and, above all, Yiddish-language schools were subject to frequent official harassment. Various pretexts were employed, including the charge that the Jewish jargon is not a language or that the buildings were unsafe, to arrest or remove teachers and to deny the renewal of school concessions over the protests of Jewish nationalist deputies in the Sejm. The government objected to the schools, especially those of *Tsisho,* as an expression of Jewish nationalism and because of their secular, leftist orientations. Between 1920 and 1922 more than twenty private Jewish schools were closed in this manner, especially in the eastern border lands (*kresy*), where both the Hebrew and Yiddish school movements were at their strongest. Moreover, supervisory state authorities gradually cancelled or reduced appropriations given by a considerable number of municipalities to *Tsisho* schools.[165] This trend, while never resulting in the outlawing of private Jewish schools, continued throughout the interwar period.

Opposition to the Yiddish secular school movement did not come exclusively, however, from the side of the Polish government. The Yiddishist *Tsisho* schools, to whose organization Folkists were leading contributors, were also decidedly unpopular among many impoverished Jewish parents once the emergency conditions of the First World War, when schools provided for the basic material needs of children of refugees, had ended. The Folksparty's work on behalf of the Yiddish secular school movement, the fundament of its program for Yiddish culture, could make little headway not only because of government policy but also because of the generally unfavourable attitudes towards the schools among both Jews and Poles and as a result of the Folkists' exclusion from school work by Jewish socialists.

Financially strapped Yiddish and Hebrew secular schools necessarily charged tuition, albeit a modest one, and relied heavily upon party funding and contributions from Jewish communities abroad, especially in the United States. Yiddishist schools were typically associated with the anti-religious, anti-Hebrew radicalism preached by Jewish socialists. Most Jewish children in the interwar period received their education in Polish state schools (although many children also attended supplementary religious schools in the afternoons), where they imbibed not only the Polish language but Polish romantic values, including an adulation of the literary and historical traditions of the Polish lands.[166]

The tuition charged by the private secular schools in either Jewish language, as well as the network of Orthodox day schools created by the

Agudat Yisrael Party, however modest,[167] became all the more decisive as Jewish economic positions were increasingly undermined by both official and non-official policy and the general economic decline of the land. Moreover, bourgeois parents recognized that Yiddish schools were poorly suited to equip children for social and economic advancement, even if they had high pedagogical standards, as a consequence of discrimination at the high school and university levels. Diplomas from Yiddish schools were frequently not recognized by the state, obliging pupils to prepare for state exams in addition to the ones administered by Jewish schools in order to gain admission to state institutions of higher learning. Parents also feared that their children would speak Polish with a stigmatizing Jewish accent.[168] Attending secondary school or university abroad, where the diplomas of Jewish secondary schools were sometimes recognized, was an option available only to the wealthy.[169] For the most part, only the most committed socialists and Yiddishists were willing to make the financial sacrifices necessary to maintain the beleaguered schools.

The Yiddish secular school, the cornerstone of the Folkist vision of national cultural autonomy for the Jews in the Diaspora, was thus unable to draw more than a fraction of Polish Jewish youth. Despite the tremendous dedication of parents and educators involved in the *Tsisho* schools, the Yiddish schools showed the weakest enrolments among the Jewish elementary schools. During the school year 1934–35, for example, they drew only 9.5 per cent of the total number of children who attended Jewish schools in comparison with roughly 25 per cent for the *Tarbut* schools and 55 per cent for religious schools (run mostly by the Agudah within the framework of the *Horev* network).[170] The Hebrew-language *Tarbut* schools fared somewhat better since they suffered less harassment from the state and because of the popularity of the Zionist pioneering ethos they imparted. Both types of secular Jewish schools were most popular in the multiethnic *kresy*, where Poles constituted a minority, thus diluting assimilatory pressures.

A lack of support for Yiddish schools and demonstrative loyalty to the language, reasoned the Vilna Yiddish activist Zalmen Reyzen, would entail a loss of Jewish livelihoods or the failure to create new ones: there would be no Yiddish teachers, no Yiddish artists, no municipally funded Yiddish theatre, no Yiddish announcements in newspapers, etc.[171] Such an argument was quite in keeping with the spirit of the Warsaw Folkists, as well. It necessarily presupposed the continued existence and, it was hoped, the expansion of a Jewish sub-economy while rejecting the full integration of Jews into Polish society, especially its cultural spheres.

Folkist school activity also met with opposition within the Yiddishist camp. Already at the School Conference in 1921, only the Independents, who represented the centrist group at the conference (it later joined the Bund), emphasized the need to cooperate with the middle class and democratic intelligentsia. The Bund and Poale Zion, on the contrary, insisted upon the exclusively socialist character of the school.[172] Prylucki complained that same year that while 84 per cent of the children attending Yiddish elementary schools in Warsaw and 80 per cent in Vilna were the children of artisans and petty merchants, the Jewish bourgeoisie was not doing enough to support the schools and was leaving their leadership to the workers' movement.[173]

His colleague Yoyne Shapiro presented a fuller picture of the Folkist position in *Dos folk* in 1922. He castigated Jewish socialists for involving the schools in party rivalries despite the need for a unified Yiddishist front to overcome the grave political and material difficulties confronting the schools. Guided by the destructive principle of separating themselves from bourgeois elements, the socialists chase after American financial support for their own educational purposes. Due to their reprehensible actions, he argued, the Yiddish secular schools as a whole had developed an unfair reputation as socialist party schools with the end result that bourgeois parents were disinclined to enrol their children. Further, he added, measures taken by the Polish Ministry of Education against Jewish schools were openly declared to be in response to what was deemed the excessively leftist orientation of the Yiddishist schools.[174]

Shapiro did not restrict his criticism to the Jewish left, however. He acknowledged that work on behalf of Yiddish was more difficult among the bourgeoisie, which, in contrast with the workers, questioned the primacy and value of Yiddish and persisted in deeming a school without Yiddish a better institution. Moreover, the politically unconscious bourgeoisie, he said, was susceptible to the 'blue-white danger' (Zionism) with its 'empty dreams' and pronounced animosity to 'jargon.'[175]

The Folkists saw their influence in the schools of the *Shul- un folksbildung-fareyn* greatly reduced in the 1920s until they were essentially excluded from *Tsisho* (except in Vilna) by the doctrinal narrowness of the Bund.[176] While only 29 per cent of *Tsisho* schools were located in Congress Poland in 1924, these institutions were rife with sectarian spirit in contrast with the bulk of the schools, which were (like those of the Hebraist *Tarbut* system) concentrated in the multiethnic regions of Vilna, Białystok, and Brześć (*Tsisho* was virtually non-existent in Galicia).[177] There also existed (at least in Congress Poland) a strong, organized Orthodox opposition to Jewish secular schools.[178]

The Folkists were impotent, however, in the *kresy* with the exception of Vilna, where a sister party, the *Folks-demokratishe partey* (People's Democratic Party), was formed under the leadership of Tsemakh Szabad and became a separate organization in August 1923 with its central council in Vilna.[179] The Jewish school movement was especially strong in Vilna, a city renowned for its Hebrew scholarly tradition and celebrated by Yiddishists for the widespread use of the language among bourgeois and intellectuals, as well as the lower classes.[180] There the Jewish upper classes switched from Russian, the prestigious and economically advantageous imperial language, to Yiddish after the tsarist retreat during the First World War. They did this largely to avoid risking the animosity of other peoples by siding overtly with any one party (Russian, Polish, Lithuanian, or German) in a multinational conflict. In the former Congress Poland and especially Galicia, where the pace of polonization was most advanced even before the First World War (because of the favoured status given the language since the 1860s by the Habsburg Empire), assimilative forces were at their strongest. Polish was not only the language of the state in these regions of Polish ethnic concentration; it was also the dominant language of non-Jewish society as a whole, including its upper classes whose conduct provided a model for the Jewish intelligentsia.[181]

Prylucki faulted Jewish socialists for refusing to cooperate with the democratic bourgeoisie and blamed them for foolishly expelling the bourgeoisie from school activity after its many contributions to the Yiddishist educational movement.[182] Purportedly out of dissatisfaction with the policies of the *Shul- un folksbildung-fareyn*, a number of teachers working under its auspices decided to transfer the schools they managed to the authority of the organization *Undzere kinder* (Our Children). These schools were subsequently incorporated into the Bundist-dominated *Tsisho*. A scandal erupted in 1922 after the state demanded that the original charter legalizing the *Shul- un folksbildung fareyn* be presented. Following the First School Conference in 1920, which was convened under the *Fareyn's* charter, all of the *Fareyn's* materials – stamp, letterhead, archive, etc. – supposedly became the property of *Tsisho*, which pronounced itself the *Fareyn*'s heir. The actual charter, however, remained in the hands of Prylucki, who considered himself the primary organizer of the *Fareyn* during the German occupation and therefore entitled to use the charter to open a new school organization in 1923, the *Folksbildung-lige* (Public Education League).[183]

The *Lige* was officially authorized in July 1924 to open new Yiddish elementary and intermediate schools along with evening courses for adults. Its stated aim was to create a broad network of Yiddish schools for the petite bourgeoisie since no schools yet existed specifically for its children and because the *Tsisho* schools taught anti-religious proletarian culture and emphasized the proletariat as the backbone of the school movement. The Folkist *Lige* opened, however, no new schools under its own aegis and was therefore excluded according to the *Tsisho* constitution from the organization's governing circle.[184] Despite the support of some Folkist intellectuals for the Hebrew-Yiddish *Shul-kult* schools opened by Poale Zion, Prylucki was unwilling to join this association.[185] The *Lige* maintained a handful of existing schools and purchased a villa in the resort area of Otwock outside Warsaw for use as an orphanage with American relief monies. The *Tsisho* organ *Shul un lebn* (School and Life) accused the Folksparty in 1922 of conducting secret negotiations with a representative of the New York–based Warsaw Relief to the detriment of *Tsisho*, whose own sanatorium had been forced to close earlier that year and which also sought money to purchase a villa.[186] The whole matter of the orphanage was forgotten until 1926, when a series of articles in *Der haynt* alleged that the *Folksbildungs-lige* terribly neglected and abused children and teachers at the Otwock villa. Prylucki was reproached with cynically seeking to exploit the orphanage to augment his party's prestige and popularity. He allegedly refused assistance from the Jewish *Yesomim-farband* (Orphans' Association) and used orphanage monies to cover his own personal expenses rather than pay for food, clothing, and other needs. 'Noah Prylucki is a has-been,' jeered the journal, 'and even his cheerleaders have turned away from him long ago.'[187] While he did not deny the orphanage faced a financial crisis, Prylucki denied any malfeasance on his part and that of his organization.[188]

The Failings of the Folksparty

The Folkist program offered little more than secular Yiddishism, which was in itself insufficiently attractive to Polish Jewry, especially as it became increasingly Polish-speaking and consumers of Polish culture in the 1920s and 1930s. Its perceived hostility to Hebrew and Palestine offended the native sympathies of many Jews.[189] In contrast, the Orthodox, who built yeshivas and other parochial institutions, were able to tap into the deeply rooted religious sentiment and respect for tradition common to most Polish Jews. While *aliyah* remained a reality for no more than a tiny fraction (albeit a growing one in the 1920s) of Polish Jewry, the Zionists could rely on the masses' instinctive sympathy for Hebrew and the cause of settlement in Palestine. Following the Balfour Declaration, they seemed to be making real progress towards the creation, even if still distant, of a self-sufficient and sovereign Jewish state. Further, the Zionist-dominated blocs in the Sejm were no less active in championing Jewish rights than the Folkists.

Jewish socialists, who were as firmly rooted as the Folkists in the claims to protect Jewish interests in situ, led a large professional movement and offered real succour to the economic interests of the impoverished and increasingly proletarian masses.[190] The Folkists had only modest success in organizing artisans and merchants despite the gratitude expressed by many for Prylucki's intercessory work on their behalf before the government and the party's efforts to rebuild petty commerce and manual industry through schools, co-operatives, and credit facilities.[191] The party, which struggled to dominate artisan associations and make them exclusively Yiddish-speaking, alienated many artisans with its position on Hebrew and Palestine and was unable to gain a foothold in the staunchly Zionist Łódź Artisans' Association. Warsaw artisans divided into separate Folkist and Zionist organizations in 1919 and reunited only in 1925.[192] Zionism, however, was also unsuited for the hundreds of thousands of pauperized Jewish craftsmen and petty traders unable to qualify for certificates of immigration to Palestine.[193] The Bund with its emphasis on daily economic struggle had the greatest influence on the Jewish trade union movement.[194]

On the whole, Prylucki's activity was, as may be anticipated from a one-man bloc, not very effective.[195] Admittedly, the Jewish bloc in the Sejm did not fare much better: the national minorities failed to cooperate among themselves because of conflicts of interest, and Polish nationalist parties, under the slogan of a 'pure Polish majority,' resolutely opposed all compromise with them in the Sejm.[196] Pointing to the isolation of the Koło, Szabad even boasted to Dubnow that Prylucki was single-handedly more effective than the entire Jewish club.[197]

Prylucki's intensive parliamentary engagement – his sixty speeches were the second-highest number among Jewish deputies[198] – was not matched in enthusiasm by a great many of his party colleagues. Prylucki found himself isolated not only in the Sejm and in the cultural realm but, increasingly, in his own party, as well. Many Yiddishist 'folk-intellectuals' formerly motivated by the romantic desire to 'unite with the interests of the Jewish masses'[199] and thrilled by the Folksparty's brash declarations and defiant posturing quickly grew cold to a party dominated by a single iron-willed personality and ideologically estranged from the 'broad masses' it claimed to represent. The party organ *Dos folk* ceased publication in April 1922 after three years of publication with interruptions and only resumed briefly in 1925 before the party split definitively the following year.[200] Disaffection and disillusionment were of course to be expected within the ranks of a self-proclaimed populist party once it became clear that it was incapable of drawing a mass following and essentially remained the province of a tiny intellectual elite. The Folkists were, so to speak, losing hold of their folk.

Prylucki's obstinacy was also bad for business. Bitter polemics between *Der haynt* and *Der moment* had long been a fixture of Polish Yiddish journalism. *Der haynt* repeatedly accused *Der moment* under Tsevi Prylucki's editorship of cowardice in its coverage of political affairs for fear of possible government fines. It charged Noah Prylucki individually with exploiting his tractable father's affection to use the paper as a second organ for the Folksparty and using his deputy status in the Sejm to further the interests of his private legal clients.[201] Normally, both papers thrived on these types of polemics and personal attacks, which riveted readers and buoyed sales. The Pryluckis' finances suffered a real blow, however, when the younger Prylucki, assuming editorial responsibilities while his father was away, refused to print an article by Yeushzon (pseudonym of Moyshe Bunem Yustman) sharply criticizing the Folksparty. Indignant at an offence that the senior Prylucki would likely have not permitted, Yeushzon, the most popular journalist in Poland, left *Der moment* for *Der haynt* in 1925 and took with him his sizable readership. His first article alone in the rival newspaper increased its circulation by 5,000 copies.[202] Formerly the richest and most widespread newspaper in Poland, *Der moment* found itself soon lagging behind *Der haynt*, whose circulation had previously been a third of that of *Der moment*.[203]

Drifting Apart

Folkist party members began to drift into various camps by the early 1920s. Internal frictions led to the eventual departure of most left-oriented elements, which found refuge among the Bundists, the Communists, the Independents, and even the Zionists. Nomberg, for one, strongly sympathized with the Bund's socialist message and declined to engage it in party polemics despite its increasingly virulent assaults on the Folkists. He gradually retreated from party activity after withdrawing from the Sejm in 1920, preferring to travel and write.[204] Still committed to Yiddish, he visited Argentina in 1922–23, where he raised money for the *Tsisho* schools and helped to organize a Yiddish writers' association that later bore his name in recognition of his contribution. This trip was followed by visits to the United States in 1924 and Palestine in 1926 prior to his death in 1927.

In 1924 he mocked as absurd and grotesque *Der haynt*'s description of him, now most emphatically a political 'non-partisan,' leading a band of Bundists in a violent assault on Grünbaum to protect Noah Prylucki's honour on the premises of the Writers' and Journalists' Association.[205] He reprimanded Grünbaum for his failure to support the Yiddish schools and characterized the episode as a 'great political crime and an act of petty personal accounts' between two deputies who, because of their insupportable egos, he implied, 'cannot dwell under the same roof.' The Jewish Koło, he cautioned, must overcome partisanship and personal ambitions to serve as an effective representative body, for responsibility for the Jewish present and future lies much more with it than with than one-man bloc presented by Noah Prylucki.[206]

A former Gerer Hasid, Shloyme Mendelson joined the Folksparty at its inception under the influence of the ex-Hasid Nomberg, with whom he enjoyed a close relationship and who served as the youth's mentor. Apart from being a leading pedagogue and school activist, he served as the co-editor of the Folkist organ *Dos folk* and member of its central council.[207] Since most school activists were 'Litvaks,' whose Yiddish dialect was foreign to the children, the Congress Poland native Mendelson stood out as the most prominent, although likely not the only, teacher to speak the 'broad Polish *Itshe-Mayer* dialect.'[208] He was offered Prylucki's forfeited Sejm mandate in 1919 but refused it because of disagreements with the party. Initially, he had joined the party because he was intimidated by the size of the Bund and felt the Zionists, with their other-worldly demands for Hebrew and Palestine, too acculturated and distant from the masses.[209] Blaming ideological alienation, he formally left the Folksparty in 1921 and eventually joined the Bund in 1928.[210] When invited to return to party work, he reportedly asked, 'How can I [as the teacher of workers' children] be a political leader of the Folkists artisans when they organize lock-outs in the factories where my pupils' parents work?'[211]

Among those who remained in the party there was strong opposition to Prylucki's views and tactics, in part because of an unwillingness to accept party politics.[212] Zeitlin, who had long stressed his opposition to any type of factionalism, ceased to write on the party's behalf by the mid-1920s. Hirschhorn also left active involvement in the party, although he maintained his loyalty to its ideals.[213]

In a time when activity in a political club became a mainstay of youth culture and a sort of surrogate home for a generation facing the breakdown of traditional culture and economic collapse, the Folksparty offered little for youth apart from Yiddish schools, libraries, and lectures held in the *Folkshoyz*. Hillel Zeitlin's son Elkhonen, Prylucki's youthful adjutant and one of the youngest party activists, organized a Folkist youth organization in the name of Y.L. Peretz but himself departed from the party in the early 1920s. He went on to become, like his father, a prominent Warsaw journalist.[214] Another promising youth active in the party, Bernard Singer, one-time secretary of the party's central committee, abandoned the pursuit of a political career after failing to be elected to the Sejm from Łódź in 1919. After returning to Warsaw, he devoted himself to journalism in the Polish-language Jewish press and became renowned under the pseudonym Regnis.[215]

Conclusion

That the Folksparty was but a 'handful of leaders without a flock,' as antagonists regularly taunted, became even more painfully obvious as the party's positions grew more rigid and exclusionary of socialist and pro-Palestine elements. Its postulates of national cultural autonomy were impossible to realize in the contemporary political conjuncture and its ardent struggle to promote Yiddish as a supreme cultural value fell on largely indifferent if not deaf ears within the bourgeoisie. Yiddish was for them a fact of life but not an ideology.

'National Personal Autonomy' – the essence of the party's platform – became a meaningless phrase for a large segment of the Jewish population since the Folkists were able to deliver on few of their promises. The Folkists' unwillingness to compromise their nationalist ideals was a source of inspiration to Jewish voters when other Jewish parties were less bold and the future of Poland, including its treatment of its minorities, was yet undecided. This same inflexibility worked to the party's deficit in the political reality of interwar Poland, where minority alliances and other coalitions were necessary to combat discrimination and to achieve, if possible, the particularistic aims of Jewish parties. Prylucki himself, the party's chief figure, was successfully isolated in political and cultural work by his opponents within and without Jewish society. Attempts to win electoral support through charitable and relief work, such as Prylucki's visit to the United States, failed to compensate for either his or the party's waning popularity.

Moreover, their limited achievements in creating schools and organizing artisans notwithstanding, the Folkists were not very successful in impressing upon the bourgeoisie and intelligentsia the crucial link between the use of Yiddish in seemingly trivial, mundane situations and the economic and material welfare of the Jews in Poland. 'To judge by the number of Yiddish signs,' the Yiddish writer Nakhmen Mayzil noted in 1926, 'Warsaw is free of Jews' in comparison with much smaller, more demonstratively pro-Yiddish Vilna. How many intellectuals, even those who claim to support 'Jewish national institutions' (press, theatre, social-philanthropic institutions), he asked, were consistent in their claims and created a Jewish environment at home by actually speaking Yiddish with their wives and children?[216] In truth, however, even in Vilna, polonization was making inroads – just not as quickly as in the former Congress Poland and Galicia. The situation in Poland was nonetheless preferable to the United States, where life as Prylucki knew it was impossible.

Prylucki himself had no children and his wife, who was active in Polish literary society, quite possibly conversed with him in Polish even if she learned Yiddish imperfectly after their marriage and produced a number of poems and plays in this language. More significantly, a few Folkists, above all such prominent party leaders as Stupnicki and Hirshhorn (who commonly spoke in Polish at party assemblies and wrote a Polish-language history of the Jews in Poland) became regular contributors to the growing Jewish press in Polish during the 1920s (if not earlier) without ever publicly recanting their allegiance to Yiddish as the singular authentic medium for the creation of a modern Jewish culture.[217] In 1923 the Folkists Hirschhorn, Sh. Vagman, and Sh. Volkovitsh joined Jakub Appenszlak and the *Haynt* writer N. Shvalbe to found *Nasz Przegląd* ('Our Review'), the major Jewish nationalist paper in Polish in the interwar period.[218]

Predictably, neither the party's atrophying nor a distressing lack of demonstrated ideological commitment to Yiddish among the Folksparty's constituency – middle-class Jews – persuaded Prylucki to revise his fundamental views. As centrifugal forces became more pronounced in the party due to dissatisfaction with its platform, tactics, and stubborn leadership, he remained committed to the course he had set.

chapter six

Compromises? The Chair of Yiddish at the University of Vilnius

Following a coup in May 1926, organized by Marshal Piłsudski in the name of the struggle against state corruption and the sanitizing (*Sanacja*) of internal relations within Poland, Jewish politics in Poland entered a new era. Dissatisfied with the isolationist course taken by the Folksparty in Poland and with what were perceived as Prylucki's hegemonic ways,[1] the substantial opposition group within the party met with its sister party, Tsemakh Szabad's Vilna-based Jewish Democratic Party, at a conference held 21–2 August in Vilna (or Vilnius, as it is known in Lithuanian). Among those in attendance from the Warsaw Folkists were Nomberg, the economist Sh. Biber, Engineer Kabatski, the journalist O. Perelman, and the writer A. Grafman – formerly among the most active writers for *Dos folk* and party activists. The executive of the Warsaw Folksparty was declared dissolved by Sh. Volkovitsh, Dr Sh. Semyatitski, and the Yiddish and Polish literary critic Leo Finkelshteyn, who officially cited the inability 'to execute the *Sanacja* in the Jewish Folksparty for reasons independent of us' and the party's failure to serve the democratic ideal.[2]

The 1926 party split effectively signalled, if it were not already clear, the demise of the Warsaw-based Folksparty as a viable political option. With it came the demise of Prylucki's political career, although neither the party nor Prylucki had officially retired from active political engagement. In the years preceding the Second World War, Prylucki returned to his scholarly interests with renewed vigour despite growing pessimism among Yiddishists regarding the future of their beloved language and aspirations for its future. While never abandoning public activity in support of his convictions, he became increasingly removed from the public light and spent much of his time abroad. Following the German

6.1 Portrait of participants at the founding conference of the Democratic Folkist Party. Declaring the Warsaw Folksparty's executive dissolved, the new party represented the fusion of the Vilnius-based Jewish Democratic Party and a splinter group of the Warsaw Folksparty. Among those seated in the second row are Borekh Lubotski, Bogen, Sh. Buber, Peysakh Kaplan, H.D. Nomberg, and Moyshe Visotski. The new party shared the emphasis of its parent parties on the propagation of secular Yiddish culture and on support for the Yiddish secular school, as well as on the general campaign for Jewish national cultural autonomy in Poland. The party differed most strikingly from the Warsaw Folkists in that it devoted greater attention to social problems and was more positively inclined towards the Hebrew language and settlement in Palestine. (YIVO Institute, record 2461, frame 5178, 49257, 49258)

invasion of Poland in September 1939, he hurriedly fled eastward with the help of the Polish government, reluctantly leaving behind his family and most valuable possessions – his books and papers. Unexpectedly, the chaos of war placed him, now a refugee in Vilna, in a position to regain much of his public stature and to see many of his lifelong goals finally realized. Both his ego and his intellect could be satisfied. But at what cost to his ideals?

This chapter will explore Prylucki's activity in the years 1926 to 1941, the final phase in his career, and the controversial decisions that he made as political horizons darkened over Europe. Prylucki had invested his energies and hopes into an ideology whose viability was already seriously in question. How did he respond to the party's failure and to the growing tide of polonization among Jewish youths? How did he and Yiddishist colleagues of different stripes gathered around YIVO understand the future of Yiddish and Eastern European Jewry itself on the eve of the Holocaust? Controversies surrounding the creation of a Chair of Yiddish at the University of Vilnius in 1940 provide a prism through which to consider these questions. They also reveal the conflicting ideologies, bitter personality conflicts, and petty jealousies which continued to divide the Yiddishist camp even a time of great calamity and uncertainty.

Party Split

The principles of a new independent party were established while Prylucki was abroad addressing the National Minorities Conference in Geneva in Yiddish in the name of Polish Jewry. The party's proclamation was approved by Dubnow, who stated in a letter to its leadership that the time had arrived to reorganize the Folksparty on the basis of its pre-1917 principles with adaptations to postwar conditions in order to provide the necessary leadership in 'our time of fascism and dictatorship.'[3] Headed by Szabad, Nomberg, and the lawyer Joseph Czernichow (one of the founders of the Kiev Folksparty in 1918), the Jewish Democratic Folkist Party (*Yidishe demokratishe-folkistishe partey*, (Żydowskie) Stronnictwo Demokratyczno-Ludowe w Polsce) shared the emphasis of its parent parties on the propagation of secular Yiddish culture and on the Yiddish school as guaranteed by international treaty, as well as on the campaign for Jewish national cultural autonomy in Poland. Its fundamental principles were expounded in its organ *Frayer gedank* (Free Thought). In the economic sphere, it specifically protested the ruinous Sunday Rest law, demanded that the same cheap credit available to Polish artisans and petty merchants be made available to Jews, and called for at least partial compensation for the victims of a taxation policy particularly baneful to the Jewish middle class.[4]

The party differed most strikingly from Prylucki's party in its greater attention to social problems and in its more positive attitude towards both settlement in Palestine and the Hebrew language. Specifically, it encouraged the efforts of the *halutsim* (pioneer) movement, which strove to build Jewish life in Palestine on the foundations of productive labour and resisted on primarily ideological grounds the transfer of traditional Eastern European Jewish economic and social structures to an embryonic Jewish state. As a Yiddishist organization, though, the new party vigorously protested the 'persecution of Yiddish in Palestine' by ardent Hebraists committed to preventing Yiddish language and culture from taking root in the Zionists settlement or 'new' *yishuv*.[5] It maintained the conviction that the Jews are a 'world people' united by Yiddish, a language on its way to becoming the Jews' national language, and a participant in 'the struggle for freedom of thought and of progressive humanity.'[6] It also encouraged Jewish emigration to democratic Western lands and promoted agricultural labour, in addition to the long-standing Folkist attachment to artisanry, as a means to further Jewish productivization in the Diaspora. From its inception, though, the party did not seek to become a mass party but rather to influence thought and work in all domains.[7]

Not all Warsaw Folkists accepted that their party had been dissolved. In December 1926, the first issue of *Oyfboy* (Construction), the new organ of the Warsaw Folkists replacing the defunct *Dos folk*, remarked that the tenth anniversary of the party was not feted. In the lead article, Noah Prylucki reflected on the dismal recent history of the party. He contrasted it with what he described as the party's 'pioneering' achievements in Jewish national politics and Yiddish culture between 1916 and 1919 – the only years when it had a 'positive balance sheet.' While the Folkists had awakened the national consciousness of the petite bourgeoisie, they were completely without influence in the important Warsaw artisan and merchant associations thanks to the efforts of the party's opponents – among them the American Joint Distribution Committee (JDC) and Zionists – to undermine it. The party had existed for three years devoid of a capable central committee and deprived of normal connections with the provinces, where Folkists were active in local *kehila* and municipal politics but seldom in contact with Warsaw. The provinces, he complained, requested money of Warsaw but paid no dues to it. Moreover, they pursued an often independent line of action. The five Folkist Warsaw city councilmen demonstrated a similar lack of party discipline. Finally, the party excluded no one, permitting disgruntled individuals to leave without bidding farewell and to return without question. 'When it comes to discussing the Jewish Folksparty in Poland as an organization,' he bitterly concluded, 'all biting words are deserved, as is contempt and even the opinion that it wouldn't be a misfortune if it were to liquidate itself because such a life is, anyway, worse than death.'[8]

His colleague Lazar Kahan expressed views no less critical but struck a more optimistic note three months later in the second and final issue of *Oyfboy* to appear. The Folkists, he maintained, are mending their ways and could supplant Zionists and 'pareve,' unaffiliated democratic elements in the leading artisan and merchant organs.[9] 'When the Jewish masses are organized, they will necessarily turn to the Folksparty or at least to our program: autonomy and secular Yiddish culture and schools.' In the meantime, 'Our slogan [remains]: organize the Jewish masses, work among them, build their positions, create new possibilities for life.'[10] Folkist delegates from Warsaw, Łódź, Lublin, Międzyrzec, Kutno, Kozienice, and Siedlce gathered in Warsaw to celebrate the party's anniversary and to express a commitment to party discipline and dissatisfaction with the Vilna splinter group. They upheld hope, though, for the reunification of all factions.[11]

From the May 1926 coup until the outbreak of the Second World War, Jewish political parties in Poland pursued a more conciliatory policy towards the government, from which they hoped for protection in an atmosphere of rising popular antisemitism, and largely forwent on national demands. Jewish representation in the Sejm on the whole declined during this period. In municipal elections in Warsaw in 1927, the Folksparty ran apart from the Jewish national bloc (Zionists, Agudat Yisrael, Central Jewish Merchants' Association, Jewish Artisans' Association, Association of Jewish Retail Merchants, and the Association of Jewish Women) on a list headed by Prylucki that included representatives from twenty professional associations, but won no mandates. In what must have appeared as a betrayal of his former positions, Prylucki, in need of an ally after his recent electoral failure, ran for the Sejm in 1928 in a technical alliance with the Agudah, the Central Association of Jewish Merchants, and the Petty Merchants' Association. The 'General Jewish National Electoral Bloc' (Ogólno-Żydowski Narodowy Blok Wyborczy) ran on a list associated with the pro-government bloc (Bezpartyjny Blok Współpracy z Rządem, Non-Partisan Bloc of Cooperation with the Government) rather than join the Zionist-headed National Minorities' Bloc organized by his nemesis Grünbaum. Folkist Chaim Rasner, head of the Association of Artisans and Petty Merchants, ran with the Jewish national bloc, as he had in the 1927 Warsaw municipal elections. So did Tsemach Szabad's Vilna Folkists. This constituted a significant achievement for

Grünbaum, who promised Szabad support for Yiddish schools. Rasner received the votes of most Jewish artisans and shopkeepers, thereby depriving Prylucki of their support, and received a Sejm mandate. Szabad earned a place in the senate. The Agudah candidate received a mandate by virtue of occupying the thirty-sixth place on the government list.[12]

Prylucki received no mandate. This was to be his last bid for the Sejm as well as what amounted to the last more or less free parliamentary elections in Poland prior to the Second World War.

Although the Warsaw Folksparty did not wholly cease to exist, the party never regained its former stature. Scattered loyalists, including in Lublin and Łódź,[13] continued their activity without broader coordination at the local level. According to an exuberant *Der haynt*, basing itself upon a report in the *Lubliner togblat* (edited by Stupnicki), 'the father, rebbe and chief of the party' Noah Prylucki had failed to appear at a 1929 conference in Lublin presided over by Stupnicki to reunite (unsuccessfully) the Vilna and Warsaw factions on a platform including support for *Eretz-yisrael*, the Jewish Agency, and the creation of Jewish schools with a broad program of Hebrew studies. Instead, he sent a letter greeting the conference and supporting the existence of the Folksparty but expressed doubts about its survival because, in language characteristic of Prylucki, 'it is the logic of abnormal Jewish life that what is necessary is hard to keep alive.'[14]

Turn from Active Politics to Scholarship

Thereafter, Prylucki, whose name was virtually synonymous with the party, largely retired into the world of his journalistic and, above all, the private scholarly pursuits from which he derived tremendous satisfaction.[15] In 1931 the Association of Jewish Writers and Journalists feted him for over thirty years of literary, cultural, and political activity on behalf of Yiddish. A number of speakers, including his wife and the important Yiddish scholar and editor Zalmen Reyzen, expressed the hope that he would one day occupy a chair of Yiddish philology at a future Yiddish university in Vilna. There he would be able to continue with an appropriate budget and prestige the vital scholarly research that he had undertaken until then without any external support.[16]

While most of the speakers congratulated Prylucki on his cultural activity, a few voices called for his return to active political life in order to reassume leadership of the Folksparty. In response to these urgings

Prylucki remarked: 'However important political work may be, it does not compare to scholarly work ... The current condition of Jewish political and organizational life convinces me even more of the national political meaning of Yiddish philological work.'

Pointing to a decline in the fate of independent Jewish politics since 1927, he continued: 'Precisely because the political struggle for national rights is so weakened among us, it is an urgent necessity to reinforce work and propaganda for the Yiddish language in order to straighten out and dignify our character and to destroy slavish mimicry tendencies.'[17]

YIVO (*Yidisher visnshaftelkher institut*, Jewish Scientific Institute), the pioneering research institute for Yiddish language and culture founded in 1925 and headquartered in Vilna, was in Prylucki's conception to become 'the Yavne of a new generation.'[18] Like the ancient rabbinic academy in Yavne that preserved Jewish learning and thus identity after the Roman destruction of the Jerusalem Temple in a time of despair, it would provide inspiration and guidance for new generations. A secular institution, however, it would study and regulate the growth of the Yiddish language and culture. Created by Yiddishist scholars in lieu of a national university, it was independent of any state apparatus and thus almost entirely dependent upon private funding. In contrast with Western Jewry, Polish Jews were accustomed, he claimed, to seeing only practical value in education and to spending their disposable income on 'petit bourgeois pleasures like trips to [the resort town of] Zakopane.' They needed to be persuaded of the social value of scholarship. 'Poland's Jews must support their one institute – YIVO – which has accomplished miracles on a "starvation budget."'[19] To this end, he took up fundraising for YIVO during his travels and contributed parts of his personal library and archives to its holdings.[20]

Following his departure from politics, Prylucki resided for extended periods in Paris, where he divided his time between visits to art exhibitions and philological research, especially about Old Yiddish. There he also founded a short-lived Yiddish daily, *Der tog*, which survived for five months in 1928 until financial disagreements among its shareholders spelled its demise.[21] At the same time, the fortunes of *Der moment*, to which he continued to contribute occasional pieces, took a turn for the worse as a result of an overly ambitious attempt to modernize the newspaper. Successive wage cuts and other attempts to shore up the newspaper's finances were unsuccessful in paying off the interest on loans taken to purchase new offices and importing printing facilities from Germany in 1928. This situation was naturally exacerbated by the ensuing world

6.2 Staff and writers of *Moment*, the Yiddish newspaper. (r-l, top to bottom) Sh. Yanovski, Y. Tunkel (Der Tunkeler), Hillel Zeitlin, D. Druk, Y. Kh. Zagorodski, Tsevi Prylucki, Yeushzon (M. B. Yustman), Bentsiyen Chilinowicz, A. Almi, Mordkhe Spektor. (YIVO Institute, record 12571, frame 6789.01; 39548, 35949)

economic crisis following the collapse of the stock market the following year. In private hands since its beginnings, the newspaper became a cooperative in 1936. It was jointly owned by its editorial board, administrative staff, and printers together with its former owners.[22]

The 1930s: Darkness and Hope

By the mid-1930s, Prylucki's dismay over politics extended beyond Poland's borders. 'The world,' Prylucki observed in 1934, 'is enslaved to dictators and degenerate tyrants.'[23] He lamented bitterly the empowerment of dictatorial strongmen in the place of social democratic governments in a number of lands. He also noted frightening similarities between Hitler's Germany and Stalin's Soviet Union. In both lands socialism had mutated into tyranny and 'racism.' In the former, chauvinistic fascism and radical antisemitism aimed at the elimination of those of the wrong 'blood'; in the latter, communist ideological intolerance victimized those born into the wrong 'class.' In both societies, a notion of 'chosenness' legitimized the persecution of the dominant 'people's' alleged enemies.[24]

In the USSR, where Jews were actually recognized as a national minority with Yiddish as their language, hypocritical Jewish communists claimed to support Yiddish culture, he argued, while 'spitting in its face.' Their oppressive ideological controls and 'Jesuit chicanery' terrorized the world of Soviet Yiddish arts and letters, leading its members to denounce their former colleagues in Poland as 'Yiddish nationalists' in order to avoid persecution for heretical 'deviations' from the party line. To demonstrate their unshakeable loyalty to the regime scholars such as Max Erik and Nokhem Shtif publicly confessed the Yiddishist sins of their youth and denounced their colleagues in the West. Thus, the very same scholars from whom Soviet Yiddish researchers had until recently solicited submissions for their publications, invited to conferences, and upon whose work they still relied (or, in the case of Shtif, plagiarized, according to Prylucki) were now supposedly enemies of the Jewish proletariat.[25] Further, the Soviet answer to Zionism – the Jewish autonomous region in Birobidzhan in Soviet East Asia – disappointed Prylucki as a rejection of the ideal of extraterritorial cultural autonomy in the regions of the Jews' historical residence.

Prylucki returned definitively to Poland in 1934 and decried there the growing influence of the Endecja and the fascist National Radical Camp (Obóz Narodowo Radykalny), an even more radical spin-off of the Endecja that was especially popular among students. Both popular and official hostility towards Jews became especially pronounced after Piłsudski's death in 1935. Thuggish violence and hypocritical discrimination, according to Prylucki, were bringing about the gradual but systematic exclusion of Jews from the economy and cultural life even without the official adoption by the government of an 'Aryan paragraph' on the model of Nazi Germany. Endeks and their allies championed, for example, the rights of the Polish minority in Czechoslovakia and elsewhere while persecuting minorities at home.[26] He adamantly rejected Foreign Minister Beck's call in 1936 for a massive wave of emigration of Jews as a 'political solution' to the 'Jewish question,' an idea proposed earlier by the Endeks and applauded by Vladimir Jabotinsky's Revisionist Zionists and by Jewish territorialists alike. The proposal, he argued, is antisemitic in its very essence since Jews are the only minority whose mass emigration is openly encouraged. The planned resettlement of Jews in Madagascar, as Beck suggested, is, moreover, a fantasy that distracts from solving the real problems of Jews in Poland. On the practical level, the plan is hopeless because the climate in most parts of the island is wholly unsuitable for Europeans and emigration will, in any case, fail to draw the wealthier, more comfortable classes of Jews. In any case, French industrialists and merchants could never tolerate competition by foreigners. Nor would France permit Jews national cultural autonomy in Madagascar. With the exception of Palestine, no land was accepting Jews in large numbers. On the contrary, the more Jews talked about emigration, he pointed out, the more countries closed their gates to them. Finally, the Madagascar plan was objectionable to him on the moral level because it ignored that colonization necessarily means the subjugation of indigenous peoples.[27]

Venting his accumulated frustration after the Nazi annexation of Austria in March 1938, Prylucki warned that it was either diplomatic opportunism or political blindness to accept Hitler's and Mussolini's claims that Nazism and Italian Fascism are internal phenomena of their respective countries and not meant for export. Intellectuals who fail to condemn their inhumane conduct were 'moral sybarites,' he maintained, whose passivity makes them complicit in the crimes of these barbarous regimes.[28] While focused mainly on the danger posed by Germany and Italy, Prylucki did not ignore events in the Soviet Union, whose Jewish communists he had previously criticized more than the regime itself. 'All Reaction – Nazi, Italian, or Soviet (Brown, Black, or Red) – cannot change its course and is dangerous to Jews and democracy.'[29] The Bolshevik Revolution was devouring its own children, accusing some of its most gifted contributors of betraying the Soviet motherland to Nazi Germany and imperialist Japan in Stalin's 'monster trials': 'This is not the first and likely not the last act of unbelievable savagery in the nightmare that has continued for the last several years ... is it not the holy duty of cultured humanity to undertake a crusade with united forces against the Kremlin, from which a demon in human form poisons the earth with his devilish immorality?'[30]

Meanwhile, Prylucki's opinion of the United States had not improved since his visit a decade earlier. Once a beacon of hope for the persecuted, it continued to enforce a draconian immigration policy (a trait he disparaged as evidence of the 'Europeanization' and 'egotism' of America). Emerging from the First World War power-drunk and filthy rich, it was ripe for social upheaval, he contended, on the scale of the Bolshevik Revolution once its poor reached awareness of their oppression by arrogant plutocrats and the professional clique of 'politicians' whom they blindly elect.[31] The working and middle classes, most of whose members remained non-unionized, as he pointed out, lacked a sense of government's responsibility to provide them with social protection. In a land where 'politics' was deemed a necessary evil with which no respectable man wishes to sully his hands, he went on, workers continued to elect the same corrupt representatives who forcefully suppress their strikes for the benefit of wealthy capitalists and industrialists.[32] Ultimately, Prylucki prophesied, the very strength of the American republic, its federal system permitting each state a high degree of autonomy, would be its undoing as states would clamour for secession to manage individually the economic crises of the era.[33]

Despite his dire warnings, Prylucki persisted in publicly reaffirming his dedication to the postulates of national cultural autonomy in the Diaspora. In contrast with Grünbaum, who, he implied, had selfishly abandoned Polish Jewry to settle in Palestine in 1933, he had remained rather than desert Jewish politics. Quite simply, he claimed, he had honestly failed and been pushed out of it in the 1928 elections.[34] After Poland formally repudiated the National Minorities Treaty in 1934, he encouraged voters to support Folkist candidates in the 1936 Warsaw *kehila* elections despite that the party had virtually ceased to exist apart from at election time.[35] As conditions worsened, Prylucki, together with other writers, denounced in *Der moment* the unprecedented wave of antisemitism that manifested itself throughout Polish society and the government in a variety of concrete forms: the boycott of Jewish businesses and manufacturers, the imposition of an unofficial *numerus clausus* in institutions of higher learning, the segregation of Jewish students in university lecture halls (the notorious 'ghetto benches'), the placing of restrictions on kosher slaughter, the exclusion of Jews from certain professional associations (law, medicine), as well as everyday acts of violence and sporadic pogroms in the latter half of the 1930s.[36]

At the same time, he continued to rejoice in the 'sacred' achievements of Yiddish culture and urged Jews to remain faithful to their 'true' nature while combating the worsening political and economic situation around them. Even more than emigration was impractical, he maintained, assimilation was futile. This left Jews no choice other than continue to build their lives and culture in Poland. Polonization of one's name would not remake the Jewish physiognomy, the Jewish gait, or remove 'Jewishness from one's eye: the nervousness of the glance (even in the healthiest people), the restless gleam (even in the most sedate), the quick little fires (even in the most phlegmatic) – the heritage of a few thousand millennia of history and culture.'[37]

Nor could the ordinary Jew adopt a 'foreign' language with complete success since the imprint of his native language was always present in his adopted one: 'When I read belletristic or poetic works by famous modern German or Polish writers of Jewish descent, I often cannot free myself from the impression that even for the linguistic virtuosos among them the psychic apparatus and the language in which they express themselves is, nonetheless, not the same as that of a born German or Pole!'[38]

On the other hand, the Yiddish of his generation of (russified) Jewish intellectuals, once they made the conscious decision to speak Yiddish, was unconsciously and inescapably influenced by the phonetic and syntactic norms and phraseology of the 'foreign language' in which they had been educated. Even the best Yiddish expert among them stumbled at times upon a syntactic or stylistic error since the foreign language remained 'our internal and external language, the language of our thinking and our speaking. When we then switched to Yiddish, adjusting to the anatomy, physiology and psychology of *mame-loshn* was extraordinarily difficult for us.' In contrast, the graduates of contemporary Yiddish secular schools enjoy the good fortune to absorb the unique atmosphere of the Yiddish language fully. They therefore learn their mother tongue with all its appropriate idioms and aphorisms. 'The basic construction of the thinking and speaking apparatus must be received through and in the mother tongue, which is the most important and most intimate [part] of the human soul.'[39]

Ironically, Prylucki did not seem to notice or mind the inherent contradiction in these premises: while successful writers in Polish and German were betrayed by their Jewish psyches (a statement with which 'zoological' antisemites who supported measures to exclude Jews from the Polish economy and cultural life would readily agree), his Yiddish and that of other intellectuals in his generation revealed that their linguistic consciousness was more Russian than Jewish! Nor does it seem to have troubled him that he, whose Yiddish was by implication imperfect as a non-native speaker of the 'mother tongue,' had arrogated to himself authority in determining correct usage. Perhaps this dismissal of Polish and German writing by Jews as 'inauthentic' reflects his own emotional distance from Polish and German cultures. He did not develop skills as an orator in Polish – a language, like Yiddish, discouraged by Russian officialdom – until adulthood and his knowledge of German was mainly for the purpose of reading.[40] Moreover, Prylucki grew up as part of a generation of Jews who continued to identify both ethnically and religiously as Jews despite russification. In contrast, Jews raised in the Polish and German cultural spheres were more likely to conceptualize Judaism as primarily a religious category and otherwise to identify with these nations. Moreover, to suggest that his Russian – a language whose native mastery was a source of pride for Jews in the late imperial period – was somehow less than perfect, would be to diminish his own youthful literary achievements in a language for which he had the greatest admiration.

In espousing since his earliest career a conventional, essentialist notion of race, Prylucki left no real opportunity for Jews to exit the biologically defined group whose characteristics allegedly marked their physical and intellectual composition.[41] Hence, his rhetoric denouncing assimilation decried it as a futile exercise in self-deception as well as a dangerous betrayal of the Jewish collective. Although he was a European cultural chauvinist, his notions of race were mainly directed at taking pride in Jewish 'difference' rather than accepting the existence of a qualitative hierarchy among human groups or suggesting Jewish superiority. On the contrary, he felt Jews had much to learn from other nations, especially those whose intellectuals toiled in fields already well tilled by previous generations of culture-builders.

Rather than pursue a career in Russian, he had chosen Yiddish, which needed him as much as he needed it:

> Intellectuals who step over to richer and happier societies find there a ready-made content for their life, disposition, and activity. One of many examples: the Jew Gershenzon, who became one of the finest scholars of Rus-

sian literary history. The atmosphere of my father's house implanted in me a natural tendency to live my life in the web (to use Mendele's expression) called the Jewish people, of which I am merely an organic little thread. Jewish life had not yet, however, made ready the conditions for a Jewish intellectual to have a normal cultural life the way a Russian intellectual could in Russian life, etc. Seeking content for my life, an application for my work, air for my lungs, a goal for my existence, I had to come to work on the Yiddish language, Yiddish folklore, Yiddish literary history and research about Jewish folk life.[42]

Apart from contributing a regular column (misleadingly) titled 'Notices without Politics' to *Der moment* in the latter half of the 1930s, Prylucki was active as a founding member of the philological section and the central administration of YIVO. He was an active participant in lively debates about language standardization, contributing his own phonetically precise and interdialectal spelling system, which he used mainly in his linguistic publications. His more idiosyncratic proposals were not included in the 1935 Rules of Standard Yiddish spelling promulgated by YIVO and approved for use in the *Tsisho* schools in 1936.

He also disagreed with the common position in favour of a normative pronunciation for Yiddish based on that of the secularized Vilna intellectual elite, that is, his Vilna-based YIVO colleagues. Instead, he supported the development of a standardized pronunciation (orthoepy) for use in the schools and in public and official life alongside the use of dialects in private life – a phenomenon analogous to the relationship between the standard German spoken in schools and in formal settings and the German dialects spoken in most people's daily interactions. Again basing his reasoning on the model of German, whose standard pronunciation was developed on the basis of theatre speech, he proposed that the Volhynian-based dialect commonly used in the Yiddish stage outside the Soviet Union (where a 'literary' pronunciation similar to that of the Vilna intellectual elite was commonly in use) also serve with some changes and elaborations as the model for elegant pronunciation.[43] It is also perhaps no coincidence that Volhynian Yiddish was his native dialect and a favourite subject of his study.[44]

In collaboration with the noted Yiddish linguists and cultural specialists Max Weinreich (born into a German-speaking family in Kurland and thus also a 'non-native' Yiddish language expert) and Zalmen Reyzen, he founded in 1937 the YIVO journal *Yidish far ale.* It aimed at an audience of both laymen and specialists interested in deciding questions of

6.3 Celebration of the twentieth anniversary of the Czernowitz Jewish Language Conference, 1928. The portrait includes Mordechai Goldberg, Herz Grossbard, Shloyme Lerner, Israel Rubin, Zalmen Reyzen, Noah Prylucki, and Itzik Manger. (YIVO Institute, groups #12, p. 8)

normative usage. Prylucki continued to edit and write articles for it and *YIVO-bleter* until the outbreak of the Second World War.

The Problem of Polonization

To be sure, Yiddish remained the native language of most Jews in Poland until the outbreak of the Second World War. It was the medium of an extremely variegated literature, press, theatre, and a wide array of cultural, political, and sporting organizations during the 1920s and 1930s.[45] Eleven Yiddish dailies, two of them afternoon papers, appeared in Warsaw alone in 1936–37.[46] Yet, as much as Prylucki rejected language shift as a futile act of inauthenticity, by the 1930s the accelerated rate of polonization, linguistic and cultural, among Jews could not be denied. The possibility of a primarily Polish-speaking Jewish population – a

CELEBRATING A YIDDISH HOLIDAY.—Here are delegates to a conference held recently at Czernowitz, Roumania, that marked the 20th anniversary of a conference in the same city when prominent Jewish writers declared Yiddish a national bone-fide tongue.

ביים 20־יעהריגען יובילעאום פון טשערנאוויצער קאנפערענץ פאר דער אידישער שפראך. — מיט 20 יאהר צוריק האבען די פראמינענטסטע אידישע שרייבער זיך פערזאמעלט אין טשערנאוויץ, בוקאווינא, און ערקלערט, אז אידיש איז א נאציאנאלע שפראך. איצט איז אין דער זעלבער שטאדט געפייערט געווארען א יובילעאום פון אט דיזער וויכטיגער פאסירונג, און אידישע שריפטשטעלער פון פיעלע לענדער זיינען זיך צוזאמענגעקומען אנטיילנעהמען אין דער דעמאנסטראציע פאר דער מאדערנער אידישער קולטור. די בילד אויבען איז פון דער הייריאהריגער קאנפערענץ. אין דער מיטעלסטער שורה (פון רעכטס צו לינקס) זיצען דר. פורמאן, דר. ריאכמאנר, ש. לערנער, א. גראסבארד, דר. ישראל רובין, דר. שעפלער, נח פרילוצקי, דר. פעלדער, זלמן רייזין, בארבו לאזעריאנו, י. קאלניק און שווערסקאיא.

6.4 A newspaper clipping and a group shot of the delegates to the twentieth-anniversary conference to commemorate the 1908 Czernowitz Conference. At the 1908 conference Yiddish was declared 'a national language' of the Jewish people, a compromise that satisfied neither staunch Yiddishists nor Hebraists. (YIVO Institute, groups #12, p. 8) menace against which Prylucki and his colleagues had long struggled – understandably terrified and demoralized those who had invested their energies, finances, and hopes in not only the survival but also in the modernization and expansion of Yiddish culture.

A climate of increasing poverty and discrimination alongside easy access to Polish primary (although not secondary) education contributed to a growing rate of linguistic assimilation without commensurate social integration among Jewish youth in the interwar period.[47] Statistics measuring the reading habits of the patrons of Jewish libraries demonstrate a marked and increasing preference over time for books in Polish rather than other languages, especially among women and children and even in the *Tsisho* schools. This inclination became more pronounced among students with age (and hence more years of exposure to Polish in school) and middle-class status. Not only were middle-class families more likely to speak Polish at home with their children than working-class ones but they were also much more likely to send their children to secondary schools, where the pace of polonization typically accelerated. Facing obstacles to admission to state institutions, in 1936–37 almost 75 per cent of Jewish high school students attended private schools that paralleled the curriculum of state institutions. Frequently offering little in the way of Judaic content, these private schools were often more Jewish in the make-up of their student bodies than in their curriculum. The vast majority of these schools taught exclusively in Polish or restricted the use of Hebrew to religious instruction while leaving Yiddish out of the curriculum altogether.[48] Thus, the bourgeoisie, the socioeconomic class which most venerated high culture – the type of culture which Prylucki and his colleagues laboured so assiduously to fashion in Yiddish – was also the class most inclined to embrace cultural life in Polish.

The Yiddish dimension of the Polish-Hebrew-Yiddish cultural polysystem in interwar Poland relied mainly on poorer and religiously conservative Jews. These sectors of Jewish society were less able financially or less ideologically inclined to support secular Yiddish culture. During a period when self-improvement through education was a cherished goal, poverty impeded the working class, the main consumers of Yiddish publications, in sustaining and helping to expand the Yiddish book market.[49] Moreover, these groups were themselves hardly immune to polonization. This was especially true of girls since, in comparison with their brothers who studied in *khadorim* and *yeshivas* (often in addition to Polish-language public schools) where Yiddish was the language of instruction, they typically received no Jewish education outside of the home.[50]

In response to the changing cultural profile of Polish Jewry in the 1920s and 1930s, a number of prominent Folkists and former Folkists advocated the creation of a Jewish press and schools in Polish to accommodate the growing number of Jews most comfortable in Polish and who desired to take part in both the Polish and Jewish worlds but were offended by the antisemitism of the Polish public sphere.[51] Indeed, Samuel Hirschhorn wrote in the 1930s specifically in favour of developing Jewish national identity via the Polish language in the face of the juggernaut of linguistic assimilation.[52]

By the outbreak of the Second World War, at least four Jewish dailies (*Nowy Dziennik* in Kraków, *Chwila* in Lwów, *Nasz Przegląd* and *5ta Rano* in Warsaw) appeared in the Polish language. Apart from familiarizing readers with issues of concern particularly to Jews, the Jewish press in Polish exposed many readers to Yiddish and Hebrew culture in translation who may have been otherwise unable or disinclined to read a book or attend a theatre performance in a Jewish language. Of decidedly Zionist-bent, it was also the vehicle for the emergence of a Jewish literature of distinction in the Polish language.[53] Polish-Jewish newspapers were thus far from being the agents of national assimilation predicted by Yiddishists and Hebraists. Nonetheless, as a forum for an emerging Jewish identity and culture expressing itself via the Polish language, they necessarily threatened the economic well-being of the more established Yiddish press. Among their readers were many who knew Yiddish but who were chiefly educated or simply preferred to read in Polish.[54]

While expressing no overt hostility to the Polish-language Jewish press in which his colleagues worked, Prylucki did not follow their example. He continued to write and edit regularly for *Der moment* until March 1938. In 1938, the co-operative owning the newspaper, on the verge of bankruptcy, attempted to settle accounts with its creditors with the assistance of a Polish court. The court entrusted supervision of the venture to the lawyer Marek Kohan. An admirer of Zabotinsky, Kohan began to convert the newspaper into a Revisionist Zionist organ, publishing materials of his own selection as well as hiring and firing staff members. In protest of what was seen as the usurpation of the newspaper by hostile forces that violated its non-partisan character and abused its personnel, members of the newspaper staff, including the editorial board, organized a three-week strike in March 1939.[55] Taking advantage of a law permitting the publication of one-time editions without a concession, they published a protest newspaper *Undzer tsaytung* (Our Newspaper) accusing Kohan of gross malfeasance: 'New staff members have come with salaries fit for ministers. All sorts of "investments" have come. Directors and vice-directors with fat salaries have come at the same time that the entire personnel have received starvation wages, wages which are a disgrace to speak of.'[56]

Kohan used his police connections, according to Tsevi Prylucki's memoirs, to have a second edition printed a week later under a different title confiscated before it could be sold. Dependent upon the newspaper for jobs but powerless to change its course, staff members abandoned the strike after Kohan promised to rehire dismissed employees – a promise he did not wholly keep.[57] Tsevi Prylucki remained until the outbreak of the Second World War the nominal editor of the *Der moment*. Its 1 January 1939 issue announced the participation of most of its former staff. Noah Prylucki, who was among the founders of *Der moment*, never wrote for it again.[58]

Between Hammer and Sickle

Following the Nazi invasion of Poland on 5 September 1939, Tsevi Prylucki, along with Hillel Zeitlin and Saul Stupnicki, continued to work for *Der moment* until German bombardments made it too dangerous for older staff members to arrive at the newspaper's offices.[59] Noah Prylucki boarded the 'journalists' train' hastily organized by the Polish government to evacuate prominent Warsaw newspapermen. He and Stupnicki were among the sixteen Jewish writers who accepted, along with forty-five or so non-Jewish journalists, official invitations to flee in secrecy with only a few hours' notice after the invasion. His father and Zeitlin opted to remain in Warsaw. After travelling a circuitous route through eastern Poland, during which passengers joined and left the group (Stupnicki, for example, returned to Warsaw), the train ultimately deposited twenty-nine members of the Warsaw Jewish Writers' and Journalists' Association in Lithuania on 10 October.[60]

Caught between the German 'hammer' and the Bolshevik 'sickle,' by late 1939 neutral Lithuania represented virtually the only escape route from Poland to the free world. The contested multiethnic city of Vilna was severed from Poland, to whom it had belonged in the interwar period, in the German-Soviet partition of that country in September 1939 and awarded by Moscow after a forty-day occupation to independent Lithuania at the end of the following month.[61] In all, more than 14,000 Polish Jews, most intending to continue on to Japan and the Western Hemisphere, gathered in Vilnius, as it was now officially called, between the outbreak of war and June 1940. Among them was Prylucki's wife Paula, who was assisted in crossing illegally into Lithuania by the young journalist Mordkhe Tsanin.[62]

In an atmosphere of intense uncertainty, the administration of YIVO, the Jewish Scientific Institute, in Vilnius found itself confronted with the dilemma of whether to continue or its suspend its operations. The war had effectively cut off YIVO from its material and cultural basis, the more than three million strong Jewish community of Poland. Communications with the outside world were impaired, and much of YIVO's academic and administrative leadership was not to be found in Lithuania. In particular, the philologist and newspaper editor Zalmen Reyzen, a pillar of YIVO, had been arrested by the Soviets.[63] And the institute's guiding spirit and research director, the internationally renowned scholar Max Weinreich, was in the West when the war broke out and unable to return home.

At the same time, Vilnius became home to an unprecedented concentration of creative forces, members of the cultural, political, and religious elites of Polish Jewry. The presence of these refugees, coupled with the absorption of tens of thousands of Jews, most of them Yiddish speakers, resulted in something of a cultural efflorescence and made possible new vistas for Jewish culture in Lithuania. Lithuanian Jewry, which had been effectively cut off culturally and otherwise from its Polish brethren throughout most of the interwar period in the absence of diplomatic relations between the two lands, received the refugees generously and was eager to benefit from their talents.[64]

The Lithuanian military's entry into the city following the Soviets' departure was inauspiciously marked by a pogrom by both Poles and the Lithuanian police. Commonplace associations of Jews with the despised Bolsheviks, who lifted discriminatory Polish measures affecting Jews and elevated many to unprecedented positions of authority and influence over non-Jews during their brief occupation, contributed to this hostility.[65] The general uncertainty of the times, the disruption of normal life and livelihoods, and resentment over the influx of refugees also undoubtedly played a role in heightening tensions between ethnic groups. Moreover, Jews understandably preferred Soviet to Nazi rule and many did not conceal their enthusiasm for the Soviet presence, a presence that offended Polish and Lithuanian national sentiments alike. Nonetheless, like members of all other national communities in Vilnius, Jews both acted in the name of Soviet authority and were arrested and deported by it.[66] Once the city changed hands, public order was restored by Lithuanian authorities and the city benefited from the general economic prosperity of the period, to which Russian soldiers' purchases and the presence of refugee consumers with foreign currency contributed.[67] Public displays of anti-Jewish sentiment subsided and the authorities evinced great sympathy for Jewish culture. At a minimum, they extended to Jewish cultural institutions in Vilnius the support they gave to them elsewhere in Lithuania.

In the early years after the First World War Lithuanian authorities had courted Jewish financial and political support for a greater Lithuania including Vilnius with promises of national cultural autonomy for Lithuanians, Jews, Poles, and Byelorussians alike. Jews made up the second largest group (37%) after Poles (45%) in the city, the rest of its interwar population of approximately 200,000 consisting of Lithuanians (10%), Byelorussians (5%), and Russians (2%).[68] Hence, their support was desirable to offset Polish demands for the city. Once Vilnius fell under Polish control (after changing hands several times it became part of Poland in 1922), however, this support was no longer crucial: the country was effectively a nation-state when deprived of the multiethnic city. Moreover, the emerging ethnic Lithuanian urban middle class, following patterns similar to those in Poland and elsewhere in the region, saw Jews (the largest national minority though making up less than 8% of the country's total population in 1923), as economic competitors. Nonetheless, while formally ending Jewish autonomy by 1926, an authoritarian Lithuanian regime that came to power after a coup d'état did not impair Jewish cultural autonomy pledged at the 1919 Paris Peace Conference. It continued to fund Yiddishist, Hebraist, and Orthodox schools (at least at the elementary level) throughout the interwar period.[69]

With Vilnius back in the picture, Lithuanian authorities likely again sought to have Jews on their side rather than that of the Poles. With the addition of some 80,000 Jews in Vilnius province (including Polish-Jewish refugees), the Jewish population of Lithuania rose to about 250,000 – nearly 10 per cent of the overall population. It was expected that Polish nationalists could never reconcile themselves to Lithuanian control over the city but Jewish nationalists could make peace with this. Indeed, many Jews had supported Lithuanian control of the city after the First World War, arousing Polish hostility. Further, seeking to Lithuanianize the city, Lithuanian officials preferred that Jews in Vilnius, few of whom knew Lithuanian well but many of whom – especially the refugees from Central Poland – spoke Polish in private life, use Yiddish as their primary language. While it was desirable for Jews to master Lithuanian, it was not a serious consideration that they be assimilated into Lithuanian society, as was hoped of Poles who were long-term residents of the Vilnius area. They were seen as renegade Lithuanians whose polonization over generations had to be undone. In contrast, refugees from 'ethnic' Poland, also numbering in the thousands, were considered an obstacle to Lithuanization of the city and were consequently to be deported.[70]

After much deliberation, the provisional administration of YIVO, a mixture of old and newly co-opted members, decided to continue its publications and scholarly work as much as possible, as well as to undertake new activities. Most conspicuous was a plan for the establishment of a state-funded chair of Yiddish language and literature. The creation of this chair in Vilnius, the unofficial capital of Yiddish culture, known to Jews as Vilna, was a long-cherished dream of the Yiddishist movement. Such public recognition for Yiddish was inconceivable in interwar Poland, whose government was openly hostile towards Yiddish and the ideals of national cultural autonomy for the Jews espoused by most of YIVO's supporters.

Although he arrived almost penniless as a refugee from Warsaw in early October 1939, Prylucki was optimistic about the horizons Vilnius offered for the propagation of secular Yiddish culture. He almost immediately became involved in cultural activities in Vilnius and enjoyed the companionship of long-time colleagues as well as promising young talents such as the young Vilnius poets Shmerke Kaczerginski, Chaim Grade, and Avrom Sutzkever.[71] He decried what he deemed pessimism and inertia in the face of the mounting calamity that was befalling Polish Jewry but whose proportions were yet unknown. He reminded his YIVO colleagues: 'The war has not destroyed us. We must work with what is available. We owe much to the Kovno Friends [of YIVO Society] for their help and making YIVO respectable in the eyes of authorities.'[72] He called for the expansion of YIVO's activities beyond its pre-war academic agenda to include more popular educational undertakings and to draw as much as possible upon the abundance of refugee talents, including his own.

Prylucki viewed the present catastrophe as the chance to build cultural institutions much in the same way that he and other Yiddishists had taken advantage of the chaos and destruction of the First World War to begin the first network of legal secular schools with Yiddish as their language of instruction. Aside from delivering popular academic lectures (such as one honouring Y.L. Peretz on the twenty-fifth anniversary of his death at the University of Vilnius, formerly the Polish Stefan Batory University in the interwar period), he prepared to give lectures on Yiddish grammar to teachers and organized a historical commission funded by the Joint Distribution Committee to document Nazi persecution of Jews.[73]

The Yiddish Chair at the University of Vilnius

In late 1939 Prylucki approached Professor Mykolas Biržiška, whom he had first met during a visit to Kaunas in the 1920s, about the possibility of creating a Yiddish Chair there. He was accompanied by Majer Balberyszki, a Lithuanian Folkist colleague who enjoyed cordial relations with Biržiška and his family, and was supported in his endeavours by the Kaunas Friends of YIVO Society.[74] Prylucki did not initially inform the YIVO administration in Vilnius, which had no legal status yet, of these meetings.

Elected rector of the Great University in Kaunas in 1940, the liberal Biržiška was a historian of Lithuanian culture and literature as well as a signatory of Lithuanian independence in 1918.[75] He was an admirer of Jewish culture who participated in the founding of a Department of Semitic Studies in the 1930s and sent salutations to the first YIVO conference in 1929.[76] He and his brother Vlaclovas, also a professor, maintained close contact with the leaders of the Lithuanian Jewish community prior to the war and Mykolas founded the Lithuanian-Jewish Friendship Association.[77] According to the Jewish writer Daniel Czarni, he even knew Yiddish and fluently read the Yiddish press.[78] Not surprisingly then, he pronounced himself in favour of a project for a Chair of Yiddish Language and Literature.

The proposed position would reside in Vilnius, where the Humanities Faculty of the Great University was to be transferred from Kaunas.[79] According to Prylucki, who subsequently explained the nature of their meeting to YIVO's temporary administration, Biržiška maintained that the greatest impediment to the endeavour was funding: it was doubtful that the state would provide funding in the early years of the chair. Biržiška suggested involving Nachman Shapiro, the professor of Semitics in Kaunas, in negotiations since Shapiro took an interest in Yiddish culture. Prylucki was, however, eager to keep the matter from him. Biržiška interpreted this as an indication of anticipated opposition on the part of local Hebraists to the plan (a subsequent YIVO delegation to Biržiška without Prylucki assured him that Yiddishists and Hebraists were capable of cooperation, as evidenced by YIVO's good relations with the Hebrew University in Jerusalem).[80] Prylucki and his local Folkist supporters, most prominently David (Vladimir) Kaplan-Kaplanski, a community activist and vice-chairman of the Vilna Society Friends of YIVO who had joined YIVO's war-time temporary administration, wanted to avoid a combined Hebrew-Yiddish Chair. They were eager to secure the position for an ideological Yiddishist who accepted the new YIVO orthography since, in Prylucki's words, 'the chair is a national and political position.'[81] He reported to his YIVO colleagues that a candidate would need neither a special linguistics diploma nor Lithuanian citizenship since Lithuanian authorities would be willing to appoint an instructor rather than a professor to teach.[82]

Prylucki's enthusiasm for the proposed chair and the expansion of YIVO's activities was matched only by Zelig Kalmanovitch's pessimism. When war broke out, Kalmanovitch, a Yiddishist linguist and translator, fled to neighbouring Latvia to escape the Soviets. Out of a sense of obligation to colleagues, Kalmanovitch, who played a key role in YIVO as an administrator, teacher, and editor, returned to Vilnius once the Red Army had departed and begrudgingly accepted appointment by the Lithuanian authorities as YIVO's curator. Born and raised (like Max Weinreich) in Kurland, he had lived for years in Vilnius and was the only remaining member of the YIVO executive who was a Lithuanian citizen.

A one-time Folkist in Lithuania (he edited there the party's daily *Letste nayes*, Latest News) and like Prylucki also a member of YIVO's philological section, Kalmanovitch had come to despair of prospects for independent Jewish cultural life in Eastern Europe long before the German invasion of Poland. In his analysis, secular Yiddish culture, with its offerings of literature and theatre, was ultimately insufficient to sustain Jewish identity in the post-Emancipation era. The Jews in Poland were linguistically acculturating despite pauperization and widespread antisemitism. And the Marxist Yiddish culture offered in the Soviet Union, divorced as it was from its roots in the Hebrew language and religious tradition, was destructive of Jewish national uniqueness. In contrast with Prylucki, who never tired of demanding state support for Yiddish culture in the name of elemental justice, Kalmanovitch became convinced by the 1930s that the Jews could not rely upon such appeals and on navigating political channels. Only the socioeconomic concentration of the Jews in a territory of their own and the embracing of the entirety of their cultural legacy could impede assimilation and guarantee Jewish national survival. Although not a Zionist, he increasingly leaned in this direction, maintaining that only the Zionists had correctly evaluated the dangers of Diaspora life.[83] On the eve of the Second World War he considered settling in Palestine, where his only son lived and where, he announced to the YIVO executive in frustration, he could have found 'an excellent position.'[84]

'The head and heart of YIVO is gone,' he lamented to his colleagues in January 1940, referring to Zalmen Reyzen's disappearance. 'How can YIVO live without him?'[85] In Kalmanovitch's appraisal, it was hopeless to carry on YIVO's activities as before, let alone expand them to include new ones, some of which, such as courses aimed at a popular audience, he felt were not in consonance with YIVO's academic mission. He enumerated a number of formal obstacles to YIVO's operations, including a paucity of funding arriving from abroad and delays in formalizing YIVO's legal status with the Lithuanian authorities – all obstacles that his more optimistic colleagues rejected as temporary inconveniences. Deploring the grievous events that had befallen Polish Jewry, he urged that all activities beyond the cataloguing of inventory be transferred to New York, the site of the *Amopteyl* (American Division), YIVO's American subsidiary. Such a move was firmly rejected by the Folkists, Bundists, and others parties alike represented in YIVO's provisional administration. They objected that it would signal to the world the demise of Eastern European Jewry and the shifting of Yiddish high culture from its centre to its periphery. From the vantage point of Eastern European Jewish intellectuals and communal activists, America was a culturally underdeveloped Jewish colony despite the presence of many talented individuals ideologically committed to Yiddish. In America, in the words of Bundist Gershon Pludermakher, 'the Yiddish movement is not faring well.'[86] To these kinds of objections, Kalmanovitch expressed his commitment to work on behalf of Jewish culture in Vilnius despite his lack of enthusiasm for its future: 'Reyzen was optimistic. He remained, and was arrested. I was pessimistic. I ran away and I am standing here now. I don't approve of Jewish life here but I work and I want there to be a Jewish life.'[87]

A YIVO delegation comprising Kalmanovitch, the lawyer and Yiddish philologist Pinkhas Kohn, and Kaplan-Kaplanski visited Biržiška on 16 January 1940 and presented him with a memorandum prepared by Weinreich regarding a chair.[88] Prylucki, feeling deliberately excluded from YIVO affairs, made clear to the YIVO administration his dissatisfaction that he had not been informed of the delegation's mission. Kohn, irritated by Prylucki's protests, retorted at the same meeting that the delegation had used at least 80 per cent of its time with the professor to correct what he described as 'fundamental errors' made previously by Prylucki in what amounted to a private initiative rather than a meeting authorized by YIVO.[89]

Regardless of this squabbling, the newly elected dean, the writer Vincas Krėvė-Mickevičius, Professor of Slavic Languages and Literautres and a former dean of the Humanities Faculty, announced to the YIVO delegation that the university faculty supported their initiative. He recommended, however, that YIVO hold out for a proper chair rather than an instructor's position as had been suggested.[90] Showing their support for YIVO and its endeavours, a group of Lithuanian professors headed by Biržiška from the Humanities Faculty of the University of Vilnius visited YIVO to acquaint itself with its contents and to view an exhibition honouring the writer Peretz in April 1940.[91] Biržiška also participated in a radio presentation in honour of Peretz to which the historian Simon Dubnow, the head of the Jewish community Dr Jacob Wigodsky, and others contributed.[92]

The matter of nominating a candidate for the position for approval by the university was entrusted by YIVO to Max Weinreich as secretary of its philological section. From Copenhagen Weinreich conducted a referendum by telegraph among the section's members Shmuel Niger, Yude Yofe, and Yudl Mark, all residents of New York City. They unanimously approved his nomination of Kalmanovitch for the chair. Kalmanovitch categorically refused, however, leaving Weinreich to nominate himself. Prylucki, who had for years aspired to an academic position, denounced the referendum as tendentious and illegitimate. Not only had Weinreich unilaterally nominated candidates and presented no alternatives, he protested. Weinreich had also failed to present him, a founding member of the philological section and the initiator of the chair, with the referendum in time to participate.[93]

Always quick to defend his honour, Prylucki threatened to leave YIVO over this insult and offered an angry critique of the institute. He decried it as a cliquish den of inertia and academic protectionism. Weinreich and Kalmanovitch discouraged independent scholarly initiative and were reluctant to permit outsiders, the refugees from Poland, to work. Prylucki alleged that Weinreich had nominated Kalmanovitch solely in order to prevent his own appointment. However, Kalmanovitch's disparaging attitude towards Yiddishism, his commitment to Jewish scholarship notwithstanding, made him an unacceptable candidate. When Kalmanovitch refused the nomination, Prylucki continued, Weinreich nominated himself in order to block Prylucki's ambitions. He further argued that Weinreich could not be relied upon to return in time for the coming academic year beginning in the fall since he had committed himself to going to New York until after the summer on YIVO business. Waiting for Weinreich, Prylucki warned, meant forfeiting the chair.[94]

The provisional administration of YIVO, which was dominated by Bundists, upheld Weinreich's candidacy because he enjoyed near universal respect for his scholarly contributions. That Weinreich quietly sympathized with the Bund's political program (although not its attitudes towards the role of YIVO) does not seem to have played a significant role. While recognizing that Prylucki had been unjustly slighted by the referendum, the administration faulted him and his Folkist colleagues for conducting what amounted to private and therefore potentially harmful negotiations with Professor Biržiška. It urged him and all others to put the needs of the institute above private interests and personal ambitions. He was asked to accept nomination as Weinreich's replacement in case Weinreich was unable to return to Vilnius.[95]

Although he was pessimistic about the chair and the Yiddishist aspirations it embodied, Kalmanovitch did not refrain from raising objections to Prylucki's candidacy. Indeed, he was Prylucki's most severe critic, if not enemy, in YIVO. Kalmanovitch, who like Weinreich possessed a doctorate (Semitic philology), denounced Prylucki without restraint as a 'simple collector,' an autodidact lacking 'the minimal scholarly qualifications' to edit the philological section's journal *Yidish far ale.*[96] He was even more explicit about Prylucki's shortcomings in a personal letter in late 1938 to linguist Yudl Mark, a former Folkist who resided in the United States from the mid-1930s. Kalmanovitch complained that *Yidish far ale* had fallen into the hands of Prylucki, who 'destroys Yiddish in his own way.' 'Poor *mame-loshn* has the misfortunate that such a scholarly graphomaniac has latched onto it and occupies its top position, driving away every expert and letting in the defect (*felenish*) of sickly egotism.' He maintained that Max Weinreich and Zalmen Reyzen concurred with him in this assessment and in the need to deprive Prylucki of the editorship of the journal.[97] Weinreich's himself penned a scathing critique of Prylucki's skills as a scholar, faulting his methodology and analysis in ways not dissimilar from Ber Borokhov's review of his folklore collections decades earlier, under the pretence of evaluating the overall quality of the journal thus far.[98] Correspondence from 1938 between the philological section and Prylucki regarding the journal suggests that colleagues sought to deprive Prylucki of final say in editorial matters of the journal but depended on his labours.[99]

In private letters to Weinreich in Copenhagen and to the secretary of YIVO's American Division in New York City, Naftali Feinerman, Kalmanovitch not only gave voice to the full extent of his personal animus towards Prylucki, whom he described as 'a personal disgrace and unpleasant – a danger to YIVO executive.'[100] He also confirmed the charges which Prylucki had laid out against him, namely, that he had allowed himself to be nominated for the express purpose of blocking Prylucki's candidacy and to save the chair for Weinreich. Kalmanovitch attributed this strategy to Professor Shapiro, who was enraged to learn that Prylucki had misrepresented him to Biržiška as hostile to the creation of a Yiddish Chair and presented himself as the only candidate for the position.[101]

Apart from these already damning objections, Kalmanovitch doubtlessly objected to Prylucki's apparent flirtation with the Soviets, expressed in his affiliation with the *Folksblat*, a formerly Folkist newspaper which had fallen into Communist hands in 1938.[102] While his hostility to communism was hardly concealed, Kalmanovitch kept silent his antipathy towards individuals for pro-Soviet sympathies during YIVO meetings. In a letter to the American Division in New York dated January 1940, however, he complained bitterly of those in YIVO 'whose heart has remained in the East [Soviet Union]' and who had the audacity to remain in YIVO even after the Soviets had, he correctly assumed, murdered Zalmen Reyzen.[103]

In contrast with Kalmanovitch, who exhibited a degree of reserve, Bundists in the provisional administration reacted openly to the tactics of the Kaunas *Folksblat.* The Bundist pedagogues Shloyme Mendelson and Shloyme Gilinski objected to the affiliation of Prylucki and unspecified others in YIVO with the newspaper. They pointed out that the *Folksblat* condemned the current administration as the 'liquidators' of YIVO and denounced socialists in general as the sell-out lackeys of British Prime Minister Chamberlain.[104] Nonetheless, the Bundists were willing to support Prylucki as a replacement for Weinreich since his attitude towards Yiddish and Yiddishism, unlike Kalmanovitch's, was ideologically correct, that is, remained committed to a Yiddish-speaking future for Eastern European Jewry. Resisting entreaties from colleagues, Prylucki, whose pride had been injured, demonstratively quit all YIVO activities in March 1940 and refused to be considered as a candidate for the chair.[105] Reporting in early June 1940 on the recent activity of YIVO, the *Folksblat* questioned, 'whether this work satisfies the broad classes of the Jewish population interested in cultural work and whether there aren't more important areas and more necessary ones than research about the archive of Grätz miracle workers, Karlin Hasidism, Yeshivat Hochmei Lublin, and the like – that is a separate question.'[106]

Negotiations between YIVO and Lithuanian academics continued without Prylucki and culminated in a plan to establish an instructor's position rather than a Chair of Yiddish at the University of Vilnius. Funding would have to be provided by the Jewish community in advance for the first three years.[107] Max Weinreich, who arrived in the United States in March 1940, was proposed for the position and he was expected to return to accept it.

Soviet Annexation of Lithuania and State Support for Yiddish Culture

These plans came to naught, however, as the Red Army occupied Lithuania in mid-June 1940 and annexed it as the sixteenth Soviet Socialist republic in August. Even then, however, departure from Lithuania via the Soviet Union remained possible for those with the requisite wherewithal, connections, and luck.[108]

Virtually overnight, private Jewish schools of all ideological directions were transformed into state-run Yiddish ones and the Soviets revived the plan for a state-funded Yiddish Chair at the University of Vilnius. At the same time, they eliminated the position for Hebrew, along with many others. Archivist Moyshe Lerer, a committed Marxist friendly with Prylucki,[109] was made YIVO's curator, displacing Kalmanovitch, who eked out a living thereafter as a copy editor.[110] From mid-August until the end of 1940, YIVO underwent a 'process of purging and reorganization,' ridding it of Bundists and pro-Yiddish Zionists and virtually anyone else judged ideologically unsuitable.[111] In an article titled 'The "YIVO" too Is Finally Dragged Out of the Swamp,' the Vilnius *Togblat* (16 August 1940) reported that the institute had 'returned' under Soviet rule to its rightful owners – the working Jewish masses:[112]

> YIVO, which was built with dedication by the folk masses, was cynically controlled by a small group of people who transformed the institute into a 'political' clique (*klayzl*). At the head of the institute stood people who related cynically to the interests, sufferings, and struggles of the folk masses and their language. The institute was transformed into a fortress behind which pronounced Zionists and Bundists barricaded themselves. United, they exploited the institute as a nest of protectionism and personal carriers, on the one hand, and struggle against the Communist Party and its friends, on the other hand. People were not allowed in the institute who could raise the institute to an appropriate level with their academic qualifications ... Having the complete protection of all prior reactionary regimes, the 'activists' of 'YIVO' were destroyers of every fertile plan for the sake of Yiddish culture.

> Thus, these people buried the plan for a Yiddish Chair at the University of Vilnius and one of the chief schemers from the Yiddish Scientific Institute travelled around preaching the dark purpose of Yiddish.[113]

The immediate imposition of Soviet nationalities policy on the tiny Baltic republic held out the promise of state-supported Yiddish culture that Poland had demonstratively refused to provide and whose institutions it even actively undermined during the preceding twenty years. In contrast with the Jews of Poland, the largest part of Jewish pupils in independent Lithuania was already enrolled in state-supported Jewish schools before the outbreak of the war. Now, virtually overnight, secular Hebrew and religious schools were transformed into state-run Yiddish schools. Elsewhere in the USSR, Jewish educational facilities were being systematically restricted to the point of disappearance. In contrast, in Soviet Lithuania, in the evaluation of historian Dov Levin, 'Jewish education seemed to be holding its own; there were almost no indications of real infringements, at least on the surface.' Despite the justified anxieties of Jewish educators, in the short term at least, plans to eliminate Jewish education were not evident here.[114]

For Prylucki, who despaired over the future of Yiddish in Poland and likely even more so in America, the prospect of mandatory Yiddish schools and state-sponsored cultural life surely held some appeal. Moreover, he was granted by Soviet authorities the recognition as a scholar which he was denied by many of his colleagues, most notably Weinreich and Kalmanovitch. In August 1940 Prylucki was nominated by YIVO as its candidate for the Yiddish Chair, as well as appointed chief instructor for Yiddish language and culture at state teachers' courses initiated through the Bureau for Minorities of the Communist Party in Lithuania – evidence of his acceptability to Soviet authorities.[115] The following month he was provided the means to publish these lectures under the title *Yidishe fonetik: Elementar kurs far lerer un aleynlerner* (Yiddish Phonetics: Elementary Course for Teachers and Autodidacts), as well as his research about Yiddish theatre (*Farvos iz dos yidishe teater azoy shpet oyfgekumen?* Why did the Yiddish Theatre Arise So Late?). The study was first published in the literary anthology *Untervegs*, which appeared with an appropriate Marxist introduction celebrating Soviet rule. It included new works by a number of now renown writers (among them Chaim Grade, Avrom Sutzkever, Yisroel Rabon, and Y.Y. Trunk) who found themselves in Vilnius and with whom the senior Prylucki cultivated close relationships of mentorship and camaraderie. His research was recognized by the Senate of the Soviet Lithuanian University in Vilnius. Although lacking formal training as a philologist, Noah Prylucki was routinely referred to in official Soviet documents as 'Professor' even prior to his appointment in October 1940 on a one-year contract as docent to the newly founded Chair of Yiddish Language and Culture.[116]

While never publicly recanting his former anti-Soviet positions, in an interview with the New York City Communist daily *Morgn-Frayhayt* appearing in December 1940, Prylucki expressed profound gratitude and admiration for the Soviet system. He noted that a 'completely equal Chair for Yiddish Language and Literature could only come to existence when the "rays of the five-point red star rose over Lithuania."' He explained that he would teach three main courses (a special Yiddish language course, history of the Yiddish language, and history of Yiddish literature) plus six special courses (phonetic characteristics of the Yiddish language, history of the Jewish people, history of Yiddish theatre, Yiddish folklore, history of Jewish art, and history of Jewish folk humour) over the course of eight semesters. Additionally, he intended to offer a course every semester on a special topic. He had already begun that semester to teach phonetic characteristics of the Yiddish language (focusing on stylistics and poetics) and history of the Yiddish language in addition to holding lectures twice weekly about Y.L. Peretz. Apart from attending his courses, Yiddish students would also study Lithuanian language, Marxism-Leninism, and introduction to language research, among other general courses required of all students in the Philology Department.[117] Thirty-five students were enrolled and more than one hundred hailing from throughout the Soviet Union were projected for the future.[118]

In order to emphasize the academic level of YIVO and to coordinate scholarly activity with the chair, Prylucki was also appointed director of YIVO on 1 January 1941 by Professor Krėvė-Mickevičius, who headed the Academy of Sciences of Soviet Lithuania following a brief stint as Lithuanian Foreign Minister the preceding summer. He worked feverishly to maintain its operations with a diminished staff. The Sovietized YIVO, now exclusively a research institution, was soon integrated into the Scholarly Academy of the Soviet Lithuanian Republic. Renamed the 'Institute for Jewish Culture,' it was thus parallel to Lithuanian, Polish, and Byelorussian institutes for the study of linguistics, history, and ethnography housed under the same authority.[119] Eager to publish new scholarly works, Prylucki undertook contacts with scholars throughout the Soviet Union.[120] Meanwhile, under the direction of Max Weinreich, who arrived in New York City in March 1940, the American branch of

YIVO expanded its operations with the help of other refugee and émigré scholars. Following the sovietization of YIVO in Vilnius, it saw itself as the institute's new world headquarters.[121]

Prylucki was well aware of the oppressive nature of the Soviet regime and, according to Mordkhe Tsanin, bore no illusion that Yiddish schools would continue there beyond the duration of the war. Commenting on the situation, he made clear his awareness of his role as an instrument of Soviet policy:

'The Soviet authority will not allow a Jewish school system in Vilna. It will want to have the Jewish children in Russian schools. So, who asks the former Hebrew teachers to give declarations for me, Noah Prylucki, that in teaching Hebrew to Jewish children they were ideationally misled by Zionist capitalism.'[122]

Nonetheless, convinced that the Soviets would defeat the Nazis quickly,[123] he preferred to take his chances as a professor among the Soviets than attempt escape to the United States. He applied for Soviet citizenship, presumably to facilitate his integration into the new order and to demonstrate his loyalty to the new masters of the land. Once he had received citizenship, he requested that he be treated on par with other university docents with regard to salary and privileges.[124]

Although Prylucki reportedly considered *Das Kapital* to be the 'best *shund* novel' he had ever read,[125] when the Soviets took control of Vilnius he was willing to enlist himself in their service in return for benefits for himself and Yiddish culture beyond the crucial protection of life and limb. 'In no other land in the world will I have such opportunities for my scholarly work as in the Soviet Union,' he explained to his Folkist colleague Balberyszski, who urged that he join him in fleeing Lithuania.

'I've seen Jewish life in America,' he explained to Balberyszski, 'and it's no place for me. Should I live from Cahan's hand-outs?' The Cahan he spoke of, was, of course, Abraham Cahan, the powerful editor of the New York Daily *Forward* and Yiddish cultural czar who advocated the americanization of his readers and the gradual disappearance of Yiddish in America. Being a sixty-year-old refugee in America meant being reduced to dependence, economic and otherwise, on his integrationist American Jewish brethren, especially the autocratic Cahan, who had little interest in encouraging Yiddish scholarship and 'serious' literature without a socialist message.[126] For Prylucki, a self-styled Jewish aristocrat who had devoted his life to the cause of Yiddish and cultural autonomy, the challenge of immigrant adjustment and the loss of personal prestige, influence, and perhaps even purpose in life were likely too much to contemplate.

In contrast with Bundists and Zionists, Prylucki maintained, Folkists had no reason to fear political repressions from the Soviets. Theirs was the only bourgeois party to join 'the popular front together with the Communists' against fascism. When questioned about the fate of their pro-Soviet colleagues Reyzen and Czernichow, who had been arrested during the initial Soviet occupation in the autumn of 1939, he suggested that they had been arrested because they constituted a political danger to the Soviets: the former for anti-Soviet statements in *Der vilner tog* (The Vilna Day), the daily he edited, and the latter for publishing his memoirs as a lawyer defending clients in Kharkov charged with 'counterrevolution and speculation' in the early Soviet period.[127]

Prylucki reported to Balberyszski on several occasions that he derived great moral and intellectual satisfaction from his work and was convinced that his students were extraordinarily pleased with him. Paula was made proud by his academic success, although she harboured doubts about the stability of the political situation.[128]

Conclusion

In trying to assess why Prylucki, given his own vehement anti-Soviet pronouncements in preceding years, remained relatively calm in the situation, it is difficult to determine whether he was making the best of a horrendous situation or in wilful, if cynical, collusion with the Soviets. Or maybe he was motivated by a combination of both. Perhaps it is best not to judge him given the extreme circumstances of the time, especially until Soviet archives yield additional information.

The journalist David Flinker, who eventually made his way to Mandate Palestine, remembers his final meeting with Prylucki in Vilnius on 25 December 1940. Prylucki asked Flinker to save his father Tsevi and to bring him from Warsaw to Palestine, to which Tsevi had dedicated his entire life. As for himself, he was resigned to his fate: 'Go, go as fast as possible. I wish I could see everyone on the train ... I am already an old man. Yes, I've grown old. [I have] no more strength to begin again. What will be, will be.'[129]

It is not clear why Prylucki was acceptable to the Soviets, especially considering that he published several articles critical of the Soviet persecution of intellectual and ideological heresy throughout the 1930s. Perhaps it was because, as Prylucki himself explained to a friend, the Folkists, unlike Zionists and Bundists, had never been significant ideological opponents or rivals of the Bolsheviks. Perhaps it was because Prylucki, frustrated by his treatment and the direction of YIVO, had expressed pro-Soviet sympathies by working in the Kaunas *Folksblat.* Quite likely, the Soviets wished to make a favourable impression on the annexed Jewish population, as well as the West, by supporting Jewish culture, at least its secular Yiddish dimension. More than Poles or Ukrainians, who saw their states dismantled by Soviet imperialism, Jews could be relied upon to support the Soviet regime, particularly when their only alternative was the Nazis. Prylucki, arguably the most qualified Yiddish scholar remaining in Vilnius after the disappearance of Zalmen Reyzen and in the absence of Max Weinreich, was willing to cooperate as a public figure in return for the fulfilment of his ideal of state-supported Yiddish culture (albeit under Soviet aegis with all its ideological strictures) and the chance to continue his own scholarly work in the 'most Yiddish' city in Eastern Europe. While he seems to have had few doubts about the long-term intentions of the Soviets to russify the Jewish population of Lithuania, in the indefinite future Soviet rule offered opportunities for himself and for Yiddish culture that independent Jewish politics had failed to create.

For one year, until the German invasion of Lithuania in the summer of 1941, Prylucki's academic star rose along with the red star over Vilnius.

Conclusion

Prominent Yiddish linguists and language ideologists in Eastern Europe may be broadly divided into two categories with a degree of overlap in activities: those chiefly occupied with status planning (e.g., Nathan Birnbaum, who championed Yiddishism and Diaspora nationalism in the journalistic and political arenas) and those who pursued mainly corpus planning (e.g., Max Weinreich, who is known almost exclusively as a scholar, his occasional journalistic activity and adolescent engagement on behalf of the Bund notwithstanding).[1] Among Jewish language ideologists none worked so assiduously and so long in both domains as Noah Prylucki. During the period examined here, Prylucki struggled to achieve official recognition and accompanying rights for the Yiddish language in the elected organs of an independent Polish state; simultaneously, he laboured on behalf of its cultivation and improved status among its own speakers. Although he did not accomplish many of his political goals, Prylucki, together with his colleagues in the Folksparty, indisputably contributed much to the defence of Jewish civil and national rights in Poland. They also helped to give form to and galvanize the movement to modernize Yiddish culture and to recast traditional, religion-based identity among Jews as a secularized Yiddish-centric one.

Noah Prylucki is distinguished among early twentieth-century Eastern European Jewish nationalists and language ideologists not merely by the sheer diversity of his political and cultural endeavours but by his upbringing in secularized, proto-nationalist circles. As demonstrated by the biographies of his colleagues active in the Folksparty, an ideological migration from a more or less traditional religious world view to Zionism and then to Diaspora nationalism and Yiddishism was hardly a rarity among contemporary intellectuals committed to defending Jewish rights and to guaranteeing continuity, even if with radical changes, in both Jewish culture and collective Jewish existence. Language-based nationalism, whether in the form of Hebraism or Yiddishism, was but one response to the crises of identity and cultural 'authenticity' engendered by the disruption of traditional Jewish society in the modern era. Both language ideologies stood in violent opposition to yet another option, linguistic (without complete cultural) assimilation.

Yiddishism combined most readily with the doctrine of national-personal autonomy in the Diaspora, although it united also with some strains of socialist Zionism and Jewish territorialism. The Hebraization of the Diaspora, in contrast with that of Palestine, was recognized as impossible by all but the most extreme ideologues. This perspective, however, did not discourage the erection of a network of Hebrew-language schools in Poland and elsewhere in Eastern Europe to prepare a generation for *aliyah.* Both language-based movements, like the whole of the 'Jewish national renaissance,' were to a large extent – albeit one greatly exaggerated by the opponents of Jewish nationalism – fostered by 'Litvaks.' They brought with them a cultural orientation and skills largely foreign to the indigenous Jewish population of Congress Poland. Meanwhile, the work of yet another Litvak (and dabbler in Yiddish linguistics), the Białystok-born inventor of the 'international' language Esperanto, Ludwig Zamenhof, presented yet another (not specifically Jewish) solution to the problem of ethnic enmity and civil and national inequality by engineering a common language for all people, one that drew on elements of many groups but which was not identified with any one.[2]

The most common linguistic response – certainly by the interwar period – was, however, the adoption of the dominant language of non-Jewish society. Such a language shift hardly implied full identification with the dominant society, however. This condition was a consequence of the apparent failure of the ideology of assimilation and practical limitations on social integration as well as personal preference. In fact, not a few champions of both Yiddishism and Hebraism failed to practise what they preached. Out of a combination of convenience and habit, they primarily spoke other languages in their private and sometimes even in their public lives.

Despite having received a prized state education in the Russian language and culture in addition to home instruction in the classical Jewish liturgical language, Noah Prylucki ceased to identify both with the 'hegemonic' language that was the chief avenue for social and economic advancement in the Russian Empire and with the revived spoken Hebrew that was the dream of his father Tsevi's youth. He thus rejected both the linguistic russification common among Jewish intellectuals and Zionists of his day and the goal of creating a new, Hebrew-speaking Jew in Palestine that he himself had endorsed in early adulthood under the influence of his father's proto-Zionist circles. Although he sympathized as a committed democrat with the Polish nationalist cause during its suppression by the tsarist regime, he also never accepted the integration of the Jews into Polish culture as a feasible, let alone desirable, goal. He made effective use of Polish as the spokesman for a Jewish nationalist party but came to the language relatively late despite living most of his life on Polish territory. In contrast with natives of Congress Poland (such as Yitshak Grünbaum and Samuel Hirschhorn), he never profoundly identified with the Polish language and culture. This undoubtedly benefited his commitment to Yiddish in a Polish-speaking milieu.

Prylucki's decision to promote Yiddish as the exclusive vehicle for modern Jewish culture did not occur overnight. It is neither explicable solely by his Romantic conception of language nor by his embrace of mass-oriented politics to redress the absence of Jewish rights in the Russian Empire. The choice of language and genre in his earliest writings indicates an ambition to join both the Russian and Hebrew literary elites. After all, Yiddish literature was scarcely known, much less respected, during his childhood and adolescence and he managed to excel in Russian schools – a source of tremendous pride – despite anti-Jewish quotas and a record of political arrests. One might speculate that as an aspiring *homme de lettres* he would not have wholeheartedly invested his energies in the development of a secular Yiddish culture had he found the accolade and acceptance in Russian and Hebrew letters which he initially sought, that is, if he were not confined to the margins of literary society both in the dominant language of European high culture in the Russian Empire and in the smaller one belonging to a tiny Jewish elite.[3]

Be that as it may, by duplicating and adapting contemporary European ideologies and cultural institutions to a Jewish context, Noah Prylucki was a primary contributor to the construction of a new Jewish culture on the foundations of traditional religious life. In lowly Yiddish, a language rooted in the Diaspora and possessing a distinguished secular cultural pedigree waiting to be 'discovered,' he found a surrogate for the territorial criterion then in vogue in European nationalist thought. Moreover, since Yiddish culture needed new leaders and heroes, it provided the opportunity to satisfy his personal ambitions for social prominence in addition to the means to promote his personal vision of a modernized

Jewish people. He was surely also drawn to Yiddish as an entrepreneur who recognized the tremendous commercial potential offered by organs of mass culture such as the press once tsarist bans had been lifted.

Like many nineteenth-century Eastern European nationalists, most early ideologists of Yiddishism and Yiddish language planners – among them Ber Borokhov and Nathan Birnbaum – were neither raised nor educated in environments where the language they promoted was widely spoken. It is understandable that they did not emerge directly from among the *folksmasn*, the 'unreflective' carriers of the language. A combination of self-conscious alienation from the folk language and a secular cosmopolitan education was necessary to create the perspective of an outsider to the culture. This perspective permitted the appreciation of Yiddish both as an instrument for the promotion of Jewish nationalism and as a cultural 'renaissance,' as well as an object of scientific study.[4]

Few of the early Yiddish language ideologists can be considered 'full' native speakers, as they were typically products of the Russian or German cultural spheres even if their parents had themselves been raised in Yiddish-speaking milieus. Prylucki, like the Soviet linguist Nokhem Shtif, was exceptional among Yiddish linguists in that he grew up and conducted his life's work amid the masses that were to provide the corpus for his linguistic research and for whose rights he militantly campaigned. Raised in bourgeois, *maskilic* homes, both politicians-turned-scholars claimed unfamiliarity with the Jews' 'mother tongue' in their childhood and report having first activated a largely passive knowledge of Yiddish in late adolescence for didactic and political aims. Their emotional distance at this time from Yiddish, which was an ever present factor in Jewish life around them, was conditioned by both ideology and social class. In the pursuit of national monolingualism, which they romantically posited as a people's natural condition, they rejected both traditional diglossia and its modernized versions (cultivation of Russian as a literary and 'high' language alongside use of Yiddish at home and with those lacking secular educations) they experienced in their youths. Parallel to other nationalists of the day, their ideology and personal proclivities dictated that they labour as politicians, community activists, and scholars to remake the national 'mother tongue' on the model of a language like French that was highly standardized and utilized for all social functions and by all segments of the national community. In short, forms of internal bilingualism that were (and remain to this day) common to that region were deemed abnormal and an impairment to the survival of the nation. Prylucki and his Folkist colleagues therefore insisted upon the use of Yiddish among all social classes to halt language shift and encouraged the expansion of a largely autarkic Yiddish-speaking sub-economy to foster the use of the language and the economic welfare of its speakers. The language's functions needed to be expanded rapidly to encompass all facets of contemporary European life without sacrificing its particularity.

For all Prylucki's devotion to democracy and the 'mother tongue of the masses,' his approach to language and linguistics reflects the inevitable tension between populism and elitism. Prylucki delighted in the dialectal variation he noted among the *folksmasn* (a term popular in his day which inherently reflects a distance between elites and non-elites) who came to him for legal consultation and was renowned for his folksy idioms. He was, however, also accused by critics of objectifying Yiddish speakers for use in his research and thereby exploiting the downtrodden for the purpose of collecting linguistics data. Indeed, it was alleged that he callously made petitioners wait and paid less attention to what they said than how they said it. The elegantly attired Jewish 'aristocrat' possessed a definite sense of his own importance and always maintained his social distance from his language informants even though he publicly praised their colourful turns of phrase and the 'national genius' directing and informing their speech.

For him the supposedly unreflective speech of the Jewish petite bourgeoisie of Congress Poland was the ultimate arbiter of naturalness and authenticity and, hence, correctness. In contrast with native speakers of German, such as the Yiddish linguists Max Weinreich and Solomon Birnbaum,[5] who worried lest Yiddish be mistaken for poor German, Prylucki was lenient towards Germanisms as long as he heard them in popular speech. Yet he detected a certain 'corruption' of the language by baneful foreign influences among more status conscious (and hence linguistically 'promiscuous') elements, as well as a pernicious trend towards linguistic polonization among segments of youth in the 'lowest of classes.'[6] He was understandably more adamant in repudiating Slavicisms freshly borrowed through direct contact with Polish and Russian than in rejecting the mainly literary influence of German on written Yiddish, though he condemned this too.

He acknowledged that Yiddish was historically open to a variety of sources for its enrichment and development. The unprecedented tide of foreign influences since the latter half of the nineteenth century needed, however, to be controlled as Jews became familiar with non-Jewish languages and cultures in growing numbers. For Yiddish to survive in a time of changing social and intellectual boundaries between Jews and

Gentiles, the *folk* that had created it could no longer remain its exclusive guardians. Instead the cultivation and regulation of the language had to be entrusted to scholars like himself who possessed the necessary sensitivity to the specificity of the language vis-à-vis closely related German and co-territorial Slavic languages to safeguard its uniqueness. He thus proposed that scholars interfere in the natural evolution of the language at the same time that he proclaimed the sovereignty of the people over its language.

Yiddishism was expected to create a democratic revolution in Jewish society by linguistically empowering the masses without access to higher education in languages other than Yiddish. Mastery of Hebrew and Aramaic, the languages of the traditional rabbinic and wealthy lay elites, or Russian and Polish, the languages of the new secular elites, would cease to convey status and power. In practice, however, Prylucki and other Yiddishists set about to create a new secular nationalist elite commanding a standardized variety of the language.[7] This new variety of Yiddish to be cultivated by scholars, the *kultursprakh*, would stand above all dialects and be used in public speaking and other occasions that required a more formal register of language. Traditional Hebrew-Yiddish diglossia, as well as Russian-Yiddish or Polish-Yiddish diglossia or bilingualism, would thus be replaced with a new diglossia joining dialects and the *kultursprakh*. The normative language was to be taught in schools and to become a mark of education and hence class. Moreover, the Yiddish secular school would produce graduates capable of understanding and appreciating scholarly literature and belle lettres in Yiddish, thus yielding a class of both consumers and producers of modern Yiddish culture. Finally, since language would replace birth or religion to define political membership in the Jewish people, language planners would thus police the boundaries not only of the language but of the national community too.

In his own speech and writing Noah Prylucki cultivated forms specific to Yiddish, drawing the mockery of satirists who ridiculed his use of seemingly obscure, antiquated or simply unheard of and outlandish forms.[8] An opponent of the Vilna-centric school of language standardization, he argued against Litvish serving as the basis for standard pronunciation since it was the Yiddish dialect closest in pronunciation to German and it was spoken by the smallest number of speakers. Instead, he supported a norm based on Volhynian Yiddish, the dialect commonly used on the Yiddish stage and, perhaps not coincidentally, the dialect he knew from his Ukrainian childhood. He argued that Yiddish orthography needed to be improved to reflect its norms, many of whose nuances were not accurately reflected in the spelling system dominant in Yiddish publishing, and insisted on using a private spelling system in his private publications.

He was thus far from the ideal of a *folks-inteligent*, the intellectual who humbly lives and works among the masses, despite his intensive work on behalf of Yiddish schools and legal and relief work undertaken to help everyday Jews in times of crisis. Prylucki enjoyed the prestige and influence accorded him and was never shy in taking credit for his achievements. While seeking to undo what he presented as his own early linguistic assimilation and to achieve the democratization of Jewish society, he also strove to preserve his own social class and standing. Given his eloquence in Yiddish – alternately erudite, alternately folksy – the quasi-myth that he promoted of being a non-native speaker could serve to bolster his status as simultaneously an insider and outsider to Jewish life.

In his later years, after having largely left political activity behind him, he openly conceded that his linguistics research was understood by few and served mainly to satisfy his own intellectual curiosity.[9] In this respect he differed little from many of his academic colleagues at YIVO, although he, a linguistics autodidact not residing in Vilna, was often made to feel an outsider to their more formally trained circles. Their linguistic purism and idealization of Yiddish as an abstract aesthetic value and object of scientific study divorced from political activism caused the organization to be reproached by the Jewish left with bourgeois remoteness from the needs and concerns of the actual speakers of the language in Poland.[10]

Prylucki's efforts on behalf of Yiddishism and Folkism notwithstanding, neither ideology took root in Poland to the extent he had hoped for reasons both internal and external to Jewish society. During the First World War the Folksparty garnered early victories among Warsaw's Jewish voters based on the strength of Prylucki's popularity as a public figure and its unrepentantly pro-Jewish and pro-Yiddish stance at a time when the future status of the Jews as a national or religious minority in a new Polish state was, it seemed, to be decided. Other Jewish parties and ideological groupings were judged to be too yielding to Polish nationalist demands and insufficiently supportive (if not hostile, as in the case of the Assimilationists) of official recognition for the primary language of most Jews in Poland. Once it become abundantly clear, however, that demands for national-cultural autonomy were supported by other Jewish parties as well and still unobtainable due to the opposition of the state in the 1920s, Folkism lost much of its meaning. Of course, the lack of a unified Jewish front, especially surrounding the language question and the authority of the *kehila*, only strengthened Polish resolve not to recognize Jewish cultural demands.

After much internal debate about for whom the party was intended – the whole of Polish Jewry or the Yiddish-speaking lower-middle class, which represented its largest part – the Folksparty opted in the inter-war period for a program hostile to both socialism and Zionism, the dominant currents in secular Jewish politics. Because of its anti-socialist platform, it lost the support of the Jewish left, its chief partner in the building of Yiddish schools. Its obstinate course of independent political action to preserve its distinct identity and uncompromising support of Yiddish at the expense of Hebrew made cooperation with the Zionists, the largest Jewish representation in the Sejm, difficult and at times impossible. Further, its relationship towards Hebrew and Jewish settlement in Palestine cost it the sympathy of the Jewish masses, which felt instinctively attached to these cultural axes even if secularized. Its secular nationalist stance was also opposed by the Agudah, which commanded the loyalty of a substantial portion of Orthodox, largely Hasidic, voters. The small number of Folkist deputies found themselves isolated in the Sejm, often without the support of either the Jewish Koło, the Polish left, or the other national minorities. Finally, the party's militancy was exploited by its enemies in the Polish right, who used the Folkists' rhetoric to foment anti-Jewish sentiment and conspired to remove Prylucki temporarily from politics. The shortcomings of Prylucki's character – his intransigence, self-importance, and easily offended pride – helped, of course, not only to create frictions between his party others in both Jewish cultural organizations and elected political bodies but also to distance him from members of his own party.

Prylucki's Folksparty never obtained a sizable following outside the Polish capital and was principally a Warsaw phenomenon. Yiddish culture alone was not sufficient to draw mass support, since most Yiddish-speaking Jews did not possess the ideological or practical attachment to the language demanded by Yiddishists. Even among themselves, the Folkists were unable to agree upon the role of Hebrew in Jewish life and some, most prominently Zeitlin, even objected to being publicly identified as Yiddishists on principle. The party's founders, reluctant to take positions that might alienate other orientations, became disaffected by its lack of followers and Prylucki's tight hold on its activity and ideology. The Yiddish secular school, the cornerstone of the Folkist vision of national cultural autonomy, was unable to draw more than a fraction of Polish Jewish youth because of its popular association with anti-religious, anti-

Hebrew radicalism and the limited socioeconomic horizons it offered graduates because of limited resources and official harassment. A secular Yiddishist education, even if including thorough instruction in both Polish and Hebrew, offered no competitive advantage in gaining places in the Polish-language state secondary schools and universities coveted by aspiring middle-class Jews. On the contrary, it was a hindrance. And admission to foreign universities as an alternative was a luxury restricted to the wealthy. As the sociolinguist Joshua Fishman observes in another context, Yiddish speakers 'were either too powerless or too mobile' for Yiddishism to succeed in the absence of an 'econo-political reality' that would protect the language in its new societal functions.[11] Quite simply, the Folksparty was unable to win the necessary recognition of cultural autonomy to make Yiddishism economically viable. Prylucki's vision of a 're-imagined' Jewish identity, one anchored primarily in language, failed to take hold among the Jews of Poland. To the contrary, despite growing secularization and the spread among Jews of a self-understanding as a national community, language continued to figure as only one element in a broader complex of factors determining an already strong sense of group belonging.

In summary, in the interwar period a climate of poverty and discrimination alongside easy access to Polish primary (although not secondary) education resulted in a growing rate of linguistic assimilation without commensurate societal integration among Jewish youth. The possibility of a primarily Polish-speaking Jewish population – a menace against which Prylucki and his colleagues had long struggled – understandably terrified and demoralized those who had invested their energies and finances in not only the survival but also the modernization and expansion of Yiddish culture. While some Folkists were willing to adapt to the changing needs of Jewish society and became active in a Jewish nationalist press in Polish, Prylucki remained committed to Yiddish, even if chiefly as an object of esoteric study.

Recognizing the impotence of political agitation on behalf of national cultural autonomy, Prylucki, like other erstwhile autonomists before him, withdrew from politics in the later half of the 1920s and retired into a world of research. His book-filled Warsaw apartment resembled more the home of a linguistics professor than that of a lawyer or politician.[12] Finally, during the Soviet occupation of Lithuania, he realized a long-held dream by holding the inaugural Chair of Yiddish at the University of Vilnius.

In their final months, Noah Prylucki and his YIVO colleagues desper-

VILNIAUS UNIVERSITETAS

Tarnautojo asmens liudijimas

Liudijamojo parašas

Noachas Priluckis

yra Humanitarinių Mokslų Fakulteto docentas, e. katedros vedėjo p.

Vilnius, 1941 m. mėn. 20 d.

Nr. 349

REKTORIUS

Administracinio Ūkinio Sektoriaus Viršininkas

Išeinant iš tarnybos liudijimas grąžinamas

7.1 Noah Prylucki's cancelled identity card from the University of Vilnius, where he was Professor of Yiddish during the Soviet occupation of Lithuania 1940–1941. He was summarily dismissed along with eight other Jewish professors in late June 1941. After being forced to catalogue rare Jewish books for the Nazi *Rosenbergstab*, he was murdered by the Germans in August 1941. (Lietuvos Centrinis Valystubehs Archyvas [LCVA], Vilnius. F. R856, Ap.2, B. 1123, Noachas Priluckis, Vilnius University Papers.)

ately debated the survival not only of Yiddish culture but of the Jewish people in Eastern Europe. Debilitated by a lung infection at the start of Operation Barbarossa, the German invasion of the Soviet Union, in June 1941, Prylucki saw little sense in accepting an invitation to join young writers attempting to escape the approaching onslaught on foot.[13] Dismissed from his university position along with eight other Jewish professors on 27 June 1941,[14] he was arrested by the Gestapo on 28 July 1941. His familiarity with YIVO collections and his expertise in the field of Old Yiddish literature and book publishing were yoked into service by the notorious Rosenbergstab (*Einsatzstab des Reichsleiters Alfred Rosenberg*), whose task was to ransack Judaica collections throughout Europe and to send their contents to the *Institut zur Erforschung der Judenfrage* in Frankfurt am Main. He and Eliyohu Yankev Goldshmidt, a Yiddish journalist and director of the Ansky Jewish Ethnographic Museum in Vilna, were transported daily from their cell in a Gestapo prison to the city's famed Strashun Judaica Library, where they were forced to compile lists of incunabula in preparation for their shipment to Germany. On 12 August 1941, the near sixty-year-old Prylucki, infirm after repeated beatings and abuse, was 'liquidated' by his captors. Goldshmidt died in his cell.[15] Prylucki's wife Paula was confined to the Vilnius ghetto and murdered a year later at the notorious killing fields at Ponar.[16] His father Tsevi, a pioneer of the Yiddish press and long-standing editor of *Der moment,* chose not to flee Warsaw with Noah and other journalists because of his age and poor health. He perished in that city's infamous ghetto.[17]

None of the other founders of the Folksparty survived the war. Hillel Zeitlin was dispatched to Treblinka in September 1942. He had rejected offers to board the journalists' train, seeing it as his fate to die, if necessary, with his brethren.[18] After spending months as a refugee in Vilna, Lazar Kahan, who did choose to board the train, was rejoined by his wife, who had also managed to make it to Vilna. After spending months there, they escaped together via Siberia to Japan. He succumbed to typhus in Japanese-controlled Shanghai in 1946 and his wife died shortly afterwards.[19] Saul Stupnicki fled Warsaw with colleagues but, unable to continue because of his age, returned to the city and resumed his cultural work in the ghetto. According to accounts, he either died of hunger there or was sent to Treblinka.[20] Samuel Hirschhorn poisoned himself during the first liquidation of the Warsaw Ghetto in May 1942.[21]

Ultimately, Noah Prylucki suffered the same fate at Nazi hands as millions of other Jews, the majority of them Yiddish speakers. He was spared, however, the experience of colleagues such as Max Weinreich and Yudl Mark. Safe in the United States, they necessarily watched from afar, powerless during the destruction of a civilization they cherished. In the postwar era they witnessed the realization of perhaps Prylucki's greatest fear – the decline of Yiddish as a language of modern, secular culture and of Yiddishism as a viable ideology.

Hebraism succeeded where Yiddishism failed. It succeeded, however, not because popular support for speaking the language exceeded that for Yiddish. Zionist pioneers who were similarly committed to language needed to overcome unprecedented barriers to revernacularize Hebrew. They were, however, able to gain international recognition for their political movement and thus able to establish the infrastructure of a proto-state during the British Mandate in Palestine, that is, *before* the arrival of mass waves of refugees in the 1930s and after the Second World War. While these immigrants often lacked deep commitment to Zionist ideology or the Hebrew language upon their arrival, they encountered in Israel the reality of a state whose normative agencies – political, social, educational, and otherwise – already functioned in Hebrew. Moreover, the state vaunted Hebrew and discouraged, if not suppressed (as is often argued in the case of Yiddish), any rivals as the primary language of the new Jewish society, particularly its high culture. Thus, Hebrew was not only the language uniting an immigrant Jewish population of diverse origins (and asserting its distinctiveness and cohesiveness vis-à-vis an Arab minority within the state and an external Arab majority in the region) but also the language for social integration and economic advancement. Unlike Yiddish in Poland (but like Polish in Poland), Hebrew in Israel was the chief, if not exclusive, vehicle for opportunity.[22]

In retrospect, it is clear that the Yiddishist experiment did not succeed in achieving its ultimate political and cultural goals, its significant accomplishments notwithstanding. While Yiddish-speaking ultra-Orthodox communities, the inheritors of pre-war religious opposition to Jewish secularism, thrive in a number of Western states and Israel, there exists no clear inheritor to the traditions of secular Yiddishism outside of academia, the dwindling circles of the organized Jewish left, and cultural festivals. Yiddish continues to be used today in many ultra-Orthodox communities, whose birthrates outstrip those of most other Jewish communities, precisely because it is but part of a larger ideology seeking to maximize Jewish distinctiveness and valuing self-segregation from broader cultural and intellectual trends. Access to higher education, which requires a mastery of the language of the state in all its written and oral registers, is largely a matter of indifference to them, because they do not desire to alter radically their community's economic profile. Language is a tool to an end, practical or otherwise, but not an independent value.[23] Thus, Yiddish continues to function, as in pre-modern Jewish society, as the language of an intensely religious subculture dwelling in close proximity to but still on the margins of the majority culture with which it is in a symbiotic relationship.

Notes

Introduction

1 From Smocza, Stawka, Gizka, Śliszka,
and from the shtetls near and far,
people are drawn to Świętokrzyśka,
eldery men, women, youth.

With packages and ragged clothes,
the people comes to Noah;

Prylucki's house is filled with suffering,
groaning, folksongs, and tears.

They are taking Jews' livelihoods away,
'O, save us, Councillor, Sir';
Noah has but one request,
'Repeat that saying carefully'...

Prylucki writes, makes records –
court decisions, songs, figures of speech.
His pen dashes in order not to miss
A Yiddish proverb, wise and sweet.

He listens and probes every face,
absorbs each one's sorrow.
And sometimes a song, a woman's prayer
is his only and highest reward.

A. Almi, *Letste gezangen* (Buenos Aires: Farband fun varshever un prager yidn in argentine, 1954), 60. This and all subsequent translations, unless otherwise noted are my own.

2 Little has been published since the Holocaust about his cultural and scholarly contributions. The linguist Yudl Mark, a Folkist while still living in Lithuania, surveyed Prylucki's accomplishments in a commemorative article, 'Noyekh prilutski – der kemfer un der forsher' in *Tsukunft* (Feb. 1945): 100–3. More recently, the linguist Christopher Hutton has contributed 'Noyekh Prylucki: Philosopher of Language,' in *History of Yiddish Studies*, ed. Dov-Ber Kerler (Chur, Switzerland: Harward Academic Publishers GmbH, 1991), 15–24. Itzik Gottesman discusses Prylucki's contributions to Yiddish folklore in his book *Defining the Yiddish Nation: the Jewish Folklorists of Poland* (Detroit: Wayne State University Press, 2003).
3 On this subject, see Jeffrey Shandler, *Adventures in Yiddishism* (Berkeley: University of California Press, 2006).
4 Ernest Gellner, *Nations and Nationalism* (Oxford: Basil Blackwell, 1983), 106.
5 EJ Hobsbawm, *Nations and Nationalism Since 1780* (Cambridge: University Press, 1990), 110–11.
6 'Noyekh Prilutski,' in Meylekh Ravitsh, *Mayn leksikon* (Montreal, 1945), vol. 1, 175–6. Ravitsh characterized him as carrying 'in one hand the warrior's sword and, in the other, the pen of the home scholar (*shtub-gelernter*), the book worm (*benkl-kvetsher*).'
7 A thorough treatment of Prylucki's linguistic works remains a desideratum. This study does not concentrate specifically on Prylucki's contributions to various fields of Yiddish linguistics, although the significant nexus between language and nationalism in his thought is examined.
8 For a schema of language-oriented nation-building activities, see Miroslav Hroch, 'The Social Interpretation of Linguistic Demands in European National Movements,' *EUI Working Paper EUF No. 94/1* (1994): 13–19.
9 'Prilutski, Noyekh,' in *Leksikon fun der nayer yidisher literatur*, Shmuel Niger and Yankev Shatski, eds., (New York: Alvetlehkher yidisher kultur-kongres, 1956–1981), vol. 7, 223. Among YIVO archival materials recently discovered in Lithuania are those pertaining to Prylucki's work in YIVO's philological section. See, e.g., YIVO Archives, YIVO-Vilna Collection RG 1-1.
10 Nakhmen Mayzil, 'Noyekh Prilutski,' *Yidishe kultur* (Jan. 1945): 25–6.
11 Uriel Weinreich, *Modern English-Yiddish Yiddish-English Dictionary* (New York: YIVO, 1990), xx–xi, xxiv–xxv.

1 Jewish Life, Language, and Politics in Poland

1 The name of a great grandson of Noah (Gen. 10: 3) in the Hebrew Bible, 'Ashkenaz' was reassigned by medieval European Jewish tradition to designate the region of northern France and western Germany. Accordingly, the

Jewish denizens of Ashkenaz came to refer to themselves as 'Ashkenazim' and their religious rite as the 'custom of Ashkenaz' (*minhag ashkenaz*).

2 For a comprehensive overview of Jewish life prior to the partitions, see Gershon David Hundert, *Jews in Poland-Lithuania in the Eighteenth Century: A Genealogy of Modernity* (Berkeley and Los Angeles: University of California Press, 2004), and Moshe Rosman, 'Innovative Tradition: Jewish Culture in the Polish-Lithuanian Commonwealth,' in *Cultures of the Jews*, ed. David Biale, (New York: Schocken, 2002), 519–70.

3 For an introduction to the history and sociology of language use among Jews, see Max Weinreich, *History of the Yiddish Language*, translated by Shlomo Noble with the assistance of Joshua A. Fishman (New Haven: Yale University Press and YIVO, 2008), and *Readings in the Sociology of Jewish Languages*, ed. Joshua A. Fishman (Leiden: E.J. Brill, 1985).

4 For the case of Latin, see Peter Burke, *Languages and Communities in Early Modern Europe* (Cambridge: Cambridge University Press, 2004).

5 Shaul Stampfer, '"Heder" Study, Knowledge of Torah, and the Maintenance of Social Stratification in Traditional East European Jewish Society,' *Studies in Jewish Education* 3 (1988): 271–89.

6 The classical theory of the genesis of Yiddish, articulated most authoritatively by Max Weinreich in his magnum opus *History of the Yiddish Language*, posits the origins of Yiddish in the fusion of variants of Old French and Italian, Hebrew-Aramaic, and medieval German dialects in the Rhine area. In recent decades, linguists have challenged this model. Robert King and Alice Farber do not question the essentials of the theory but place the origins of the language further east, in the medieval Jewish communities of Bavaria and eastern Germany due to the greater similarities between features of Yiddish and the German dialects spoken there ('Yiddish and the Settlement History of Ashkenazic Jews,' *Mankind Quarterly* 24/4 (1984): 393–425). Paul Wexler offers a more radical challenge, arguing that Yiddish arose as a Jewish variant of Sorbian (Judeo-Sorbian) that was relexified with German vocabulary (while preserving its basic Slavic structure) in the mixed German-Slavic linguistic territory that is now eastern Germany ('Yiddish: the Fifteenth Slavic Language – A Study of Partial Language Shift from Judeo-Sorbian to German,' *International Journal of the Sociology of Language* 91 (1991): 9–150).

7 M. Weinreich, *History of the Yiddish Language*, vol. 1, 315–27.

8 Richard Pipes, 'Catherine II and the Jews: The Origins of the Pale of Settlement,' *Soviet Jewish Affairs* 5/2 (1975): 3–20.

9 Paul Robert Magosci, *A History of Ukraine* (Toronto: University of Toronto Press, 1996), 12–16.

10 Theodore R. Weeks, 'The Best of Both Worlds: Creating the *Żyd-Polak*,' *East European Jewish Affairs* 34/2 (2004): 6.
11 Theodore R. Weeks, *Nation and State in Late Imperial Russia* (Dekalb: Northern Illinois University Press, 1996), 50–68, 113–29.
12 Michael Stanislawski, 'The Russian Empire,' in *YIVO Encyclopedia of Jews in Eastern Europe* (New Haven and London: Yale University Press and YIVO, 2008), vol. 2, 1607–15.
13 Dan Miron, *A Traveler Disguised* (Syracuse, NY: Syracuse University Press, 1996), ch. 2, 'The Language as Caliban.'
14 On Zederbaum's career as a journalist, see Alexander Orbach, *New Voices of Russian Jewry* (Leiden: E.J. Brill, 1980).
15 On this subject, see Steven Aschheim, *Brothers and Strangers: The East-European Jew in German and German-Jewish Consciousness* (Madison: University of Wisconsin Press, 1982).
16 See Michael Stanislawski, *Tsar Nicholas and the Jews* (Philadelphia: Jewish Publication Society, 1983).
17 Yehuda Slutsky, *Ha-'itonut ha-yehudit-rusit ba-me'a ha-'esrim* (Tel-Aviv: Ha-aguda le-heker toldot ha-yehudim, ha-makhon le-heker ha-tefutsot, 1978), 9. See also, Gennadi Estraich, 'On the Acculturation of Jews in Late Imperial Russia,' *La Rassegna Mensile Israel* 62/1–2 (1996): 217–26.
18 Even when a group of Jewish writers, scholars, and community activists in St Petersburg gathered at a banquet to honour the visiting Yiddish and Hebrew writer Peretz in 1906, all present spoke Russian in their speeches. Outraged, Peretz slammed his hand on the table and unceremoniously announced that it was a grievous insult to him that Jewish intellectuals spoke no Yiddish in his presence at the same time that they acknowledged his cultural contributions in that language. (Shoel Ginzburg, 'Ershte yidishe tsaytung in rusland, "der fraynd,"' in his *Amolike peterburg* (New York: Shoel Ginzburg shriftn-komitet, 1944), 201–2.) Twenty-five years earlier, the poet Judah Leib Gordon attacked Russian Jewish notables honouring his literary achievements in Hebrew at a sumptuous dinner in the Russian capital for their ignorance of the language of his works. Rather than make an indignant pronouncement, however, Gordon veiled his linguistic condescension in the form of an ironic Yiddish poem since he was quite certain that few in the Russian-speaking audience could comprehend Yiddish. (Michael Stanislawski, *For Whom Do I Toil?* (New York and Oxford: Oxford University Press, 1988), 174–5.) Both episodes serve to demonstrate just how distant the St Petersburg Jewish elite were in their daily linguistic behaviour, regardless of public loyalties, from the ideals promoted by Jewish cultural heroes.

19 Gennady Estraikh, *Soviet Yiddish: Language Planning and Linguistic Development* (Oxford: Clarendon, 1999), 5–11.

20 Michael Stanislawski, *Zionism and the Fin-de-Siècle: Cosmopolitanism and Nationalism from Nordau to Jabotinski* (Los Angeles: University of California Press, 2001).

21 Marcin Wodziński, 'Good Maskilim and Bad Assimilationists, or Toward a New Historiography of the Haskalah in Poland,' *Jewish Social Studies* 10/3 (2004): 87–122.

22 Ibid.

23 Stanislaw Blejwas, 'The Failure of Assimilation 1864–1895,' review of Alina Cała, *Asymilacja Żydów w Królestwie Polskim (1864–1897)* (Warsaw: Państwowy Instytut Wydawniczy, 1989), *Polin* 8 (1994): 326.

24 Gershon Bacon, 'La société juive dans le royaume de la Pologne du Congrès (1860–1914),' in *Société juive à travers l'histoire,* ed. Shmuel Trigano (Paris: Fayard, 1992), vol. 1, 659.

25 Ezra Mendelsohn introduces the term *integrationist* to describe this school of thought in the Polish-Jewish context to indicate that 'what its adherents really wanted the Jews to do was to integrate into the majority society without being entirely swallowed up by it' (*On Modern Jewish Politics* (New York and Oxford: Oxford University Press, 1993), 16).

26 Direct Jewish (as well as peasant) participation in the January Insurrection was limited, although many Jews played important roles in furnishing intelligence, arms, and uniforms to the combatants; most Jews seem to have maintained neutrality (Stanislaw Blejwas, 'Polish Positivism and the Jews,' *Jewish Social Studies* 46 (1984): 25). Theodore Weeks notes: 'While one can certainly argue that this much-touted "brotherhood" of Jews and Poles was both superficial and short-lived, it was nonetheless very strong both as a reality in the early 1860s and as a myth that survived in various ways into the twentieth century' – Weeks here understands 'myth' as not '"falsehood" but rather a deeper, almost metaphysical belief that resists cold logic' ('Polish "Progressive Antisemitism," 1905–1914,' *East European Jewish Affairs* 25/2 (1995): 50). The Insurrection of 1863 served as a symbol well into the twentieth century of Polish-Jewish cooperation against a common foe. The figure of the patriotic Jew has been immortalized in Polish literature, as well, most notably in Polish national poet Adam Mickiewicz's epic work *Pan Tadeusz* (1834). On the issue of Polish-Jewish relations as depicted in literature, see Magdalena Opalski and Israel Bartal, *Poles and Jews: A Failed Brotherhood* (Hanover, NH: Brandeis University Press, 1992).

27 See Robert Blobaum, *Rewolucja: Russian Poland, 1904–1907* (Ithaca: Cornell University Press, 1995); Weeks, 'Polish "Progressive Antisemitism"'; Piotr

S. Wandycz, *The Lands of Partitioned Poland, 1795–1918* (Seattle and London: University of Washington Press, 1974), ch. 10; Stephen D. Corrsin, 'Language Use in Cultural and Political Change in pre-1914 Warsaw: Poles, Jews, and Russification,' *Slavonic and East European Review* 68/1 (1990): 75–6.

28 Stephen D. Corrsin, *Warsaw before the First World War: Poles and Jews in the Third City of the Russian Empire, 1880–1914* (Boulder: East European Monographs, 1989), 11; Michael Jerry Ochs, 'St Petersburg and the Jews of Russian Poland, 1862–1905' (PhD diss., Harvard University, 1986), ch. 2; Weeks, *Nation and State*, 59.

29 Bacon, 'La société juive,' 635.

30 Gershon Bacon, 'Poland from 1795 to 1939,' in *YIVO Encyclopedia of Jews in Eastern Europe*, vol. 2, 1394.

31 Blejwas, 'Polish Positivism,' 32.

32 Abraham Ascher, *The Revolution of 1905: Russia in Disarray* (Stanford: Stanford University Press, 1988), 155.

33 Blejwas, 'Polish Positivism,' 30–3.

34 Weeks, 'Progressive Antisemitism,' 65.

35 Bacon, 'La société juive,' 661, 663.

36 Blejwas, 'Polish Positivism,' 21; Theodore R. Weeks, 'Fanning the Flames: Jews in the Warsaw Press, 1905–1912,' *East European Jewish Affairs* 28/2 (1998–9): 66.

37 Corrsin, *Warsaw before the First World War*, 18–19.

38 Yankev Shatski, *Geshikhte fun yidn in varshe* (New York: YIVO, 1953), vol. 3, ch. 4; Frank Golczewski, *Polnisch-Jüdische Beziehungen, 1881–1922* (Wiesbaden: Franz Steiner, 1981), 41–51.

39 For a more extensive survey of the development of Polish nationalism from the Partitions until 1966, see Peter Brock, 'Polish Nationalism,' in *Nationalism in Eastern Europe*, ed. Peter F. Sugar and Ivo J. Lederer (Seattle: University of Washington Press, 1969), 310–72.

40 Corrsin, *Warsaw*, 80–3.

41 The great financial and industrial potentate Jan Bloch, a childhood convert to Catholicism, together with the Assimilationist leader Henryk Natanson, convinced the Warsaw Stock Exchange to prepare a document arguing vehemently on behalf of the necessary role played by Poland's Jews in agriculture, trade, and artisanship. This document, submitted to Russian authorities in 1886, was instrumental in averting the introduction of restrictive laws affecting the Jews. (Joseph Lichten, 'Notes on the Assimilation, 1863–1943,' in *The Jews in Poland*, ed. Chimen Abramsky, Maciej Jachimczyk, and Antony Polonsky (Oxford: Basil Blackwell, 1986), 113.)

42 Jonathan Frankel, *Prophecy and Politics: Socialism, Nationalism, and the Russian Jews, 1862–1917* (Cambridge: Cambridge University Press, 1981), 140.

43 Joshua D. Zimmerman, *Poles, Jews, and the Politics of Nationality* (Madison: University of Wisconsin Press, 2004), 229–30.

44 Benjamin Nathans, 'Integration and Modernity in Fin-de-Siècle Russia,' in *The Emergence of Jewish Politics: Bundism and Zionism in Eastern Europe*, ed. Zvi Gitelman (Pittsburgh: University of Pittsburgh Press, 2003), 20–34.

45 Ruth R. Wisse, *I.L. Peretz and the Making of Modern Jewish Culture* (Seattle: University of Washington Press, 1991), 6.

46 Wisse, ibid., 3–36; Ken Frieden, *Classic Yiddish Fiction: Abramovitsh, Sholem Aleichem, and Peretz* (Albany: State University of New York Press, 1995), 231–58.

47 Nathan Cohen, *Sefer, sofer ve-'iton: Merkaz ha-tarbut ha-yehudit be-varsha, 1918–1942* (Jerusalem: Magnes, 2003), 9.

48 Frieden, *Classic Yiddish Fiction*, 232.

49 For a history of events during the year 1905 in Congress Poland, see Blobaum, *Rewolucja*, and Ascher, *Revolution of 1905.*

50 Weeks, 'Progressive Antisemitism,' 67.

51 Ibid., 55.

52 Michael Steinlauf, 'Fear of Purim: Y.L. Peretz and the Canonization of Yiddish Theatre,' *Jewish Social Studies* 1/3 (1995): 46. Piotr Wróbel, 'Jewish Warsaw before the First World War,' in *The Jews in Warsaw*, 267.

2 The Making of a Jewish Nationalist

1 'And just as his name was prominent in Warsaw, so was the figure he cut: a tall, heroic appearance, an expressive, albeit a bit fleshly face, a brunet, of course, a short but satisfied beard ... between moustache and beard peer out full, red lips and between the lips, a brown cigar. He still wears a broad-brimmed hat and, when he goes down the street, all look and Jews whisper, "Noah Prylucki," and greetings do not cease to be exchanged' (Ravitsh, *Mayn leksikon*, vol. 1, 175).

2 'He had quick reflexes and it was dangerous when he felt like giving a jab. He gave a jab with an aphorism, a quickly formulated interjection ... He could speak well' (Shloyme Belis, 'Dos gantse lebn farn mame-loshn,' *Folksshtime* (Buenos Aires), 13 Aug. 1966). Warsaw grew accustomed to the trembling and nervous contraction of his mouth and shoulder when he spoke; this defect, however, in no way impeded his speech, which seldom failed to make an impression on listeners (Ravitsh, *Mayn leksikon*, vol. 1,

176; Mordkhe Tsanin, interview by author, Tel Aviv, 4 July 1999; Prof. Shmuel Verses, conversation with author, Jerusalem, autumn 1998).

3 'From all of the flirtations with politics, with theatre, with folklore, with poetry, with journalism and law,' writes Noah Prylucki's arch-rival in the domain of Yiddish theatre criticism, Alexander Mukdoni, 'his true and genuine love for Yiddish shines forth ... It was true love, the love that depends on nothing' (*In varshe un in lodzh* (Buenos Aires: Tsentral farband fun poylishe yidn in argentine, 1955), 241).

4 According to B. Khilinovitsh's biographical account in Noah Prylucki's *In poyln: kimat a publitsist togbukh, 1905–1911* (Warsaw, 1921, II), the Hebraist education that Prylucki received as a child imparted to him a certain condescension towards Yiddish that conflicted with his innate attraction to the songs and speech of the *folksmasn.*

5 N. Prilutski, '"Der veg" a bintl zikhroynes,' *Der moment* 176, 15 Aug. 1930.

6 Nokhum Shtif, 'How I Became a Yiddish Linguist' in *The Golden Tradition,* ed. Lucy S. Dawidowicz (Boston: Beacon, 1967), 259. The lives and careers of the two men warrant further comparison in light of the many similarities in their upbringing, education, and political and cultural activism.

7 According to Eliyahu Prylucki, a relative who lived in Tsevi Prylucki's home in Warsaw in 1932–33, the Prylucki household was decidedly a Yiddish-speaking one; further, the Jews of Kremenets, where Eliyahu Prylucki resided during his childhood prior to relocating to study in Warsaw in 1932, were primarily Yiddish speakers (interview with author, Haifa, 20 Dec. 1998). Tsevi and his wife Pesye Prylucki (née Bekelman), whom he wed in January 1882, had, in addition to Noah, two sons, Nakhmen and Joseph, and two daughters, Sara (Sonia) and Yehudes (Ida). Noah's younger siblings Nakhmen and Sonia were also literate in Yiddish: Nakhmen, a Bialystok physician, contributed medical articles to the Yiddish press; Sonia, the director of a gymnasium for girls at Nowolipski 6 in Warsaw, recorded their father's Yiddish memoirs. Little is known, however, of Ida, who resided in Warsaw, or Joseph, who lived in Odessa and had a son, Vitaly. *Der moment* regularly included advertisements for 'Froyen-gimnazium sh. prilutska,' e.g., *Der moment* 208, 6 Sept. 1920. See Nathan Cohen, 'Zikhronot Tsvi Prilutski: Te'uda merateket le-heker 'itonut yidish be-varsha,' in *Mi-vilna le-yerushalayim: Mehkarim be-toldoteihem ve-tarbutam shel yehudei mizrah eiropa, mugashim le-profesor Shmuel Verses,* ed. David Assaf et al. (Jerusalem: Magnes, 2002); N. Priluckis, 'Anketa,' 11 Dec. 1940, Lietuvos Centrinis Valstybės Archyvas, Vilnius (hereafter LCVA), F. R856, Ap. 2, B. 1123, Noachas Priluckis, Vilnius University Papers (hereafter NP VUP).

8 Yitshak Grünbaum, *Penei ha-dor* (Jerusalem: Ha-sifria ha-tsionit al yad hanhalat ha-histadrut ha-tsionit, 1957–60), 59–95.

9 To cite only a few examples: Poale Zion theoretician and Yiddish linguist Ber Borokhov, Bundist leader Vladimir Medem, the founder of Revisionist Zionism Vladimir Jabotinsky (all three native Russian speakers) and the Bundist-turned-deacon of Yiddish linguistics Max Weinreich (raised in a German-speaking family in Kurland).

10 See, e.g., *Dos gevet* (Warsaw, 1923). The book represents a series of five dialogues between Kalmen, an amateur philologist bearing a strong resemblance to Prylucki (he even mentions the time he spent, like Prylucki, in Pawiak prison), and Sender, an interested friend. Sender has come to Kalmen for aid in proving to a third party that *lokshn* (noodle) is a Yiddish word for the purpose of winning a bet. In the course of the discussions, which emphasize the national value of folklore and ethnography, Kalmen specifies having heard a number of folk sayings in either Warsaw or Kremenets, the locations where Prylucki spent most of his life.

11 On Russian Jewish cosmopolitanism, see Michael Stanislawski's treatment of Vladimir Jabotinsky in his *Zionism and the Fin-de-Siècle.*

12 On the problems of reading Jewish autobiographies, see Michael Stanislawski, *Autobiographical Jews: Essays in Jewish Self-Fashioning* (Seattle: University of Washington Press, 2004).

13 On Grünbaum's early life and political activity, see Shlomo Netzer, 'Yitshak Grinboym ke-ish tsa'ir: tsmihato shel manhig tsioni be-polin,' *Kivunim* 10 (Nov. 1980): 73–92. Hartglas's memoirs have been published as *Na pograniczu dwóch światów,* ed. Jolanta Żyndul (Warsaw: Oficyna Wydawnicza, 1996).

14 Marian Fuks, 'Poczet Publicystów i Dziennikarzy Żydowskich,' *Biuletyn Żydowskiego Instytutu Historycznego w Polsce* 1–2/133–4 (1985): 69.

15 Memoirs of Tsevi Prylucki, Yad Vashem Archives, M10/175 I, 144.

16 The 'Precise (or clear, correct) Language' (*Safa brura*) Society was founded in Jerusalem in 1889 by two Ashkenazi and three Sephardi Jews (including Lithuanian-born Eliezer ben Yehuda, the most celebrated activist for the revernacularization of Hebrew as the condition of the Jews' national revival and unity in Palestine). It strove to promote Sephardi Hebrew pronunciation as the singular standard of use. It also combated the Diaspora 'jargons' (i.e., Yiddish, Judezmo, Judeo-Arabic) habitually spoken as in-group languages by Sephardim and Ashkenazim in Palestine as a source of interethnic tension and, consequently, an impediment to Jewish unity. (Benjamin Harshav, *Language in Time of Revolution* (Berkeley: University of California Press, 1993), 84.)

17 H. Hoykhgelernter, 'Kurtse geshikhte fun kremenits,' in *Kremenits, vizshgorodek un potshayev yizker-bukh* (Buenos Aires: landslayt-fareyn fun kremenits un umgegnt in argentine, 1965), 59. N. Prilutski, 'Koshere asimilatorn,' *Der moment,* Jan. 1910, repr. in his *Barg-aroyf* (Warsaw: Nayer farlag, 1917), 166–88. For a discussion of the early Hebrew-speaking circles in Eastern and Central Europe, see Yisrael Klausner, 'Halutsei ha-dibur ha-'ivri ba-'artsot ha-gola,' *Leshonenu la-'am* 15/1–2 (1966): 3–47. Klausner (at 26) cites a dissatisfied participant in the meetings of the Warsaw branch of *Safa brura* who, not surprisingly, lamented that 'in our discussion of everyday matters, our language was lent the flavour of the corrupt *jargon* commonly uttered by our mouths or the flavour of Russian, German or French.'

18 Ibid., 29.

19 Slutsky, *Ha-'itonut ha-yehudit-rusit,* 9. See also Estraich, 'On the Acculturation.'

20 Founded in 1899, the semi-secret society *Bnei moshe* was 'dedicated to the notion that moral and cultural preparation had to precede the material salvation of the Jews' (David Vital, *The Origins of Zionism* (Oxford: Clarendon, 1975), 156; Shmuel Ettinger, 'Le-toldot ha-yishuv ha-yehudi be-kremenits,' in his *Bein polin le-rusyah* (Jerusalem: Merkaz Zalman Shazar le-toldot Yisra'el, 1994), 356; 'Tsvi Prilutski,' in Zalmen Reyzen, *Leksikon fun der yidisher literatur, prese un filologye* (Vilna: B. Kletzkin, 1930), vol. 2, 967; H. Hoykhgelernter, *Kremenits,* 84–8; Ts. Prilutski, 'Fun der noenter fargangenheyt (material tsu der biografye fun d'r t. hindes, z'l),' *Der moment* 202, 30 July 1920; 209, 9 Aug. 1920; 'Prylucki, Cwi,' in *Polski Słownik Biograficzny* (Warsaw: Polska Akademia Nauk Institut Historii, 1982–84), vol. 28, 628–9; 'Prilutski, Tsvi Hirsh,' in Sh.L. Tsitron, *Leksikon tsioni* (Warsaw: Sh. Shreberek, 1924), 543–7; M. Fuks, 'Poczet Publicystów,' 69–72.

21 Khilinovitsh, 'Noyekh Prilutski,' in N. Prilutski, *In poyln,* I–IV.

22 'Noyekh Prilutski,' *Literarishe bleter* 18 (1931): 329.

23 *Noyekh Prilutskis zamlbikher far yidishn folklor, filologye un kultur-geshikhte* (Warsaw: Nayer farlag, 1912).

24 Khilinovitsh, 'Noyekh Prilutski,' IV.

25 Dovid Druk, *Tsu der geshikhte fun der yidisher prese* (Warsaw: Hatsefira, 1920), 23; Marian Fuks, *Prasa żydowska w Warszawie, 1823–1939* (Warsaw: Panstwowe, Naukowe, 1979), 70.

26 'Noyekh Prilutski,' *Literarishe bleter,* 330; Khilinovitsh, 'Noyekh Prilutski,' V; Druk, *Tsu der geshikhte,* 15, 18–19; M. Fuks, *Prasa żydowska,* 129–30; 'Tsvi Prilutski,' in Reyzen, *Leksikon,* vol. 2, 969.

27 'Noyekh Prilutski,' *Literarishe bleter,* 330.

28 Ibid.; 'Tsvi Prilutski,' in Reyzen, *Leksikon,* vol. 2, 969.

29 Khilinovitsh, 'Noyekh Prilutski,' VI–VII.

30 An examination of the biographies of the leaders of the *Endecja*, for example, reveals many superficial similarities with those of Jewish political leaders during their student days: law studies in Warsaw, liberal or radical student activism, and subsequent ejection from the university. About the *Endecja* in its earliest years, see, e.g., Brian Porter, *When Nationalism Began to Hate: Imagining Modern Politics in Nineteenth-Century Poland* (New York: Oxford University Press, 2000).

31 On Russian universities during this period, see Samuel Kassow, *Students, Professors, and the State in Tsarist Russia* (Berkeley: University of California Press, 1989).

32 N. Prilutski, 'Bratnya pomots,' *Der moment* 281, 4 Dec. 1931; 'Prylucki, Noë,' in *Polski Słownik Biograficzny*, vol. 28, 629; Avrom-Yitskhok Grafman, 'Di geveylte yidishe ratmener,' *Der moment* 165, 167–8, 18, 20–1 July 1916; Nahum Nir Rafalkes, *Ershte yorn: in rod fun dor un bavegung*, translated from Hebrew by Y. Bregman (Tel Aviv: Y.L. Peretz, 1960–66), 51. For Apolinary Hartglas's recounting of the episode, see his memoir, *Na pograniczu dwóch światów*, 66–70.

33 His behaviour was part of a general shift towards socialism among Jews around 1905. See Frankel, *Prophecy and Politics.*

34 Netzer, 'Yitshak Grinboym,' 73–92.

35 Grafman, 'Di gevelte yidishe ratmener'; Khilinovitsh, 'Noyekh Prilutski,'VIII; N. Prilutski, 'Koshere asimilatorn,' 170; Matityahu Mintz, *Ber Borokhov: Ha-ma'agal ha-rishon, 1900–1906* (Tel Aviv: Tel Aviv University, 1976), 271; Matityahu Mintz and Tseviah Balshan, *Igrot Ber Borokhov, 1897–1917* (Tel Aviv: Am Oved, 1989), 155.

36 Nir Rafalkes, *Ershte yorn*, 75, 109.

37 N. Prilutski, 'Bratnya pomots II,' *Der moment* 282, 6 Dec. 1931; 'Vegn der letster farzamlung in varshever universitet,' *Der veg* 26, 28 Sept. 1905.

38 Grafman, 'Di gevelte yidishe ratmener.' For more on the strike, see Sabina Levin's study of the history of Jewish education in Poland in the eighteenth and early twentieth centuries (*Prakim be-toldot ha-hinukh ha-yehudi be-polin ba-me' a ha-tesha-'esre uve-reshit ha-me'a ha-'esrim* (Tel Aviv: Center for the History of Polish Jewry. Diaspora Research Institute, Tel Aviv University, 1997)).

39 I have not been able to locate the novel that he claims to have written ('Noyekh Prilutksi,' *Literarishe bleter* (1931)) and believe that it may have actually been published the preceding year.

40 Collections of his early newspaper articles are found in his *Natsionalizm un demokratizm (tsayt-artiklen)* (Warsaw: Yeshurun, 1907) and *In poyln.*

41 Khone Shmeruk, 'Strikhn tsu der geshikhte fun dem yidishn literarishn

tsenter in varshe,' in his *Prokim fun der yidisher literatur-geshikhte* (Jerusalem: Yiddish Department, Hebrew University; and Tel Aviv: Y.L. Peretz, 1988), 304.

42 Shoel Ginzburg, 'Ershte yidishe tsaytung in rusland, "der fraynd,"' in his *Amolike peterburg*, 184–6; David Fishman, 'The Politics of Yiddish in Tsarist Russia,' in *From Ancient Israel to Modern Judaism: Intellect in Quest of Understanding – Essays in Honor of Marvin Fox*, ed. Jacob Neusner, Ernest S. Fredrichs, and Nahum M. Sarna (Providence: Brown University Press, 1989), 161–2; M. Fuks, *Prasa żydowska*, 130.

43 Fishman, 'The Politics of Yiddish,' 162. Ginzburg suggests that Plehve hoped to use a Yiddish newspaper in order to agitate for mass Jewish immigration from Russia ('Ershte yidishe tsaytung,' 187).

44 Druk, *Tsu der geshikhte*, 23–4; Fishman, 'The Politics of Yiddish,' 161–3; Ginzburg, 'Ershte yidishe tsaytung,' 186–9.

45 On *Der fraynd*, see Sarah Stein, *Making Jews Modern: The Yiddish and Ladino Press in the Russian and Ottoman Empires* (Bloomington and Indianapolis: Indiana University Press, 2004).

46 Simkhe Lev, 'Tsu der geshikhte fun der yidisher prese in poyln,' in his *Prokim yidishe geshikhte* (Brooklyn: Shulsinger Bros., 1941), 179.

47 Druk, *Tsu der geshikhte*, 24; A. Kirzhnits, *Di yidishe prese in der gevezener rusisher imperye (1823–1916)* (Moscow, Kharkov, and Minsk: Tsentral felker-farlag fun fssr, 1930), 18–20.

48 N. Prilutski, 'Der veg.' With his customary attentiveness to language and dialect, Prylucki identifies this financial agent as 'a quiet person, quite distant even from an elementary intellectual. A typical *Litvak* who still could not grasp the secrets of Russian phonetics after thirty years of residence in the Crown City. He was convinced that "shubota" [*subota*, Saturday] and "sapka" [*shapka*, hat] were the classic pronunciation.' Here Prylucki is poking fun at the 'confusion' of sibilants common in Lithuanian Yiddish dialect, a phenomenon popularly known in Yiddish linguistics literature as *sabesdiker-losn* (Sabbath tongue). It is known as such because the customary /š/ in both words (*shabes, loshn*) is realized instead as a sound approaching /s/. Conversely, in this dialect /s/ sounds to speakers of other dialects like /š/. Actually, speakers of this dialect produce an intermediary sound in both cases.

49 Druk, *Tsu der geshikhte*, 33–4; M. Fuks, *Prasa żydowska*, 134–5; N. Prilutski, 'Der veg.'

50 Corrsin, 'Language Use,' 81; S. Hirszhorn, 'Początki żydowskiego ruchu narodowego w Polsce,' *Nasz Przegląd*, 18 Sept. 1938.

51 A postcard, sent during Passover 1905, by Noah Prylucki in St Petersburg to Zionist leader Menachem Ussishkin in Ekaterinoslav suggests the trans-

fer was the idea of Prylucki *père*: 'I report to you that my father received a permit to publish here a daily newspaper in the jargon language. Its name is "The Way" (Der veg). The permit was given for Petersburg but my father wishes to transfer the newspaper to the Pale of Settlement.' (Ussishkin Collection, Central Zionist Archives (hereafter CZA), A24/117/II). In his reminiscences, Prylucki attributes the decision to himself (see his, 'Der veg.')

52 Memoirs of Ts. Prylucki, III, 381–5; Druk, *Tsu der geshikhte*, 35; N. Prilutski, 'Der veg.' Noah Prylucki's memoirs seem to confirm the suspicions of Simkhe Lev: 'But in the Prylucki affair, the Governor General acted in a strange manner, a manner until then unknown in the practice of the highest tsarist authority in Poland. The Warsaw Governor General gave his approval before being asked by St Petersburg. In the days of Chertkov [the previous Governor General] such a thing could not have been imagined. It is difficult to determine whether it was the effect of the revolutionary mood in the country or whether personal connections and Khodak's [the newly appointed Jewish censor, a man positively disposed to a Yiddish daily in Warsaw] influence were at work ... Prylucki's request was submitted to the Warsaw General Governor. He gave his approval and sent off the request with his positive position on the matter to the Chief Administration for Press Affairs. This was the shorter path, but therefore a dangerous one. Prylucki let himself slide on this dangerous path, so he probably knew that he would not skid' (*Prokim yidishe geshikhte*, 197).

53 Memoirs of Ts. Prylucki, I, 1–2.

54 Shatski, *Di geshikhte fun yidn in varshe*, vol. 3, ch. 5; Blejwas, 'Failure of Assimilation,' 125–7. Cała distinguishes three streams of 'assimilation' post-1863: the 'moderate Assimilationists,' whose message of secular learning and secular social activism as a means to acculturation while respecting religious observance was carried by the Hebrew journal *Ha-tsefira* (founded in 1862); the 'Poles of Mosaic Confession'; and the 'Radical Assimilationists,' who broke entirely with Judaism and the Jewish Community. (Alina Cała, *Asymilacja Żydów w Królestwie Polskim (1864–1897)* (Warsaw: Państwowy Instytut Wydawniczy), 1989.)

55 Memoirs of Ts. Prylucki, I, 21.

56 See Shmuel Leyb Tsitron, *Di geshikhte fun der yidisher prese: 1. fun yor1863 biz 1889* (Vilna, 1923); Yisroel Tsinberg, 'Di bli-tkufe fun der haskole,' published posthumously as ch. 9 of his pre–Second World War magnum opus *Geshikhte fun der literatur bay yidn* (Buenos Aires: Alveltlekher yidisher-kultur-kongres, 1964); available in English translation as Israel Zinberg, 'Haskalah at Its Zenith,' ch. 12 of his *A History of Jewish Literature*, trans. and ed. Bernard Martin (New York: Ktav, 1978.); also Orbach, *New Voices*, 72–154.

57 Tony Michels, *A Fire in Their Hearts: Yiddish Socialists in New York* (Cambridge: Harvard University Press, 2005), 109–10; Shmeruk, 'Strikhn tsu der geshikhte,' 307; Scott Ury, 'Red Banner, Blue Star: Radical Politics, Democratic Institutions and Collective Identity among Jews in Warsaw, 1904–1907' (PhD diss., Hebrew University, 2006), 175. Khone Shmemk, 'Shtrikhn tsu der geshikhte fun dem yidishn literarishn tsenter in Varshe,' in his *Prokim fun der yidisher literatur-geshikhte* (Jerusalem: Yiddish Department, Hebrew University, and Tel Aviv: Farlag Y.L. Perets, 1988).

58 See, e.g., his brochure on the importance of Hanukkah as a struggle against cultural assimilation: Pi (Tsvi Prilutski), 'Vos dertseyln di khanuke-likhtlekh?' (Warsaw, 1913).

59 Yoysef Heftman, 'Tsvi prilutski,' in *Pinkas Kremenits* (Tel Aviv: Irgun olei kremenits be-yisrael, 1954), 189. He was reportedly less attentive to paying his writers and staff on time (Cohen, 'Zikhronot Tsvi Prilutski,' 388).

60 'And the Polish Jews were a mix of *beys-medresh-yidn* or *shtibl-yidn* [frequenters of synagogues and Hasidic prayer houses] and agile merchants, so they delighted in Tsevi Prylucki's articles about world politics' (Mukdoni, *In varshe un in lodzh,* 232). The term *lezhanke* denotes the oven itself around which men gathered.

61 'Tsvi prilutski' in Reyzen, *Leksikon,* vol. 2, 967; Ravitsh, *Mayn leksikon,* vol. 2, 137–8; Avrom Zak, who was referred by Tsevi Prylucki to the Yiddish writers Yankev Dinezon and Y.L. Peretz for a critique of his work when he first arrived in Warsaw, describes the elderly editor in a decidedly more positive light: 'Tsevi Prylucki was a handsome man with a clipped greyish beard, with spectacles on his eagle-nose and an ample, shining bald spot' (*In onheyb fun a friling* (Buenos Aires: Tsentral-farband fun poylishe yidn in argentine, 1962), 79).

62 According to Ravitsh, 'Panie Redaktorze' and 'Her redaktor' were his favourite addresses: 'To address him correctly when requesting something was half of having the request granted' (*Leksikon,* vol. 2, 137).

63 Cohen, 'Zikhronot Tsvi Prilutski,' 388. For Tsevi Prylucki's trials as editor of *Der veg,* see, e.g., Memoirs of Ts. Prylucki, III, 1–16.

64 'Tsvi prilutski mit zayn zun,' *Di bin,* 29 March 1906.

65 Memoirs of Ts. Prylucki, I, 7.

66 'One could find in the entire bourgeois press sharp articles against the autocratic regime and bourgeois exploitation no less than in the socialist press. This was not because the publishers and editors were such terrible revolutionaries or supporters of socialism or because all journalists were socialists. Quite the contrary. In the Jewish newspapers for the most part worked Zionists or Zionist-sympathizers, representatives of the bourgeois

ideology and many were outspoken opponents of socialism and especially the Jewish workers' party, the Bund ... The spirit of the time was such that one could not but be controlled by it. First, the agitation against the government was enormous even in the highest salons. Who did not want to get rid of the autocratic arbitrariness, of the entire inquisitorial order that did not let any citizen of the land breathe freely? Hatred for the tsar ruled especially in Jewish society, which had suffered enough from pogroms, "oblaves" [police raids], and in general from the entire arbitrariness of each policeman. As for the labour questions, even the "bourgeois" writer had unwillingly to sympathize with the worker because he saw that the only one to sacrifice himself to overthrow the tsarist order and bring freedom through struggle was, after all, the worker' (Druk, *Tsu der geshikhte,* 56). On the eagerness of the newspaper to receive Zionist financial support and its willingness to become a party organ, see the correspondence between Tsevi Prylucki and Menachem Ussishkin (Ussishkin Collection, CZA, A24/117/II).

67 N. Prilutski, 'Der veg.' About the 'Progressives,' see Golczewski, *Polnisch-Jüdische Beziehungen,* 93, and Weeks, 'Polish "Progressive Antisemitism."'

68 The newspaper was long owned by Salomon Lewental (Franciszek Salezy, 1839 or 1841–1902). Lewental, a bookseller and publisher long active in Jewish community affairs, was a graduate of the Warsaw rabbinical seminary and a convert to Catholicism towards the end of his life. His wife Hortensja, the daughter of the Warsaw Jewish *dozor* and philanthropist Mathias Berson, became the newspaper's owner after his death. ('Lewental, Salomon (Franciszek Salezy),' in *Polski Słownik Biograficzny,* vol. 17, 220–1; Corrsin, *Warsaw before the First World War,* 36.) Initially reluctant to advertise *Der veg, Kurjer Warszawski* was willing to announce the arrival of the newspaper in Latin but not Hebrew letters, allegedly because doing so would oblige it on principle to publish announcements in Russian too (Memoirs of Ts. Prylucki, I, 18–19).

69 Memoirs of Ts. Prylucki, I, 28–9.

70 Shmeruk, 'Shtrikhn,' 304n29.

71 Druk, *Tsu der geshikhte,* 34; N. Prilutski, 'Der veg.' Memoirs of Ts. Prylucki, I, 13.

72 N. Prilutski, 'Der veg.'

73 Ibid. N. Prilutski, 'Tsu der frage vegn varshever universitet,' 26 April 1906, repr. in *In poyln.*

74 Memoirs of Ts. Prylucki, I, 22; Khilonovitsh, 'Noyekh Prilutski,' IX; 'Noyekh Prilutski,' in Niger and Shatski, *Leksikon,* vol. 7, 218.

75 Memoirs of Ts. Prylucki, I, 32; M. K-ski [Magnus Krinski], 'Di yoyvl-fayerung fun noyekh prilutski,' *Der moment* 106, 8 May 1931; Golczewski, *Polnisch-Jüdische Beziehungen,* 88–9.

76 A summary of the chief principles adopted by the Zionist party at the Helsinfors Party Congress (Dec. 1905), many of which Prylucki expressed in his writings, can be found in Adolf Böhm, *Die Zionistische Bewegung* (Berlin: Jüdischer Verlag, 1935), vol. 1, 339.

77 N. Prilutski, *Natsionalizm un demokratizm*, 1, 4–5.

78 Ibid., 13–14.

79 Ibid., 15.

80 Ibid., 8, 20, 24.

81 Roni Gechtman, 'Conceptualizing National-Cultural Autonomy: From the Austro-Marxists to the Jewish Labor Bund,' *Simon-Dubnow-Institut Jahrbuch* 4 (2005): 17–49.

82 For the program of Dubnow's Folksparty and an evaluation of its activity, see Zvi Gitelman, *Jewish Nationality and Soviet Politics* (Princeton: Princeton University Press, 1972), 49–52; Robert M. Seltzer, 'Jewish Liberalism in Late Tsarist Russia,' *Contemporary Jewry* 9 (1987–88): 47–66.

83 The conservative Realist party, compelled by their poor showing in the First Duma election to cooperate with the Endeks, initially also joined the 'Concentration' but dropped out due to the Endeks' manifest domination of the alliance (Blobaum, *Rewolucja*, 217).

84 'Vegn yidishe deputatn fun poyln,' *Der veg* 32, 19 Feb. 1906; 'Tsvey natsionalizmen,' *Der veg* 254, 25 Nov. 1906; *Der veg* 255, 26 Nov. 1906; 'Finsterkeyt geyt tsu finsterkeyt,' *Der veg* 294, 3 Jan. 1907, repr. in *In poyln*, 16–19, 83–91, 102–3.

85 'Der yidisher valkomitet un zayn program,' *Der veg* 285, 31 Dec. 1906; 'Evolutsye fun poylishn antisemitizm,' *Der veg* 295, 11 Jan. 1907, repr. in *In poyln*, 95–6, 107–11.

86 'Di farfoylte, di umfarshemte,' *Der veg* 86, 2 May 1906; *Der veg* 87, 3 May 1906, repr. in *In poyln*, 23–31.

87 'An onheyb,' *Der veg* 242, 11 Nov. 1906, and 'Dos shtilshvaygn iz a shand,' *Der veg* 246, 15 Nov. 1906, repr. in *In poyln*, 64–9, 76–9.

88 Corrsin, *Warsaw*, 84–7.

89 Ibid., 85, 89; Blobaum, *Rewolucja*, 232; Stephen D. Corrsin, 'The Jews, the Left, and the State Duma Elections in Warsaw in 1912: Selected Sources,' *Polin* 9 (1996): 45.

90 Druk, *Tsu der geshikhte*, 39–42; Stein, *Making Jews Modern*, 34–5.

91 Both the printed word and theatre fell under the purview of the Warsaw Censorship Board, which implemented Empire-wide censorship statutes. It decided what could be published or printed in Poland, as well as what could be imported from abroad. For more about censorship in Poland in this period, see Zenon Kmiecik, 'Prasa polska w królestwie polskim i

imperium rosyjskim w latach 1865–1904,' in Zenon Kmiecik, *Prasa polska w latach 1864–1918* (Warsaw: Państwowe Naukowe, 1976), 11–13; Ochs, *St Petersburg*, 122–3.

92 M. Fuks, *Prasa żydowska*, 137; Druk, *Tsu der geshikhte*, 38–9; N. Prilutski, 'Der veg.'

93 *Der veg* 67, 24 Nov. 1905.

94 Druk, *Tsu der geshikhte*, 45, 49.

95 The circulation of the newspaper, as estimated by Tsevi Prylucki, declined from 16,000–18,000 on weekdays and 25,000 on the weekend during the summer of 1906 to 13,000–14,000 daily (Letter from T. Prylucki to Ussishkin, 13 Nov. 1906, Central Zionist Archives, Jerusalem, Ussishkin Collection, A24/117/II). Fuks, citing the figures of the Warsaw Censor Committee, offers the more modest circulation figure of 9,000 for 1906 (M. Fuks, *Prasa żydowska*, Appendix 2; see also Ury, 'Red Banner, Blue Star,' 176).

96 Corrsin, *Warsaw*, 71. Noah Prylucki convinced his father to cease paying bribes to the censor, who eventually 'took vengeance' according to Noah. Tsevi Prylucki was defended in a number of lawsuits by Henryk Ettinger and Bronisław Sobolew (twice Justice Minister in the Founding Sejm of Independent Poland); N. Prilutski, 'Der veg.'

97 Memoirs of Ts. Prylucki, I, 35–8.

98 'H.d. nomberg,' in Niger and Shatski, *Leksikon*, vol. 6, 160–3; 'H.D. Nomberg,' in *Polski słownik biograficzny*, vol. 23, 173–4.

99 Druk, *Tsu der geshikhte*, 42–4, 45–9; N. Prilutski, 'Der veg'; M. Fuks, *Prasa żydowska*, 137; Reyzen, 'Tsvi Prilutski,' 969; Kirzhnits, *Di yidishe prese*, 29.

100 M. Fuks, *Prasa żydowska*, 138; Druk, *Tsu der geshikhte*, 79–80.

101 Leszek Olejnik, 'The Emergence of the Yiddish Press in Łódź,' *Polin 6* (1991): 108.

102 Druk, *Tsu der geshikhte*, 79–80.

103 Ibid., 139–41.

104 E.g., his 'Fir yor yidish teater in rusland un poyln,' *Unzer lebn* 37, 1910, repr. in N. Prilutski, *Yidish teater 1901–1921* (Bialystok: A. Albek, 1921), 31–62.

105 Druk, *Tsu der geshikhte*, 88.

106 Mendl Mozes, 'Der moment,' in *Yidishe prese in varshe*, vol. 2, *Fun noentn over* (New York: Congress for Jewish Culture, 1956), 243.

107 Yosef Regev, 'Ha-'itonut be-yidish,' in *Entsiklopedya shel galuyot-varsha*, Yitzhak Grünbaum, ed. (Jerusalem and Tel Aviv: Encyclopaedia of the Jewish Diaspora, 1959), vol. 1, 499.

108 Avraham Levinson, *Toldot yehudei varsha* (Tel Aviv: Am oved, 1953), 302–3; Druk, *Tsu der geshikhte*, 87–8, 103; Mozes, 'Der moment,' 242.

109 Druk, *Tsu der geshikhte*, 88.

110 Ibid., 103.

111 N. Prilutski, 'Di grindung fun "moment,"' *Der moment* 265, 19 Nov. 1920. Memoirs of Ts. Prylucki, I, 64–5.

112 Kirzhnits, *Di yidishe prese*, 39; Memoirs of Ts. Prylucki, I, 66–7.

113 Y.D. Berkovitsh, *Undzere rishoynim: Zikhroynes-dertseylungen vegn sholem aleykhem un zayn dor* (Tel Aviv: Ha-menora, 1966), 20.

114 Elkhonen Zeitlin, *In a literarisher shtub* (Buenos Aires: Tsentral farband fun poylishe yidn in argentine, 1946), 169.

115 On Jewish lawyers, see Benjamin Nathans, *Beyond the Pale: The Jewish Encounter with Late Imperial Russia* (Berkeley: University of California Press, 2004). Prylucki also put the innovation of newspaper advertising to his professional service. He regularly advertised in a number of newspapers his readiness to receive in his office at Świętokrzyska 48 'special criminal cases, questions of military service, bills of exchange, and legalization of statuses.' For one such announcement, see *Der fraynd* (Warsaw) 130, 21 June 1911.

116 'Noyekh Prilutski,' in Niger and Shatski, *Leksikon*, 218.

117 This technique was employed in order to make the departure of popular writers from one newspaper to another, then a common occurrence, less noticeable to readers.

118 Druk, *Tsu der geshikhte*, 105. Hillel Zeitlin, according to the memoirs of Tsevi Prylucki (I, 65–71), was dismayed by the 'pornographic stories' printed in *Der haynt*.

119 Kirzhnits, *Di yidishe prese*, 39.

120 Memoirs of Ts. Prylucki, I, 66; N. Prilutski, 'Di grindung fun "moment"'; Kirzhnits, *Di yidishe prese*, 18; Druk, *Tsu der geshikhte*, 102–7. According to Druk (at 102), the plan to start a new daily was hatched by himself, Noah Prylucki, and Hillel Zeitlin, long before *Der fraynd* transferred to Warsaw in Dec. 1909.

121 According to Marian Fuks, government documents indicate that the concession was granted in the name of Magnus Krinski in 1907; due to the relative ease of obtaining newspaper concessions at this time, many potential publishers and editors applied for them and created a 'reserve' that they did not necessarily use (*Prasa żydowska*, 143n 47).

122 Memoirs of T. Prylucki, I, 72–5; N. Prilutski, 'Di grindung fun "moment"'; Druk, *Tsu der geshikhte*, 107. *Unzer lebn* continued to be published in Warsaw until 1912, when it moved to Odessa, and continued there until 1917 (Kirzhnits, *Di yidishe prese*, 32).

123 Michael Weichert, *Zikhroynes – varshe* (Tel-Aviv: Ha-menora, 1960–70), 53.

124 Memoirs of Ts. Prylucki, I, 134. In the early days of *Der moment*, the paper

was also defended by Yitshak Grünbaum, later the leader of the Zionist party in Poland and Noah Prylucki's fiercest political rival. Once friends, the two lawyers-turned-politicians eventually developed an intense personal animosity between them (Ravitsh, *Mayn leksikon,* 176).

125 Itzhak Borenstein, *Varshe fun nekhtn* (São Paulo: Author, 1967), 75.

126 Mozes, 'Der moment,' 245.

127 According to Aleksander Hafftka, it regularly sold 60,000 copies on weekdays and 90,000 on Fridays in Warsaw and the Polish provinces prior to the outbreak of the First World War, and its circulation is claimed to have climbed as high as 150,000 in 1913 during the Beilis blood libel trial in Kiev, to which it sent a team of correspondents, including Noah Prylucki. In his memoirs, Tsevi Prylucki places the newspaper's circulation at 100,000 on weekdays and at even higher on Friday nights. Memoirs of Ts. Prylucki, I, 77–8, 114–21, 125; Mozes, 'Der moment,' 246–7; Aleksander Hafftka, 'Prasa żydowska w Polsce (do 1918 r.),' in *Żydzi w Polsce Odrodzonej,* ed. Ignacy Schiper, A. Tartakower, and Aleks. Hafftka (Warsaw, 1932–35), vol. 2, 157.

128 E. Zeitlin, *In a literarisher shtub,* 74.

129 I thank Edward Portnoy for pointing out to me this alternate 'crime scene.'

130 According to E. Zeitlin (*In a literarisher shtub,* 166), the Yatskan-Zeitlin scandal did not cease until it was interrupted by the blood libel of Mendel Beilis. See also Mozes, 'Der moment,' 247–9; Memoirs of Ts. Prylucki, I, 114. In defending *Haynt*'s publisher in 1912 against accusations that it had repeatedly insulted Krinski as revenge for his partnership in *Moment,* attorney Yatskan Grünbaum offered the following explanation for Yatskan's tone: 'It is true that in Yatskan's articles against Krinski are found many sharp expressions, which must be deemed defamatory by intelligent people. One must, however, recall that *Haynt* is a boulevard-newspaper, a street rag for the simple rabble and a salon-style is not relevant in such a newspaper. *Haynt* has a style of its own. The defamations in such a newspaper are not defamations. One must also know Yatskan and in what kind of environment he grew up and lived. There was no other style in Yatskan's environment. Yatskan was raised on the Talmud and Talmudic scholars, when they quarrel with each other, use the most abusive language' (in Mozes, 'Der moment,' 247–9).

131 Moshe Arye-Leon Waldoks, 'Hillel Zeitlin: The Early Years' (1894–1919) (Phd diss., Brandeis University, 1984), 99.

132 The region is called 'Lite' in Yiddish and associated with a Yiddish dialect and cultural stereotypes distinct from those belonging to Poland or Ukraine. Among these stereotypes is a penchant for cold rationalism and

scepticism supposedly foreign to the 'emotional' Hasidic Jews of Poland and Galicia.

133 Samuel Hirszhorn, 'Litwaki,' *Głos Żydowski,* 29 April 1906; cited in Corrsin, *Warsaw,* 34.

134 François Guesnet, 'Migration et Stéréotype: Le cas des juifs russes au Royaume de Pologne à la fin du XIXe siècle,' *Cahiers du Monde russe* 41/4 (2000): 505–18.

135 Bacon, 'Poland from 1795 to 1939,' 1394.

136 Shmarya Levin, *The Autobiography of Shmarya Levin,* translated and edited by Maurice Samuel (Philadelphia: Jewish Publication Society, 1967), 262.

137 A popular Yiddish proverb relates that 'a Litvak has a cross in his head' (*a litvak hot a tseylem in kop*), an illusion to his embrace of 'non-Jewish,' i.e., heretical ideas.

138 Ochs mentions the Director of the Second Russian Gymnasium praising the success of the 'Litvaks' in *Varshavskii Dnevnik* as early as 1866 ('St Petersburg and the Jews,' 196).

139 Citation in Wróbel, 'Jewish Warsaw before the First World War,' 252; Bacon, 'La société juive,' 639–43.

140 Berkovitsh, *Undzere rishoynim,* 66.

141 Olejnik, 'Emergence of the Yiddish Press,' 115.

142 Bacon, 'La société juive,' 639–44; François Guesnet, *Polnische Juden im 19. Jahrhundert* (Köln: Böhlau, 1998), 61–78.

143 On Jewish literacy, see Shaul Stampfer: 'Gender Differentiation and Education of the Jewish Woman in Nineteenth-Century Eastern Europe,' *Polin* (1992): 63–87, and 'What Did "Knowing Hebrew" Mean in Eastern Europe?' in *Hebrew in Ashkenaz,* ed. Lewis Glinert (New York: Oxford University Press, 1993), 129–40.

144 The average subscription price for dailies in the Russian Empire at this time was 4 to 17 roubles per year. Jewish artisans, who composed up to 90 per cent of the Jewish workforce in some regions, generally earned 3 to 8 roubles weekly and received paid employment only ten weeks annually; 88% of their salary was eaten up by weekly necessities, leaving little for leisure reading (Stein, *Making Jews Modern,* 32; statistics from Ezra Mendelsohn, *Class Stuggle in the Pale* (Cambridge: Cambridge University Press), 1970).

145 The tallies are Shmeruk's ('Strikhn,' 304) based on the statistics of the Warsaw Censor Committee for 1906, published as an appendix in M. Fuks, *Prasa żydowska,* 308.

146 Shmeruk, 'Strikhn,' 304.

147 A famous example in the Jewish context is Y.L. Peretz, who spent most of

his professional life as an employee of the Warsaw *kehila.* See Wisse, *I.L. Peretz.* Similarly, the Discount Bank was sometimes called the 'Polish Academy of Sciences' and the Commercial Bank 'the Polish Literary Club.' Both firms were owned by polonized Jews. Similarly, the Warsaw-Vienna railway was an 'asylum for Polish learning' (Corrsin, *Warsaw,* 60–1).

148 Weeks, 'Fanning the Flames,' 66. See also François Guesnet, '"Wir müssen Warschau unbedingt russisch machen": Die Mythologisierung der russisch-jüdischen Zuwanderung ins Königreich Polen zu Beginn unseres Jahrhunderts am Beispiel eines polnischen Trivialromans,' in *Geschichtliche Mythen in den Literaturen und Kulturen Ostmittel- und Suedosteuropas,* ed. Eva Behring, Ludwig Richter, and Wolfgang F. Schwarz (Stuttgart: Franz Steiner, 1999); Dr Yankev Vigodski, 'Di "litvakes" in poyln,' in *'Haynt' yoyvl-bukh (1908–1938)* (Warsaw, 1938), 219–22.

149 N. Prilutski, 'Tsi zenen di "zhargonistn" gemanizatorn?' *Der moment* 15, 31 Jan. 1911; 'Votslavker "simulyatse,"' *Der moment* 86, 28 April 1911; 'Yidn tsi daytshn,' *Der moment* 20, 6 Feb. 1911; 'Vegn der kloymershter sine fun di yidn tsum poylishn folk,' *Der moment* 24, 10 Feb. 1911. All repr. in *In poyln,* 226–8, 242–6, 232–4, 235–8.

150 Cited in Lambda, 'Żargonówcy między sobą,' *Izraelita,* 5 Jan. 1912.

151 They did, however, manage to obtain the financially strapped *Unzer lebn,* renamed *Nayes,* for their cause to campaign in the 1912 Duma elections. The Assimilationist organ in 'jargon,' *Nayes* saw a dwindling readership until it closed at the end of Oct. 1912. (Memoirs of Ts. Prylucki, I, 81–4; Kirzhnits, *Di yidishe prese,* 45; M. Fuks, *Prasa żydowska,* 141.)

152 Weeks, 'Fanning the Flames,' 75.

153 Corrsin, 'Language Use,' 81.

3 Creating Modern Yiddish Culture

1 Prylucki angered Yitshak Grünbaum by speaking in the name of Poale Zion at an assembly in 1905 despite having left it (Nir Rafalkes, *Ershte yorn,* 109).

2 Delphine Bechtel, 'Les chercheurs en linguistique et histoire littéraire yiddish: une génération d'intellectuels engagés dans la première moitié du XXe siècle,' in *Ecriture de l'histoire et identité juive,* Delphine Bechtel et al., eds. (Paris: Les Belles Lettres, 2003), 253–78.

3 On Zhitlovski, see David H. Weinberg, *Between Tradition and Modernity: Haim Zhitlowski, Simon Dubnow, Ahad Ha-Am, and the Shaping of Modern Jewish Identity* (New York: Holmes and Meier, 1996).

4 Prylucki's work in this period on behalf of Yiddish combines elements of Phases B and C of Hroch's schema of the development of language-based

nationalist movements. In Phase A, a small group of intellectuals devotes itself to scholarly enquiry into all aspects of the culture it seeks to promote (e.g., language, history, folk culture, etc.). The results of its findings are often published in languages of the dominant culture among which or under whose hegemony the non-dominant group dwells and in whose language and culture its proto-elite has likely been educated. In Phase B, a new range of activists emerges who continue work undertaken in the previous phase but also begin to agitate for others to join in creating a 'fully fledged nation.' In order to achieve this aim, three goals must be accomplished: (1) the formation of a national community possessing an economically varied social structure and its own ruling classes; (2) self-administration, usually in the form of local or territorial autonomy or, alternately, the realization of independence; (3) the elaboration or even the establishment of a national high culture based on a written variant of the national language and the use of this language within a specific territory. Phase B is characterized (to varying extents according to case) by programs of language planning, as well as by political and social demands. Hroch divides language programs into five phases: (1) a phase of celebration and defence of the language during which demands are generally directed both upwards towards ruling elites of a dominant group speaking another language and downwards towards the peer group of language activists; (2) language planning and codification directed at the creation of norms for use by the nation-building collective; (3) intellectualization of the national language, i.e., its promotion and use in journals, the collection and imitation of folk songs, the writing of new literary and dramatic works, the improvement or 'invention' of a register of the national language suitable for scientific and scholarly writings; (4) the introduction of the codified language into national schools, where it will be most effectively disseminated among the younger generation of speakers and contribute to a sense of national community through the spread of affective, language-based concepts; (5) the realization of full equality for the language, i.e., its use in administration, courts, postal systems, commerce, and politics. In Phase C a mass movement is formed on behalf of the patriotic cause, a full social structure is usually achieved, and political differentiation begins to emerge. (Hroch, 'The Social Interpretation of Linguistic Demands,' 13–19.) The formation of Jewish national community meant largely the replacement of a religion-based sense of identity as a people with a secular concept of nationhood and the supplanting of old elites not supportive of the nationalist cause. Additionally, Jewish self-administration would necessarily exist on an extra-territorial basis because of the Jews' scattering across Eastern Europe. Finally, it was precisely the question of which tongue would serve as the national language that was the cause of so much division and rancour among Jewish nationalists.

5 David Fishman, *The Rise of Modern Yiddish Culture* (Pittsburgh: University of Pittsburgh Press, 2005), 98–99.

6 Slutsky, *Ha-'itonut ha-yehudit-rusit,* 42.

7 The protocols of the well-known conference were never published but contemporary newspaper reports and conference speeches were collected and published by YIVO, *Di ershte yidishe shprakh-konferents: Barikhtn, dokumentn un opklangen fun der tshernovitser konferents 1908* (Vilna, 1931). Discussions and accounts of the conference are also to be found in Joshua A. Fishman, *Ideology, Society and Language* (Ann Arbor: Karoma, 1987), and Emanuel Goldsmith, *Modern Yiddish: The Story of a Language Movement* (New York: Fordham University Press, 1997).

8 N. Priltuski, 'Di tshernovitser konferents,' (1908) in *Barf-aroyf,* 147–51.

9 N. Prilutski, untitled reprint of article from Lemberg *Togblat* 178, 15 Sept. 1908, in YIVO, *Di ershte yidishe shprakh-konferents,* 217.

10 H.D. Nomberg, 'Tsu vos a natsionale shprakh?' *Teater velt* 1–2 (8 Oct. 1908), 7–8, repr. in Abraham Menes, *Der yidisher gedank in der nayer tsayt* (New York: Congress for Jewish Culture, 1957), 266.

11 Hilel Tseytlin, untitled reprint of article from *Haynt* 196, 18 Sept. 1908, in *YIVO, Di ershte yidishe shprakh-konferents,* 212–14.

12 H. Tseytlin, 'An emes vegn hebreish un yidish,' *Haynt* 67, 19 Feb. 1910; *Haynt* 70, 23 Feb. 1910; *Haynt* 73, 26 Feb. 1910; *Haynt* 76, 30 March 1910.

13 Waldoks, 'Hillel Zeitlin,' 77.

14 'Noyekh Prilutski,' in YIVO, *Di ershte yidishe shprakh-konferents,* 217.

15 Fishman, *Rise of Modern Yiddish Culture,* 58–9.

16 Steven J. Zipperstein, *Elusive Prophet: Ahad Ha'am and the Origins of Zionism* (London: Peter Halban, 1993), 222–3, 266. Until the 'battle of languages' pitting Hebrew and Yiddish against each other, the term *zhargon* (a borrowing from the pejorative French term *jargon*) was not negatively coloured among Jews in Eastern Europe. 'In the battle of languages before and after Czernowitz, when the opponents again took to stressing the pejorative connotation of the word *zhargon,* the adherents of Yiddish finally rejected the word and began to regard it is an insult ... For the speakers of the language, *zhargon* was only a book word. It was never accepted in daily usage' (M. Weinreich, *History of the Yiddish Language,* vol. 1, 322).

17 Ibid., 205.

18 Ibid., 210.

19 N. Prilutski, 'Akhad hoom vegn "zhargon,"' in *Barg-aroyf,* 194–5. The article originally appeared in *Unzer lebn,* 67–73, 1–8 April 1910.

20 Slutsky, *Ha-'itonut ha-yehudit-rusit,* 10.

21 N. Prilutski, 'Akhad hoom vegn "zhargon,"' 211.

22 Ibid., 171, 175–9, 186–7.

23 Ibid., 210. Perhaps because he never visited Palestine and did not consider Palestine an adequate solution to the plight of the Jews, Prylucki never comments on the degree to which Yiddish was actually used there in daily life. By the late nineteenth century, Ashkenazim constituted the majority of the Jewish population of Palestine and resided mainly in Jerusalem. For reasons of practicality rather than ideology, Yiddish was the chief language of the diverse Jewish population of Palestine, much of which had been dwelling there for generations. Zionist pioneers contemptuously referred to the pre-existing Jewish community, which they deemed a bastion of negative Diaspora values, as the 'old *yishuv*' to distinguish it from the new community, 'the *yishuv,*' which they had created. As Yael Chaver observes, however, 'Yiddish was also the language of the old *yishuv* and of early Jewish farmers' community, as well as the officially repressed but nonetheless native and spoken tongue of most of the pioneers' in the late nineteenth and early twentieth centuries ('From Mother Tongue to the Voice Within: The Marginalization of Yiddish in Zionist Palestine,' in *The Life and Times of Yiddish: Studies in the Past and Present of the Language,* ed. Joseph C. Landis (Flushing, NY: Yiddish Books, 2000), 152–4).

24 N. Prilutski, 'Akhad hoom vegn "zhargon,"' 171, 175–9, 186–7.

25 YIVO, *Di ershte yidishe shprakh-konferents,* 83.

26 N. Prilutski, 'Akhad hoom vegn "zhargon,"' 173.

27 See Ahad Ha'am, 'Ver iz der "yud"?' *Der yud* 7 (April 1899), repr. in Zalmen Zilbertsvayg, *Akhad hoom un zayn batsiung tsu yidish* (Los Angeles: Farlag 'Elisheve,' 1956), 14–18.

28 Noyekh Prilutski, 'Koshere asimilatorn,' first appeared in *Unzer lebn,* 1–6, 14–20 Jan. 1910, and is repr. in *Barg-aroyf,* 166–88.

29 Ibid., 171–2.

30 Prylucki tells of a visitor to his law office, a man quite familiar with his articles in the Yiddish press and therefore his stance as a Yiddishist, who nonetheless feels obliged to address a lawyer in Polish. 'He sweats, is embarrassed and asks fearfully, "*Czy można mówić po żargonu?*" And I hear the same question ten times a day, which upsets me greatly. "Certainly! You've come, it would seem, to a Jew!" "But for a lawyer to speak Yiddish??" "What's the surprise? Haven't I written that a Jew should never be ashamed of his mother tongue?" "There's no telling what they'll write [in newspapers]!"' (N. Prilutski, 'Male vos m'shraybt!' in *Der zhurnalist: A zamlung aroysgegebn lekoved dem zhurnalistn-bal dem tsveytn tog peysakh 5672* (Warsaw, 1912), 34–5.)

31 N. Prilutski, 'Ver darf dos? (di rusish-yidishe prese),' *Unzer lebn* 13, 28 Jan. 1910, repr. in *Barg-aroyf*, 212–15.
32 N. Prilutski, 'Mekoyekh a barikht,' 12 May 1911, repr. in *Barg-aroyf*, 220–3; 'Der eltster yidisher muzikfareyn,' 17 April 1911, repr. in *Barg-aroyf*, 224–5.
33 N. Prilutski, 'Kleynikeytn,' *Unzer lebn*, Spring 1910, repr. in *Barg-aroyf*, 216–19.
34 N. Prilutski, 'Tsi zenen di "zhargonistn" germanizatorn?' *Der moment* 15, 31 Jan. 1911; 'Votslavker "simulyatse,"' *Der moment* 86, 28 April 1911; 'Yidn tsi daytshn,' *Der moment* 20, 6 Feb. 1911; 'Vegn der kloymershter sine fun di yidn tsum poylishn folk,' *Der moment* 24, 10 Feb. 1911 – all repr. in *In poyln.*
35 N. Prilutski, 'Mir vartn oyf tshuve.'
36 N. Prilutski, 'Farzhaverte shverd,' *Unzer lebn*, 18 March 1910, repr. in *In poyln*, 173–8.
37 N. Prilutski, 'Vegn poylishn kongres in vashington,' *Unzer lebn*, 31 May 1910, repr. in *In poyln*, 179–84.
38 N. Prilutski, 'M'tor nisht tseygern,' *Der moment* 4, 22 Nov. 1910, 'Gekokht tsi gebrotn,' *Der moment* 6, 24 Nov. 1910, 'Eygene un fremde,' *Der moment* 10, 29 Nov. 1910, 'Di rikhtike fon,' *Der moment* 17, 7 Dec. 1910, 'Mir vartn oyf tshuve,' *Der moment* 24, 15 Dec. 1910 – all repr. in *In poyln.*
39 N. Prilutski, 'Mir vartn oyf tshuve.'
40 N. Prilutski, 'Tsu vos es firt der veg fun asimilatsye!' *Der moment* 139, 30 July 1912.
41 N. Prilutski, *Farn mizbeyekh: gedikhtn, ershte serye* (Warsaw: Ha-tsefirah, 1908).
42 Michael Charles Steinlauf, 'Polish-Jewish Theatre: The Case of Mark Arnstein – A Study of the Interplay among Yiddish, Polish, and Polish-Language Jewish Culture in the Modern Period' (doctoral dissertation, Brandeis University, 1988), 164–6. Among the other Polish writers who attended her salon were Stanisław Brzozowski, Dawid, Gorczyński, Adolf Nowaczyński, Leon Rygier, and Zofia Rygier Nałkowska ('Paula, R.,' in Niger and Shatski, *Leksikon*, vol. 7, 63).
43 'Prylucki, Noë,' in *Polski słownik biograficzny*, vol. 28, 630. 'Paula, R.' in Niger and Shatski, *Leksikon*, vol. 7, 63. Her husband founded a Yiddish summer theatre on Arnstein's initiative in the 'Bagatela,' which later performed in the 'Jardin d'hiver' and 'Muranower Theatre' in Warsaw. 'Prilutski, Paula,' in Zalmen Zilbertsvayg, *Leksikon fun yidishn teater* (New York: Farlag 'Elisheve,' 1959), vol. 3, 1884.
44 'She was much older than Noah Prylucki,' A. Almi recalls, 'but a real beauty' ('Fun amolikn varshe,' *Der poylisher yid* 2 (1944): 28; see also Zak, *In onheyb fun a friling*, 127). Tsevi and especially his wife Pesye Prylucki were reluctant to receive Paula in their home. Even ninety years later (and more

than fifty after Noah and Paula Prylucki's deaths), Noah Prylucki's cousin Eliyahu was uncomfortable speaking with me about their marriage (Eliyahu Prylucki, interview with author, Haifa, 20 Dec. 1998).

45 Martha Bohacehevsky-Chomiak and Bernice Glazer Rosenthal, eds., Marian Schwartz, trans., *A Revolution of the Spirit: Crisis of Value in Russia, 1890–1918* (Newtonville, MA: Oriental Research Partners, 1982), 32.

46 A. Almi, *Mentshn un ideyen* (Warsaw: Goldfarb, 1933), 201.

47 'Nem arum,' in Prilutski *Farn mizbeyekh,* 6.

48 E. Zeitlin, *In a literarisher shtub,* 171.

49 N. Prilutski, 'Kunst un pornografye,' *Teater-velt,* 1–2 (1908): 29–32.

50 Ibid., 30.

51 Ibid., 31.

52 A. Lazar (Yitskhok-Eliezer Leyzerovitsh), 'Kinstler un verk: V. Noyekh Prilutski,' *Roman-tsaytung* 2/33 (1908): 1031–8.

53 'Fester!' in *Farn mizbeyekh,* 7.

54 Sh. Niger, 'Shpinvebs,' *Der fraynd* 45, 9 March 1909.

55 Lazar, 'Kinstler un verk.'

56 Niger, 'Shpinvebs.'

57 Lazar, 'Kinstler un verk.'

58 The polemic surrounded Niger's criticism of *Farn mizbeyekh,* as well as an allegation by Niger that Prylucki had denigrated the 'older' generation of Yiddish writers – Mendele, Sholem Aleichem, and Peretz – in order to laud the 'younger' generation. Prylucki's rebuttal (N. Prilutski, 'A briv in der redaktsye,' *Der fraynd* 62, 29 March 1909) pointed to his essays about these three authors as proof of his respect for them. Niger remained unconvinced, however, that 'a person with respect for and a love of literature and modesty would defend the "young" against the "old" with such words and such a tone' and would introduce 'such a "style" into literature with which only Yatskan can compete' (Sh. Niger, 'A briv in der redatktsye (an entfer h' noyekh prilutski),' *Der fraynd* 87, 8 (21) April 1909).

59 N. Prilutski, *Ertselung vegen zieben gehongene* (Warsaw: Ferlag byuro, 1908). A second edition of his translation was published in New York in 1916 or 1917 by the 'Literarisher ferlag.'

60 Among those who began their literary careers with a visit to Peretz were the most prominent Yiddish literary figures of the twentieth century, including H.D. Nomberg, Sholem Asch, Sh. An-ski (Rapoport), Joseph Opatoshu, Dovid Bergelson, Bal-Makhshoves (Dr. Eliashiv), Yehoyesh (Solomon Bloomgarten), Itshe Meyer Vaysenberg, Yekhiel Yeshaye Trunk, Efraim Kaganovski, Alter Kacyzne, Der Nister (Pinkhas Kaganovitch), Avrom Reyzen, and Lamed Shapiro (Wisse, *I.L. Peretz,* 39).

61 Almi, 'Fun amolikn varshe,' 28–9.

62 Ibid., 29.
63 Levinson, *Toldot yehudei varsha*, 279.
64 Shraga Bar-Sella, 'On the Brink of Disaster: Hillel Zeitlin's Struggle for Survival in Poland,' *Polin* 11 (1998): 79.
65 Waldoks, 'Hillel Zeitlin,' 72–3.
66 'Hilel tseytlin,' in Niger and Shatski, *Leksikon*, vol. 7, 576. 'Hilel tseytlin,' in Reyzen, *Leksikon*, vol. 3, 304–5. Shloyme Mendelson, 'Hilel tseytlin,' in Shloyme Mendelson, *Shloyme mendelson: zayn lebn un shafn* (New York: Farlag 'Unzer tsayt,' 1949), 393–4.
67 Cited in Wisse, *I.L. Peretz*, 98.
68 Bar-Sella, 'On the Brink,' 79–84.
69 Waldoks, 'Hillel Zeitlin,' 78–9, 89, 92–5; Niger and Shatski, *Leksikon*, vol. 7, 578.
70 Almi, 'Fun amolikn varshe,' 29.
71 For a description of Jewish neighbourhoods and population distribution in Warsaw, see Wróbel, 'Jewish Warsaw,' 256–7.
72 E. Zeitlin, *In a literarisher shtub*, 170.
73 Almi, *Mentshn un ideyen*, 200–2.
74 N. Prilutski, ed., *Der yunger gayst* (Warsaw: Progres, 1909); N. Prilutski, ed., *Goldene Funken* (Warsaw: Ferlag byuro, 1909).
75 Almi recalls of Paula R. that 'when Noah Prylucki met her, she knew almost no Yiddish but he taught her Yiddish and she wrote, in later years, beautiful, delicate poems and plays for Yiddish theatre.' Her first Yiddish drama, *Eyne fun yene* (One of Those), which depicts a prostitute in the Warsaw Jewish underworld, was written in Latin letters. So primitive and at times even incomprehensible was its language that Prylucki requested that Almi rewrite the play ('Fun amolikn varshe,' 28).
76 E. Tseytlin, *In a literarisher shtub*, 171.
77 E. Tseytlin (at 175) notes that 'Prylucki was considered one of the best, if not actually the best, speakers of Yiddish literary Warsaw.'
78 Almi, 'Fun amolikn varshe,' 29.
79 N. Prilutski, 'Kunst un lebn,' in *Goldene Funken*, 87.
80 E. Tseytlin, *In a literarisher shtub*, 170.
81 Zak, *In onheyb fun a friling*, 113.
82 Dan Miron, 'Folklore and Antifolklore in the Yiddish Fiction of the Haskalah,' in *Studies in Jewish Folklore*, Frank Talmage, ed. (Cambridge, MA: Association for Jewish Studies, 1980), 219–49.
83 Shatski, 'Perets-shtudyes,' 50–2.
84 Mark Kiel, 'Vox Populi, Vox Dei: The Centrality of Peretz in Jewish Folkloristics,' *Polin* 7 (1992): 91.
85 Ibid., 93. Perhaps the first to claim that Yiddish folk songs proved the exist-

ence of a Yiddish-speaking *folk* was Yoysef-Yehude Lerner who, also following the thought of Herder, proclaimed in his article 'The Jewish Muse: Yiddish Folk songs' (*Hoyzfraynd*, 1889) that the songs were the creation and reflection of a singular national genius. Additional voices speaking on behalf of its collection include Mordkhe Spektor, who published his own collection of Yiddish proverbs in Yiddish in *Yidishes folksblat* (1886), and Ignatz Bernstein, who published the largest collection to date (more than 2,000 proverbs) in Spektor's *Hoyzfraynd* in 1895 (Gottesman, *Defining the Yiddish Nation*, xvii–xxii).

86 Ignats Bernshteyn, *Yidishe shprikhverter un redensarten* (Warsaw: Ha-tsefirah, 1908).

87 Mark, 'Noyekh prilutski,' 82.

88 'Draysik yor literarishe tetikeyt fun noyekh prilutski,' *Literarishe bleter* 18, 1 May 1931, 330.

89 N. Prilutski, *Yidishe folkslider: gezamlt, derklert un aroysgegebn fun noyekh prilutski*,vol. 1, *Religyezishe un yontevdike* (Warsaw: Farlag 'Bikher far ale,' 1911), 10.

90 N. Prilutski, 'Sholem aleykhem (tsum 25-yerikn yubileum fun zayn literarisher tetikeyt),' *Teater velt* 3–4 (1908), 5.

91 Gottesman, *Defining the Yiddish Nation*, 5.

92 Almi, *Mentshn un ideyen*, 202.

93 A. Almi, *Momentn fun a lebn* (Buenos Aires: Tsentral farband fun poylishe yidn in argentine, 1948), 121–8. Almi was eventually released for fear that Prylucki and others knew his whereabouts and would bring the brothel to the attention of the police. Years later, the pimp requested that Prylucki defend him in a criminal case since Prylucki owed him a 'favour.'

94 N. Prilutski, *Yidishe folkslider* (1911) and (1913).

95 Although he wrote the article in Yiddish, Prylucki's contribution to the folklore journal *Reshumot* (Odessa, 1918) about the language of klezmer musicians ('Lashon ha-klezmorim be-poloniya') appeared in Hebrew translation. Certainly, Prylucki could have written the article himself in Hebrew but likely refrained from doing so as a matter of personal ideology.

96 N. Prilutski, *Yidishe folkslider*, III.

97 L. Vilenski [pseud. Y.L Cahan], 'Yidishe folklore,' in *Der pinkes*, Shmuel Niger, ed. (Vilna: B. Kletskin, 1913); Alfred Landoy, 'Bamerkungen tsu noyekh prilutskis "yidishe folkslider,"' *Yidishe filologye* 1 (1924): 151–60.

98 N. Prilutski, 'Polemik: A tshuve eynem a retsenzent,' in *Noyekh prilutskis zamlbikher far yidishn folklor, filologye un kultur-geshikhte*, N. Prilutski and Shmuel Lehman, eds. (Warsaw: Nayer farlag, 1912), 155–69. Sh. An-ski's review of Prylucki's collection is found in *Evreiskaya Starina* 4 (1911): 591–4. For Y.L. Cahan's views, see Gottesman, *Defining the Yiddish Nation*, 42.

99 Gottesman, *Defining the Yiddish Nation*, 42–3. See in particular, *Bay unz yudn: zamelbukh far folklor un filologye*, ed. M. Vanvild (Warsaw: P. Graubard, 1923) which Lehman published in Warsaw. Prylucki contributed a philological study and Lehman and Graubard folklore studies.

100 N. Prilutski, *Yidishe folkslider* (1911), VI.

101 Ibid., VI.

102 Ibid., X.

103 Ibid., X–XII.

104 'Draysik yor literarishe tetikeyt fun Noyekh Prilutski,' 331.

105 N. Prilutski, *Yidishe folkslider*, XII.

106 Ber Borokhov, 'Di oyfgabn funem yidishn filolog' in Niger, *Der pinkes*, 1–22.

107 N. Prilutski, *Yidishe folkslider*, XIV.

108 'Draysik yor literarishe tetikeyt fun noyekh prilutski,' 331. Literary Yiddish lexically and grammatically gravitates towards the southern dialects of Yiddish but is typically pronounced with a pronunciation similar to that then customary among Vilna intellectuals. The sound inventory of standard Yiddish, a codified version of literary Yiddish, may be found in U. Weinreich, *Modern English-Yiddish Yiddish-English Dictionary*, xxi. For a discussion of the features and evolution of a literary pronunciation in Yiddish, see Yudl Mark, *Gramatik fun der yidisher klal-shprakh* (New York: Alveltlekher yidisher kultur-kongres, 1978), 15–31, and Kalmen Vayzer, 'Di debate arum aroysred in der yidish-veltlekher shul in mizrekh-eyrope,' *Yidishe shprakh* (forthcoming).

109 To this day, all major systems of Yiddish spelling allow speakers to a large degree to interpret vowels according to the values of their own dialects rather than according to a single phonetic standard. The relatively democratic nature of Yiddish spelling, however, makes it unsuitable for accurate phonetic transcriptions without modification.

110 M. Spektor, 'Yidishe oytsres,' *Der moment* 225, 12 Oct. 1911.

111 The publishing house seems to have printed exclusively the work of Noah Prylucki and his wife. An announcement at the end of the *Noyekh prilutskis zamlbikher* lists among its publications three of Paula R.'s dramas (*Yerushe*, *Der aktyor*, and *Eyne fun yene*) and Prylucki's second volume of *Yidishe folkslider*. It also lists in preparation an additional volume of *Yidishe folkslider*, *Dembes (portretn un skitsn, literarishe un gezelshaftlekhe)*, *Yidishe shprikhverter un rednsartn*, vol. 1, *In vald fun der yidisher folksfantazye: mayses un zagn*, vol. 1, Paula R.'s drama *Er un zi*, and the second volume of the *Noyekh prilutskis zamlbikher*. Of these, only the last item ever appeared in print.

112 N. Prilutski, *Noyekh prilutskis zamlbikher*, preface.

113 M. Veynger, 'Dialektologishe bamerkungen,' in *Noyekh prilutskis zamlbikher*, 126–33. The article dispels the notion that the Lithuanian pronunciation

of Yiddish forms the basis for the literary language and that the Ukrainian and Polish dialects of Yiddish developed from the Lithuanian one. Basing his arguments on analogy with the history of other literary languages, Veynger proposes that the literary pronunciation of Yiddish must have derived from the speech of an early prestige group, one that existed already in Germany prior to massive Jewish settlement in Eastern Europe.

114 N. Prilutski, 'A filologishe fenomen,' in *Noyekh prilutskis zamlbikher,* 134–7. The article first appeared under the same title in the literary anthology *Nisn: Literarishe zamlung lekoved peysakh* (Warsaw), which Prylucki edited in 1912.

115 It is likely that Prylucki's sharp attacks on An-ski discouraged the latter from inviting Prylucki to join in his famed folklore expedition in 1912. In a letter to An-ski, the Hebrew poet Bialik chides him for excluding Prylucki from the project for personal reasons: 'In my opinion, without a doubt, you should have invited Peretz and Dinezon. And you should have invited somebody else: N. Prylucki. He has been dealing with folklore for a long time and he could be useful. It is not a matter of honour; it's a matter of getting the work done' (F. Lahover, ed., *Igrot Hayim Nahman Bialik* (Tel Aviv: Devir, 1937–39), vol. 2, 134). I thank Phillip Hollander for bringing this letter to my attention and for the translation from the Hebrew.

116 Benjamin Lukin, 'From Folklore to Folk: An-Sky and Jewish Ethnography,' in *Back to the Shtetl: An-Sky and the Jewish Ethnographic Expedition, 1912–1914. From the Collections of the State Ethnographic Museum in St. Petersburg,* ed. Rivka Gonen (Jerusalem: Israel Museum, 1994), xiv.

117 Ber Borokhov in *Der pinkes,* 351–2; Gottesman, *Defining the Yiddish Nation,* 41–3.

118 Anonymous review of Prylucki 1913, *Vokhenblatt* (Warsaw) 82, 5 April 1914, 16 (cited in Gottesman, *Defining the Yiddish Nation,* 47).

119 Alfred Landoy, 'Bamerkungen tsu noyekh prilutskis "yidishe folklider,"' *Yidishe filologye* 1 (1924), 151–60. In an introduction to Landau's comments, Prylucki states that he had intended to publish the review, sent to him in the form of letters during the summer and autumn of 1913, in the third volume of his *Noyekh prilutskis zamlbikher,* but the volume never materialized (ibid., 151).

120 Gottesman, *Defining the Yiddish Nation,* 5–6.

121 Y.D. Berkowitz recalls that Noah Prylucki began propagandizing for a phonetic spelling of Yiddish around the time that *Moment* debuted; in negotiating the purchase of the novel *Blonzhende shtern,* he wrote its author Sholem Aleichem using his own orthographic system in 1910 (*Undzere rishoynim,* vol. 4, 103–4). Borokhov mentions Prylucki (along with Zhitomirski, Hokh-

berg, Veynger, and the Brothers Gordin) as a champion of the 'pedagogic phonetic school' of Yiddish spelling in a letter dated 19 Dec. 1913 to Shmuel Niger (Mintz and Balsan, *Igrot Ber Borokhov*, 563).

122 Zalmen Reyzen, *Gramatik fun der yidisher shprakh* (Vilna: Sh. Shrebek, 1920), 119. Solomon Birnbaum, 'Two Problems in Yiddish Linguistics,' in *The Field of Yiddish*, ed. Uriel Weinreich (New York: Linguistic Circle of New York), 68.

123 Mark, *Gramatik*, 26.

124 Yudl Mark, 'Noyekh Prilutski (1882–1941),' *Yivo Bleter* 26 (1945): 94. Characteristically, he rejected words that had entered Yiddish only from the New High German literary language and not through oral contact, e.g., via merchants or from occupying troops during the First World War. Essentially, almost any word heard in the mouths of the *folksmentshn* was acceptable to him. See Noyekh Prilutski, 'Metodologishe bamerkungen tsum problem daytshmerish,' *Yidish far ale* 1 (1938): 201–9. A summary of standpoints regarding *daytshmerish* among Prylucki and his YIVO colleagues (most notably Zelig Kalmanovitch and Max Weinreich) can be found in Rakhmiel Peltz, 'The Undoing of Language Planning from the Vantage of Cultural History: Two Twentieth-Century Yiddish Examples,' in *Undoing and Redoing Corpus Planning*, ed. M. Clyne (Berlin: Mouton de Gruyter, 1997), 327–56.

125 N. Prilutski, 'Materialn far yidisher gramatik un ortografye,' *Lebn un visnshaft* 5 (1909): 61–8.

126 N. Prilutski, 'Heymishe tipn. I. Sholem ash,' *Der veg* 2, 2 (15) Jan. 1907.

127 On the development of a literary dialect of Russian combining various layers of the language together with European influences, see Lawrence L. Thomas, condensed adaptation into English of V.V. Vinogradov's *The History of the Russian Literary Language from the Seventeenth Century to the Nineteenth* (Madison: University of Wisconsin Press, 1969).

128 N. Prilutski, 'Mekoyekh dem "printsip fun daytshmerish,"' *Der moment* 42, 3 March 1911, repr. in *Barg-aroyf*, 231–2.

129 N. Prilutski, 'Undzer vald,' *Der moment* 97, 8 May 1914, repr. in *Barg-aroyf*, 234–7.

130 N. Prilutski, 'Nosn birnboym,' *Der moment* 5, 19 Jan. 1911.

131 Mark, 'Noyekh Prilutski,' 94. See Der Tunkeler's parody in Yoysef Tunkel, *Seyfer ha-humoreskes*, ed. Yehiel Szajntukh (Jerusalem: Magnes, 1990), 207–9.

132 Joseph Gutmann, 'Is There a Jewish Art?' in *The Visual Dimension: Aspects of Jewish Art*, ed. Clare Moore (Boulder: Westview, 1993), 5.

133 Kalman P. Bland, 'Antisemitism and Aniconism: The Germanophone Requiem for Jewish Visual Art,' in *Jewish Identity in Modern Art History*,

ed. Catherine M. Soussloff (Berkeley: University of California Press, 1999), 41–66.

134 N. Prilutski, 'Undzere natsionsale altertimer,' *Teater velt* 10 (1908): 5–9, repr. in *Barg-aroyf,* 77.

135 N. Prilutski, 'Vos eyner ken oyfton,' *Der moment* 35, 28 Dec. 1910, repr. in *Barg-aroyf,* 101.

136 N. Prilutski, 'Undzere natsionale altertimer,' 80.

137 N. Prilutski, 'Vos eyner,'101.

138 Iks (Noyekh Prilutski), 'Opklangen fun der betsalel-oysshtelung,' *Der moment* 2, 6 Jan. 1911, repr. in *Barg-aroyf,* 105.

139 N. Prilutski, 'Vegn natsionalistisher kunst,' *Der moment* 149, 13 July 1913, repr. in *Barg-aroyf,* 118–19.

140 N. Prilutski, 'Der yidisher kinstler un di yidishe gas,' *Der moment* 83, 25 April 1911; *Der moment* 84, 26 April 1911; *Der moment* 85, 27 April 1911, repr. in *Barg-aroyf,* 112.

141 N. Prilutski, 'Di yidishe kinstler un di yidishe gas,' 108–16.

142 N. Prilutski, 'M. Minkovski,' *Unzer lebn* (?) March 1909, repr. in *Barg-aroyf,* 95–9; 'Di tsveyte yidishe kunst-oysshtelung in varshe,' *Der moment* 278, 17 Dec. 1913; *Der moment* 285, 25 Dec. 1913, repr. in *Barg-aroyf,* 123–6. On Minkowski, see Zachary Baker, 'Art Patronage and Philistinism in Argentina: Maurycy Minkowski in Buenos Aires, 1930,' *Shofar* 19/3 (2001): 107–19.

143 For a description of centuries of rabbinic censor of theatrical spectacles (apart from the venerable *purim-shpil*) see Nahma Sandrow, *Vagabond Stars: A World History of Yiddish Theater* (Syracuse, NY: Syracuse University Press, 1996).

144 Ibid.

145 Yitskhok Turkov-Grudberg, *Yidish teater in poyln* (Warsaw: Farlag 'yidish-bukh,' 1951), 24–5.

146 Steinlauf, 'Fear of Purim,' 46.

147 A. Mukdoni, 'Zikhroynes fun a yidishn teater-kritiker (yidisher teater in poyln fun 1909 biz 1915),' in *Arkhiv far der geshikhte fun yidishn teater un drame,* ed. Yankev Shatski (Vilna and New York: YIVO, 1930), 343–4; A. Mukdoni, *In varshe un in lodzsh,* 233–5; 'Noyekh Prilutski,' in Zilbertsvayg, *Leksikon,* vol. 3, 1881.

148 N. Prilutski, 'Der veg.' While recognizing the importance of Prylucki's contribution to the development of Yiddish theatre arts, Mukdoni, perhaps Prylucki's sharpest critic in all endeavours, describes his theatre reviews as 'not very competent but they were intelligent and warmly written. He did not study theatre. He believed, like the most part of Yiddish theatre critics in Europe and America, that Yiddish theatre needs nothing in expert thea-

tre criticism. It needs, like a pauper, not Torah but a piece of bread ... But Noah Prylucki was truly a prince among theatre critics ... He had at least read Russian theatre critics for several years, from which one could really learn something' (Mukdoni, 'Zikhroynes,' 235).

149 N. Prilutski, 'Der yidisher inteligent un dos yidishe teater,' *Teater velt* 66 (repr. from *Fayerlekh*, April 1910).

150 Mukdoni, 'Zikhroynes,' 344.

151 N. Prilutski, 'Fragmentn,' in N. Prilutski, *Yidish teater* (Bialystok: A. Albek, 1921), 5, repr. from *Der veg* 8, 22 Jan. 1907; *Der veg* 9, 23 Jan. 1907; *Der veg* 14, 29 Jan. 1907.

152 N. Prilutski, 'Undzer teater-kritik,' *Teater velt* 7 (1908): 5.

153 N. Prilutski, 'Feliks fridman (tsu zayn oysshtelung),' *Der moment* 271, 22 Sept. 1929.

154 N. Prilutski, 'Krizis fun undzer dramatish teater,' *Lebn un visnshaft* 1 (Summer 1909), repr. in *Yidish teater*, 22–9.

155 Zilbertsvayg, *Leksikon*, vol. 3, 1880.

156 'Un mayne oygn hobn derzen,' *Der moment* 176, 13 Aug. 1911, repr. in *Barg-aroyf*, 33–5.

157 N. Prilutski, 'Moyshe hes,' *Der moment* 24, 9 Feb. 1912; *Der moment* 30, 16 Feb. 1912; *Der moment* 36, 23 Feb. 1912; *Der moment* 42, 1 March 1912; *Der moment* 48, 8 March 1912; *Der moment* 54, 15 March 1912 – all repr. in *Barg-aroyf*, 3–25.

158 N. Prilutski, 'Akhad Hoom vegn zhargon,' *Unzer lebn* 67–73, 19, 22–7 March 1910.

159 For a treatment of Hess's life and philosophy, see Frankel, *Prophecy and Politics*, 6–28.

160 N. Prilutski, 'Moyshe hes.'

161 N. Prilutski, 'Maks nordoy,' *Der moment*, Aug. 1911, repr. in *Barg-aroyf*, 36–9. According to Michael Berkowitz, 'Although Nordau did not often deal with specifically Jewish subjects in his books and articles before 1897, his traditional Jewish background – he was the son of a rabbi – constituted part of the mythology that formed his public image. This fact lent itself to the appropriation of Nordau as a Zionist icon. Many Jews identified Nordau as a teacher and as an exemplar of Jewish characteristics' ('Art in Zionist Popular Culture and Jewish National Self-Consciousness, 1897–1914,' *Studies in Contemporary Jewry* 6 (1990): 30).

162 N. Prilutski, 'Shpil-zhe mir a lidl khotsh in mitn gas!' *Der moment* 187, 25 Aug. 1911; *Der moment* 190, 29 Aug. 1911, repr. in *Barg-aroyf*, 40–6.

163 N. Prilutski, 'Yekheskl nisanov,' *Der moment* 79, 18 April 1911, repr. in *Barg-aroyf*, 29–32.

164 N. Prilutski, 'D'r yoysef khazanovitsh (impresye),' *Der moment* 45, 6 March 1914; *Der moment* 49, 11 March 1914, repr. in *Barg-aroyf*, 293–7; 'Nokh vegn der yidisher natsionaler bibliotek,' *Der moment* 63, 27 Nov. 1914, repr. in *Barg-aroyf*, 298–300; 'A dor geyt unter (Shoel pinkhes rabinovitsh), nekrolog,' *Der moment* 19, 19 Dec. 1910, repr. in *Barg-aroyf*, 26–8.

165 N. Prilutski, 'Nosn birnboym,' *Der moment* 5, 19 Jan. 1911.

166 On the term *Ausbau* language, see Fishman, *Ideology, Society, and Language*, 250.

167 Mark, 'Noyekh Prilutski,' 81.

4 Cultural Politics in Action: The Birth of Folkism

1 N. Prilutski, 'Anumelt (bimkom zikhroynes),' *Der moment* 210, 7 Sept. 1928; B. Khilinovitsh, introduction to N. Prilutski, *In poyln*, XI.

2 For fuller treatments of Polish-Jewish relations and conditions in occupied Poland during the First World War, see Konrad Zieliński, *Stosunski polsko-żydowskie na ziemach Królestwa Polskiego w czasie pierwszej wojny światowej* (Lublin: Uniwesytetu Marii Curie-Skłodowskiej, 2005), and Piotr Wróbel, 'Przed odzyskaniem niepodległości,' in *Najnowe Dzieje Żydów w Polsce*, ed. Jerzy Tomaszewski (Warsaw: Wydawnictwo Naukowe PWN, 1993), 104–39.

3 Alexander Carlebach, 'A German Rabbi Goes East,' *Leo Baeck Institute Year Book* 6 (1961): 61.

4 S. Adler Rudel, *Ostjuden in Deutschland 1880–1940* (Tübingen: J.C.B. Mohr, 1959), 38. On the plight of refugees in the Russian Empire during the First World War, see Peter Gatrell, *A Whole Empire Walking: Refugees in Russia during World War I* (Bloomington: Indiana University Press, 1999).

5 Bina Garncarska-Kadari, *Di linke poyeley-tsien in poyln biz der tsveyter veltmilkhome* (Tel Aviv: Y.L. Perets, 1995), 24.

6 Corrsin, *Warsaw*, 145.

7 Wynot, 'Jews in Inter-war Poland,' 292.

8 Julius Berger, 'Deutsche Juden und polnische Juden,' *Der Jude* 3 (1916): 144.

9 Zosa Szajkowski, 'Jewish War Relief Work,' *American Jewish Year Book 5678* (1917–18): 213–14.

10 Elimeylekh Rak, *Zikhroynes fun a yidishn hantverker-tuer* (Buenos Aires, 1958), 33.

11 On the activity of EKOPO, see Steven Zipperstein, 'The Politics of Relief: The Transformation of Russian Jewish Communal Life During the First World War,' *Studies in Contemporary Jewry* 4 (1988): 22–40.

12 Ibid., 30.

13 A. Grafman, 'Di gevelte yidishe ratmener,' *Der moment* 165, 18 July 1916.

14 Testimonials of programs and petitions to the government on behalf of Polish Jews recorded by Prylucki in 1915 are to be found in the *Shrayber zamlung*, YIVO Archives, M16-24.

15 Khilinovitsh, 'Noyekh Prilutski,' XII.

16 N. Prilutski, 'Anumlt'; Memoirs of Ts. Prylucki, I, 137–8; M. K-ski [Magnus Krinski], 'Banket lekoved noyekh prilutskin,' *Der moment* 107, 10 May 1931. On one occasion he personally loaded document-laden boxes while under heavy surveillance onto a St Petersburg–bound train aboard which Alfred Ginzburg, son of the Jewish notable Baron Ginzburg, was travelling. Careful to conceal the boxes in a car other than the one in which he was seated, Ginzburg had them transported on his arrival in St Petersburg to the Jewish Relief Committee. From there they were forwarded to Finland for publication.

17 R.F. Leslie, ed., *The History of Poland since 1863* (Cambridge: Cambridge University Press, 1980), 116; Leo Fuks and Renate Fuks, 'Yiddish Publishing Activities in the Weimar Republic, 1920–1933,' *LBIYB* 32 (1988): 419.

18 The memoirist is Stanisław Dzierzbicki, a co-founder of the Central Citizens Committee whom Wróbel describes as 'a moderate and certainly not deserving of the designation antisemite' (cited in Wróbel, 'Przed odzyskaniem niepodległości,'122).

19 Golczewski, *Polnisch-Jüdische Beziehungen*, 125–6.

20 For a discussion of this period, see Steven Aschheim, *Brothers and Strangers: the East-European Jew in German and German-Jewish Consciousness* (Madison: University of Wisconsin Press, 1982).

21 Ezra Mendelsohn, *Zionism in Poland, the Formative Years, 1915–1926* (New Haven and London: Yale University Press, 1981), 48. On the development of Zionist activity in Congress Poland during the First World War, see Piotr Wróbel, 'Wielka roszda: Śyjoniści warszawscy pomiędzy Niemcami a Rosją w czasie pierwszej wojny światowej,' in *Żydzi Warszawy*, Eleonora Bergman and Olga Zienkiewicz, eds. (Warsaw: Zydowski Instytut Historyczny, 2000), 159–92.

22 Zosa Szajkowski, 'The Struggle for Yiddish during World War I,' *LBIYB* 9 (1964): 143–5; Wolfgang Heinze, 'Die polnisch-jiddische Presse,' *Preußische Jahrbücher* 163 (Jan.–March, 1916): 498–9.

23 Druk, *Tsu der geshikhte*,125; Yeshaye Unger, 'Hindenburg kegn "Haynt,"' in *'Haynt': a tsaytung bay yidn, 1908–1939*, Chaim Finkelstein, ed. (Tel Aviv: Velt-federatsye fun poylishe yidn, 1978), 401–4.

24 Party representatives Noah Prylucki (Folkist), Yitshak Grünbaum (Zionist), and Pinhas Mints (Bundist) joined the board in its first meeting after the

First World War in May 1919. (Weichert, *Zikhroynes*, vol. 2, 194; Cohen, *Sefer, sofer ve-'iton*, 18, 33.)

25 Egmont Zechlin, *Die deutsche Politik und die Juden im ersten Weltkrieg* (Göttingen: Vanderhoeck and Ruprecht, 1969), 175. 'The *Lodzher Folksblat* has been described as "a paper which seemed to be defending Jewish interests, but in reality tried to win Jews over to the German side"' (Olejnik, 'Emergence of the Yiddish Press in Łódź,' 114).

26 Leslie, *History of Poland*, 112–13, 116–17. On German and Austrian policy and Jewish plans for autonomy in Congress Poland during the First World War, see Marcos Silber, 'Shepolin ha-hadasha tiye em tova lekhol yeladeha' (doctoral dissertation, Tel Aviv University, 2001).

27 'Kahan, Lazar,' in Reyzen, *Leksikon*, vol. 3, 392–5. Druk, *Tsu der geshikhte*, 135. On Kahan's journalistic career, see Olejnik, 'Emergence of the Yiddish Press,' 111–12. Leszek does not mention Kahan in connection with the *Lodzher nakhrikhtn*, of which no copies have survived in public collections, but with the similarly titled *Di nakhrikht*.

28 'Tsu der hayntiker derefnung fun seym,' *Der moment* 34, 9 Feb. 1919; A. Grafman, 'Di gevelte yidish ratmener: Shmuel hirshhorn,' *Der moment* 167, 20 July 1916; 'Hirshhorn, Shmuel,' in Reyzen, *Leksikon*, vol. 1, 847–8.

29 'Stupnitski, Shoyl,' in Reyzen, *Leksikon*, vol. 2, 623; Niger and Shatski, vol. 6, 388; Mendelson, *Shloyme Mendelson*, 385.

30 Regev, 'Ha-'itonut be-yidish,' 503–4.

31 Mordkhe Breuer, 'Rabanim-doktorim be-polin-lita ba-yemei ha-kibush ha-germani, 1914–1918,' *Bar-Ilan* 24–5 (1989): 130.

32 Paul Roth, *Die politische Entwicklung in Kongreß-Polen während der deutschen Okkupation* (Leipzig: K.F. Koehler, 1919), 150.

33 Druk, *Tsu der geshikhte*, 131.

34 So familiar was Prylucki with the more than 2,000 *shtetlekh* in Poland that when the writer Meylekh Ravitsh told him that he came from Radimno, Prylucki inquired why his visitor did not identify his home town by its Yiddish name, Reydim. Ravitsh was astonished by Prylucki's familiarity with the *shtetl*, including its abundance of rope makers, and claimed that Prylucki knew 'every nuance of every dialect' (Ravitsh, 'Noyekh Prilutski,' in *Mayn leksikon*, 175).

35 N. Prilutski, 'Materialn far yidishe vort-forshungen' and 'Dos tsayt-umshtandvort *frier*: zayn etimologishe mishpokhe un zayne sinonimen,' both in *In shturem*, L. Kestin, ed. (Warsaw: Farlag yungt, 1917); *Der yidisher konsonantizm* (Warsaw: Nayer farlag, 1917).

36 On the first illegal attempts to create a Yiddish school in Warsaw, see Khayim Shloyme Kazdan, *Fun kheyder un 'shkoles' biz tsisho* (Mexico City: Gezelshaft 'Kultur un hilf,' 1956), 408–10.

37 For a history of the Yiddish secular school system, see the works of Khayim Shloyme Kazdan, *Di geshikhte fun yidishn shulvezn in umophengikn poyln* (Mexico City: Gezelshaft 'Kultur un hilf,' 1947), and *Fun kheyder un 'shkoles' biz tsisho.*

38 'Von den neuen Schulen in Warschau,' *Jüdische Rundschau* 29, 21 July 1916, 242.

39 Zechlin, *Die deutsche Politik*, 171–2, 178; Szajkowski, 'The Komitee fuer den Osten and Zionism,' *Herzl Year Book* 7 (1971): 224; Breuer, 'Rabanim-dokotrim,' 128. For a history of the Agudah in Poland, see Gershon Bacon, *The Politics of Tradition: Agudat Yisrael in Poland, 1916–1939* (Jerusalem: Magnes, 1986).

40 The system employs toys to provide pre-school children with practice in creating useful, artistic, and geometric constructions as well as lessons with numbers.

41 Rak, *Zikhroynes*, 42.

42 Tonja S. Lewit, 'Die Entwicklung des jüdischen Volksbildungswesens in Polen' (doctoral dissertation, Thüringische Landesuniversität zu Jena, 1931), 98.

43 Kazdan, *Fun kheyder*, 214–15.

44 'Fun yidishn shulvezn in poyln,' *Literarishe bleter* 4/38 (23 Sept. 1927): 750.

45 Otto Eberhard, 'Zur Schulfrage der Ostjuden,' *Neue Jüdische Monatshefte* 23 (1915); Roth, *Die politische Entwicklung*, 156.

46 For the case of Łódź, see Marcos Silber, 'Ruling Practices and Multiple Cultures: Jews, Poles, and Germans in Łódź during WWI,' *Simon Dubnow Institute Yearbook* 5 (2006): 189–208.

47 'Dos amerikaner gelt un di varshaver klal-tuer,' *Lebnsfragn* 4, 25 Feb. 1916.

48 Zosa Szajkowski, 'Jewish Relief in Eastern Europe 1914–1917,' *LBIYB* 10 (1965): 36.

49 Kazdan, *Fun kheyder*, 415; 'Dos amerikaner gelt.'

50 The Jewish People's Relief Committee, *Di pipels relief fun amerike: Faktn un dokumentn, 1915–1924* (New York: Author, 1924), 31.

51 S.Y. Londinksi, 'Vegn a konferents fun yidish-lerer,' *Lebnsfragn* 4, 25 Feb. 1916.

52 Kazdan, *Di geshikhte*, 28. For a full version of the declaration, see 'Resolution der jüdischen Arbeitervereine in Warschau bezüglich der jiddischen Schulsprache,' *Jüdische Rundschau* 46, 12 Nov. 1915, 37.

53 'Noë Prylucki,' *Polski Słownik Biograficzny*, vol. 28, 630; Y.Sh. Hertz, *Di geshikhte fun bund in lodz* (New York: Farlag 'Undzer tsayt,' 1958), 256; N. Prilutski, 'Oyf der vakh,' *Der moment* 293, 21 Dec. 1924.

54 Roth, *Die politische Entwicklung*, 153; Szajkowski, 'Struggle for Yiddish,' 137–9.

55 See Szajkowski, 'Struggle for Yiddish'; Szajkowski, 'Jewish Relief in Eastern Europe'; Golczewski, *Polnisch-Jüdische Beziehungen,* 152–8.

56 N. Prilutski, 'Tsi zenen di "zhargonistn" germanizatorn?' *Der moment* 15, 31 Jan. 1911, repr. in *Barg-aroyf,* 226–8.

57 On the history of Yiddish studies, see Max Weinreich, *Geschichte der jiddischen Sprachforschung,* ed. Jerold Frakes (Atlanta: Scholars' Press, 1993); Dovid Katz, 'On Yiddish, in Yiddish and for Yiddish: 500 Years of Yiddish Scholarship,' in *Identity and Ethos: a Festschrift for Sol Liptzin on the Occasion of His 85th Birthday,* ed. Mark H. Gelber (New York, Berne, Frankfurt am Main: Peter Lang, 1986), 23–36; Gabriele L. Strauch, 'Methodologies and Ideologies: the Historical Relationship of German Studies to Yiddish,' in *Studies in Yiddish Linguistics,* ed. Paul Wexler (Tübingen: Max Niemeyer, 1990), 83–100.

58 On Mieses, see Goldsmith, *Modern Yiddish,* ch. 6.

59 On *Seyfer-refues,* see Alexander Guterman, '"Sefer-refuot," le-d'r markuze ve-hatsaotav le-tikunim ha-yehudim,' in his *Perakim be-toldot yehudei polin ba-'et ha-hadasha* (Jerusalem: Karmel, 1999).

60 N. Prilutski, 'Vos iz yidish?' in *Barg-aroyf.*

61 Silber, 'Ruling Practices and Multiple Cultures,' 196–7.

62 'Polnisch-assimilatorische Propaganda in Lodz,' *Jüdische Rundschau* 46, 12 Nov. 1915, 371. The report notes that 'several thousand' signatures were collected for the petition; Zieliński, *Stosunki polsko-żydowskie,* 196.

63 'Aus Aller Welt,' *Jüdische Rundschau* 43, 22 Oct. 1915, 350.

64 Eberhard, 'Zur Schulfrage der Ostjuden,' 672.

65 The petition is reprinted in the original German with a Yiddish translation in 'Dokumentn, materialn un barikhtn: Dos yidishe shul-vezn in poyln ba der daytsher okupatsye,' *Di naye shul* 6–7/11–12 (1922).

66 'Tsu der hayntiker derefnung fun seym,' *Der moment* 34, 9 Feb. 1919.

67 'Dokumentn, materialn un barikhtn,'100–2.

68 Prylucki was one of the first to propose representing the distinction between the vowels /o/ and /u/ in southern dialects in words such as /got/, /dort/ and /vus/, /zugn/ through the use of diacritics. In northern dialect and the literary language of the day (and of today), no distinction is made – the vowel in all of these words is written identically and realized as /o/. (Mordkhe Schaechter, *Der eynheytlekher yidisher oysleyg* (New York: YIVO and the Yiddish Language Resource Center of the League for Yiddish, 1999), 9.)

69 N. Prilutski, *Der yidisher konsonantizm,* in *Noyekh prilutskis ksovim* (Warsaw: 1917), vol. 7, IX, XI.

70 Steven Aschheim, 'Eastern Jews, German Jews and Germany's Ostpolitik in the First World War,' *LBIYB* 28 (1983): 357; Golczewski, *Polnisch-Jüdische Beziehungen,* 129.

71 Golczewski, *Polnisch-Jüdische Beziehungen*, 157.

72 Roth, *Die politische Entwicklung*, 155–6; Szajkowski, 'Struggle for Yiddish,' 139, 154–6; Hertz, *Di geshikhte*, 256–8.

73 Zechlin, *Die deutsche Politik*, 194; Kazdan, *Di geshikhte*, 225.

74 H. Tseytlin, '"Zhargon" tsi "yidish,"' *Der moment* 39, 15 Feb. 1916. The article to which Zeitlin refers is printed in *Varshaver tageblat* 35 (1916).

75 Golczewski, *Polnisch-Jüdische Beziehungen*, 159, 161.

76 Ibid., 160.

77 Mark W. Kiel, 'The Ideology of the Folks-Partey,' *Soviet Jewish Affairs* 2 (1975): 77. Hertz, *Di geshikhte*, 287.

78 Kiel, 'Ideology of the Folks-Partey,' 77; Hertz, *Di geshikhte*, 299–300.

79 Druk, *Tsu der geshikhte*, 131.

80 Isaac Nissenbaum, *Alei Heldi* (Jerusalem: R. Mas, 1968), 324; Druk, *Tsu der geshikhte*, 133.

81 Nissenbaum, *Alei Heldi*, 324; Wróbel, 'Przed odzyskaniem niepodległości,' 129.

82 *Jüdische Rundschau* 27, 7 July 1916, 221.

83 Guterman, *Kehilat varsha*, 51.

84 Roth, *Die politische Entwicklung*, 160–1.

85 Shmuel Hirshhorn, 'Der sakh-hakl (tsu der geshikhte fun der folks-partey),' *Dos folk* 20, 29 June 1917, 9–10; Kiel, 'Ideology of the Folks-Partey,' 77–8.

86 Roth, *Die politische Entwicklung*, 161.

87 Khilinovitsh, 'Noyekh Prilutski,' XIV; 'Undzer farhaltn zikh tsu di valn in varshever shtot-rat,' *Der moment* 154, 5 July 1916.

88 Khilinovitsh, 'Noyekh Prilutski,' XIV.

89 Druk, *Tsu der geshikhte*, 131; Rak, *Zikhroynes*, 47.

90 Roth, *Die politische Entwicklung*, 161.

91 Rak, *Zikhroynes*, 47, 61.

92 'Tsu di yidishe veler,' *Der moment* 151, 2 July 1916.

93 Kiel, 'Ideology of the Folks-Partey,' 78.

94 According to *Haynt* 153 ('Der bashlus fun fareyniktn yidishn val-komitet vegn prilutskis kampanye,' 4 July 1916), Prylucki initially demanded that the Assimilationists in the UJEC sign a declaration not to oppose the Yiddish school and theatre, etc. He reduced this demand to an essentially meaningless phrase opposing 'forced assimilation' that the Assimilationists as 'men of culture' could not reject. He announced these compromises with a letter to the UJEC but was still refused a mandate.

95 Druk, *Tsu der geshikhte*, 131–3.

96 Guterman, *Kehilat varsha*, 115–16.

97 Druk, *Tsu der geshikhte*, 130–1.

98 Sh.Y. Yatskan: 'Fun tog tsu tog – di fareynikung,' *Der haynt* 152, 3 July 1916, and 'Undzer val-kampanye,' *Der haynt* 154, 5 July 1916.
99 Yatskan, 'Fun tog tsu tog,' *Der haynt* 159, 11 July 1916.
100 'Der val-kamf,' *Der haynt* 156, 7 July 1916; 'An ofener briv fun di hale-hendler,' *Der haynt* 161, 13 July 1916.
101 'Undzer val-kampanye,' *Der haynt* 151, 2 July 1916; E.N. Frenk, 'Undzer val-kampanye: H.d. nomberg vegn noyekh prilutskin,' *Der haynt* 151, 2 July 1916.
102 Sh.Y. Yatskan: 'Undzer val-kampanye,' *Der haynt* 158, 10 July 1916, and 'Val-bamerkungen,' *Der haynt* 159, 11 July 1916.
103 'Val-kamf (bamerkungen),' *Der haynt* 158, 10 July 1916.
104 'Di farval-bavegung tsum shtotrat,' *Der moment* 158, 9 July 1916.
105 N. Prilutski, 'Oyf der vakh (val-notitsn),' *Der moment* 157, 8 July 1916.
106 'Di poylishe prese vegn der val-fareynikung,' *Der haynt* 152, 3 July 1916.
107 Yatskan, 'Fun tog tsu tog,' *Der haynt* 159, 11 July 1916.
108 Golczewski, *Polnisch-Jüdische Beziehungen,* 160.
109 Ibid., 160.
110 Guterman, *Kehilat varsha,* 116; Kiel, 'Ideology of the Folks-Partey,' 78.
111 *Der moment* 163, 16 July 1916; *Ha-tsefira* 158, 16 July 1916, cited in Golczewski, *Polnisch-Jüdische Beziehungen,* 160.
112 N. Prilutski, 'Dos iberkerenish,' *Der moment* 166, 19 July 1916.
113 Druk, *Tsu der geshikhte,* 132–3.
114 'Briv in redaktsye,' *Der haynt* 164, 17 July 1916.
115 *Jüdische Rundschau* 31, 4 Aug. 1916, 258; Roth, *Die politische Entwicklung,* 164; Golczewski, *Polnisch-Jüdische Beziehungen,* 161; Bernard K. Johnpoll, *The Politics of Futility* (Ithaca: Cornell University Press, 1967), 307.
116 Breuer, 'Rabanim-doktorim,' 128; Marcos Silber, '"Ha-legionot shel has" – nisayon ba-milhemet ha-'olam ha-rishona la'asot et ha-yehudim 'uma mamlahtit,' in *Olam yashan adam hadash: kehilot yisra'el be'idan ha-modernizatsya,* Eli Tsur, ed. (Be'er Sheva: Mehon Ben-Guryon, 2005), 5–13.
117 Mendelsohn, *Zionism,* 41.
118 *Jüdische Rundschau* 6, 9 Feb. 1917.
119 The German press department estimated the following political breakdown of Polish Jewry in 1917: 3–5% Assimilationists, 40% petit bourgeois nationalists (including Folkists) and Zionists of all classes, 8% Bundists and supporters of Poale Zion, and close to 50% supporters of the Agudah (Wolfgang Heinze, 'Internationale jüdische Beziehungen,' *Preußische Jahrbücher* 168 (April 1917): 363).
120 Breuer, 'Rabanim-doktorim,' 130; Roth, *Die politische Entwicklung,* 175–6; Druk, *Tsu der geshikhte,* 135–9.

121 Golczewski, *Polnisch-Jüdische Beziehungen,* 161–2; Hertz, *Di geshikhte,* 3, 283.
122 O. Perelman, 'Der sakh-hakl,' *Dos folk* 20, 29 July 1917.
123 N. Prilutski, 'Vegn der yidisher shulfrage,' in *Noyekh prilutskis redes in varshever shtot-rat* (Warsaw, 1922), 48; 'Der Warschauer Magistrat und die Juden,' *Jüdische Rundschau* 10, 9 March 1917; 'Eine stürmische Sitzung im Warschauer Stadtrat,' *Jüdische Rundschau* 13, 30 March 1917; 'Im Warschauer Stadtrat,' *Jüdische Rundschau* 22, 1 June 1917.
124 Golczewski, *Polnisch-Jüdische Beziehungen,* 167–8.
125 Wróbel, 'Przed odzyskaniem niepodległości,' 131.
126 Golczewski, *Polnisch-Jüdische Beziehungen,* 235.
127 Ibid., 161; Wróbel, 'Wielka roszada,' 175–6. 'We are not Russians, we are not Germans, we are also not Poles. We were, we are, and we will remain Jews ... Jews who feel solidarity with the Polish people but demand for themselves full civil and national rights.' (N. Prilutski, 'Di redes beshas der diskusye iber der interpelatsye mekoyekhn opshteln durkhn magistrat di efntlekhe arbetn,' in *Redes in varshever shtot-rat,* 5).
128 N. Prilutski, *Redes,* 5.
129 Golczewski, *Polnisch-Jüdische Beziehungen,* 166.
130 Ibid., 164. M. Fridlender, 'Di taktik fun der folksgrupe un ir derfolg,' *Der moment* 77, 30 March 1917.
131 Hili, 'Fun dem letsn miting fun der folks-partey,' *Der moment* 27, 31 Jan. 1917; *Der moment* 28, 1 Feb. 1917; *Der moment* 30, 3 Feb. 1917; *Der moment* 33, 6 Feb. 1917; *Der moment* 34, 7 Feb. 1917.
132 L. Finklshteyn, 'Inm amolikn varshe,' in *Shloyme Mendelson,* 89.
133 Zionism never formally accepted the autonomist doctrine, but its program of *Gegenwartsarbeit* (Helsingfors, 1906), especially in Eastern Europe, shared most of its goals, including championing the right of Yiddish in the Diaspora (despite the opposition of some Hebraists). The acceptance of the principle of *Gegenwartsarbeit* marks a rejection of the prior Zionist doctrine of directing all energies towards the creation of a future state in Palestine and eschewing involvement in sustained Diaspora life. Although the recognition of the legitimacy of *Gegenwartsarbeit* meant a willingness to fight for Jewish emancipation in Russia, it did not, however, mean the acceptance of emancipation as a solution to the plight of the Jews.
134 Shimon Frost, 'Jewish School System in Interwar Poland,' in *The Jews in Poland,* 241–2; Jonathan Frankel, 'The Dilemmas of Jewish National Autonomism: The Case of the Ukraine 1917–1920,' in *Ukrainian-Jewish Relations in Historical Perspective,* ed. Howard Aster and Peter J. Potichnyj (Edmonton: University of Alberta Press, 1990), 263–4; Seltzer, 'Jewish Liberalism,' 65.
135 N. Prilutski, *Natsionalizm un demokratizm,* 20.

136 See, e.g., Khayim Zhitlovski, 'Far vos dafke yidish?' (1897), repr. with introduction in Dr Khayim Zhitlovski, *In kamf far folk un shprakh* (New York: Dr kh. zhitlovski ferlag gezelshaft, 1917), 31–43. On Dubnow's concept of the *kehila*, see Fishman, *Rise of Modern Yiddish Culture*, 62–8.
137 Guterman, *Kehilat varsha*, 116–17.
138 Shoyl Stupnitski, 'Der shtandpunkt fun klal-yisroel,' *Dos folk* 21, 6 July 1917; 'Surogatn II,' *Dos folk* 31, 14 Sept. 1917; N. Shvalbe, 'Fraye tribune,' *Dos folk* 29, 1 Aug. 1917; Lazar Kahan, 'Di partey fun mitlshtand,' *Dos folk* 20, 29 June 1917; Shoyl Stupnitski, *Oyfn veg tsum folk* (Warsaw: Nayer farlag, 1920), 121–3.
139 'Tsu undzere lezer,' *Dos folk* 5, 16 March 1917.
140 'Der folks-groshn,' *Dos folk* 20, 29 July 1917.
141 Sh. Stupnitski: 'Tsienizm, teritorializm un folkism,' *Dos folk* 20–1, 29 June and 6 July 1917, and 'Undzer shtelung tsum palestine-problem,' *Dos folk*, 7 Dec. 1917.
142 'Natsionale yidishe parteyen (referat fun h.d. nomberg),' *Dos folk* 5, March 1917.
143 Guterman, *Kehilat varsha*, 115.
144 H. Tseytlin, 'Parteyen tsi folk?' *Der moment* 116, 18 May 1917; 'Tsi zenen yidn nor a religye,' *Der moment* 41, 16 Feb. 1917, and *Der moment* 47, 23 Feb. 1917; 'Vegn a yidish-natsionaler partey,' *Der moment* 21, 24 Jan. 1917.
145 N. Prilutski, undated photocopy from *Dos folk*, 1917, in *Shrayber zamlung*, YIVO Archives, RG-3, Folder 2610; 'Di araber git men oykh havtokhes,' *Dos folk* 33, 28 Aug. 1918.
146 H. Tseytlin, 'Tsi darf men grobn umziste tehumes?' *Der moment* 35, 9 Feb. 1917.
147 Translation in Kiel, 'Ideology of the Folks-Partey,' 86.
148 Ibid., 86.
149 Ibid., 86.
150 'Tsum program fun der yidisher folks-partey,' *Dos folk* 33, 30 Nov. 1917.
151 H. Tseytlin, 'Tsi zenen yidn nor a religye,' *Der moment* 47, 23 Feb. 1917.
152 H. Tseytlin, 'Tsi iz der natsionalizm fayndlekh oder glaykhgilitk tsu religye,' *Der moment* 144, 22 June 1917.
153 H. Tseytlin: 'A vort tsu di rodfim,' *Der moment* 93, 20 April 1917, and 'Mit vemen darfn mir khsidim geyn?' *Der moment* 23, 26 Jan. 1917.
154 H. Tseytlin, 'Tsi darfn zikh frume yidn opteyln fun ale iberike yidn?' *Der moment* 59, 9 March 1917.
155 N. Prilutski, 'Oyf der vakh,' *Dos folk* 36, 31 Dec. 1917.
156 Shoyl Stupnitski, *Oyfn veg tsum folk* (Warsaw: Nayer farlag, 1920), 140–2.

157 'Tsum program fun der yidisher folks-partey,' *Dos folk* 34, 7 Dec. 1917; *Dos folk* 35, 14 Dec. 1917.

158 Guterman, *Kehilat varsha*, 116–17.

159 Ibid., 116–19. On Folkist attitudes towards the elections, see 'Verhinderung der jüdischen Gemeindewahlen in Polen,' *Jüdische Rundschau* 42, 18 Oct. 1918; Shmuel Hirshhorn, 'Der ershter shrit tsum tsvek,' *Der moment* 82, 11 April 1918; H. Tseytlin, 'Vos far a gmine darf varshe hobn,' *Der moment* 88, 26 April 1918, and *Der moment* 91, 30 April 1918; 'In vos bashteyt zeyer zind,' *Der moment* 186, 1918.

160 On the role of Zionism in promoting Yiddish letters in *Der yud*, see Ruth Wisse, 'Not the "Pintele Yid" but the Full-Fledged Jew,' in *Prooftexts* 15/1 (1995): 33–61.

161 A. Aynhorn, 'Folkizm,' *Der haynt* 14, 16 Jan. 1917; *Der haynt* 18, 21 Jan. 1917; *Der haynt* 23, 16 Jan. 1917; *Der haynt* 35, 9 Feb. 1917; *Der haynt* 47, 23 Feb. 1917.

162 Druk, *Tsu der geshikhte*, 142.

163 V. Medem, 'Folkizm, tsienizm un andere – me zukht an armey,' *Lebnsfragn* 9, 2 March 1917; *Lebnsfragn* 11, 16 March 1917; 'Oyf der organizatsions-farzamlung fun der "folkspartey,"' *Lebnsfragn* 11, 13 March 1917.

164 Sh. Hirshhorn, 'Di tragedye fun "bundizm" in poyln beys der milkhome,' *Dos folk* 30, 7 Sept. 1917.

165 H. Tseytlin, 'Di ershte yidishe kultur-konferents in varshe,' *Der moment* 64, 15 March 1917; N. Prilutski, 'Oyf der vakh,' *Der moment* 71, 23 March 1917.

166 'Di yidishe kultur-kongres,' *Der haynt* 74, 27 March 1917; *Der haynt* 75, 28 March 1917; 'Di ershte yidishe kultur-konferents,' *Der moment* 74, 27 March 1917; 'Die Kulturtagung in Warschau,' *Jüdische Rundschau*, 14/15, 6 April 1917; Kazdan, *Di geshikhte fun yidishn shulvezn*, 38.

167 'Di ershte yidishe kultur-konferents,' *Der moment* 74, 28 March 1917.

168 Ibid.; *Der moment* 75, 29 March 1917; *Der moment* 76, 30 March 1917; *Der moment* 77, 31 March 1917.

169 *Haynt* mocked Samuel Hirschhorn, e.g., for publishing bowdlerized Polish-language translations of his 'rebbe's' poetry from *Farn mizbeyekh* (1908) in the Jewish paper *Glos Żydowski* (No. 5, 1917): 'Why shouldn't Jews know that their "people's leader" "wants to be wild and impudent" and "rings white bodies of marble women with locks"?' ('In undzer veltl,' *Der haynt* 74, 27 March 1917.)

170 'In undzer veltl,' 'Di yidishe kultur-konferents,' *Der haynt* 76, 29 March 1917.

171 Ployni, 'Vos shraybn di tsaytungen?' *Dos folk* 9, 12 April 1917.

172 Medem, 'Oyf der kultur-konferents,' *Lebnsfragn* 13, 30 March 1917.

173 'Der miting vegn der kultur-konferents,' *Der moment* 96, 24 April 1917.
174 H. Tseytlin, 'Di kultur-baderfenishn fun der poylisher provints,' *Der moment* 144, 22 June 1917; *Der moment* 150, 29 June 1917.
175 H. Tseytlin, 'Yidish in religyez-natsionaln bavustzayn fun folk,' *Der moment* 300, 29 Dec. 1916.
176 Ibid.
177 H. Tseytlin and Shoyl Stupnitski, eds., *Ersht yudish entsiklopedish verterbukh* (Warsaw: Verlag 'Hantbücher,' 1917), viii.
178 Ibid., iii–iv.
179 Shmuel Hirshhorn, 'Mitlshuln far yidn,' *Shul un dertsiung* 8 (1 June 1917): 5–12.
180 N. Prilutski, 'Oyf der vakh,' *Der moment* 116, 18 May 1917.
181 Ibid.
182 N. Prilutski, 'Oyf der vakh,' *Dos folk* 33, 28 Aug. 1918.
183 M. Fuks, *Prasa żydowska,* 153.
184 L. Kahan, 'A shlogvort oder a program?' *Dos folk* 15, 25 May 1917.
185 N. Shvalbe, 'Fraye tribune: Folks-sotsializm,' *Dos folk* 29, 31 Aug. 1917.
186 Y. Kabantski, 'Notitsn,' *Dos folk* 6, 15 Feb. 1918.
187 Karlinius, 'Di frayhayt fun gayst,' *Dos folk* 21, 6 July 1917.
188 Sh.Y. Stupnitski, 'Natsionalizm un religye,' *Dos folk* 22, 13 July 1917; *Dos folk* 23, 20 July 1917
189 Sh. Hirshhorn, 'Dos natsionale un religyeze yidntum,' *Dos folk* 25, 3 Aug. 1917.
190 Isaac Lewin, *A History of Polish Jewry during the Revival of Poland* (New York: Shengold, 1990), 13–20; 'Di valn tsu der melukhe-rat,' *Der moment* 78, 7 April 1918; H.D. Nomberg, 'Vegn a fartreter in melukhe-rat,' *Der moment* 80, 9 April 1918.
191 Lewin, *History of Polish Jewry,* 34–6; Zieliński, *Stosunki polsko-żydowskie,* 328–9.
192 Bina Garncarska-Kadari, *Di linke poyeley-tsien in polyn biz der tsveyter velt-milkhome* (Tel Aviv: Y.L. Perets Farlag, 1995), 34.
193 Perelman, 'Der sakh-hakl.'
194 Mendelsohn, *Zionism,* 67.
195 Sh. Hirshhorn, 'Der nitsokhn fun undzer idee,' *Dos folk* 7, 22 Feb. 1918; H., 'Di folkspartey in rusland,' *Dos folk* 14, 12 April 1918. On Jewish politics in independent Ukraine, see Henry Abramson, *A Prayer for the Government: Ukrainians and Jews in Revolutionary Times, 1917–1920* (Cambridge, MA: Harvard University Press, 1999).
196 Levinson, *Toldot yehudei varsha,* 271.
197 Weichert, *Zikhroynes,* vol. 2, 16.
198 Ibid., 50.

5 From Avant- to Arrière-garde: The Folksparty in Interwar Poland

1 For an overview of nationalities issues in interwar Poland, see Jerzy Tomaszewski, *Rzeczpospolita wielu narodów* (Warsaw: Czytelnik, 1985).

2 Ezra Mendelsohn, *The Jews of East Central Europe between the World Wars* (Bloomington: Indiana University Press, 1983), 14–15, 23; Leslie, *History of Poland,* 126–7.

3 'Grinboym, yitskhok,' in Reyzen, *Leksikon,* vol. 1, 631–2; Chaim Finkelstein, *Haynt: A tsaytung bay yidn, 1908–1939* (Tel Aviv, 1978), 134; Mendelsohn, *Zionism,* 74–5.

4 Shlomo Netzer, *Ma'avak yehudei polin 'al zekhuyoteyhem ha-ezrahiot veha-le'umiyot* (Tel Aviv: Tel Aviv University Press, 1980), 58–9; Aleksander Hafftka, 'Di yidishe politik in poyln,' in *Yidisher gezelshaftlekher leksikon: Poyln I Varshe,* ed. Ruvn Feldshuh (Warsaw: Yidisher leksikografisher farlag, 1939), 157–8; Mendelsohn, *Zionism,* 51–3.

5 Lewin, *History of Polish Jewry,* 78, 98.

6 Netzer, *Ma'avak yehudei polin,* 81; Lewin, *History of Polish Jewry,* 86.

7 Netzer, *Ma'avak yehudei polin,* 82; Hafftka, 'Di yidishe politik,' 158–9; Arye Tartakover, 'Yidn in poylishn parlament,' *Sefer ha-shana/yorbukh* 3 (1970): 211; Aleksander Hafftka, 'Życie parlmentarne Żydów w Polsce Odrodzonej,' in *Żydzi w Polsce odrodzonej,* ed. Ignacy Schipper, A. Tartakower, Aleks. Hafftka (Warsaw: 'Żydzi w Polsce Odrodzonej,' 1932), 288–9.

8 Bacon, *Politics of Tradition,* 239.

9 Mendelsohn, *Zionism,* 108–9, 129.

10 Ludwik Hass, *Wybory Warszawskie 1918–1926* (Warsaw: Państwowe Naukowe, 1972), 96.

11 Mendelsohn, *Zionism,* 109n59.

12 Szymon Rudnicki, *Żydzi w Parlamencie II Rzeczypospolitej* (Warsaw: Sejmowe, 2004), 117. The Polish government press report is based on a description of the meeting published in *Goniec Krakowski* on 21 Feb. 1919 (Press Department, Office for Jewish Matters, Meeting of Prime Minister with Representatives of Jewish Parties, *Prasa żydowska* 41, 21 Feb. 1919, AAN, MSZ, 7970A, k. 103–5).

13 Bacon, *Politics of Tradition,* 240; Hafftka, 'Di yidishe politik,' 159–60; Netzer, *Ma'avak yehudei polin,* 84, 93–5.

14 Leslie, *History of Poland,* 140–1.

15 Netzer, *Ma'avak yehudei polin,* 180–1. Tobacco and alcohol concessions, areas of production in which Jews were traditionally strongly represented, were granted to Poles supposedly in order to benefit war invalids. But this law was also aimed at reducing the proportion of Jews active in commerce to a level

commensurate with their part of the overall population. According to statistics published by Y. Schipper in 1928, 41.2% of Jews were engaged in commerce and Jews made up 76.3% of those engaged in commerce in Poland (ibid., 191).

16 Mendelsohn, *Jews of East Central Europe*, 43.

17 'Di yidn-frage in seym,' *Der moment* 84, 8 April 1919.

18 Netzer, *Ma'avak yehudei polin*, 86–90.

19 Bacon, *Politics of Tradition*, 244; Hafftka, 'Di yidishe politik,' 163.

20 Rudnicki, *Żydzi w Parlamencie*, 36.

21 Bacon, *Politics of Tradition*, 230; Mendelsohn, *Jews*, 61–2.

22 Bacon, *Politics of Tradition*, 243.

23 N. Prilutski, 'Politik un shtadlones,' *Der moment* 229, 8 Oct. 1920.

24 Hafftka, 'Di yidishe politik,' 165.

25 Netzer, *Ma'avak yehudei polin*, 99–102.

26 Rudnicki, *Żydzi w Parlamencie*, 38–9.

27 Netzer, *Ma'avak yehudei polin*, 144.

28 On pogroms, see Golczewski, *Polnisch-Jüdische Beziehungen*, 181–208.

29 'Zydzi a wschód,' *Gazeta Warszawska*, 27 Jan. 1919.

30 E.g., 'Der sensatsionaler protses in vladave,' *Der moment* 21, 25 Jan. 1920.

31 'Opklangen fun di troyerike geshenishn in pinsk,' *Der moment* 101, 4 May 1919; Netzer, *Ma'avak yehudei polin*, 126; Golczewski, *Polnisch-Jüdische Beziehungen*, 219–29; Zosa Szajkowski, 'Disunity in the Distribution of American Jewish Overseas Relief 1919–1939,' *American Jewish Quarterly* 58 (1969): 381.

32 Pawel Korzec, *Juifs en Pologne* (Paris: Presses de la fondation nationale des sciences politiques, 1980), 111–12.

33 Mendelsohn, *Jews in East Central Europe*, 41.

34 Golczewski, *Polnisch-Jüdische Beziehungen*, 325.

35 Prylucki was assaulted by the Endek deputies Ludwik Dobiją and Mateusz Manterys, leaving him with a bandaged head ('Nokhn brutaln onfal oyfn dep' prilutski,' *Der moment* 161, 11 July 1924). A photo of him recuperating in his office graces the cover of *Ilustrirte vokh* (Illustrated Week) (17 July 1924), a journal edited by the Folkist A. Grafman; Rudnicki, *Żydzi w Parlamencie*, 221. Dobija's remark is cited in Grzegorz Radomski, *Narodowa Demokracja wobec problematyki mniejszości narodowych w Drugiej Rzeczypospolitej w latach 1918–1926* (Toruń: Wydawnictwo Adam Marszałek, 2000), 61.

36 Lewin, *History of Polish Jewry*, 115–18; Netzer, *Ma'avak yehudei polin*, 96; Rudnicki, *Żydzi w Parlamencie*, 47–8; Sprawozdanie Stenograficzne Sejmu Ustawodawczego (SSSU), 27 Feb. 1919 (8/332, 343–5); SSSU, 28 Feb. 1919 (9/352–3).

37 Rudnicki, *Żydzi w Parlamencie,* 47; *Prasa żydowska* 52, 3 March 1919, AAN, MSZ, 7970A, k.129.

38 Netzer, *Ma'avak yehudei polin,* 222–8; N. Prilutski, 'Oyf der vakh,' *Der moment* 63, 14 March 1919; Hafftka, 'Di yidishe politik,' 161–2; Tartakover, 'Yidn in poylishn parlament,' 213; SSSU, 18 March 1919 (15/807–13).

39 SSSU, 24 May 1919 (5/184).

40 'Di birgershaft-frage in seym. di rede fun dep' hirshhorn,' *Der moment* 19, 22 Jan. 1920.

41 *Nowy Dziennik,* 1 April 1919, as reported in *Przegląd prasy* 86, 1 April 1919, AAN, MSZ, 7970A, k.217.

42 SSSU, 31 March 1919 (22/3–17); Rudnicki, *Żydzi w Parlamencie,* 69–70.

43 See, e.g., Sh. Hirshhorn, 'Der konstitutsye-proyekt un di yidishe rekht,' *Der moment* 122, 27 May 1920; *Der moment* 124, 30 May 1920; 'Forshlog fun deputat sh.hirshhorn u. and. vegn farefntlekhn di ofitsiele materialn vegn der kloymershter umloyalitet fun der yidisher bafelkerung beshas der bolshevistisher invazye,' *Der moment* 231, 11 Oct. 1920; 'Interpelatsye fun deputat hirshhorn un andere tsum krigs-minister vegn shlogn un baroybn oyf kovler vokzal un varshe dem soldat yoysef sosnavitsh durkh a vakh fun der banzhandarme,' *Der moment* 241, 22 Oct. 1920.

44 Rudnicki, *Żydzi w Parlamencie,* 41.

45 Netzer, *Ma'avak yehudei polin,* 169–75; Lewin, *History of Polish Jewry,* 139; 'Prylucki, Noë,' in *Polski słownik biograficzny,* vol. 28, 173–4; Rudnicki, *Żydzi w Parlamencie,* 69.

46 Rudnicki, *Żydzi w Parlamencie,* 81.

47 Netzer, *Ma'avak yehudei polin,* 146–60; Mendelsohn, *Zionism,* 35; Oscar I. Janowsky, *The Jews and Minority Rights (1898–1919)* (New York: Columbia University Press, 1933), 340–69; Shimon Frost, *Schooling as a Socio-Political Expression* (Jerusalem: Magnes, 1998), 19–22.

48 'Fun groysn yidishn miting in kaminskis teater: di rede fun n. prilutski,' *Der moment* 144, 25 June 1919.

49 N. Pryłucki, *Mowy* (Warsaw: Nakładem Radu Centralnej Żydowskiego stronnicta ludowego w Polsce, 1920).

50 Yitzhak Grünbaum, *Milhamot yehudei polania 5673–5700* (Jerusalem and Tel Aviv: 'Hotsa'at 'Haverim,' 1940–41).

51 N. Prilutski, *Sholem-yankev abramovitsh* (Warsaw: Nayer farlag, 1920); *Tsum yidishn vokalizm: etyudn* (Warsaw: Nayer farlag, 1920).

52 Mark, 'Noyekh Prilutski,' 88. Based on the realization of the dipthong in the words *kleyd* (dress) and *fleysh* (meat) as either /aa/, /aj/, or /ej/, the schema divides the Yiddish-speech territory into western (Germany, Austria, Bohemia, Moravia, and Hungary), middle (Poland minus a small strip

in the east of Congress Poland and a part of eastern Galicia), and eastern (Lithuania, Belorussia, Ukraine, Bessarabia, Bukovina, and Rumania) dialect regions, respectively.

53 N. Prilutski, *In poyln.*

54 'A kleyne hakdome,' in Lazar Kahan, *Di folksbildung bay laytn un bay undz* (Łódź: Author, 1918), 2.

55 Garncarska-Kadari, *Di linke poyeley-tsien in poyln*, 270; Kazdan, *Di geshikhte*, 25.

56 'Fun groysn yidishn miting in kaminskis teater,' *Der moment* 142, 23 June 1919.

57 Lazar Kahan, *Di lage un di oyfgabn fun yidishn hantverker* (Łódź: Author, 1918).

58 N. Prilutski , 'Der yidisher bal-melokhe un dos yidishe lern-yingl,' *Der moment* 233–4, 3–4 Nov. 1911; 'Fun tsuzamenlebn tsu tsuzamenvirken,' *Der moment* 261, 24 Nov. 1911.

59 S. Londinski, 'Vegn a konferents fun yidish-lerer,' *Lebnsfragn* 4, 25 Feb. 1916.

60 Frost, *Schooling*, 37–8.

61 Zalmen Reyzen, *Yidishe literatur un yidishe shprakh*, vol. 24, *Musterverk fun der yidisher literatur*, Shmuel Rozhanski, ed. (Buenos Aires: Literatur-gezelshaft baym YIVO in argentine, 1965), 24, 155; Mordkhe Schaechter, *Der eynheytlekher yidisher oysleyg* (New York: YIVO and the Yiddish Language Resource Center of the League for Yiddish, 1999), 9.

62 Estraikh, *Soviet Yiddish*, 117.

63 In treating orthography, Prylucki advanced two contradictory premises at this time. On the one hand, he argued that Yiddish orthography must reflect the as yet unfixed pronunciation of the literary language. The literary language, he explained, is based largely on the works of speakers of southern (Polish and Ukrainian) Yiddish, and contrary to popular misconception, is not identical in pronunciation with that of the intellectual elite of Vilna. On the other hand, an improved spelling system must bear a one-to-one correspondence between phoneme and grapheme in order accurately to represent the full vowel inventory of those dialects that 'assign' more than one vowel to a given sign according to the 'old' system in use since before the war, e.g., /o/ and /u/ are both represented in some instances in Polish and Ukrainian Yiddish by אָ while the same אָ corresponds exclusively to /o/ in Lithuanian Yiddish. Since the average reader in Poland intuits that אָ always corresponds to /u/ in his speech apart from certain familiar exceptions (such as the word *hot* ((he) has), which is realized as /hot/ in all dialects) he typically errs in the pronunciation of foreign words (including internationalisms) and proper names containing the vowel /o/. To dem-

onstrate the inadequacy of the current orthography, Prylucki offered the example of the daily he founded with Hillel Zeitlin, which was commonly called *Mument* by less sophisticated Warsaw Jews (N. Prilutski, 'Undzer ortografishe komisye (fun a referat),' in *Naye himlen: Literarish zamelbukh,* ed. L. Kestin (Warsaw: L. Kestin, 1921)).

64 Rakhmiel Peltz, 'The Dehebraization Controversy in Soviet Yiddish Language Planning: Standard or Symbol?' in *Readings in the Sociology of Jewish Languages,* ed. Joshua A. Fishman (Leiden: E.J. Brill, 1985), 145–7.

65 Elkhonen Zeitlin, e.g., remembers Prylucki presenting his brother, the future poet Aaron Zeitlin, with a volume of Bialik's Hebrew poetry as a bar-mitzvah gift (*In a literarisher shtub,* 176).

66 N. Prilutski, 'A shmues vegn gringe zakhn, vos vern kinstlekh farplontert,' *Der moment* 147, 26 June 1931.

67 On Soviet orthographic policy, see Estraikh, *Soviet Yiddish,* ch.5. On the dehebraization controversy, in particular, see Peltz, 'Dehebraization Controversy.'

68 Kazdan, *Di geshikhte,* 69–73; 'Kultur baratung in varshe,' *Di naye shul* (1920).

69 H.D. Nomberg, 'Vokhndike shmuesn: ortografye,' *Der moment* 253, 7 Nov. 1919.

70 H.D. Nomberg, 'Notitsn: hefker-petrishke,' *Der moment* 67, 20 March 1918.

71 N. Prilutski, 'Oyf der vakh,' *Der moment* 20, 23 Jan. 1920.

72 Bacon, *Politics of Tradition,* 250–1.

73 H. Tseytlin, 'Es tor nisht geduldet vern,' *Der moment* 19, 22 Jan. 1920; 'Gegn vos tret ikh oys,' *Der moment* 26, 30 Jan. 1920.

74 Regev, 'Ha-'itonut be-yidish,' 503–4; Druk, *Tsu der geshikhte,* 133–4.

75 'Der Parteikampf im polnischen Judentum,' *Jüdische Rundschau* 25, 20 April 1920, 189–90.

76 Ibid.

77 'Voser akhdes ken un darf hershn in der yidisher gas (referat fun h' n. prilutski),' *Der moment* 34, 10 Feb. 1920.

78 See, e.g., B. Khilinovitsh, 'Hinter di kulisn-politik (tsu der geshikhte fun politik kegn h' noyekh prilutski),' *Der moment* 247 and 248, 29 and 30 Oct. 1920; 'A protest kegn onfaln oyf noyekh prilutski (a briv in der redaktsye),' *Der moment* 234, 14 Oct. 1920; *Der moment* 236–42, 17–24 Oct. 1920.

79 E. Tseytlin, *In a literarisher shutb,* 176. It is notable that Tsevi Prylucki scarcely mentions his other children in his memoirs while Noah figures prominently in them.

80 Szajkowski, 'Disunity,' 385.

81 On Boris Bogen's experiences in Poland at this time, see his *Born a Jew* (New York: Macmillan, 1930).

82 Bogen, *Born a Jew,* 135–6.
83 Szajkowski, 'Disunity,' 385–7.
84 Mendelsohn, *Zionism,* 47.
85 Korzec, *Juifs en Pologne,* 107–10.
86 Golczewski, *Polnisch-Jüdische Beziehungen,* 240.
87 Memoirs of Ts. Prylucki, II, 207–8; Netzer, *Ma'avak yehudei polin,* 141–2.
88 'Melukhe-shef bafelt tsu bafrayen n. prilutskin fun arest,' *Der moment* 175, 4 Aug. 1930.
89 'Noyekh Prilutski ongekumen in nyu-york tsu helfn di heymloze ukrayner karbones,' *Morgn-zhurnal* 19 Sept. 1921.
90 N. Prilutski, 'Oyf der vakh,' *Der moment* 289, 19 Dec. 1919; *Der moment* 89, 16 April 1920.
91 *Morgn-zhurnal,* 19 Sept. 1921.
92 Eugene P. Trani and David L. Wilson, *The Presidency of Warren G. Harding* (Kansas City: Regents Press of Kansas, 1977), 60–1; John Higham, *Strangers in the Land* (New Brunswick, NJ: Rutgers University Press, 1955), 282–6.
93 A. Goren, 'New York City,' *Encyclopaedia Judaica* (Jerusalem, 1971), vol. 12, 1078.
94 'Baym gezegenen zikh mit h' noyekh prilutski,' *Der moment* 168, 25 July 1921; F. Rodilski, 'A briv fun berlin (a geshprekh mit h' noyekh prilutski),' *Der moment* 178, 5 Aug. 1921; N. Prilutski, 'Oyf der vakh,' *Der moment* 51, 4 March 1921.
95 Memorandum from Dr B.D. Bogen, 20 July 1921, JDC Archives, New York, AR 2132, File 405. For refutations of accusations levelled against Prylucki, see, e.g., 'A beyzvilike intrige kegn h' n. prilutski (an erklerung fun tsentral ukrayner komitet),' *Der moment* 218, 21 Sept. 1921; Sh. Biber, 'Tsu der beyzviliker intrige kegn h'noyekh prilutski,' *Der moment* 221, 25 Sept. 1921.
96 Report from Dr Senator to AJD, Refugee Dept., Warsaw, 7 Nov. 1921, JDC Archives, New York, AR2132, File 405.
97 On the cohort of Eastern European Jewish politician-scholars resident in Berlin at this time, see Cecile Kuznitz, 'The Origins of Jewish Scholarship and the YIVO Institute for Jewish Research' (doctoral dissertation, Stanford University, 2000), 41–52.
98 Kuznitz, 'Origins of Jewish Scholarship,' 46.
99 F. Rodilski, 'A briv fun berlin,' *Der moment* 180, 8 Aug. 1921.
100 'Ukrainian Jews Seek Aid,' *New York Times,* 16 Oct. 1921.
101 D. Druk, 'N. Prilutski,' *Der moment* 225, 11 Nov. 1921. See, e.g., an advertisement announcing that he, together with Joseph Krimski (president of the National Federation of Ukrainian Jews in America) and Dr Stephen Wise, will address the public in Carnegie Hall (*Forverts,* 15 Oct. 1921).

102 Cable from JDC New York to Vienna, JDC Archives, AR 2132, File 405, 2 Nov. 1921.

103 Cable from JDC Bucharest to New York, ibid., 3 Nov. 1921.

104 Moyshe Leyzerovitsh, 'Der koyekh fun sheker,' *Der haynt* 269, 271, and 272, 28 and 30 Nov. 1921, 1 Dec. 1921.

105 Sh. Volkovitsh, 'Di hent avek,' *Der moment* 272, 1 Dec. 1921.

106 Cable from JDC Berlin to Vienna, JDC Archives, AR 2132, File 405, 9 Nov. 1921. Kahn wrote, 'Have no objection working with Prilutzki in spite of his being ambitious reckless politician stop Prilutzki represents only small part of Jewish population Poland stop his party out of power at present stop He is trying by suspicious relations to polish government and by handling big welfare work to strengthen his personal political influence and influence of his party stop in spite of these motives his work has many good results.'

107 Cable from JDC Berlin to NYC, JDC Archives, AR 2132, File 405, 7 Nov. 1921.

108 YIVO Archives, RG 245.4.12 (HIAS Europe), MKM 15.23 XII-Europe-3.

109 Letter from Lucas to Prilutski, JDC Archives, AR 2132, File 405, 17 Nov. 1921.

110 Letter from Dr N. Prilutzky to JDC, New York, ibid., 22 Nov. 1921.

111 Letter from James N. Rosenberg to Dr Bernard Kahn, ibid., 20 May 1922.

112 N. Prilutski, 'Lui marshal,' *Der moment* 221, 20 Sept. 1929.

113 Dovid Druk, 'Noyekh prilutski baym president (a briv fun amerike),' *Der moment* 19, 22 Jan. 1922.

114 'Noyekh prilutski baym president,' *Idishes tageblat*, 18 Dec. 1921.

115 Druk, 'Noyekh prilutski baym president (a briv fun amerike).'

116 N. Prilutski; 'Harding,' *Der moment* 182, 7 Aug. 1923.

117 N. Prilutski, 'Untervegs: Nyu-york,' *Der moment* 180, 8 Aug. 1922.

118 N. Prilutski, 'Lui marshal.'

119 N. Prilutski, 'Amerikaner "blofer" un undzere "ernste" layt,' *Literarishe bleter* 1/2 (16 May 1924): 2.

120 On this phenomenon, see Michael Brown, *The Israeli-American Connection: Its Roots in the Yishuv, 1914–1945* (Detroit: Wayne State University Press, 1996).

121 Nomberg, e.g., felt that the Jewish immigrants to Argentina were on a higher cultural level than those in the United States (Shmuel Rozhanski, ed., *H.d. nomberg oysgeklibene shriftn* (Buenos Aires, 1958)). Nina Warnke notes of Sholem Aleichem: 'Whereas he acknowledges the benefits of political freedom and economic opportunity for Jews in America, he continuously mocked in his writings the low level of the immigrants' culture and the shallowness of their values' ('Of Plays and Politics: Sholem Aleichem's

first visit to America,' *YIVO Annual* 20 (1991): 251). Similarly, Khone Shmeruk notes the degradation of Eastern European Jewish 'aristocrats' in the United States ('Sholem Aleichem and America,' *YIVO Annual* 20 (1991): 227).

122 Y. Mark, 'Yidishe anglitsizmen,' *Yorbukh fun amopteyl* 1 (1938): 296–321; Y. Yofe, 'Yidish in amerike,' *YIVO-bleter* 10 (1936): 127–45. Prylucki penned one article about Yiddish in North America: N.P., 'Yidish folkslider oys kanade,' *Yidishe filologye* 1 (1924): 235–6.

123 Netzer, *Ma'avak yehudei polin,* 285. On the d'Hondt method by which the apportionment of mandates was determined, see Joseph Marcus, *Social and Political History of the Jews 1919–1939* (Berlin: Mouton, 1983), 262–3.

124 Mendelsohn, *Zionism,* 137.

125 Citation of the writer Tadeusz Holowko in *Robotnik,* 26 Sept. 1922, in Korzec, *Juifs en Pologne,* 127.

126 He was likely chosen for this role as intermediary by the Germans because he was not a Sejm member and was not seen as hostile to the state (Netzer, *Ma'avak yehudei polin,* 292). Korzec suggests that, apart from combating the discriminatory electoral rules, German diplomats were eager to initiate a minorities bloc in order to impair the process of Poland's internal stabilization (Korzec, *Juifs en Pologne,* 126).

127 N. Prilutski. 'Oyf der vakh,' *Der moment* 189, 15 Aug. 1922.

128 N. Prilutski, 'Diskusye tsu der val-kampanye. der val-platform,' *Der moment* 225–7, 27–9 Sept. 1922; Netzer, *Ma'avak yehudei polin,* 299.

129 'Tsum yidishn folk!' *Der moment* 228, 1 Oct. 1922; 'Diskusye tsu der val-kampanye: der natsionaler blok un zayn farteydiker,' *Der moment* 245, 24 Oct. 1922.

130 N.P., 'Diskusye tsu der val-kampanye: a bisl kheshbn,' *Der moment* 233, 9 Oct. 1922.

131 Y. Khm., 'Der "folks-demokratisher" blok,' *Folkstsaytung* 39, 20 Oct. 1922.

132 Y. Grinboym, 'Ibergedreyt dem dishl,' *Der haynt* 224, 22 Sept. 1922.

133 A. K-n, 'Di melukhe-liste fun der folks-partey,' *Der haynt* 226, 28 Sept. 1922; 'Di balagerung fun minderheyts-blok,' *Der haynt* 234, 8 Oct. 1922.

134 'Di mapole fun di folkistishe redlfirer,' *Der haynt* 219, 18 Sept. 1922.

135 Netzer, *Ma'avak yehudei polin,* 301.

136 'Di yidishe literatn vegn sh. hirshhorn,' *Der haynt* 238, 16 Oct. 1922; A. Goldberg, 'Der urteyl fun literatn-fareyn,' *Der haynt* 241, 19 Oct. 1922; *Jüdische Rundschau* 75 (22 Sept. 1922): 507; Cohen, *Sefer, sofer ve-'iton,* 26–7.

137 B. Yeushzon, 'Klore diburim,' *Der moment* 231, 6 Oct. 1922.

138 S. Dubnow, 'Antwort an die Fanatiker,' *Jüdische Rundschau* 10, 3 Feb. 1925.

139 H. Tseytlin, 'On a zayt funem groysn tuml,' *Der moment* 266, 17 Nov. 1922.

140 H. Tseytlin, 'Di boykotistn bay der arbet,' *Der moment* 227, 29 Sept. 1922.

141 Netzer, *Ma'avak yehudei polin,* 309–10; Korzec, *Juifs en Pologne,* 128.

142 Netzer, *Ma'avak yehudei polin,* 310–13.

143 Moshe Landau, *Mi'ut le'umi lohem: Ma'avak yehudei polin ba-shanim 1918–1928* (Jerusalem: Merkaz Zalman Shazar, 1986), 167–8.

144 Hafftka, 'Di yidishe politik,' 170–1.

145 According to Rudnicki, the Koło rejected Prylucki in a 10–8 vote on grounds of his campaigning with its opponents during the electoral campaign (*Żydzi w Parlamencie,* 152).

146 Jolanta Żyndul, *Panstwo w panstwie?: autonomia narodowo-kulturalna w Europie Środkowowschodniej w XX wieku* (Warsaw: DiG, 2000), 126, 149.

147 'Minister mikloshevski vider bakumen umtsutroy fun seym,' *Der moment* 285, 11 Dec. 1924.

148 Żyndul, *Panstwo w panstwie?* 132–4.

149 N. Prilutski, 'Vi azoy iz dos tsugegangen,' *Der moment* 287, 14 Dec. 1924.

150 'Di nisht-tsushtand gekumene forlezung fun dep' grinboym,' *Der moment* 287, 14 Dec. 1924.

151 A. Aynhorn, 'Der rebe un zayne talmidim,' *Der haynt* 226, 28 Sept. 1922.

152 S. Dubnow, 'Antwort an die Fanatiker,' *Jüdische Rundschau* 10, 3 Feb. 1925.

153 Undated letter from Dubnow to Prylucki, Central Archives for the History of the Jewish People, Arkhion Dubnov, P1/12.

154 Bacon, *Politics of Tradition,* 184, 192–3.

155 N. Prilutski, 'Val-notitsn,' *Der moment* 137, 13 June 1924.

156 N. Prilutski, 'Oyf der vakh,' *Der moment* 76, 28 April 1924.

157 N. Prilutski, 'A briv in redaktsye,' *Literarishe bleter* 1/4 (1924): 5. While the journal only printed three issues, it was of tremendous symbolic importance in helping to promote the conviction that Yiddish scholarship was sufficiently mature to support its own institution. This institution was YIVO, which began its history the following year in Berlin (Kuznitz, 'Origins of Jewish Scholarship,' 30).

158 Guterman, *Kehilat varsha,* 191, 197.

159 Ibid., 198–206; Bacon, *Politics of Tradition,* 196–8; Rak, *Zikhroynes,* 100.

160 Korzec, *Juifs en Pologne,* 152–60; Frost, *Schooling,* 24–5; Finkelstein, *Haynt,* 143–5; Mendelsohn, *Zionism,* ch.7.

161 During the Second Polish Republic only one grant was made by the Ministry of Education to Jewish schools, a one-time allocation for 45,000 złoty in 1927; communal allocations were made more often, although irregularly, and, on the whole, grudgingly (Frost, *Schooling,* 26).

162 Stanisław Mauersberg, *Szkolnictwo poweszechne dla mniejszości narodwych w Polsce w latach 1918–1939* (Wrocław: Polskiej akademii nauk, 1968).

163 On Ukrainian schools in Poland, see George Y. Shevelov, *The Ukrainian Language in the First Half of the Twentieth Century (1900–1941)* (Cambridge, MA: Harvard University Press), 178–81.

164 Albert S. Kotowski, *Polens Politik gegenüber seiner deutschen Minderheit 1919–1939* (Wiesbaden: Harrassowitz, 1998), 101–4.

165 Żyndul, *Panstwo w panstwie?* 123–6; Nathan Eck, 'The Educational Institutions of Polish Jewry (1921–1939),' *Jewish Social Studies* 9/1 (Jan. 1947): 11, 15. Eck notes (at 11) that during this same period, 'government reports bewailed the fact that, due to lack of funds, hundreds of rural public schools were housed in dilapidated huts.'

166 On the attitudes of Jewish children to Polish schools, see Jeffrey Shandler, ed., *Awakening Lives: Autobiographies of Jewish Youth in Poland before the Holocaust* (New Haven: Yale University Press, 2002).

167 Gershon Bacon, 'National Revival, Ongoing Acculturation: Jewish Education in Interwar Poland,' *Simon Dubnow Institut Jahrbuch* 1 (2002): 71–92.

168 E.g., Szabad requested in 1923 that Dubnow use his influence in order that German universities and *Hochschulen* recognize the diploma of the Vilna Yiddish *Realshule* since this was not accepted by Polish institutions of higher learning (Letter from Tsemakh Szabad to Simon Dubnow, 9 June 1923, Central Archives for the History of the Jewish People, Arkhion Dubnov P1/11).

169 Chone Shmeruk, 'A Trilingual Jewish Culture,' in *The Jews of Poland between Two World Wars*, ed. Y. Gutman, E. Mendelsohn, J. Reinharz, and C. Shmeruk (Hanover and London: University Press of New England, 1989), 292–6. According to JDC statistics, in 1936, 'of the one-half million Jewish children of school age, 64 percent studied or were supposed to study in public schools in Polish, some of which were intended exclusively for Jewish children' (ibid., 292). Official Polish government figures for the same year show some 80% of Jewish school age children registered in state public schools (Bacon, 'National Revival,' 84). Gershon Bacon approvingly cites Shimon Frost's assessment that 'all statistical data on the Jewish educational networks in interwar Poland are flawed with inaccuracies and overlapping figures. This is particularly true of the orthodox sector which included a great number of small hadarim, many of which in the words of Tartakower, "did not deserve to be called schools"' (ibid., 74).

170 Nathan Cohen, 'The Jews of Independent Poland: Linguistic and Cultural Changes,' *Starting the Twenty-First Century*, ed. Ernest Krausz and Gitta Tulea (New Brunswick, NJ: Transaction Publishers, 2002), 164.

171 Kassow, *Students, Professors, and the State*, 75–6.

172 Garncarska-Kadari, *Di linke poyeley-tsien*, 282.

173 N. Prilutski, 'Oyf der vakh,' *Der moment* 191, 15 Aug. 1921.
174 Yoyne Shapiro, 'Undzere noentste oyfgabn,' *Dos folk* 12, 1 June 1922.
175 Ibid.
176 Mayzil, 'Noyekh prilutski,' 27.
177 Mendelsohn, *Zionism*, 204. On the whole, despite government harassment and financial difficulties the number of *Tsisho* schools actually grew between 1921 and 1925. In 1921, *Tsisho* possessed 69 elementary schools and 35 kindergartens – a total of 381 classes with 13,457 children in 44 cities. Four years later, it had 91 elementary schools with 455 classes and 16,364 pupils in addition to three secondary schools with 780 pupils (Kh.Sh. Kazdan, 'Education,' in *Encyclopaedia Judaica*, vol. 6, 435).
178 Mendelsohn, *Zionism*, 193; Miriam Eisenstein, *Jewish Schools in Poland 1919–39* (New York: King's Crown Press, 1950), 35.
179 Sh. Biber, 'Folks-partey,' in Mab, *Politish-ekonomish verterbukh* (Warsaw: Kultur-lige, 1936), 296.
180 On the topic of Yiddish cultural work in Vilna at this time, see Shmuel D. Kasov, 'Zalmen reyzen un zayn gezelshaftlekh-politishe arbet, 1915–1922,' *YIVO-bleter* 2 (1994): 67–97.
181 Mendelsohn, *Jews of East Central Europe*; Dawidowicz, *From That Place and Time.*
182 N. Prilutski, 'Oyf der vakh,' *Der moment* 109, 12 May 1922.
183 'Vegn inyen prilutski-trop,' *Shul un lebn* 8/15 (1922); Kazdan, *Di geshikhte*, 160, 342; Gancarska-Kadari, *Di linke poyeley-tsien*, 285.
184 'Funem gezelshaftlekhn lebn: Di grindings-farzamlung fun der folksbildungs-lige,' *Der moment* 185, 8 Aug. 1924; 'Fayerlekher oysflug in otvotsker dertsiungs-hoyz fun der folksbildungs-lige,' *Der moment* 163, 14 July 1924; Kazdan, *Di geshikhte*, 352.
185 H. Tseytlin, 'Un vos hert zikh epes mekoyekh der folkspartey,' *Der moment* 135, 12 June 1931.
186 'Vegn inyen trop-prilutski.'
187 'Fun tog tsu tog,' *Der haynt* 137, 16 June 1926. See also, 'A shoyderhafte geshikhte mit dem otvotsker yesomim-hoyz,' *Der haynt* 136, 15 June 1926; 'Der skandal arum otvotsker beys-yesomim,' *Der haynt* 137, 16 June 1926.
188 'Hakhkhoshe n. prilutski,' *Der haynt* 136, 15 June 1926; 'Di tsveyte hakhkhoshe,' *Der haynt* 141, 21 June 1926.
189 Warsaw artisan-activist Elimeylekh Rak complained that the Zionists neglected the needs of artisans in both Poland and Palestine: 'The relationship of the Zionist organization to the artisans used to vex us so that I often thought that, had the Folkists a positive position vis-à-vis Palestine, the artisans would really have to join their party' (*Zikhroynes*, 110).

190 Finkelstein, *Haynt,* 92.

191 Levinson, *Toldot yehudei varsha,* 271; Ruvn Feldshuh, *Yidisher gezelshaftlekher leksikon: poyln I varshe* (Warsaw: Yidisher leksikografisher farlag, 1939), 218; N. Prilutski, 'Oyf der vakh,' *Der moment* 67, 19 March 1920.

192 Rak, *Zikhroynes,* 65–6, 110; N. Prilutski, 'Oyf der vakh,' *Der moment* 29, 3 Feb. 1920.

193 Mendelsohn, 'Reflections on East European Jewish Politics,' 29.

194 Mendelson, *Jews of East Central Europe,* 61.

195 Guterman, *Kehilat varsha,* 196.

196 Korzec, *Juifs en Pologne.* 134–5; Mendelsohn, *Zionism,* 222.

197 Letter from Tsemakh Szabad to Simon Dubnow, 9 June 1923, Central Archives for the History of the Jewish People, Arkhion Dubnov, P1/11.

198 Hafftka, 'Di yidishe politik,' 174.

199 Mark Turkov, 'Elkhonen tseytlin un zayn svive,' in E. Tseylin, *In a literarisher shtub,* xxiii.

200 Yechel Szeintuch, *Preliminary Inventory of Yiddish Dailies and Periodicals Published in Poland between the Two World Wars* (Jerusalem: Hebrew University, Center for Research on the History and Culture of Polish Jews, 1986), 140. The newspaper seems to have been published in 1917, 1918, and 1922. I was able to locate part of one issue from 1925 (fourth year of publication according to the masthead) dated 5 April in the Bund Archive in YIVO (RG 1400, MG2-520).

201 Finkelstein, *Haynt,* 118–19.

202 B[unem] Yeushzon, *Nekhtn: a bukh felyetonen* (Ramat-Gan, Israeli: Bar-Ilan University, 1988), 35.

203 M. Fuks, *Prasa żydowska,* 197.

204 L. Finkelshteyn recalls Nomberg reproaching Rasner for an anti-Bundist pronouncement in the Warsaw City Council: '"Why did you attack the Bund? We are travelling a parallel path with it." "Comrade Nomberg, don't forget that we are not merely a cultural party. We have also economic interests. The Bund organizes strikes in our workshops"' (Finkelshteyn, 'Inm amolikn varshe,' 90).

205 H.D. Nomberg, 'Di geshenishn in literatn-fareyn,' *Der moment* 289, 16 Dec. 1924.

206 H.D. Nomberg, 'Provokatsye,' *Der moment* 287, 14 Dec. 1924.

207 M. Shulman, 'Zayn lebn un veg,' in *Shloyme mendelson,* 16–18.

208 Finkelshteyn, 'Inm amolikn varshe,' 86. The term *Itshe-Mayer* as a derisive designation for Polish Jews among other Yiddish-speaking Jews stems from the frequency with which the name was encountered among males, many of whom were named in memory of the founder of influential Gerer

dynasty, Isaac Meir Rothenberg Alter (1789–1866, *Itshe Mayer* in Polish Yiddish).

209 Ibid.

210 'Mendelson, Shloyme,' in Niger and Shatski, *Leksikon*, vol. 6, 44; M. Shulman, 'Zayn lebn un veg,' 17.

211 Finkelshteyn, 'Inm amolikn varshe,' 92.

212 Turkov, 'Elkhonen tseytlin un zayn svive,' xxiii; Sh. Biber, 'Folks-partey,' 296.

213 Finkelshteyn, 'Inm amolikn varshe,' 92.

214 Aaron Tseytlin, 'Nokhvort fun aren tseytlin,' in E. Zeitlin, *In a literarisher shtub*, 223.

215 Janina Katarzyna Rogozik, 'Bernard Singer, the Forgotten "Most Popular Jewish Reporter of the Inter-War Years in Poland,"' *Polin* 12 (1999): 188.

216 Nakhmen Mayzel, 'Yidishe shildn,' *Literarishe bleter* 3/132 (1926): 747–8.

217 Samuel Hirszhorn, *Historja Zydów w Polsce: od Sejmu Czteroletnego do wojny europejskiej (1788–1914)* (Warsaw: B-cia Lewin-Epstein, 1921).

218 Michael C. Steinlauf, 'The Polish Jewish Daily Press,' *Polin* 2 (1987): 219–45.

6 Compromises? The Chair of Yiddish at the University of Vilnius

1 Sh. Biber, *Der krizis funem yidish politishn gedank: a vendung tsu der yidisher demokratye* (Warsaw, 1927), 22.

2 'Di demokatish-folkistishe konferents,' *Frayer gedank* 1, 29 Oct. 1926.

3 Response of Dubnow to the declaration of the Jewish Democratic Party in Vilna of 10 Aug. 1926, Central Archives for the History of the Jewish People, Arkhion Dubnov, no date, P1/12.

4 'Di demokratish-folkistishe konferents,' *Frayer gedank* 1, 29 Oct. 1926; Czesław Brzoza, *Żydowska Mozaika Polityczna w Polsce 1917–1927: Wybór Dokumentów* (Kraków: Księgarnia Akademicka, 2003), 114–15.

5 'Di demokratish-folkistishe konferents,' *Frayer gedank* 1, 29 Oct. 1926. On the attitude towards Yiddish in the *yishuv*, see Chaver, 'From Mother Tongue.'

6 'Undzer platform,' *Frayer gedank* 1, 29 Oct. 1926.

7 Sh. Biber, 'Folks-partey,' in *Politish-ekonomish verterbukh*, 296.

8 N. Prilutski, 'A shtikl khezhbn-hanefesh,' *Oyfboy* 1, 15 Dec. 1926.

9 Lazar Kahan, 'Di folkspartey un di hantverker,' *Oyfboy* 2, 15 Feb. 1927.

10 Lazar Kahan, 'Di yidishe kleynhendler un di folkspartey,' *Oyfboy* 1.

11 'Di plener-zitsung fun tsentral rat mitn onteyl fun delegatn fun di provintser organizatyes,' *Oyfboy* 2.

12 Yankev Shatski, 'Yidishe politik in poyln tsvishn di tsvey velt-milkhomes,' in *Algemeyne entsiklopedye yidn* vol. 4 (New York: Dubnov-fond un tsiko, 1950), 229–33; Haya Meller, 'Mifleget ha-folkistim (folkspartey) be-polin [1915–1939]' (PhD diss., Bar-Ilan University, 2004), 309–11; Rudnicki, *Żydzi w parlamencie*, 253–5; A.J. Groth, 'Polish Elections 1919–1928,' *Slavic Review* 24/4 (Dec., 1965): 653–65.

13 In municipal elections in 1927, 1929, and 1934, Folkists won 6 mandates in Lublin (Zbigniew Zaporowski, 'Żydzi w Radzie Miejskiej Lublina 1919–1939,' in *Żydzi w Lublinie*, ed, Tadeusz Radzik (Lublin: Wydawnictwo Uniwersytetu Marii Curie-Skłodowkiej, 1995), 238). Folkists in Łódź independently won one mandate in 1923, 1927, and 1936. They received votes as part of blocs with other Jewish parties in 1934 and 1938 (one mandate) (Maria Nartonowicz-Kot, 'Obliczne polityczne samorządu miejskiego Łódzi w latach 1919–1939,' *Rocznik Łódzki* 31 (1982): 107–8, 113, 118, 138; Barbara Wachowska, 'The Jewish Electorate of Interwar Łódź in the Light of the Local Government Elections (1919–1938),' *Polin* 6 (1991): 154–72).

14 B. Yeushzon, 'Folkizm,' *Der haynt* 259, 14 Nov. 1929.

15 'To tell the truth, I have mainly worked for myself alone. The interest in philology in the broadest sense of the concept is an inborn quality. The social instinct that determines the relationship of the individual to the milieu directed this interest towards the Yiddish camp' ('Draysik yor literarishe tetikeyt fun noyekh prilutski,' 332). He later described himself in Lithuanian-Soviet documents as having headed the Folksparty until 1929 and thereafter being almost completely passive politically ('Anketa,' p. 1).

16 M. K-ski [Magnus Krinski], 'Di yoyvl-fayerung fun noyekh prilutski,' *Der moment* 106, 8 May 1931; 'Banket lekoved noyekh prilutski,' *Der moment* 107, 10 May 1931.

17 'Banket lekoved noyekh prilutski,' *Der moment* 107, 10 May 1931.

18 Ibid.

19 N. Prilutski, 'Mir nitsn nisht keyn bilder,' *Der moment* 59, 10 March 1935.

20 See, e.g., correspondence between YIVO and Prylucki dated 20 and 29 Nov. 1929 (YIVO, Vilna Collection, RG 1.1, Box 3, Folder 65).

21 'Noyekh prilutski (tsu zayn tsurikkumen keyn varshe),' *Der moment* 17, 19 Jan. 1934.

22 Mozes, 'Der moment,' in *Fun noentn over*, 280–90.

23 N. Prilutski, 'Di ideale folkseynikeyt fun der drangizm,' *Der moment* 162, 13 July 1934; 'Notitsn on politik,' *Der moment* 175, 27 July 1934.

24 N. Prilutski, 'Notitsn on politik,' *Der moment* 122, 27 May 1932; *Der moment* 123, 29 May 1932.

25 N. Prilutski, 'Notitsn on politik,' *Der moment* 240, 18 Oct. 1931; 'Oy, doles, doles!' *Der moment* 197, 25 Aug. 1933.

26 N. Prilutski, 'An elementare foderung,' *Der moment* 114, 16 May 1934; 'Abetse un alef-beys,' *Der moment* 120, 25 May 1934; 'Vaser oyf undzere mil-reder,' *Der moment* 186, 10 Aug. 1934; 'A mayse mit an adres un ir muser-haskl,' *Der moment* 11, 13 Jan. 1935.

27 N. Prilutski, 'Hava melodyes,' *Der moment* 1, 1 Jan. 1937; 'Meshugene shvomen,' *Der moment* 302, 31 Dec. 1937; Carla Tonini, 'The Polish Plan for a Jewish Settlement in Madagascar 1936–1939,' *Polin* 19 (2007): 467–7.

28 N. Prilutski, 'Der seykhl iz a krikher,' *Der moment* 211, 9 Sept. 1938.

29 N. Prilutski, 'Alef-beys,' *Der moment* 153, 2 July 1937.

30 N. Prilutski, 'Moskve un di velt,' *Der moment* 60, 11 March 1938.

31 N. Prilutski, 'Ay, dobl yu, dobl yu-organizatyse. (Fun der serye 'amerike un amerikaner'),' *Der moment* 66, 17 March 1933.

32 N. Prilutski, 'Notitsn on politik,' *Moment* 104, 6 May 1932; 'Amerike un amerikaner vi ikh hob zey gezen,' *Der moment* 61, 12 March 1933.

33 N. Prilutski, 'Der psikhos fun diktatur in di fareynikte shtatn,' *Der moment* 88, 14 April 1933.

34 N. Prilutski, 'Vu iz eyner? Un vu iz der tsveyter?' *Der moment* 53, 2 March 1934.

35 See N. Prilutski, *Bay di kehile-valn* (Warsaw: Lodzsher organizatsye fun der yidisher demokratisher folkspartey in poyln, 1936).

36 For a survey of antisemitism in this period, see William H. Hagen, 'Before the "Final Solution": Toward a Comparative Analysis of Political Anti-Semitism in Interwar Germany and Poland,' *Journal of Modern History* 68/2 (June 1996): 351–81. On the *numerus clausus*, see Szymon Rudnicki, 'From "Numerus Clausus" to "Numerus Nullus,"' *Polin* 2 (1987): 246–68.

37 N. Prilutski, 'Ven di ganz vil vern a shlayen,' *Der moment* 5, 5 Jan. 1934.

38 N. Prilutski, 'Notitsn on politik,' *Der moment* 183, 7 Aug., 1931.

39 N. Prilutski, 'Triumf fun heyliker arbet,' *Der moment* 198, 24 Aug. 1934.

40 According to the information he provided Soviet Lithuanian authorities, Prylucki spoke and wrote Yiddish, Russian, and Polish well; he read French, English, and German weakly and spoke German weakly ('Anketa,' p. 2).

41 On racial science and Jewish nationalists, see John M. Efron, *Defenders of the Race: Jewish Doctors and Race Science in Fin-de-Siècle Europe* (New Haven: Yale University Press, 2004).

42 M. K-ski, 'Di yoyvl-fayerung fun noyekh prilutski.'

43 N. Prilutski, 'Di yidishe bineshprakh,' *Yidish teater* 4/1 (1927): 130–44. For a discussion of debates surrounding standard pronunciation in Yiddish schools in Eastern Europe, see Kalmen Vayzer, 'Di debate arum aroysred in der yidish-veltlekher shul in mizrekh-eyrope,' *Yidishe shprakh* (forthcoming).

44 On the issue of local patriotism among Yiddish language standardizers, see

Hirsh-Dovid Kats, 'Naye gilgulim fun alte makhloykesn; di litvishe norme un di sikhsukhim vos arum ir,' *YIVO-bleter* 2 (1994): 205–57.

45 On Jewish sports in Poland, see Roni Gechtman, 'Socialist Mass Politics through Sport: The Bund's Morgnshtern in Poland, 1626–1939,' *Journal of Sport History* 26/2 (1999): 326–52.

46 Shmeruk, 'Trilingual Jewish Culture,' 305.

47 Celia Heller, *On the Edge of Destruction* (New York: Columbia University Press, 1977); Mendelsohn, *Jews of East Central Europe.*

48 Cohen, 'Jews of Independent Poland,' 166–8.

49 Ibid., 172; Ellen Deborah Kellman, 'Dos yidishe bukh alarmirt,' *Polin* 16 (2003): 226.

50 On the inroads of the Polish language among strictly religious girls, a phenomenon noted before the interwar period in predominately Hasidic Galicia and Congress Poland, see Bacon, 'La société juive,' 647, 656; Moyshe Prager, 'Dos yidishe togblat,' in *Yidishe prese in varshe,* vol. 2, *Fun noentn over* (New York: Congress for Jewish Culture, 1956), 488–9.

51 'W młynie opinji: Czy potrzebne jest pismo polsko-żydowski?' *Nasz Przegląd,* 14 June 1928.

52 Eugenia Prokop-Janiec, *Polish-Jewish Literature in the Interwar Years* (Syracuse, NY: Syracuse University Press, 2003), translation by Abe Shenitzer of *Miedzywojenna literatura polsko-żydowska jako zjawisko kulturowe i artystyczne* (Kraków: 'Universitas,' 1992), 36. On the subject of Jewish national identity and culture as expressed in the Polish-language Jewish press, see Katrin Steffen, *Jüdische Polonität: Ethnizität und Nation im Spiegel der polnischsprachigen jüdischen Presse, 1918–1939* (Göttingen: Vandenhoeck and Ruprecht, 2004).

53 On this subject, see Prokop-Janiec, *Polish-Jewish Literature.*

54 Cohen, 'Jews of Independent Poland,' 170.

55 Mark Turkov, 'Der emes vegn "moment"-shtrayk' and Tsvi Prilutski, '30 yor "moment,"' *Unzer tsaytung,* 3 March 1939; Mendl Mozes, 'Der moment,' in *Fun noentn over,* 280–90.

56 Redaktsye-kolegium fun 'Moment,' 'Tsu der efntlekhkeyt!' *Unzer tsaytung,* 3 March 1939.

57 Memoirs of Ts. Prylucki, III, 304–5.

58 Mozes, 'Der moment,' 291.

59 Ibid., 293.

60 Cohen, *Sefer, sofer ve-'iton,* 297–9.

61 Dov Levin, *The Lesser of Two Evils* (Philadelphia and Jerusalem: Jewish Publication Society, 1995), 198–217.

62 Mordkhe Tsanin, *Grenetsn biz tsum himl* (Tel Aviv: Ha-menorah, 1969).

63 Dov Levin, 'The Jews of Vilna under Soviet Rule, 19 September–28 October 1939,' *Polin* 9 (1996): 117.

64 See, e.g., Moyshe Mandelman, 'In freyd un leyd tsvishn litvishe yidn (fun 1938 biz 1940),' in *Lite*, ed. Mendel Sudarsky et al. (New York: Jewish-Lithuanian Cultural Society 'Lite,' 1951), 1333–58.

65 On the notion of Żydo-Komuna (Yid-Communist Conspiracy), see Jan Gross, *Fear: Anti-Semitism in Poland after Auschwitz – An Essay in Historical Interpretation* (New York: Random House, 2006).

66 On this period, see Sarunas Liekis, 'Jewish-Polish Relations and the Lithuanian Authorities in Vilna 1939–1940,' *Polin* 19 (2007): 521–36; Marek Wierzbicki, 'Polish-Jewish Relations in Vilna and the Region of Western Vilna under Soviet Occupation, 1939–1941,' *Polin* 19 (2007): 487–516.

67 Aziel Shochat, 'Jews, Lithuanians and Russians 1939–1941,' in *Jews and Non-Jews in Eastern Europe (1918–1945)*, ed. Bela Vago and George L. Mosse (New Brunswick, NJ: Transaction Books, 1974), 304–5.

68 Levin, 'Jews of Vilna,' 117.

69 Mendelsohn, *Jews of East Central Europe*, 217–25; Levin, 'Lithuania,' *YIVO Encyclopedia of Jews in Eastern Europe*, vol. 2, 1071–3.

70 Liekis, 'Jewish-Polish Relations,' 533; Levin, 'Lithuania,' 1073.

71 Hirsh-Dovid Kats, 'Kapitelekh yidish: A merkvirdike froy,' *Forverts*, 17 March 2000.

72 'Protokol fun der ferter shlus zitsung, zuntik dem 10tn detsember 1939,' 35–42.

73 Majer Balberyszski, *Shtarker fun ayzn* (Tel Aviv: Ha-menorah, 1967), 88, 118; Herman Kruk, *Togbukh fun vilner geto* (New York: YIVO, 1961), 535n425.

74 Balberyszki, *Shtarker fun ayzn*, 79.

75 Julija Šukys, '"And I burned with shame": The Testimony of Ona Šimaite, Righteous Among the Nations. A Letter to Isaac Nachman Steinberg,' *Search and Research – Lectures and Papers* (Jerusalem: Yad Vashem, 2007), 38.

76 Izraelis Lempertas, 'Uzmirsta jidis puoseletoja: Nojaus Priluckio katedra Vilniaus universitete,' in *Vilniaus Zydu intelektualinis gyvenimas*, ed. Larisa Lempertiene (Vilnius: Mokslo aidai, 2004), 185; Mandelman, 'In freyd un leyd,' 1335n.

77 Avraham Tory, *Surviving the Holocaust: The Kovno Ghetto Diary* (Cambridge, MA: Harvard University Press, 1990), 317

78 Daniel Tsharni, 'In kovner lite in 1933,' in Sudarsky, *Lite*, vol. 1, 1326.

79 Tomas Venclova, 'Four Centuries of Enlightenment: A Historic View of the University of Vilnius, 1579–1979,' *Lithuanian Quarterly Journal of Arts and Sciences*, 27/1 (Summer 1981). http://www.lituanus.org/1981_2/81_2_01.htm (accessed 10 Dec. 2008).

80 'Barikht vegn dem bazukh fun der delegatsye fun yivo bay prof' birzhishko vegn dem inyen katedre far yidisher shprakh un literatur baym vilner universitet,' undated, YIVO Archives, RG 1.1, Box 31, Folder 633.

81 'Protokol fun der zitsung fun der tsaytvayliker farvaltung fun yivo, vilne, dem 27tn yanuar 1940,' ibid., Folder 631, p. 19.
82 Ibid.
83 Joshua Karlip, 'At the Crossroads between War and Genocide: A Reassessment of Jewish Ideology in 1940,' *Jewish Social Studies* 11/2 (2005): 170–201.
84 'Protokol fun der zitsung fun der tsaytvayliker farvaltung fun yivo, 10tn marts 1940,' YIVO Archives, RG 1.1, Box 31, Folder 631, p. 19.
85 'Protokol fun der zitsung fun der tsaytvayliker farvaltung fun yivo, vilne, dem 27tn yanuar 1940,' ibid., p. 13.
86 Ibid., p. 12.
87 'Protokol fun der driter zitsung, zuntik dem 10tn detsember, 1939, 11 a zeyger f'm,' ibid., p. 33.
88 Lempertas, 'Uzmirsta jidis puoseletoja,' 186.
89 'Protokol fun der zitsung fun der tsaytvayliker farvaltung fun yivo, vilne, dem 27tn yanuar 1940,' YIVO Archives, RG 1.1, Box 31, Folder 631, p. 20.
90 Lempertas, 'Uzmirsta jidis puoseletoja: Nojaus Priluckio katedra Vilniaus universitete,' 187.
91 'Profesorn fun vilner universitet oyf der perets-oysshtelung yivo,' YIVO Archives, RG 584, Box 30, Folder 293; Mandelman, 'In freyd un leyd,' 1349.
92 Levin, 'Tsvishn hamer un serp,' 85.
93 'Protokol fun der zitsung fun der tsaytvayliker farvaltung fun yivo, vilne, dem 27tn yanuar 1940,' YIVO Archives, RG 1.1, Box 31, Folder 631, pp. 16–21; 'Zitsung fun der tsaytvayliker farvaltung fun yivo, 10tn marts 1940,' ibid., pp. 3–5.
94 'Protokol fun der zitsung fun der tsaytvayliker farvaltung fun yivo, 10tn marts 1940,' ibid., pp. 15–17, 21.
95 Undated, handwritten note in name of Central Administration of YIVO, ibid., Folder 633.
96 'Protokol fun der zitsung fun der tsaytvayliker farvaltung fun yivo, 10tn marts 1940,' ibid., Folder 631, pp. 19, 18–19.
97 Letter from Kalmanovitch to Mark, 8 Dec. 1938, ibid., RG 540, Box 9, Folder 161.
98 Summarizing some of Prylucki's chief faults as a scholar, Weinreich writes: 'I wouldn't "bother with trifles" if I didn't see evidence here of a method. The excess of Old Yiddish, of Yiddish dialectal materials, of copying from books, of relying on foreign languages whether it is directly relevant or not to the matter – it is consistent. L. Olitski recently wrote in a review of *Yidish far ale* that the journal is "too philological-scientific." He certainly meant all the elements that I mention here. I would, however, not call that "philological-scientific," but simply cloudy because [true] scholarship, I believe,

really benefits nothing from all of these accessories of scholarship' (Maks Vaynraykh, 'Zibn numern "yidish far ale,"' *Yidish far ale* 10 (Dec. 1938): 288). Understandably indignant, Prylucki responded with characteristic discursiveness, alternately refuting and confirming Weinreich's criticisms, in a series of lengthy articles in the journal titled 'A vort in a min general-diskusye,' *Yidishe far ale* 1 (11) (Jan. 1939): 1–23; 2 (12) (Feb.–March 1939): 33–46; 3 (13) (April–May 1939): 65–80.

99 Signature cut off, letter from YIVO Vilna to Prylucki, 4 April 1938; Prylucki, for his part, protested that the articles were sent to him late and without any prior corrections (Noah Prylucki to YIVO, unspecified addressee, 1 Jan. 1939, YIVO Archives, RG 1.1, Box 3, Folder 65).

100 Letter from Kalmanovitch to Feinerman (Amopteyl), 9 Nov. 1939, YIVO Archives, RG 100A, Box 24.

101 Letter from Kalmanovitch to Weinreich, undated, YIVO Archives, RG 584, Box 30, Folder 293b.

102 Yosef Gar, 'Di kovner togtsaytung "folksblat,"' in *Lite*, Ch. Leikowicz, ed. (Tel Aviv: I.L. Peretz, 1965), vol. 2, 419–39. Gar submits that those who worked in the communist *Folksblat* were either convinced communists or opportunists who understood that the Soviets were soon to take over Lithuania and wished to advance their careers. Remembering Prylucki on the 25th anniversary of his death in the Polish communist *Folksshtime*, the writer Shloyme Belis recalls that Prylucki sympathized ideologically with the *Folksblat*, which Belis describes as a 'progressive' newspaper that had many enemies. Upon his request, Prylucki joined the circle of 'Friends of the *Folksblat*,' in 1939 in Vilnius. Belis does not, however, explain the nature of this organization's activities ('Dos gantse lebn farn mame-loshn').

103 Letter from Kalmanovitch to Amopteyl, 1 Jan. 1940, excerpt in *Der yivo un zayne grinder: Katalog fun der oysshtelung tsum 50-yorikn yoyvl fun yidishn visnshaftlekhn institut*, ed. Zosa Szajkowski (New York: YIVO, 1975), 56.

104 YIVO Executive minutes, Fragment, date unspecified, YIVO Archives, RG 1.1, Box 31, Folder 629, pp. 32–3.

105 'Protokol fun der zitsung fun der tsaytvayliker farvaltung fun yivo, 10tn marts 1940,' ibid., Folder 631, 21.

106 'Vos tut der "yivo" in milkhome tsayt?' *Folksblat* 147, 7 June 1940.

107 S., 'An intervyu mit profesor noyekh prilutski,' *Morgn-frayhayt*, 15 Dec. 1940.

108 Levin, *Lesser of Two Evils*, 198–21; Dawidowicz, *From That Place and Time*, 215; Mordkhe Tsanin, himself a refuge in Vilnius at this time, depicts frantic attempts to secure visas and permission to exit Soviet Lithuania in his wartime memoirs, *Grenetsn biz tsum himl*.

109 Balberyszski, *Shtarker fun ayzn*, 103.

110 Kaczerginski, 'Tsvishn hamer un serp,' 28.

111 Levin, 'Tsvishn hamer un serp,' 86; Kaczerginski, *Tsvishn hamer un serp*, 20, 28.

112 Levin, 'Tsvishn hamer un serp,' 88–91; Yisroel Lempert, 'Der goyrl fun yivo in historishn iberbrokh (1939–1941),' *YIVO-bleter* 3 (1997): 9–42.

113 'Oykh der "yivo" vert endlekh aroysgetsoygn fun zumf,' *Tageblat*, 16 Aug. 1940; Leyzer Ran, *Ash fun yerushalayim de'lite* (New York: Vilner Farlag, 1959), 176–9.

114 Levin, *Lesser of Two Evils*, 111.

115 Letter from M. Lerer to Prof. Mykolas Biržiška, 20 Aug. 1940, LCVA, F. R856, Ap.2, B. 1123, NP VUP; a letter from the editor of the 'Vilnius daily [Yiddish] newspaper' to the rector certified that Prylucki is a specialist in his field and 'has always been friendly to the USSR' (Letter to Rector of Vilnius University, 24 Aug. 1940).

116 Lempert, 'Der goyrl fun yivo,' 21; letter from N. Prylucki to Vilnius University Humanities Faculty, 3 April 1941, LCVA, F. R856, Ap.2, B. 1123, NP VUP.

117 S., 'An intervyu mit profesor noyekh prilutski.'

118 Lempertas, 'Uzmirsta jidis puoseletoja,' 189.

119 Levin, 'Tsvishn hamer un serp,' 88–91; Lempert, 'Der goyrl fun yivo'; Lempertas, 'Uzmirsta jidis puoseletoja,' 190. On the political career of Vincas Krėvė-Mickevičius, see Alfred Erich Senn, *Lithuania 1940: Revolution from Above* (Amsterdam and New York: Rodopi, 2007), 139ff.

120 Khaym Beyder, 'Noyekh prilutskis briv tsu aren gurshteyn,' *Di pen* 32 (Summer 1997): 41–5.

121 On the impact of Weinreich and other refugees on the *Amopteyl* in this period, see Dawidowicz's memoir, *From That Place and Time.*

122 Tsanin, *Grenetsn biz tsum himl*, 13–14.

123 Avrom Sutzkever, *Vilner geto, 1941–1944* (Paris: Farband fun di vilner in pariz, 1946), 3.

124 Levin, 'Tsvishn hamer un serp,' 89; letter from N. Prylucki to Vilnius University Humanities Faculty, 3 April 1941, LCVA, F. R856, Ap.2, B. 1123, NP VUP.

125 Mordkhe Tsanin, interview by author, Tel Aviv, 4 July 1999.

126 On Cahan and his policies in *Forward*, see Irving Howe, *World of Our Fathers* (New York: Schocken, 1989); Ellen Deborah Kellman, 'The Newspaper Novel in the Jewish Daily *Forward*: Fiction as Entertainment and Serious Literature' (PhD diss., Columbia University, 2000).

127 Yisroel Lempert reports that it was believed then in Vilna that Reyzen was arrested specifically for his denunciation of the Hitler-Stalin Pact ('Der

goyrl fun yivo in historishn iberbrokh,' 9; Yoysef Tshernikhov, *In Revtribunal: zikhroynes fun a farteydiker* (Vilna: Author, 1932); Hirsz Abramowicz, *Profiles of a Lost World*, ed. Dina Abramowicz and Jeffrey Shandler, trans. Eva Zeitlin Dobin (Detroit: YIVO and Wayne State University Press, 1999), 286.) Balberyszski attributes the following statement to Prylucki: 'The Bolsheviks are applying repressions against the Bund because Lenin and Stalin were already combating the Bund as a counterrevolutionary, Menshevik movement. The Bund was dangerous for them for decades because it agitates among workers and speaks in the name of socialism. They combat Zionism, on the other hand, as a reactionary, pro-English movement' (*Shtarker fun ayzn*, 105).

128 Basing himself on a conversation in the Warsaw ghetto with Rabbi Kurlianczik, who supervised the Chair as Commissar for Cultural Affairs in Lithuania, Balberyszski maintained that the Soviets intended to replace Prylucki with a more reliable scholar from Minsk in the next academic year. His interpretations, to the disappointment of students, were not appropriately Marxist and often contrary to the Marxist line. A new school year did not come, however. The Nazis invaded Lithuania in late June 1941 (Balberyszski, 'Di yidishe katedre baym vilner univerzitet,' *Driter oystralyish-yidisher almanakh* (1967): 382–3).

129 David Flinker, 'Noyekh Prilutski,' in '*Arim ve-imahot be-yisra'el*, ed. Judah Leib Maimon (Jerusalem: Mosad ha-rav Kuk, 1945), vol. 3, 289, 292.

Conclusion

1 On Weinreich, see the introduction in Jeffrey Shandler, ed., *Awakening Lives.*

2 A one-time Zionist and student of Yiddish linguistics, Zamenhof came to reject all forms of nationalism and understood his chief contribution to be the creation of an international language and a universal, neutral religion conceived to promote mutual understanding and harmony between peoples (Detlev Blanke, *Internationale Plansprachen* (Berlin: Akademie-Verlag, 1985), 220–3).

3 Hroch emphasizes barriers to social advancement experienced by members of a non-dominant ethnic group educated in the language and culture of a dominant group as an important motivating factor in the creation of language-based nationalism in Europe (Hroch, 'Social Interpretation of Linguistic Demands,' 22).

4 Christopher Hutton, *Linguistics and the Third Reich: Mother-Tongue Fascism, Race, and the Science of Language* (London and New York: Routledge, 1998), 190.

5 On their positions, see Christopher Hutton, 'Normativism and the Notion of Authenticity in Yiddish Linguistics,' in *The Field of Yiddish, Fifth Collection*, ed. David Goldberg (Evanston: Northwestern University Press and YIVO, 1993): 14–28.

6 N. Prilutski, 'Kleynikeytn,' 216.

7 Hroch, 'Social Interpretation of Linguistic Demands,' 19, 34.

8 See, e.g., Der Tunkeler (Yoysef Tunkel), 'Folklor un filologye: a lektsye fun noyekh prilutski,' in Yechiel Szeintuch, ed., *Der Tunkler: seyfer fun humoreskes un literarishe pardoyes* (Jerusalem: Mount Scopus Publications by the Magnes Press, Hebrew University, 1990), 207–9.

9 'To tell the truth, I have mainly worked for myself alone. The interest in philology in the broadest sense of the concept is an inborn quality. The social instinct that determines the relationship of the individual to the milieu directed this interest towards the Yiddish camp' ('Draysik yor literarishe tetikeyt fun noyekh prilutski,' 332).

10 Hutton, *Linguistics and the Third Reich*, 231–2.

11 Fishman, *Ideology, Society and Language*, 62.

12 Mayzil, 'Noyekh prilutski,' 27.

13 Balberyszski, *Shtarker fun ayzn*, 119.

14 Declaration signed by M. Biržiška, 27 June 1941, LCVA, F. R856, Ap. 2, B. 1123, NP, VUP.

15 L. Beder and M. Yelin, 'Di letste yorn fun noyekh prilutskin,' *Sovetish heymland* (March 1965): 146–8; David E. Fishman, *Embers Plucked from the Fire: The Rescue of Jewish Cultural Treasures in Vilna* (New York: YIVO, 1996), 4; Shmerke Katsherginski, *Khurbn vilne* (New York: United Vilner Relief Committee, 1947), 203–4; Sutzkever, *Vilner geto*, 108.

16 Balberyszski, *Shtarker fun ayzn*, 146.

17 'Prilutski, Tsvi,' in Niger and Shatski, *Leksikon*, vol. 7, 222.

18 Ber Y. Rozen, *Portretn* (Buenos Aires: Tsentral-farband fun poylishe yidn in argentine, 1956), 126–7.

19 Ibid., 175–9; Yonas Turkov, *Farloshene shtern* (Buenos Aires: Tsentral farband fun poylishe yidn in argentine, 1953), vol. 2, 238–44.

20 *Pinkes varshe* (Buenos Aires, 1955), 795; Yonas Turkov, *Azoy is dos geven* (Buenos Aires, 1948), 454.

21 Turkov, *Azoy is dos geven*, 377; 'Hirszhorn, Samuel,' in *Posłowie i Senatorowie Rzeczypospolitej Polskiej 1919–1939: Słownik biograficzny*, ed. Małgorzata Smogorzewska (Warsaw: Sejmowe, 2000), vol. 2, 226.

22 On the revival of Hebrew, see Jack Fellman, *The Revival of a Classical Tongue* (The Hague: Mouton, 1973); Harshav, *Language in Time of Revolution*. On the relationship between Yiddish and Hebrew, see Arye-Leyb Pilovski,

Tsvishn yo un neyn: Yidish un yidish-literatur in erets-yisroel, 1907–1948 (Tel Aviv: Veltrat far yidish un yidisher kultur, 1986).

23 On the relationship of contemporary ultra-Orthodox Jews to Yiddish, see Miriam Isaacs and Lewis Glinert, eds., *Pious Voices: Languages among Ultra-Orthodox Jews*, special issue of the *International Journal of the Sociology of Language* 138 (1999); Lewis Glinert and Yosseph Shilhav, 'Holy Land, Holy Language: A Study of an UltraOrthodox Jewish Ideology,' *Language and Society* 20 (1991): 59–86.

Bibliography

Primary Sources

Interviews

Eliyahu Prylucki, Haifa, 20 December 1998
Mordkhe Tsanin, Tel Aviv, 4 July 1999

Archival Materials

Archiwum Akt Nowych (AAN), Warsaw
Ministerstwo Spraw Wewnętrznych (MSW), Wydział Narodowościowy
Ministerstwo Spraw Zagranicznych (MSZ), Wydział prasowy, Referat spraw żydowskich
Archiwum Sejmu, Warsaw
Delegates' interpellations
Central Archives for the History of the Jewish People, Jerusalem
P1/11, 12 Arkhion Dubnov
Central Zionist Archives, Jerusalem
A24/117/II, Ussishkin Collection
Joint Distribution Committee (JDC), New York
AR 2132, File 405, Refugees (Feb.) 1921–22
AR 2132, File 406, Refugees (Mar.) 1922–23
Lietuvos Centrinis Valystubės Archyvas (LCVA), Vilnius
F. R856, Ap.2, B. 1123, Noachas Priluckis, Vilnius University Papers
Yad Vashem Archives, Jerusalem
AR II/175/M/10, Memoirs of Tsevi Prylucki
YIVO Institute for Jewish Research, New York

RG 1-1, Box 31, 9 Vilna Collection
RG 3, Folder 2610, Shrayber zamlung
RG 100A, Box 24, Amopteyl
RG 208, Series III, no. 739, Chaim Zhitlowsky Papers
RG 245, Box 4.12, Hias Europe
RG 584, Box 30, Max Weinreich Papers
RG 1400, MG2-520, Bund Archive
RG M16-24, Shrayber zamlung

Daily and Periodical Press

Di bin (Warsaw)
Evreiskaya Starina (St Petersburg)
Filologishe shriftn (Warsaw)
Dos folk (Warsaw)
Di folksshtime (Buenos Aires)
Di folksshtime (Warsaw)
Di folkstsaytung (Warsaw)
Der forverts (New York)
Frayer gedank (Vilna)
Der fraynd (St Petersburg, Warsaw)
Gazeta Warszawska (Warsaw)
Der haynt (Warsaw)
Idishes tageblat (New York)
Ilustrirte bleter (Warsaw)
Izraelita (Warsaw)
Jüdische Rundschau (Berlin)
Lebn un visnshaft (Vilna)
Lebnsfragn (Warsaw)
Literarishe bleter (Warsaw)
Der moment (Warsaw)
Der morgn-frayhayt (New York)
Der morgn-zhurnal (New York)
Nasz Przegląd (Warsaw)
Di naye shul (Warsaw)
Neue Jüdische Monatshefte (Berlin)
New York Times (New York)
Nowa Gazeta (Warsaw)
Oyfboy (Warsaw)

Preußische Jahrbücher (Berlin)
Reshumot (Odessa)
Roman-tsaytung (Warsaw)
Shul un dertsiung (Warsaw)
Shul un lebn (Warsaw)
Tageblat (New York)
Teater velt (Warsaw)
Unzer lebn (Warsaw)
Der veg (St Petersburg, Warsaw)
Yidish far ale (Warsaw)
Yidishe filologye (Warsaw)

Published Materials

Works by Noah Prylucki

Barg-aroyf. Warsaw: Nayer farlag, 1917.
Bay di kehile-valn. Warsaw: Lodzsher organizatsye fun der yidisher demokratisher folkspartey in poyln, 1936.
Ertselung vegen zieben gehangene. Warsaw: Ferlag byuro, 1908.
Farn mizbeyekh: gedikhtn, ershte serye. Warsaw: Ha-tsefira, 1908.
Dos gevet. Warsaw, 1923.
ed. *Goldene funken.* Warsaw: Ferlag byuro, 1909.
In poyln: kimat a publitsist togbukh, 1905–1911. Warsaw, 1921.
(Nojach Pryłucki) *Mowy.* Warsaw: Nakładem Radu Centralnej. Żydowskiego stronnicta ludowego w Polsce, 1920.
Natsionalizm un demokratizm (tsayt-artiklen). Warsaw: Yeshurun, 1907.
Noyekh prilutksis ksovim. Warsaw: 1917.
Noyekh prilutskis redes in varshever shtot-rat. Warsaw, 1922.
eds. Noyekh Prilutski and Shmuel Lehman. *Noyekh prilutskis zamlbikher far yidishn folklor, filologye un kultur-geshikhte.* Warsaw: Nayer farlag, 1912.
Sholem-yankev abramovitsh. Warsaw: Nayer farlag, 1920.
Tsum yidishn vokalizm: etyudn. Warsaw: Nayer farlag, 1920.
Yidish teater, 1901–1921. Bialystok: A. Albek, 1921.
Yidishe folkslider: gezamlt, derklert un aroysgegebn fun noyekh prilutski, vol. 1, *Religyezishe un yontevdike.* Warsaw: Farlag 'Bikher far ale,' 1911.
Yidishe folkslider. vol. 2. *I. Lider un mayselekh fun toyt. II.*
Balades un legendes mit un on a muser-haskl. Warsaw: Nayer farlag, 1913.
Der yidisher konsonantizm. Warsaw: Nayer farlag, 1917.
Yidish teater 1901–1921. Bialystok: A. Albek, 1921.

ed. *Der yunger gayst.* Warsaw: Progres, 1909.
Der zhurnalist: A zamlung aroysgegebn lekoved dem zhurnalistn-bal dem tsveytn tog peysakh 5672. Warsaw, 1912.

Works by Lazar Kahan
Di folksbildung bay laytn un bay unz. Lodz: Author, 1918.
Di lage un di oyfgabn fun yidishn handverker. Lodz: Author, 1918.

Works by H.D. Nomberg
Dos bukh felyetonen. Warsaw: Sh. Yatshkovski, 1924.
Y.L. Perets. Buenos Aires: Tsentral farband fun poylishe yidn in argentine, 1946.

Work by Saul Stupnicki (Polish; Yiddish: Shoyl Stupnitski)
Oyfn veg tsum folk. Warsaw: Nayer farlag, 1920.
eds. Hilel Tseytlin and Shoyl Stupnitski. *Ersht yudish entsiklopedish verterbukh.* Warsaw: Verlag 'Hantbücher,' 1917.

Secondary Sources

Abramowicz, Hirsz. *Profiles of a Lost World.* Ed. Dina Abramowicz and Jeffrey Shandler, transl. Eva Zeitlin Dobin. Detroit: YIVO and Wayne State University Press, 1999.
Abramsky, Chimen, Maciej Jachimczyk, and Antony Polonsky, eds. *The Jews in Poland.* Oxford: Basil Blackwell, 1986.
Abramson, Henry. *A Prayer for the Government: Ukrainians and Jews in Revolutionary Times, 1917–1920.* Cambridge, MA: Harvard University Press, 1999.
Aleksandrov, H. *Forsht ayer shtetl.* Minsk: Institut far vaysruslendisher kultur, 1928.
Almi, A. *Humoristishe shriftn.* Warsaw: A. Gitlin, 1928.
– *Mentshn un ideyen.* Warsaw: Goldfarb, 1933.
– 'Fun amolikn varshe.' *Der poylisher yid* 2 (1944): 27–30.
– *Momentn fun a lebn.* Buenos Aires: Tsentral farband fun poylishe yidn in argentine, 1948.
– *Letste gezangen.* Buenos Aires: Farband fun varshever un prager yidn in argentine, 1954.
Apenszlak, P. 'Ha-'itonut (ha-yehudit) be-polanit (be-varsha),' in *Entsiklopedya shel galuyot-varsha,* vol. 1, ed. Y. Grünbaum. Jerusalem and Tel Aviv: Encyclopaedia of the Jewish Diaspora, 1953, 505–14.

Armon, Witold, et al. *Historia Etnografi Polskiej.* Wróclaw: Zaklad narodowy Imienia Ossolinskich Wydawnictwo Polskiej Akademii Nauk, 1973.

Ascher, Abraham. *The Revolution of 1905: Russia in Disarray.* Stanford: Stanford University Press, 1988.

Aschheim, Steven. *Brothers and Strangers: The East-European Jew in German and German-Jewish Consciousness.* Madison: University of Wisconsin Press, 1982.

– 'Eastern Jews, German Jews and Germany's Ostpolitik in the First World War.' *Leo Baeck Institute Yearbook* (hereafter *LBIYB*) 28 (1983): 351–65.

Assaf, David, Israel Bartal, Shmuel Feiner, Yehuda Friedlander, Avner Holtzman, and Chava Turniansky, eds. *Mi-vilna le-yerushalayim: Mehkarim be-toldoteihem ve-tarbutam shel yehudei mizrah eiropa, mugashim le-profesor Shmuel Verses.* Jerusalem: Magnes, 2002.

Aster, Howard, and Peter J. Potichnyj, eds. *Ukrainian-Jewish Relations in Historical Perspective.* Edmonton: University of Alberta Press, 1990.

Auty, R. 'The Linguistic Revival among the Slavs of the Austrian Empire, 1780–1850: The Role of Individuals in the Codification and Acceptance of New Literary Languages.' *Modern Language Review* 53 (1958): 392–404.

Bacon, Gershon. *The Politics of Tradition: Agudat Yisrael in Poland, 1916–1939.* Jerusalem: Magnes, 1986.

– 'La société juive dans le royaume de la Pologne du Congrès (1860–1914),' in *Société juive à travers l'histoire,* ed. S. Trigano. Paris: Fayard, 1992, vol.1, 623–64.

– 'National Revival, Ongoing Acculturation: Jewish Education in Interwar Poland.' *Simon-Dubnow-Institut Jahrbuch* 1 (2002): 71–92.

– 'Poland from 1795 to 1939,' in *YIVO Encyclopedia of Jews in Eastern Europe,* ed. G.D. Hundert. New Haven: YIVO and Yale University Press, 2008, vol.2, 1390–1403.

Baker, Zachary. 'Art Patronage and Philistinism in Argentina: Maurycy Minkowski in Buenos Aires, 1930.' *Shofar* 19/3 (2001): 107–19.

Balberyszski, M. *Shtarker fun ayzn.* Tel Aviv: Ha-menorah, 1967.

– 'Di yidishe katedre baym vilner univerzitet.' *Driter oystralyish-yidisher almanakh* (1967): 376–83.

Bar-Sella, Shraga. *Bein sa'ar le-demama: hayav u-mishnato shel Hilel Tseytlin.* Tel Aviv: Kibuts he-me'uhad, 1999.

– 'On the Brink of Disaster: Hillel Zeitlin's Struggle for Survival in Poland.' *Polin* 11 (1998): 77–93.

Bartal, Yisrael, and Yisrael Gutman, eds. *Kiyum ve-shever: yehudei polin le-doroteihem.* Jerusalem: Merkaz Zalman Shazar le-toldot yisrael, 1997.

Bartoszewski, Władysław, and Antony Polonsky, eds. *The Jews in Warsaw.* Oxford: Institute for Polish-Jewish Studies, 1991.

Bauer, Ela. *Between Poles and Jews: The Development of Nahum Sokolow's Political Thought.* Jerusalem: Magnes, 2005.

Bechtel, Delphine. 'Les chercheurs en linguistique et histoire littéraire yiddish: une génération d'intellectuels engagés dans la première moitié du XXe siècle.' In *Ecriture de l'histoire et identité juive*, ed. Delphine Bechtel et al., Paris: Les Belles Lettres, 2003, 253–78.

– ed. *Ecriture de l'histoire et identité juive: l'Europe ashkénaze, XIXe–XXe siècle.* Paris: Les Belles Lettres, 2003.

Beder, L., and M. Yelin. 'Di letste yorn fun noyekh prilutskin.' *Sovetish heymland* 3 (March 1965): 146–8.

Behring, Eva, Ludwig Richter, and Wolfgang F. Schwarz, eds. *Geschichtliche Mythen in den Literaturen und Kulturen Ostmittel- und Suedosteuropas.* Stuttgart: Franz Steiner, 1999.

Belis, Shloyme. 'Dos gantse lebn farn mame-loshn.' *Folksshtime* (Buenos Aires), 13 Aug. 1966.

Ben-shem (Feldshuh), R. 'Ha'folkistim' (Folks-partey), in *Entsiklopedya shel galuyot-varsha.* Vol. 6, ed. Y. Grünbaum. Jerusalem and Tel Aviv: Encyclopaedia of the Jewish Diaspora, 1959.

Berditshevski, Mikhah Yosef (M.Y. Bin-Goryon), and Yosef Hayim Brener. *Halifat igrot (667–681).* Holon: Bet Devorah ve-Imanuel; and Tel Aviv: Reshafim, 1984.

Bergman, Eleonora, and Olga Zienkiewicz, eds. *Żydzi Warszawy.* Warsaw: Żydowski Instytut Historyczny, 2000.

Bergman, Olaf. *Narodowa Demokracja wobec problematyki żydowkiej w latach 1918–1929.* Poznań: Poznańskie, 1998.

Berkovitsh, Y.D. *Undzere rishoynim: Zikhroynes-dertseylungen vegn sholem aleykhem un zayn dor.* Tel Aviv: Ha-menora, 1966.

Berkowitz, Michael. 'Art in Zionist Popular Culture and Jewish National Self-Consciousness, 1897–1914.' *Studies in Contemporary Jewry* 6 (1990): 9–42.

Beyder, Khaym. 'Noyekh prilutskis briv tsu aren gurshteyn.' *Di pen* 32 (Summer 1997): 41–5.

Biale, David, ed. *Cultures of the Jews.* New York: Schocken, 2002.

Biber, Sh. *Der krizis fun yidishn politishn gedank: a vendung tsu der yidisher demokratye.* Warsaw, 1927.

Birnbaum, Pierre, and Ira Katznelson, eds. *Paths of Emancipation: Jews, State, and Citizenship.* Princeton: Princeton University Press, 1995.

Birnbaum, Solomon. 'Two Problems in Yiddish Linguistics,' in *The Field of Yiddish*, ed. U. Weinreich. New York: Linguistic Circle of New York, 63–72.

Blanke, Detlev. *Internationale Plansprachen.* Berlin: Akademie-Verlag, 1985.

Blejwas, Stanislaus A. 'Polish Positivism and the Jews.' *Jewish Social Studies* 46 (1984): 21–37.

– '"The Failure of Assimilation 1864–1895": Review of Alina Cała, *Asymilacja Żydów w Królestwie Polskim (1864–1897)* (Warsaw: Państwowy Instytut Wydawniczy, 1989).' *Polin* 8 (1994): 325–9.

Blobaum, Robert. *Rewolucja: Russian Poland, 1904–1907.* Ithaca: Cornell University Press, 1995.

Böhm, Adolf. *Die Zionistische Bewegung.* Vol. 1. Berlin: Jüdischer Verlag, 1935.

Bogen, Boris. *Born a Jew.* New York: Macmillan, 1930.

Bohachevsky-Chomiak, Martha, and Bernice Glazer Rosenthal, eds. *A Revolution of the Spirit: Crisis of Value in Russia, 1890–1918.* Trans. Marian Schwartz. Newtonville, MA: Oriental Research Partners, 1982.

Borenstein, Izhak. *Varshe fun nekhtn.* São Paulo: Author, 1967.

Botoshanski, Yankev. *Di lebnsgeshikhte fun a yidishn zhurnalist.* Buenos Aires, 1942.

Breuer, Mordkhe. 'Rabanim-doktorim be-polin-lita ba-yemei ha-kibush ha-germani, 1914–1918.' *Bar-Ilan* 24–5 (1989): 117–53.

Brock, Peter. 'Polish Nationalism,' in *Nationalism in Eastern Europe*, ed. Peter F. Sugar and Ivo J. Lederer. Seattle: University of Washington Press, 1969, 310–72.

Brown, Michael. *The Israeli-American Connection: Its Roots in the Yishuv, 1914–1945.* Detroit: Wayne State University Press, 1996.

Brzoza, Czesław. *Żydowska Mozaika Polityczna w Polsce, 1917–1927: Wybór Dokumentów.* Kraków: Księgarnia Akademicka, 2003.

Burke, Peter. *Languages and Communities in Early Modern Europe.* Cambridge: Cambridge University Press, 2004.

Chaver, Yael. 'From Mother Tongue to the Voice Within: The Marginalization of Yiddish in Zionist Palestine,' in *The Life and Times of Yiddish: Studies in the Past and Present of the Language*, ed. J.C. Landis. Flushing, NY: Yiddish Books, 2000, 145–76.

Clyne, M.G. *Language and Society in the German-Speaking Countries.* Cambridge: Cambridge University Press, 1984.

– ed. *Undoing and Redoing Corpus Planning.* Berlin: Mouton de Gruyter, 1997.

Cohen, Nathan. 'Zikhronot Tsvi Prilutski: Te'uda merateket le-heker "itonut yidish be-varsha,"' in *Mi-vilna le-yerushalayim: Mehkarim be-toldoteihem ve-tarbutam shel yehudei mizrah eiropa, mugashim le-profesor Shmuel Verses.* ed. David Assaf et al. Jerusalem: Magnes, 2002, 385–402.

– 'The Jews of Independent Poland: Linguistic and Cultural Changes,' in *Starting the Twenty-First Century*, ed. E. Krausz and G. Tulea. New Brunswick, NJ: Transaction Publishers, 2002, 161–75.

– *Sefer, sofer ve-'iton: Merkaz ha-tarbut ha-yehudit be-varsha, 1918–1942.* Jerusalem: Magnes, 2003.

Congress for Jewish Culture. *Yidishe prese in varshe*, vol. 2, *Fun noentn over.* New York: Author, 1956.

Coulmas, Flourian, ed. *With Forked Tongues.* Ann Arbor: Karoma, 1988.

Corrsin, Stephen D. 'Political and Social Change in Warsaw from the January 1863 Insurrection to the First World War: Polish Politics and the "Jewish Question."' Doctoral dissertation, University of Michigan, 1981.

– 'Polish-Jewish Relations before the First World War: The Case of the State Duma Elections in Warsaw.' *Gal-Ed* 11 (1989): 31–53.

– *Warsaw before the First World War: Poles and Jews in the Third City of the Russian Empire, 1880–1914.* Boulder: East European Monographs, 1989.

– 'Language Use in Cultural and Political Change in pre-1914 Warsaw: Poles, Jews, and Russification.' *Slavonic and East European Review* 68/1 (1990): 69–90.

– 'Works on Polish Jewry, 1990–1994: A Bibliography.' *Gal-Ed* 14 (1995): 131–233.

– 'The Jews, the Left, and the State Duma Elections in Warsaw in 1912: Selected Sources.' *Polin* 9 (1996): 45–54.

– '"The City of Illiterates"? Levels of Literacy among Poles and Jews in Warsaw, 1882–1914.' *Polin* 12 (1999): 221–41.

Davies, Norman. *Poland, Past and Present: A Select Biography of Works in English.* Newtonville, MA: Oriental Research Partners, 1972.

– 'Great Britain and the Polish Jews, 1918–1920.' *Journal of Contemporary History* 8 (1973): 119–42.

– *God's Playground: A History of Poland.* Oxford: Clarendon, 1981.

Dawidowicz, Lucy. *From That Place and Time.* New York: Norton, 1989.

– ed. *The Golden Tradition.* Boston: Beacon, 1967.

Druk, Dovid. *Tsu der geshikhte fun der yidisher prese.* Warsaw: Ha-tsefira, 1920.

Dubnow, Simon. *Nationalism and History.* Philadelphia: Jewish Publication Society of America, 1958.

– *Kniga zhizni: vospominaniia i razmyshleniia: materialy dlia istorii moego vremeni.* St Petersburg: Peterburgskoe vostokovedenie, 1998.

Eck, Nathan. 'The Educational Institutions of Polish Jewry (1921–1939).' *Jewish Social Studies* 9/1 (1947): 3–32.

Efron, John M. *Defenders of the Race: Jewish Doctors and Race Science in Fin-de-Siècle Europe.* New Haven: Yale University Press, 2004.

Eisenstein, Miriam. *Jewish Schools in Poland 1919–39.* New York: King's Crown Press, 1950.

Endelman, Todd M. 'Jewish Converts in Nineteenth-Century Warsaw: A Quantitative Analysis.' *Jewish Social Studies* 4/1 (1997): 28–59.

Estraikh, Gennadi. 'Languages of "Yehupets" Students.' *Eastern European Jewish Affairs* 22/1 (1992): 63–71.

– 'Pyrrhic Victories of Soviet Yiddish Language Planners.' *Eastern European Jewish Affairs* 23/2 (1993): 23–32.

– 'Yiddish Language Conference Aborted.' *Eastern European Jewish Affairs* 25/2 (1995): 91–6.

– 'On the Acculturation of Jews in Late Imperial Russia.' *La Rassegna Mensile Israel* 62/1–2 (1996): 217–26.

– *Soviet Yiddish: Language Planning and Linguistic Developments.* Oxford: Clarendon, 1999.

Ettinger, Shmuel. *Bein polin le-rusya.* Jerusalem: Merkaz Zalman Shazar le-toldot Yisra'el, 1994.

Fasold, R. *The Sociolinguistics of Society.* Oxford: Basil Blackwell, 1984.

Feldshuh, Ruvn. *Yidisher gezelshaftlekher leksikon: poyln,* vol. 1, *varshe.* Warsaw: Yidisher leksikografisher farlag, 1939.

Fellman, Jack. *The Revival of a Classical Tongue.* The Hague: Mouton, 1973.

Finkelstein, Chaim. *'Haynt': A tsaytung bay yidn, 1908–1939.* Tel Aviv: Velt-federatsye fun poylishe yidn, 1978.

Finkelshteyn, L. 'Inm amolikn varshe,' in Shloyme Mendelson, *Shloyme mendelson: zayn lebn un shafn.* New York: 'Unzer tsayt,' 1949, 77–99.

Fishman, David E. 'The Politics of Yiddish in Tsarist Russia,' in *From Ancient Israel to Modern Judaism: Intellect in Quest of Understanding – Essays in Honor of Marvin Fox,* ed. Jacob Neusner, Ernest S. Fredrichs, and Nahum M. Sarna. Providence: Brown University Press, 1989), 155–71.

– *Russia's First Modern Jews: The Jews of Shklov.* New York: New York University Press, 1995.

– *Embers Plucked from the Fire: The Rescue of Jewish Cultural Treasures in Vilna.* New York: YIVO, 1996.

– *Shaytlekh aroysgerisn fun fayer: dos oprateven yidishe kultur-oytsres in vilne.* New York: YIVO, 1996.

– *The Rise of Modern Yiddish Culture.* Pittsburgh: University of Pittsburgh Press, 2005.

Fishman, Joshua A. *Advances in the Creation and Revision of Language Systems.* The Hague: Mouton, 1977.

– *Ideology, Society and Language.* Ann Arbor: Karoma, 1987.

– ed. *Readings in the Sociology of Jewish Languages.* Leiden: E.J. Brill, 1985.

Flinker, David. 'Varshe,' in *'Arim ve-imahot be-yisra'el,* ed. J.L. Maimon. Jerusalem: Mosad ha-rav Kuk, 1945, vol. 3.

Flinker, David, Mordkhe Tsanin, and Sholem Rozenfeld, eds. *Di yidishe prese vos iz geven.* Tel Aviv: Velt-farband fun di yidishe zhurnalistn, 1975.

Fountain, Alvin Marcus. *Roman Dmowski: Politics, Tactics, Ideology, 1895–1907.* Boulder: East European Monographs, 1980.

Frankel, Jonathan. *Prophecy and Politics: Socialism, Nationalism, and the Russian Jews, 1862–1917.* Cambridge: Cambridge University Press, 1981.

– 'The Dilemmas of Jewish National Autonomism: The Case of the Ukraine 1917–1920,' in *Ukrainian-Jewish Relations in Historical Perspective,* ed. Howard Aster and Peter J. Potichnyj. Edmonton: University of Alberta Press, 1990, 263–79.

Freilich, Miri. 'Assimilationists in the Polish Freethinkers Movement.' *Gal-Ed* 12 (1991): 37–60.

Frieden, Ken. *Classic Yiddish Fiction: Abramovitsh, Sholem Aleichem, and Peretz.* Albany: State University of New York Press, 1995.

Frost, Shimon. 'Jewish School System in Interwar Poland,' in *The Jews in Poland,* ed. C. Abramsky, M. Jachimczyk, and A. Polonsky. Oxford: Basil Blackwell, 1986, 235–44.

– *Schooling as a Socio-Political Expression.* Jerusalem: Magnes, 1998.

Fuks, Leo, and Renate Fuks. 'Yiddish Publishing Activities in the Weimar Republic, 1920–1933.' *LBIYB* 32 (1988): 417–34.

Fuks, Marian. *Prasa żydowska w Warszawie, 1823–1939.* Warsaw: Państwowe Naukowe, 1979.

– 'Di yidishe prese in der poylisher shprakh.' *Bleter far geshikhte* 19 (1980): 181–218.

– 'Poczet Publicystów i Dziennikarzy żydowskich.' *Biuletyn żydowskiego Instytutu Historycznego w Polsce* 1–2/133–4 (1985): 69–72.

Garncarska-Kadari, Bina. *Di linke poyeley-tsien in poyln biz der tsveyter velt-milkhome.* Tel Aviv: Y.L. Perets, 1995.

Gassenschmidt, Christoph. *Jewish Liberal Politics in Tsarist Russia, 1900–1914.* New York: New York University Press, 1995.

Gatrell, Peter. *A Whole Empire Walking: Refugees in Russia during World War I.* Bloomington: Indiana University Press, 1999.

Gechtman, Roni. 'Socialist Mass Politics through Sport: The Bund's Morgnshtern in Poland, 1926–1939.' *Journal of Sport History* 26/2 (1999): 326–52.

– 'Conceptualizing National-Cultural Autonomy: From the Austro-Marxists to the Jewish Labor Bund.' *Simon-Dubnow-Institut Jahrbuch* 4 (2005): 17–49.

Gelber, Mark H., ed. *Identity and Ethos: A Festschrift for Sol Liptzin on the Occasion of His 85th Birthday.* New York: Peter Lang, 1986.

Gellner, Ernest. *Nations and Nationalism.* Oxford: Basil Blackwell, 1983.

Ginzburg, Shoel. *Amolike peterburg.* New York: Shoel Ginzburg shriftn-komitet, 1944.

Gitelman, Zvi, ed. *Jewish Nationality and Soviet Politics.* Princeton: Princeton University Press, 1972.

– *The Emergence of Jewish Politics: Bundism and Zionism in Eastern Europe.* Pittsburgh: University of Pittsburgh Press, 2003.

Glinert, Lewis, ed. *Hebrew in Ashkenaz.* New York and Oxford: Oxford University Press, 1993.

Glinert, Lewis, and Yosseph Shilhav. 'Holy Land, Holy Language: A Study of an UltraOrthodox Jewish Ideology.' *Language and Society* 20 (1991): 59–86.

Golczewski, Frank. *Polnisch-Jüdische Beziehungen, 1881–1922.* Wiesbaden: Franz Steiner, 1981.

Gold, David. 'Some Notes on Yiddish and Judezmo.' *History of European Ideas* 13/1–2 (1991): 41–9.

Goldberg, David, ed. *The Field of Yiddish, Fifth Collection.* Evanston: Northwestern University Press and YIVO, 1993.

Goldsmith, Emanuel. *Modern Yiddish Culture: The Story of the Yiddish Language Movement.* New York: Fordham University Press, 1997.

Gonen, Rivka, ed. *Back to the Shtetl: An-Sky and the Jewish Ethnographic Expedition, 1912–1914.* From the Collections of the State Ethnographic Museum in St Petersburg. Jerusalem: Israel Museum, 1994.

Gottesman, Itzik Nakhmen. *Defining the Yiddish Nation: The Jewish Folklorists of Poland.* Detroit: Wayne State University Press, 2003.

Gross, Jan. *Fear: Anti-Semitism in Poland after Auschwitz: An Essay in Historical Interpretation.* New York: Random House, 2006.

Groth, A.J. 'Polish Elections 1919–1928.' *Slavic Review* 24/4 (1965): 653–65.

Grünbaum, Yitshak. *Der tsaytvayliker yidisher natsional-rat un der seym-klub ba im. barikht fun der tetikeyt fun yanuar 1919 biz yuli 1923.* 2 vols. Warsaw, 1923.

– *Milhamot yehudei polania 5673–5700.* Jerusalem and Tel Aviv: Hotsa'at 'Haverim,' 1940–41.

– *Penei ha-dor.* Jerusalem: Ha-sifria ha-tsionit al yad hanhalat ha-histadrut ha-tsionit, 1957–60.

– *Ne'umim ba-seym ha-polani.* Jerusalem and Tel Aviv: M. Neuman, 1963.

Guesnet, François. *Polnische Juden im 19. Jahrhundert: Lebensbedingungen, Rechtsnormen und Organisation im Wandel.* Köln: Böhlau, 1998.

– '"Wir müssen Warschau unbedingt russisch machen": Die Mythologisierung der russisch-jüdischen Zuwanderung ins Königreich Polen zu Beginn unseres Jahrhunderts am Beispiel eines polnischen Trivialromans,' in *Geschichtliche Mythen in den Literaturen und Kulturen Ostmittel- und Suedosteuropas,* ed. Eva Behring, Ludwig Richter and Wolfgang F. Schwarz. Stuttgart: Franz Steiner, 1999, 99–116.

– 'Migration et Stéréotype: Le cas des juifs russes au Royaume de Pologne à la fin du XIXe siècle.' *Cahiers du Monde russe* 41/4 (2000): 505–18.

Guterman, Alexander. *Kehilat varsha bein shete milhamot ha-'olam.* Tel Aviv: Tel Aviv University Press, 1997.

– *Perakim be-toldot yehudei polin ba-'et ha-hadasha.* Jerusalem: Karmel, 1999.

Hafftka, Aleksander. 'Życie parlmentarne Żydów w Polsce Odrodzonej,' in *Żydzi w Polsce Odrodzonej,* ed. I. Schipper, A. Tartakower, A. Hafftka. Warsaw: 'Żydzi w Polsce Odrodzonej,' 1932–35, vol. 2, 286–311.

– 'Prasa żydowska w Polsce (do 1918 r.),' in *Żydzi w Polsce Odrodzonej,* ed. I. Schiper, A. Tartakower, and A. Hafftka. Warsaw: '*Żydzi* w Polsce Odrodzonej,' 1932–35, vol. 2, 148–61.

– 'Di yidishe politik in poyln,' in *Yidisher gezelshaftlekher leksikon: Poyln I Varshe,* R. Feldshuh, ed. Warsaw: Yidisher leksikografisher farlag, 1939, 157–212.

Hagen, William H. 'Before the "Final Solution": Toward a Comparative Analysis of Political Anti-Semitism in Interwar Germany and Poland.' *Journal of Modern History* 68/2 (1996): 351–81.

Halpern, Israel, ed. *Beit yisra'el be-polin.* Jerusalem: Youth Department of Zionist Organization, 1948 (vol. 1), 1953 (vol. 2).

Halpern, Leopold. *Polityka żydowska w Sejmie i Senacie Rzeczypospolitej Polskiej 1919–33.* Warsaw: Instytut Badan Spraw Narodowościowych, 1933.

Harshav, Benjamin. *Language in Time of Revolution.* Berkeley: University of California Press, 1993.

Hartglas, Apolinary. *Na pograniczu dwóch światów.* Ed. Jolanta Żyndul. Warsaw: Oficyna Wydawnicza, 1996.

Hass, Ludwik. *Wybory Warszawskie 1918–1926.* Warsaw: Państwowe Naukowe, 1972.

'Haynt' yoyvl-bukh (1908–1938). Warsaw, 1938.

Heftman, Yoysef. 'Tsvi prilutski,' in *Pinkas Kremenits,* ed. A.Sh. Shteyn. Tel Aviv: Irgun 'olei kremenits be-yisra'el, 1954, 189–90.

Heinze, Wolfgang. 'Die polnisch-jiddische Presse.' *Preußische Jahrbücher* 163 (Jan.–March 1916): 496–509.

– 'Internationale jüdische Beziehungen.' *Preußische Jahrbücher* 168 (April 1917): 340–66.

Heller, Celia. *On the Edge of Destruction.* New York: Columbia University Press, 1977.

Hertz, Y.Sh. *Di geshikhte fun bund in lodzsh.* New York: 'Undzer tsayt,' 1966.

Higham, John. *Strangers in the Land.* New Brunswick, NJ: Rutgers University Press, 1955.

Hirszhorn, Samuel. 'Początki żydowskiego ruchu narodowego w Polsce.' *Nasz Przegląd,* 18 Sept. 1938.

– *Historja Żydów w Polsce: od Sejmu Czteroletnego do wojny europejskiej (1788–1914).* Warsaw: B-cia Lewin-Epstein, 1921.

Hobsbawm, E.J. *Nations and Nationalism since 1780.* Cambridge: Cambridge University Press, 1990.

Hobsbawm, E.J., and T. Ranger, eds. *The Invention of Tradition.* Cambridge: Cambridge University Press, 1993.

Horak, Stephan. *Poland and Her National Minorities, 1919–39.* New York: Vantage, 1961.

Howe, Irving. *World of Our Fathers.* New York: Schocken, 1989.

Hoykhgelernter, H. 'Kurtse geshikhte fun kremenits,' in *Kremenits, vizshgorodek un potshayev yizker-bukh,* ed. Falik Lerner. Buenos Aires: landslayt-fareyn fun kremenits un umgegnt in argentine, 1965, 13–82.

Hroch, Miroslav. 'The Social Interpretation of Linguistic Demands in European National Movements.' *EUI Working Paper EUF No.94/1* (1994).

Hundert, Gershon David. *Jews in Poland-Lithuania in the Eighteenth Century: A Genealogy of Modernity.* Berkeley and Los Angeles: University of California Press, 2004.

Hundert, Gershon David, and Gershon C. Bacon. *The Jews in Poland Russia: Bibliographical Essays.* Bloomington: Indiana University Press, 1984.

Hutton, Christopher. 'Noyekh Prylucki: Philosopher of Language,' in *History of Yiddish Studies,* ed. Dov-Ber Kerler. Chur, Switzerland: Harward Academic, 1991, 15–24.

– 'Normativism and the Notion of Authenticity in Yiddish Linguistics,' in *The Field of Yiddish, Fifth Collection,* ed. D. Goldberg. Evanston: Northwestern University Press and the YIVO, 1993.

– *Linguistics and the Third Reich: Mother-Tongue Fascism, Race, and the Science of Language.* London and New York: Routledge, 1998.

Isaacs, Miriam, and Lewis Glinert, eds. *Pious Voices: Languages among Ultra-Orthodox Jews.* Special issue of the *International Journal of the Sociology of Language* 138 (1999).

Janowsky, Oscar I. *The Jews and Minority Rights, 1898–1919.* New York: Columbia University Press, 1933.

Jewish People's Relief Committee. *Di pipels relief fun amerike: faktn un dokumentn, 1915–1924.* New York: Author, 1924.

Johnpoll, Bernard K. *The Politics of Futility.* Ithaca: Cornell University Press, 1967.

Jusdanis, Gregory. *Belated Modernity and Aesthetic Culture.* Minneapolis: University of Minnesota Press, 1991.

Kaganowski, Ephraim. *Yidishe shrayber in der heym.* Paris: Ofsnay, 1956.

Karlip, Joshua. 'At the Crossroads between War and Genocide: A Reassessment of Jewish Ideology in 1940.' *Jewish Social Studies* 11/2 (2005): 170–201.

Kassow, Samuel D.(Yidish: Shmuel D. Kasov). *Students, Professors, and the State in Tsarist Russia.* Berkeley: University of California Press, 1989.

– 'Zalmen reyzen un zayn gezelshaftlekh-politishe arbet, 1915–1922.' *YIVO-bleter* 2 (1994): 67–97.

Kats, Hirsh-Dovid. 'Naye gilgulim fun alte makhloykesn: di litvishe norme un di sikhsukhim vos arum ir.' *YIVO-bleter* 2 (1994): 205–57.

– 'Kapitelekh yidish: A merkvirdike froy.' *Forverts,* 17 March 2000.

Katsherginski, Sh. *Khurbn vilne.* New York: United Vilner Relief Committee, 1947.

– *Tsvishn hamer un serp: Tsu der geshikhte fun der likvidatsye fun der yidisher kultur in sovetn-rusland.* Paris, 1949.

Katz, Dovid. (Yiddish: Hirsh-Dovid Kats). 'On Yiddish, in Yiddish and for Yiddish: 500 Years of Yiddish Scholarship,' in *Identity and Ethos: A Festschrift for Sol Liptzin on the Occasion of His 85th Birthday,* ed. M.H. Gelber. New York, Berne, and Frankfurt am Main: Peter Lang, 1986, 23–36.

Kazdan, Khayim Shloyme. *Di geshikhte fun yidishn shulvezn in umophengikn poyln.* Mexico City: Gezelshaft 'Kultur un hilf,' 1947.

– *Fun kheyder un 'shkoles' biz tsisho.* Mexico City: Gezelshaft 'Kultur un hilf,' 1956.

Kellman, Ellen Deborah. 'The Newspaper Novel in the Jewish Daily *Forward*: Fiction as Entertainment and Serious Literature.' Doctoral dissertation, Columbia University, 2000.

– 'Dos yidishe bukh alarmirt.' *Polin* 16 (2003): 213–41.

Kerler, Dov-Ber, ed. *History of Yiddish Studies.* Chur, Switzerland: Harward Academic, 1991.

– *The Origins of Modern Literary Yiddish.* New York: Clarendon, 1995.

– *The Politics of Yiddish: Studies in Language, Literature, and Society.* Walnut Creek, CA: Altamira Press, 1998.

Kestin, Lipe, ed. *In shturem.* Warsaw: Farlag yungt, 1917.

– ed. *Naye himlen: Literarish zamelbukh.* Warsaw: L. Kestin, 1921.

Kiel, Mark W. 'The Ideology of the Folks-Partey.' *Soviet Jewish Affairs* 2 (1975): 75–89.

– 'Vox Populi, Vox Dei: The Centrality of Peretz in Jewish Folkloristics.' *Polin* 7 (1992): 88–120.

Kieniewicz, Stefan. 'Review of Stephen D. Corrsin, *Warsaw before the First World War: Poles and Jews in the Third City of the Russian Empire, 1880–1914.*' *Polin* 8 (1994): 388–92.

King, Robert, and Alice Farber. 'Yiddish and the Settlement History of Ashkenazic Jews.' *Mankind Quarterly* 24/4 (1984): 393–425.

Kirzhnits, A. *Di yidishe prese in der gevezener rusisher imperye (1823–1916).* Moscow, Kharkov, and Minsk: Tsentral felker-farlag fun fssr, 1930.

Klausner, Yisrael. 'Halutsei ha-dibur ha-'ivri be-'artsot ha-gola.' *Leshonenu la-'am* 15/1–2 (1966): 3–47.

Kmiecik, Zenon. 'Prasa polska w królestwie polskim i imperium rosyjskim w latach 1865–1904,' in Zenon Kmiecik, *Prasa polska w latach 1864–1918*. Warsaw: Państwowe Naukowe, 1976, 11–57.

– *Prasa polska w rewolucji 1905–1907*. Warsaw: Państwowe Wydawnictwo Naukowe, 1980.

– et al. *Prasa polska w latach 1864–1918*. Warsaw: Państwowe Naukowe, 1976.

Kohn, Hans. *Pan-Slavism: Its History and Ideology*. New York: Bantam, 1960.

Konopczynski, Władysław, et al. *Polski słownik biograficzny*. Kraków: Nakl. Polskiej Akademii Umiejetności, 1935–1991.

Korzec, Pawel. *Juifs en Pologne*. Paris: Presses de la fondation nationale des sciences politiques, 1980.

Kotowski, Albert S. *Polens Politik gegenüber seiner deutschen Minderheit 1919–1939*. Wiesbaden: Harrassowitz, 1998.

Krausz, Ernest, and Gitta Tulea, eds. *Starting the Twenty-Firsty Century*. New Brunswick, NJ: Transaction Publishers, 2002.

Kremenits, vizshgorodek un potshayev yizker-bukh. Falik Lerner, ed. Buenos Aires: Landslayt-farband fun kremenits un umgegnt in argentine, 1965.

Kruk, Herman. *Togbukh fun vilner geto*. New York: YIVO, 1961.

Kuznitz, Cecile. 'The Origins of Jewish Scholarship and the YIVO Institute for Jewish Research.' Doctoral dissertation, Stanford University, 2000.

Lachower, F., ed. *Igrot Hayim Nahman Bialik*. 5 vols. Tel Aviv: Devir, 1937–39.

Landau, Moshe. *Mi'ut le'umi lohem: Ma'avak yehudei polin ba-shanim 1918–1928*. Jerusalem: Merkaz Zalman Shazar, 1986.

Landis, Joseph C.,ed. *The Life and Times of Yiddish: Studies in the Past and Present of the Language*. Flushing, NY: Yiddish Books, 2000.

Landoy, Alfred. 'Bamerkungen tsu noyekh prilutskis "yidishe folkslider,"' *Yidishe filologye* 1 (1924): 151–60.

Lazar, Izidor. 'Kinstler un verk noyekh prilutski.' *Roman-tsaytung* 2/33(67) (Aug./Sept. 1908), 1031–38.

Leikowicz, Ch., ed. *Lite*. 2 vols. Tel Aviv: I.L. Peretz, 1965.

Lempert, Yisroel (Yiddish; Lithuanian: Izraelis Lempertas). 'Der goyrl fun yivo in historishn iberbrokh (1939–1941).' *YIVO-bleter* 3 (1997): 9–42.

Lempertiene, Larisa, ed. *Vilniaus Zydu intelektualinis gyvenimas*. Vilnius: Mokslo aidai, 2004.

Lerski, George J., and Halina T. Lerski. *Jewish-Polish Coexistence, 1772–1939*. Westport: Greenwood, 1986.

Leslie, R.F., ed. *The History of Poland since 1863*. Cambridge: Cambridge University Press, 1980.

Lev, Simkhe. *Prokim yidishe geshikhte.* Brooklyn: Shulsinger Bros., 1941.

Levin, Dov. 'Tsvishn hamer un serp.' *YIVO-bleter* 46 (1975): 78–97.

– *The Lesser of Two Evils.* Philadelphia and Jerusalem: Jewish Publication Society, 1995.

– 'The Jews of Vilna under Soviet Rule, 19 September–28 October 1939.' *Polin* 9 (1996): 107–37.

– 'Lithuania,' in *YIVO Encyclopedia of Jews in Eastern Europe,* ed. G.D. Hundert. New Haven: YIVO and Yale University Press, 2008, vol. 2, 1068–75.

Levin, Sabina. *Perakim be-toldut ha-hinuh ha-yehudi be-polin be-me'a ha-tesha-'esre uve-reshit ha-me'a ha-'esrim.* Tel Aviv: Center for the History of Polish Jewry, Diaspora Research Institute, Tel Aviv University, 1987.

Levin, Shmarya. *The Autobiography of Shmarya Levin.* Translated and edited by Maurice Samuel. Philadelphia: Jewish Publication Society, 1967.

Levinson, Avraham. *Toldot yehudei varsha.* Tel Aviv: 'Am 'oved, 1953.

Lewin, Isaac. *The Jewish Community in Poland.* New York: Philosophical Library, 1985.

– *A History of Polish Jewry during the Revival of Poland.* New York: Shengold, 1990.

Lewit, Tonja S. 'Die Entwicklung des jüdischen Volksbildungswesens in Polen.' Doctoral dissertation, Thüringische Landesuniversität zu Jena, 1931.

Lichten, Joseph. 'Notes on the Assimilation and Acculturation of Jews in Poland, 1863–1943,' in *The Jews in Poland.* ed. C. Abramsky, M. Jachimczk, and A. Polonsky. Oxford: Basil Blackwell, 1986, 106–29.

'List (Tentative) of Jewish Cultural Treasures in Axis-Occupied Countries.' Commission on Jewish Cultural Reconstruction. Supplement to *Jewish Social Studies* 8/1 (1946).

Liekis, Sarunas. 'Jewish-Polish Relations and the Lithuanian Authorities in Vilna 1939–1940.' *Polin* 19 (2007): 521–36.

Lockwood, W.B. *An Informal History of the German Language.* Oxford and London: Basil Blackwell, André Deutsch, 1985.

Lukin, Benjamin. 'From Folklore to Folk: An-Sky and Jewish Ethnography,' in *Back to the Shtetl: An-Sky and the Jewish Ethnographic Expedition, 1912–1914. From the Collections of the State Ethnographic Museum in St Petersburg,* ed. R. Gonen. Jerusalem: Israel Museum, 1994, xiv.

Mab, A. *Politish-ekonomish verterbukh.* Warsaw: Kultur-lige, 1936.

Magosci, Paul Robert. *A History of Ukraine.* Toronto: University of Toronto Press, 1996.

Maimon, Judah Leib, ed. *'Arim ve-imahot be-yisrael.* Jerusalem: Mosad ha-rav Kuk, 1945.

Mandelman, Moyshe. 'In freyd un leyd tsvishn litvishe yidn (fun 1938 biz

1940),' in *Lite*, ed. Mendel Sudarsky et al. New York: Jewish-Lithuanian Cultural Society 'Lite,' 1951, 1333–58.

Marcus, Joseph. *Social and Political History of the Jews in Poland, 1919–1939*. Berlin: Mouton, 1983.

Mark, Yudl. 'Noyekh prilutski: der kemfer un der forsher.' *Tsukunft* (Feb. 1945): 100–3.

– 'Noyekh prilutski (1882–1944).' *YIVO-bleter* 26 (1945): 79–95.

– 'Di geshikhte fun yidishn oysleyg gor bekitser.' *Yidishe shprakh* 12/1 (1952): 23–9.

– *Gramatik fun der yidisher klal-shprakh*. New York: Alveltlekher yidisher kultur-kongres, 1978.

Mauersberg, Stanisław. *Szkolnictwo poweszechne dla mniejszości narodwych w Polsce w latach 1918–1939*. Wrocław: Polskiej akademii nauk, 1968.

Mayzil, Nakhmen. 'Noyekh prilutski.' *Yidishe kultur* (Jan. 1945): 25–30.

– *Geven a mol a lebn: Dos yidishe kultur-lebn in poyln tsvishn beyde velt-milkhomes*. Buenos Aires: Tsentral-farband fun poylishe yidn in argentine, 1951.

McReynolds, Louise. *The News under Russia's Old Regime*. Princeton: Princeton University Press, 1991.

Meller, Haya. 'Mifleget ha-folkistim (folkspartey) be-polin [1915–1939].' Doctoral dissertation, Bar-Ilan University, 2004.

Mendelsohn, Ezra. 'Jewish Assimilation in Lvov: The Case of Wilhelm Feldman.' *Slavic Review* 28 (1969): 577–90.

– *Class Struggle in the Pale*. Cambridge: Cambridge University Press, 1970.

– *Zionism in Poland: The Formative Years, 1915–1926*. New Haven and London: Yale University Press, 1981.

– *The Jews of East Central Europe between the World Wars*. Bloomington: Indiana University Press, 1983.

– 'Reflections on East European Jewish Politics in the Twentieth Century.' *YIVO Annual* 20 (1991): 23–37.

– *On Modern Jewish Politics*. New York and Oxford: Oxford University Press, 1993.

Mendelson, Shloyme. *Shloyme mendelson: zayn lebn un shafn*. New York: 'Unzer tsayt,' 1949.

Menes, Abraham. *Der yidisher gedank in der nayer tsayt*. New York: Congress for Jewish Culture, 1957.

Micgiel, John, Robert Scott, and H.B. Segel, eds. *Conference on Poles and Jews: Myth and Reality in the Historical Context (1983: Columbia University)*. New York: Institute on East Central Europe, Columbia University, 1986.

Michels, Tony. *A Fire in Their Hearts: Yiddish Socialists in New York*. Cambridge: Harvard University Press, 2005.

Mintz, Matityahu. *Ber Borokhov: Ha-ma'agal ha-rishon, 1900–1906.* Tel Aviv: Tel Aviv University Press, 1976.

Mintz, Matityahu, and Tseviah Balshan. *Igrot Ber Borokhov, 1897–1917.* Tel Aviv: Am Oved, 1989.

Miron, Dan. *A Traveler Disguised: A Study in the Rise of Modern Yiddish Fiction in the Nineteenth Century.* New York: Schocken, 1973.

– 'Folklore and Antifolklore in the Yiddish Fiction of the Haskalah,' in *Studies in Jewish Folklore,* ed. F. Talmage. Cambridge, MA: Association for Jewish Studies, 1980, 219–49.

Moore, Clare, ed. *The Visual Dimension: Aspects of Jewish Art.* Boulder: Westview, 1993.

Mukdoni, Alexander. 'Zikhroynes fun a yidishn teater-kritiker (yidisher teater in poyln fun 1909 biz 1915),' in *Arkhiv far der geshikhte fun yidishn teater un drame,* ed. Y. Shatski. Vilna and New York: YIVO, 1930, 341–4.

– *In varshe un in lodzh.* Buenos Aires: Tsentral farband fun poylishe yidn in argentine, 1955.

Nartonowicz-Kot, Maria. 'Obliczne polityczne samorządu miejskiego Łódzi w latach 1919-1939.' *Rocznik Łódzki* 31 (1982): 99–130.

Nathans, Benjamin. 'Integration and Modernity in Fin-de-Siècle Russia,' in *The Emergence of Jewish Politics: Bundism and Zionism in Eastern Europe,* ed. Z. Gitelman. Pittsburgh: University of Pittsburgh Press, 2003, 20–34.

– *Beyond the Pale: The Jewish Encounter with Late Imperial Russia.* Berkeley: University of California Press, 2004.

Netzer, Shlomo. *Ma'avak yehudei polin 'al zekhuyoteihem ha-'ezrahiot ve-ha-le'umiot 1918–1922.* Tel Aviv: Tel Aviv University Press, 1980.

– 'Yitshak Grinboym ke-ish tsa'ir: tsmihato shel manhig tsioni be-polin.' *Kivunim* (Nov. 1980): 73–92.

Neusner, Jacob, Ernest S. Frerichs, and Nahum M. Sarna, eds. *From Ancient Israel to Modern Judaism: Intellect in Quest of Understanding – Essays in Honor of Marvin Fox.* Providence: Brown University, 1989.

Niger, Shmuel. *Der pinkes.* Vilna: B. Kletskin, 1913.

Niger, Shmuel, and Yankev Shatski, eds. *Leksikon fun der nayer yidisher literatur.* New York: Alveltlekher yidisher kultur-kongres, 1956–81.

Nir Rafalkes, Nahum. *Ershte yorn: in rod fun dor un bavegung.* Translated from Hebrew by Y. Bregman. Tel Aviv: I.L. Peretz, 1960–66.

Nissenbaum, Isaac. *Alei heldi.* Jerusalem: R. Mas, 1968.

Ochs, Michael Jerry. 'St Petersburg and the Jews of Russian Poland, 1862–1905.' Doctoral dissertation, Harvard University, 1986.

Olejnik, Leszek. 'The Emergence of the Yiddish Press in Łódź.' *Polin 6* (1991): 105–18.

Opalski, Magdalena, and Israel Bartal. *Poles and Jews: A Failed Brotherhood.* Hanover, NH: Brandeis University Press, 1992.

Orbach, Alexander. *New Voices of Russian Jewry.* Leiden: E.J. Brill, 1980.

Picchio, Riccardo, and Harvey Goldblatt, eds. *Aspects of the Slavic Language Question.* vol. 1. New Haven: Yale Concilium on International and Area Studies, 1984.

Peltz, Rakhmiel. 'The Dehebraization Controversy in Soviet Yiddish Language Planning: Standard or Symbol?' in *Readings in the Sociology of Jewish Languages,* ed. J.A. Fishman. Leiden: E.J. Brill, 1985, 125–50.

– 'The Undoing of Language Planning from the Vantage of Cultural History: Two Twentieth-Century Yiddish Examples,' in *Undoing and Redoing Corpus Planning,* ed. M. Clyne. Berlin: Mouton de Gruyter, 1997, 327–56.

Pilovski, Arye-Leyb. *Tsvishn yo un neyn: Yidish un yidish-literatur in erets-yisroel, 1907–1948.* Tel Aviv: Veltrat far yidish un yidisher kultur, 1986.

Pinye, Kats, Motl Zakin, Gedalye Kalikshteyn, and Shmuel Kaminski, eds. *Pinkes Varshe.* Buenos Aires: Landslayt-fareyn fun varshe un umgegnt in argentine, 1955.

Pipes, Richard. 'Catherine II and the Jews: The Origins of the Pale of Settlement.' *Soviet Jewish Affairs* 5/2 (1975): 3–20.

Pograbinsky, J. 'Ha-'itonut be-'ivrit (be-varsha),' in *Entsiklopedya ha-galuyot-varsha.* Vol. 1, ed. Y. Grünbaum. Jerusalem and Tel Aviv: Encyclopaedia of the Jewish Diaspora, 1959, 479–94.

Polonsky, Antony. *Politics in Independent Poland, 1921–1939.* London: Oxford University Press, 1972.

Porter, Brian. 'Social Darwinism without Empiricism, Romanticism without Ethics: Polish National Democracy and the Concept of the "Nation," 1863–1905.' Doctoral dissertation, University of Wisconsin, 1994.

– *When Nationalism Began to Hate: Imagining Modern Politics in Nineteenth-Century Poland.* New York: Oxford University Press, 2000.

Prager, Moyshe. 'Dos yidishe togblat,' in *Yidishe prese in varshe,* vol. 2, *Fun noentn over.* New York: Congress for Jewish Culture, 1956, 443–534.

Prokop-Janiec, Eugenia. *Polish-Jewish Literature in the Interwar Years.* Syracuse: Syracuse University Press, 2003, translation by Abe Shenitzer of *Miedzywojenna literatura polsko- żydowska jako zjawisko kulturowe i artystyczne* (Kraków: 'Universitas,' 1992).

Rabinowicz, Harry M. *The Legacy of Polish Jewry.* New York: Thomas Yoseloff, 1965.

Radomski, Grzegorz. *Narodowa Demokracja wobec problematyki mniejszości narodowych w Drugiej Rzeczypospolitej w latach 1918–1926.* Toruń: Adam Marszałek, 2000.

Radzik, Tadeusz. *Żydzi w Lublinie.* Lublin: Uniwersytetu Marii Curie-Skłodowskiej, 1995.

Rak, Elimeylekh. *Zikhroynes fun a yidishn hantverker-tuer.* Buenos Aires: Tsentral-farband fun poylishe yidn in argentine, 1958.

Ran, Leyzer. *Ash fun yerushalayim de'lite.* New York: Vilner Farlag, 1959.

Ravitsh, Meylekh. *Mayn leksikon,* 5 vols. Montreal, 1945.

Regev, Yosef. 'Ha-'itonut be-yidish,' in *Entsiklopedya shel galuyot-varsha,* vol. 1, ed. Y. Grünbaum. Jerusalem and Tel Aviv: Encyclopaedia of the Jewish Diaspora, 1959, 495–504.

Reyzen, Zalmen. *Gramatik fun der yidisher shprakh.* Vilna: Sh. Shrebek, 1920.

– *Leksikon fun der yidisher literatur, prese un filologye.* 4 vols. Vilna: B. Kletzkin, 1930.

– *Yidishe literatur un yidishe shprakh.* vol. 24. *Musterverk fun der yidisher literatur,* ed. Sh. Rozhanski. Buenos Aires: Literatur-gezelshaft baym YIVO in argentine, 1965.

Rogozik, Janina Katarzyna. 'Bernard Singer, the Forgotten "Most Popular Jewish Reporter of the Inter-War Years in Poland."' *Polin* 12 (1999): 179–97.

Rosman, Moshe. 'Innovative Tradition: Jewish Culture in the Polish-Lithuanian Commonwealth,' in *Cultures of the Jews,* ed. D. Biale. New York: Schocken, 2002, 519–70.

– 'Poland before 1795,' in *YIVO Encyclopedia of Jews in Eastern Europe,* ed. G.D. Hundert. New Haven: YIVO and Yale University Press, 2008, vol. 2, 1381–9.

Roth, Paul. *Die politische Entwicklung in Kongreß-Polen während der deutschen Okkupation.* Leipzig: K.F. Koehler, 1919.

Rothstein, Robert A. 'Spelling and Society: The Polish Orthographic Controversy of the 1930s.' *Papers in Slavic Philology* 1 (1977): 225–36.

Rozen, Ber Y. *Tlomatske 13.* Buenos Aires: Tsentral-farband fun poylishe yidn in argentine, 1950.

– *Portretn.* Buenos Aires: Tsentral-farband fun poylishe yidn in argentine, 1956.

Rozhanski, Shmuel, ed. *H.d. nomberg oysgeklibene shriftn.* Buenos Aires: Argentinian Division of the Alvetlekher yidisher kultur kongres, 1958.

– ed. *Varshe in der yidisher literatur.* vol. 80, *Musterverk fun der yidisher literatur.* Buenos Aires: Literatur-gezelshaft baym YIVO in argentine, 1979.

Rudnicki, Szymon. 'From "Numerus Clausus" to "Numerus Nullus."' *Polin* 2 (1987): 246–68.

– *Żydzi w parlamencie II Rzeczypospolitej.* Warsaw: Sejmowe, 2004.

Ruud, Charles A. 'The Printing Press as an Agent of Political Change in Early Twentieth-Century Russia.' *Russian Review* 40/4 (1981): 378–96.

Sandrow, Nahma. *Vagabond Stars: A World History of Yiddish Theater.* Syracuse: Syracuse University Press, 1996.

Schaechter, Mordkhe. 'Tsum akhtsikstn yoyvl fun der tshernovitser shprakh-konferents. Mates mizeses farteydikung fun der yidisher shprakh.' *Afn shvel* 271 (1988): 1–4.

– *Der eynheytlekher yidisher oysleyg.* New York: YIVO and the Yiddish Language Resource Center of the League for Yiddish, 1999.

Schapiro, Robert Moses. 'Jewish Self-government in Poland: Lodz, 1914–1939.' Doctoral dissertation, Columbia University, 1987.

Schipper, Ignacy, A. Tartakower, Aleks. Hafftka, eds. *Żydzi w Polsce Odrodzonej.* Warsaw: 'Żydzi w Polsce Odrodzonej,' 1932.

Schwarzbart, Isaac. *Tsvishn beyde velt-milkhomes.* Buenos Aires: Tsentral-farband fun poylishe yidn in argentine, 1958.

Segal, Simon. *The New Poland and the Jews.* New York: Lee Furman, 1938.

Sejm Ustawodawczy. Sprawozdanie stenograficzne. (Transcript of the Polish parliament's sessions.) Warsaw: Sejm, 1918–1938.

Seltzer, Robert M. 'Jewish Liberalism in Late Tsarist Russia.' *Contemporary Jewry* 9 (1987–88): 47–66.

Senn, Alfred Erich. *Lithuania 1940: Revolution from Above.* Amsterdam and New York: Rodopi, 2007.

Shandler, Jeffrey. *Adventures in Yiddishism.* Berkeley: University of California Press, 2006.

– ed. *Awakening Lives: Autobiographies of Jewish Youth in Poland before the Holocaust.* New Haven: Yale University Press, 2002.

Shatski, Yankev (Jacob Shatzky), ed. *Arkhiv far der geshikhte fun yidishn teater un drame.* Vilna and New York: YIVO, 1930.

– 'Yidishe politik un poyln tsvishn di tsvey velt-milkhomes,' in vol. 9 (Yidn, vol. 4), cols. 195–248. *Algemeyne entsiklopedye.* New York: CYCO, 1950.

– *Di geshikhte fun yidn in varshe.* 3 vols. New York: YIVO, 1953.

Shevelov, George Y. *The Ukrainian Language in the First Half of the Twentieth Century (1900–1941).* Cambridge, MA: Harvard University Press, 1989.

Shmeruk, Chone. (In English titles, Khone Shmeruk in Yiddish ones, and Hone Shmeruk in Hebrew.) 'A Pioneering Study of the Warsaw Jewish Press.' *Soviet Jewish Affairs* 11/ 3 (1981): 36–53.

– *Prokim fun der yidisher literatur-geshikhte.* Jerusalem: Yiddish Department, Hebrew University; and Tel Aviv: Y.L. Perets, 1988.

– 'Hebrew-Yiddish-Polish: A Trilingual Jewish Culture,' in *The Jews of Poland between Two World Wars,* ed. Yisrael Gutman, Ezra Mendelsohn, Jehuda Reinharz, and Chone Shmeruk. Hanover and London: University Press of New England, 1989, 295–311.

– 'Sholem Aleichem and America.' *YIVO Annual* 20 (1991): 211–38.

– 'Strikhn tsu der geshikhte fun dem yidishn literarishn tsenter in varshe,' in *Prokim fun der yidisher literatur-geshikhte,* 292–308.

Shochat, Aziel. 'Jews, Lithuanians and Russians 1939–1941,' in *Jews and Non-Jews in Eastern Europe (1918–1945)*, ed. Bela Vago and George L. Mosse. New Brunswick, NJ: Transaction Books, 1974, 301–14.

Shteyn, A.Sh., ed. *Pinkas Kremenits.* Tel Aviv: Irgun 'olei kremenits be-yisrael, 1954.

Shtif, Nokhem. 'Tsu der historisher antviklung fun yidishn oysleyg.' *Di yidishe shprakh* 2/1–2(8–9) (1928): 33–60.

– 'How I Became a Yiddish Linguist,' in *The Golden Tradition*, ed. L.S. Dawidowicz. Boston: Beacon, 1967, 257–63.

Shulman, V. 'Zayn lebn un veg,' in Shloyme Mendelson, *Shloyme mendelson: zayn lebn un shafn.* New York: 'Unzer tsayt,' 1949, 11–34.

Silber, Marcos. 'Shepolin ha-hadasha tiye em tova lekhol yeladeha.' Doctoral dissertation, Tel Aviv University, 2001.

– 'Reshuyot germaniot, reshuyot polaniot ve-takanon ha-kehila ha-yehudit be-milhemet ha-'olam ha-rishona.' *Gal-Ed* 18 (2002): 173–86.

– '"Ha-legionot shel has": nisayon be-milhemet ha-'olam ha-rishona la'asot et ha-yehudim 'uma mamlakhtit,' in *'Olam yashan adam hadash: kehilot yisra'el be'idan ha-modernizatsya*, ed. E. Tsur. Be'er Sheva: Mehon Ben-Guryon, 2005, 5–19.

– 'Ruling Practices and Multiple Cultures: Jews, Poles, and Germans in Łódź during WWI.' *Simon Dubnow Insitute Yearbook* 5 (2006): 189–208.

Singer, Bernard. *Moje Nalewki.* Warsaw: Czytelnik, 1993.

Slutsky, Yehuda. *Ha-'itonut ha-yehudit-rusit ba-me'a ha-tesha'esre.* Jerusalem: Bialik Institute, 1970.

– *Ha-'itonut ha-yehudit-rusit be-reshit ha-me'a ha-'esrim.* Tel Aviv: ha-agudah le-heker toldot ha-yehudim, ha-makhon le-heker ha-tefutsot, 1978.

Smogorzewska, Małgorzata, ed. *Posłowie i Senatorowie Rzeczypospolitej Polskiej 1919–1939: Słownik biograficzny.* Warsaw: Sejmowe, 2000.

Soussloff, Catherine M., ed. *Jewish Identity in Modern Art History.* Berkeley: University of California Press, 1999.

Stampfer, Shaul. '"Heder" Study, Knowledge of Torah, and the Maintenance of Social Stratification in Traditional East European Jewish Society.' *Studies in Jewish Education* 3 (1988): 271–89.

– 'Gender Differentiation and Education of the Jewish Woman in Nineteenth-Century Eastern Europe.' *Polin* 7 (1992): 63–87.

– 'What Did 'Knowing Hebrew' Mean in Eastern Europe?' in *Hebrew in Ashkenaz*, ed. L. Glinert. New York: Oxford University Press, 1993, 129–40.

Stanislawski, Michael. *Tsar Nicholas and the Jews.* Philadelphia: Jewish Publication Society, 1983.

– *For Whom Do I Toil?* New York and Oxford: Oxford University Press, 1988.

– *Zionism and the Fin-de-Siècle: Cosmopolitanism and Nationalism from Nordau to Jabotinski.* Los Angeles: University of California Press, 2001.
– *Autobiographical Jews: Essays in Jewish Self-Fashioning.* Seattle: University of Washington Press, 2004.
– 'The Russian Empire,' in *YIVO Encyclopedia of Jews in Eastern Europe.* Vol. 2, ed. G.D. Hundert. New Haven: Yale University Press and YIVO, 2008, 1607–15.
Steffen, Katrin. *Jüdische Polonität: Ethnizität und Nation im Spiegel der polnischsprachigen jüdischen Presse, 1918–1939.* Göttingen: Vandenhoeck and Ruprecht, 2004.
Stein, Sarah. *Making Jews Modern: The Yiddish and Ladino Press in the Russian and Ottoman Empires.* Bloomington and Indianapolis: Indiana University Press, 2004.
Steinlauf, Michael C. 'Jews and the Polish Theater in Nineteenth-Century Warsaw.' *Polish Review* 32/4 (1987): 439–58.
– 'The Polish Jewish Daily Press.' *Polin* 2 (1987): 219–45.
– 'Polish-Jewish Theatre: The Case of Mark Arnstein – A Study of the Interplay among Yiddish, Polish, and Polish-Language Jewish Culture in the Modern Period.' Doctoral dissertation, Brandeis University, 1988.
– 'Fear of Purim: Y.L. Peretz and the Canonization of Yiddish Theatre.' *Jewish Social Studies* 1/3 (1995): 44–65.
– 'Sources for the History of Jewish Theatre.' *Gal-Ed* 15–16 (1997): 83–104.
Strauch, Gabriele L. 'Methodologies and Ideologies: The Historical Relationship of German Studies to Yiddish,' in *Studies in Yiddish Linguistics,* ed. P. Wexler. Tübingen: Max Niemeyer, 1990, 83–100.
Sudarsky, Mendel, et al., eds. *Lite.* New York: Jewish-Lithuanian Cultural Society 'Lite,' 1951.
Sugar, Peter F., and Ivo J. Lederer, eds. *Nationalism in Eastern Europe.* Seattle: University of Washington Press, 1969.
Šukys, Julija. '"And I Burned with Shame": The Testimony of Ona Šimaite, Righteous among the Nations. A Letter to Isaac Nachman Steinberg.' *Search and Research: Lectures and Papers.* Jerusalem: Yad Vashem, 2007.
Sutzkever, Avrom. *Vilner geto, 1941–1944.* Paris: Farband fun di vilner in pariz, 1946.
Szajkowski, Zosa. 'The Struggle for Yiddish during World War I.' *LBIYB* 9 (1964): 131–58.
– 'Jewish Relief in Eastern Europe, 1914–1917.' *LBIYB* 10 (1965): 24–56.
– 'Disunity in the Distribution of American Jewish Overseas Relief 1919–1939.' *American Jewish Quarterly* 58 (1969): 376–407, 484–506.

– 'The Komitee fuer den Osten and Zionism.' *Herzl Year Book* 7 (1971): 199–240.

– ed. *Der yivo un zayne grinder: Katalog fun der oysshtelung tsum 50-yorikn yoyvl fun yidishn visnshaftlekhn institut.* New York: YIVO, 1975.

Szeintuch, Yechiel. (English; Yiddish: Yekhiel Shayntukh). *Preliminary Inventory of Yiddish Dailies and Periodicals Published in Poland between the Two World Wars.* Jerusalem: Hebrew University, Center for Research on the History and Culture of Polish Jews, 1986.

Szeintuch, Yechiel, ed. 'Der Tunkler (Yoysef Tunkel),' in *Der seyfer fun humoreskes un literarishe parodyes.* Jerusalem: Mount Scopus Publications by the Magnes Press, the Hebrew University, 1990.

Tartakover, Arye. 'Yidn in poylishn parlament.' *Sefer ha-shana/yorbukh* 3 (1970): 197–232.

Thomas, Lawrence L. Condensed adaptation into English of V.V. Vinogradov's *The History of the Russian Literary Language from the Seventeenth Century to the Nineteenth.* Madison: University of Wisconsin Press, 1969.

Tikotshinski, Pinkhes. 'Shul un shprakh-frages in der konstitutsye-debate in poylishn grindungseym.' *YIVO-bleter* 12/4–5 (1937): 433–42.

Tomaszewski, Jerzy. *Rzeczpospolita wielu narodów.* Warsaw: Czytelnik, 1985.

– *Najnowe Dzieje Żydów w Polsce.* Warsaw: Naukowe PWN, 1993.

Tonini, Carla. 'The Polish Plan for a Jewish Settlement in Madagascar, 1936–1939.' *Polin* 19 (2007): 467–77.

Tory, Avraham. *Surviving the Holocaust: The Kovno Ghetto Diary.* Cambridge, MA: Harvard University Press, 1990.

Trani, Eugene P., and David L. Wilson. *The Presidency of Warren G. Harding.* Kansas City: Regents Press of Kansas, 1977.

Trigano, Shmuel, ed. *Société juive à travers l'histoire.* Paris: Fayard, 1992.

Tsanin, Mordkhe. *Grenetsn biz tsum himl.* Tel Aviv: Ha-menorah, 1969.

– 'Der oyfgang un untergang fun der yidisher prese in poyln.' *Kesher* 6 (Nov. 1989): 108–19.

Tseytlin, Elkhonen. (Yiddish; English: Elkhonen Zeitlin). *In a literarisher shtub.* Buenos Aires: Tsentral farband fun poylishe yidn in argentine, 1946.

Tshernikhov, Yoysef. *In Revtribunal: zikhroynes fun a farteydiker.* Vilna: Author, 1932.

Tsitron, Shmuel Leyb. *Di geshikhte fun der yidisher prese: 1. fun yor 1863 biz 1889.* Vilna, 1923.

– *Leksikon tsioni.* Warsaw: Sh. Shreberek, 1924.

Tsur, Eli. *'Olam yashan adam hadash: kehilot yisra'el ba-'idan ha-modernizatsya.* Be'er Sheva: Mehon Ben-Guryon, 2005.

Tunkel, Yoysef. Edited by Yekhiel Shayntukh. *Der seyfer fun humoreskes un parodyes.* Jerusalem: Magnes, 1990.

Turkov, Mark. *Di letse yorn fun a groysn dor.* Buenos Aires, 1954.

Turkov, Yonas. *Azoy is dos geven.* Buenos Aires, 1948.

– *Farloshene shtern.* vol. 2. Buenos Aires: Tsentral farband fun poylishe yidn in argentine, 1953.

Turkav-Grudberg, Yitskhok. *Yidish teater in poyln.* Warsaw: Farlag 'yidish-bukh,' 1951.

Unger, Yeshaye. 'Hindenburg kegn "Haynt,"' in *'Haynt': a tsaytung bay yidn, 1908–1939,* ed. Ch. Finkelstein. Tel Aviv: Velt-federatsye fun poylishe yidn, 1978, 401–4.

Ury, Scott. 'Red Banner, Blue Star: Radical Politics, Democratic Institutions and Collective Identity among Jews in Warsaw, 1904–1907.' Doctoral dissertation, Hebrew University, 2006.

Vago, Bela, and George L. Mosse, eds. *Jews and Non-Jews in Eastern Europe (1918–1945).* New Brunswick, NJ: Transaction Books, 1974.

Vanvild, M., ed. *Bay unz yudn: zamelbukh far folklor un filologye.* Warsaw: P. Graubard, 1923.

Venclova, Tomas. 'Four Centuries of Enlightenment: A Historic View of the University of Vilnius, 1579–1979.' *Lithuanian Quarterly Journal of Arts and Sciences* 27/1 (summer 1981). http://www.lituanus.org/1981_2/81_2_01.htm (accessed 10 Dec. 2008).

Veynger, M. *Vos, vi un bay vemen tsu klaybn un farshraybn.* Minsk, 1925.

Vigodski, Yankev. 'Di "litvakes" in poyln,' in *'Haynt' yoyvl-bukh (1908-1938),* ed. M. Balaban. Warsaw, 1938, 219–23

Vital, David. *The Origins of Zionism.* Oxford: Clarendon, 1975.

Vlavianos, Basil J., and Feliks Gross, eds. *Struggle for Tomorrow.* New York: Arts, Inc., 1954.

Wachowska, Barbara. 'The Jewish Electorate of Interwar Łódź in the Light of the Local Government Elections (1919–1938).' *Polin* 6 (1991): 154–72.

Waldoks, Moshe-Arye Leon. 'Hillel Zeitlin: The Early Years (1894–1919).' Doctoral dissertation, Brandeis University, 1984.

Walkin, Jacob. 'Government Controls over the Press in Russia, 1905–1914.' *Russian Review* 13/3 (1954): 203–9.

Wandycz, Piotr S. *The Lands of Partitioned Poland, 1795–1918.* Seattle and London: University of Washington Press, 1974.

Warnke, Nina. 'Of Plays and Politics: Sholem Aleichem's First Visit to America.' *YIVO Annual* 20 (1991): 239–76.

Weeks, Theodore R. 'Polish "Progressive Antisemitism," 1905–1914.' *East European Jewish Affairs* 25/2 (1995): 49–68.

– *Nation and State in Late Imperial Russia.* Dekalb: Northern Illinois University Press, 1996.

– 'Fanning the Flames: Jews in the Warsaw Press, 1905–1912.' *East European Jewish Affairs* 28/2 (1998–9): 63–82.

– 'Poles, Jews, and Russians, 1863–1914: The Death of the Ideal of Assimilation in the Kingdom of Poland.' *Polin* 12 (1999): 242–56.

– 'The Best of Both Worlds: Creating the *Żyd-Polak.*' *East European Jewish Affairs* 34/2 (2004): 1–20.

– *From Assimilation to Antisemitism: The 'Jewish Question' in Poland, 1850–1914.* Dekalb: Northern Illinois University Press, 2006.

Weichert, Michael. *Zikhroynes.* 4 vols. Tel Aviv: Ha-menora, 1960–70.

– *Varshe,* vol. 2, of *Zikhroynes.* Tel Aviv: Ha-menora, 1960–70.

Weinberg, David H. *Between Tradition and Modernity: Haim Zhitlowski, Simon Dubnow, Ahad Ha-Am, and the Shaping of Modern Jewish Identity.* New York: Holmes and Meier, 1996.

Weinreich, Max. 'Zibn numern "yidish far ale."' *Yidish far ale* 10 (Dec. 1938): 280–90.

– *Modern English-Yiddish Yiddish-English Dictionary.* New York: YIVO, 1990.

– *Geschichte der jiddischen Sprachforschung.* Ed. Jerold Frakes. Atlanta: Scholars' Press, 1993.

– *History of the Yiddish Language,* 2 vols. Trans. Shlomo Noble, with the assistance of Joshua A. Fishman, ed. Paul Glasser. New Haven: Yale University Press, 2008.

Weinreich, Uriel, ed. *The Field of Yiddish.* New York: Linguistic Circle of New York, 1954.

Weiser, Kalman. 'The "Orthodox" Orthography of Solomon Birnbaum.' *Studies in Contemporary Jewry* 20 (2004): 275–95.

Wells, C.J. *German: A Linguistic History to 1945.* Oxford: Oxford University Press, 1985.

Wexler, Paul, ed. *Studies in Yiddish Linguistics.* Tübingen: Max Niemeyer, 1990.

– 'Yiddish: The Fifteenth Slavic Language – A Study of Partial Language Shift from Judeo-Sorbian to German.' *International Journal of the Sociology of Language* 91 (1991): 9–150.

Wierzbicki, Marek. 'Polish-Jewish Relations in Vilna and the Region of Western Vilna under Soviet Occupation, 1939–1941.' *Polin* 19 (2007): 487–516.

Wiles, Timothy, ed. *Poland between the Wars: 1918–1939.* Bloomington: Indiana University Press, 1989.

Wilson, William A. 'Herder, Folklore and the Romantic Nationalism.' *Journal of Popular Culture* 6/4 (1973): 819–35.

Wininger, S. *Große Jüdische National-Biographie.* Cernauti: 'Arta,' 1925.

Wisse, Ruth R. *The I.L. Peretz Reader.* New York: Schocken, 1990.

– *I.L. Peretz and the Making of Modern Jewish Culture.* Seattle: University of Washington Press, 1991.

– 'Not the "Pintele Yid" but the Full-Fledged Jew.' *Prooftexts* 15 (1995): 33–61.

Wodziński, Marcin. 'Good Maskilim and Bad Assimilationists, or Toward a New Historiography of the Haskalah in Poland.' *Jewish Social Studies* 10/3 (2004): 87–122.

Wróbel, Piotr. 'Jewish Warsaw before the First World War,' in *The Jews in Warsaw,* ed. Władysław Bartoszewski and Antony Polonsky. Oxford: Institute for Polish-Jewish Studies, 1991, 246–77.

– 'Przed odzyskaniem niepodległości,' in *Najnowe Dzieje Żydów w Polsce,* ed. J. Tomaszewski. Warsaw: Naukowe PWN, 1993, 104–39.

– 'Wielka roszda: Śyjoniści warszawscy pomiędzy Niemcami a Rosją w czasie pierwszej wojny światowej,' in *Żydzi Warszawy,* ed. Eleonora Bergman and Olga Zienkiewicz. Warsaw: Żydowski Instytut Historyczny, 2000, 159–92.

Yeushzon, B[unem]. *Nekhtn: a bukh felyetonen.* Ramat Gan, Israel: Bar-Ilan University, 1988.

YIVO. *Vos iz azoyns yidishe etnografe: Hantbikhl far zamler.* Vilna: Author, 1931.

– Di ershte yidishe shprakh-konferents: barikhtn, dokumentn un opklangen fun der tshernovitser konferents, 1908. Vilna: Yidisher visnshaftlekher institut, 1931.

Zak, Avrom. *In onheyb fun a friling.* Buenos Aires: Tsentral-farband fun poylishe yidn in argentine, 1962.

Zaporowski, Zbigniew. 'Żydzi w Radzie Miejskiej Lublina 1919–1939,' in *Żydzi w Lublinie,* ed. T. Radzik. Lublin: Uniwersytetu Marii Curie-Skłodowskiej, 1995, 237–44.

Zechlin, Egmont. *Die deutsche Politik und die Juden im ersten Weltkrieg.* Göttingen: Vanderhoeck and Ruprecht, 1969.

Zhitlovsky, Khayim. *In kamf far folk un shprakh.* New York: Dr kh. zhitlovski ferlag gezelshaft, 1917.

Zieliński, Konrad. 'Aktywność polityczna Żydów na Lubelszczyźnie w latach 1914–1918.' *Studia Judaica* 1/2 (1998): 221–42.

– *Żydzi Lubelszczyzny, 1914–1918.* Lublin: Lubelskie Towarzystwo Naukowe, 1999.

– *Stosunski polsko-żydowskie na ziemach Królestwa Polskiego w czasie pierwszej wojny światowej.* Lublin: Uniwesytetu Marii Curie-Skłodowskiej, 2005.

Zilbertsvayg, Zalmen. (English, Polish; Yiddish: Zalmen Zilbertsvayg). *Akhad hoom un zayn batsiung tsu yidish.* Los Angeles: Farlag 'Elisheve,' 1956.

– *Leksikon fun yidishn teater.* New York: Farlag 'Elisheve,' 1931–69.

Zimmerman, Joshua D. *Poles, Jews, and the Politics of Nationality.* Madison: University of Wisconsin Press, 2004.

Zinberg, Israel. *A History of Jewish Literature.* Trans. and ed. Bernard Martin. New York: Ktav, 1978.

Zinger, Y.Y. 'A vikhtike frage.' *Literarishe bleter* 3/103 (1925): 260–1.

Zipperstein, Steven. 'The Politics of Relief: The Transformation of Russian Jewish Communal Life during the First World War.' *Studies in Contemporary Jewry* 4 (1988): 22–40.

– *Elusive Prophet: Ahad Ha'am and the Origins of Zionism.* London: Peter Halban, 1993.

Żyndul, Jolanta. *Panstwo w panstwie? Autonomia narodowo-kulturalna w Europie Środkowowschodniej w XX wieku.* Warsaw: DiG, 2000.

Index

Page numbers in italics indicate a reference to maps or illustrations.

www.ingramcontent.com/pod-product-compliance
Lightning Source LLC
LaVergne TN
LVHW090801070826
844660LV00022B/1048

* 9 7 8 0 8 0 2 0 9 7 1 6 3 *